AF822717

THE MANUAL OF MALE PHOTOGRAPHY

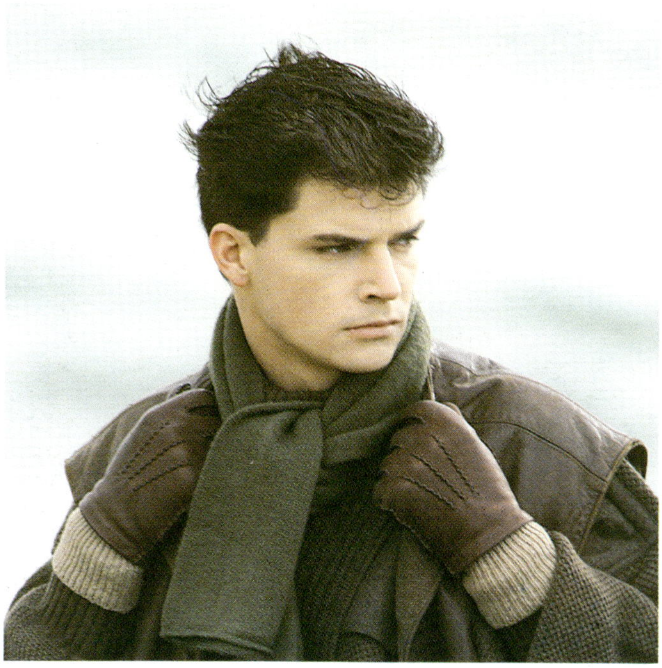

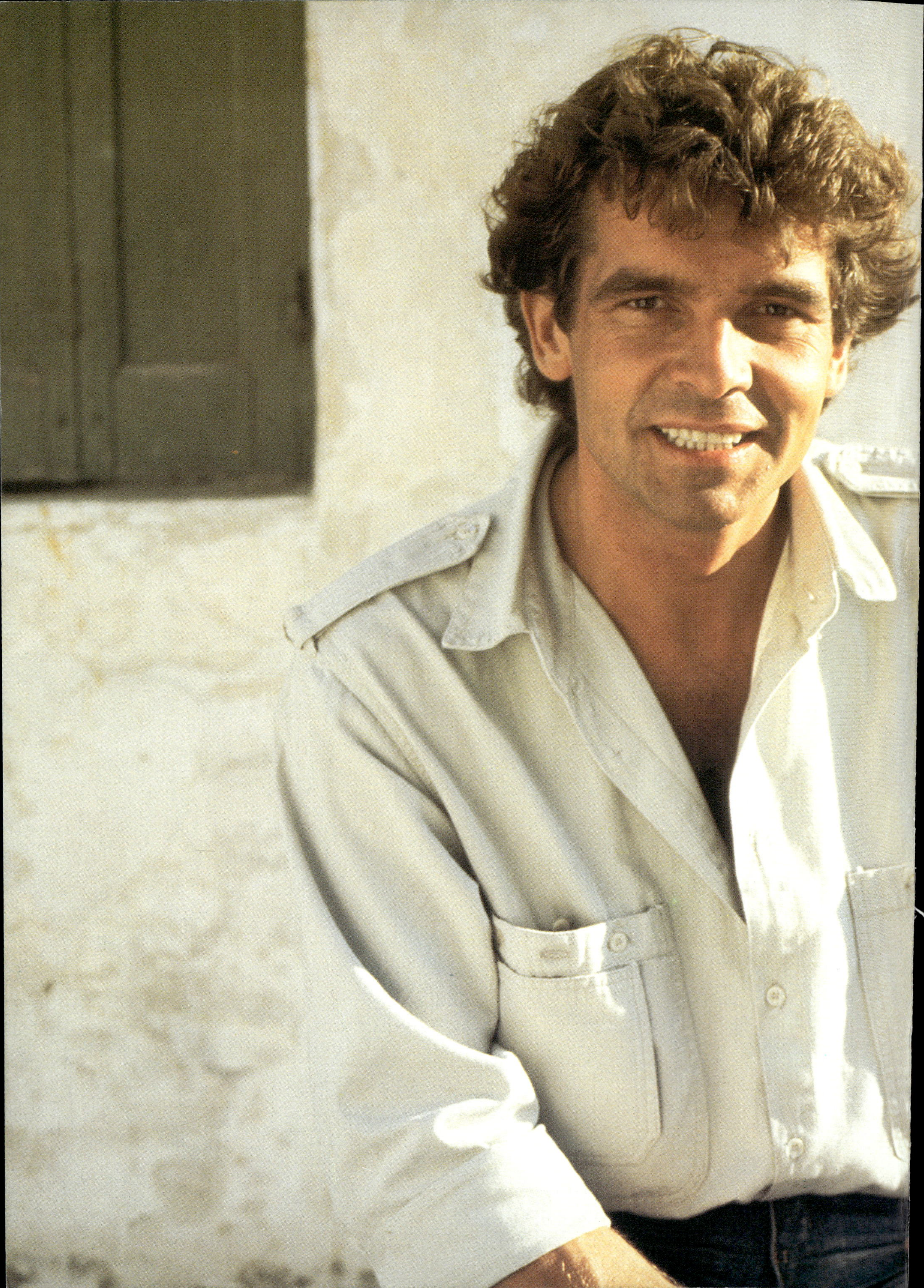

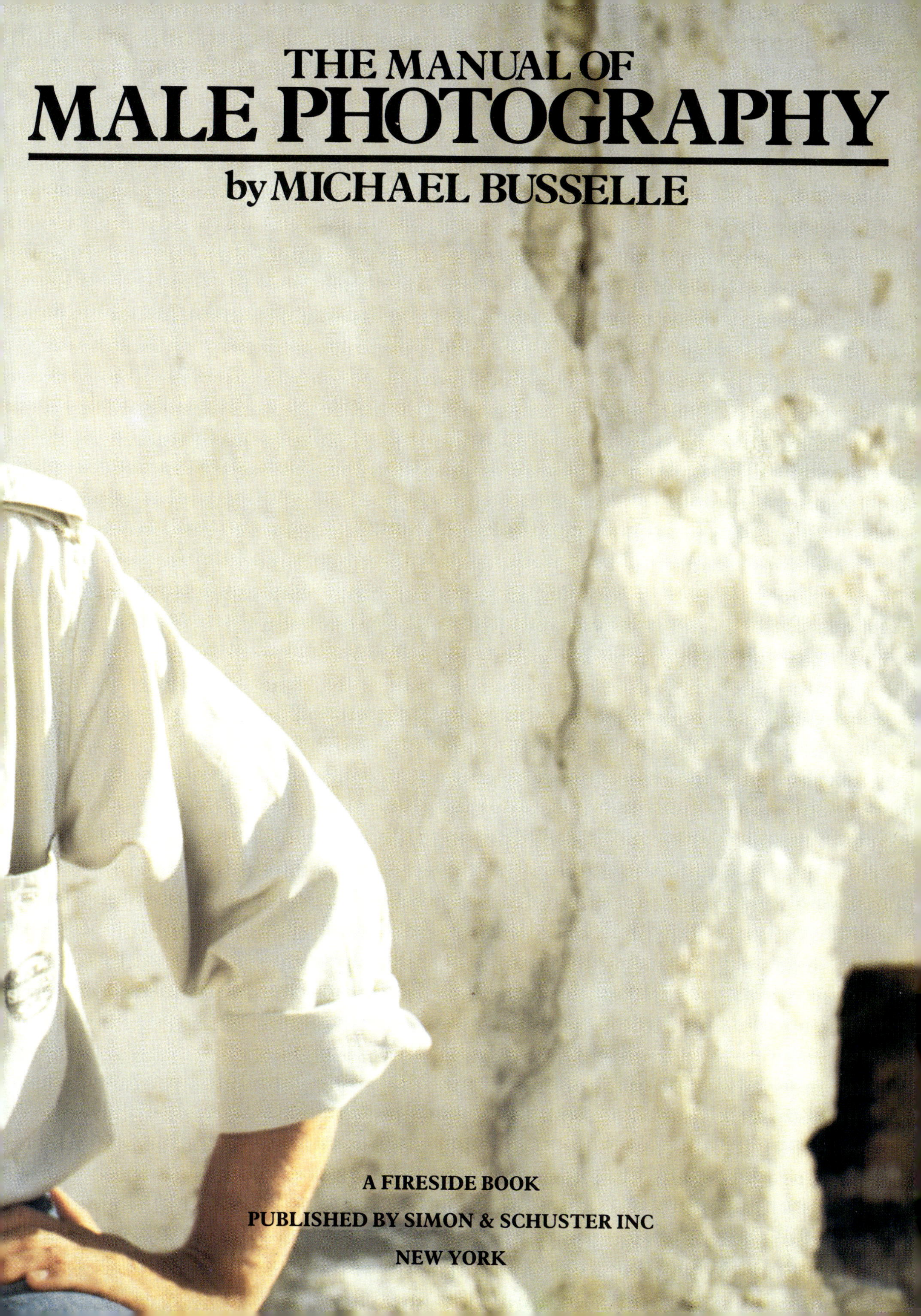

THE MANUAL OF MALE PHOTOGRAPHY

by MICHAEL BUSSELLE

A FIRESIDE BOOK
PUBLISHED BY SIMON & SCHUSTER INC
NEW YORK

A Fireside Book
Published by
Simon and Schuster
A Division of
Simon & Schuster, Inc.
Simon & Schuster Building
Rockefeller Center
1230 Avenue of the
Americas, New York,
New York, 10020

FIRESIDE
and colophon are
registered trademarks of
Simon & Schuster, Inc.

ISBN 0-671-60556-9

Designed and produced by
**Robert Adkinson Limited,
London**

Phototypesetting by
Ashwell Print Services Ltd.
Norwich

Color and black-and-white
illustration origination by
East Anglian Engraving
Limited, Norwich

Printed and bound in Italy
by New Interlitho, S.p.A.

1 2 3 4 5 6 7 8 9 10

CONTENTS

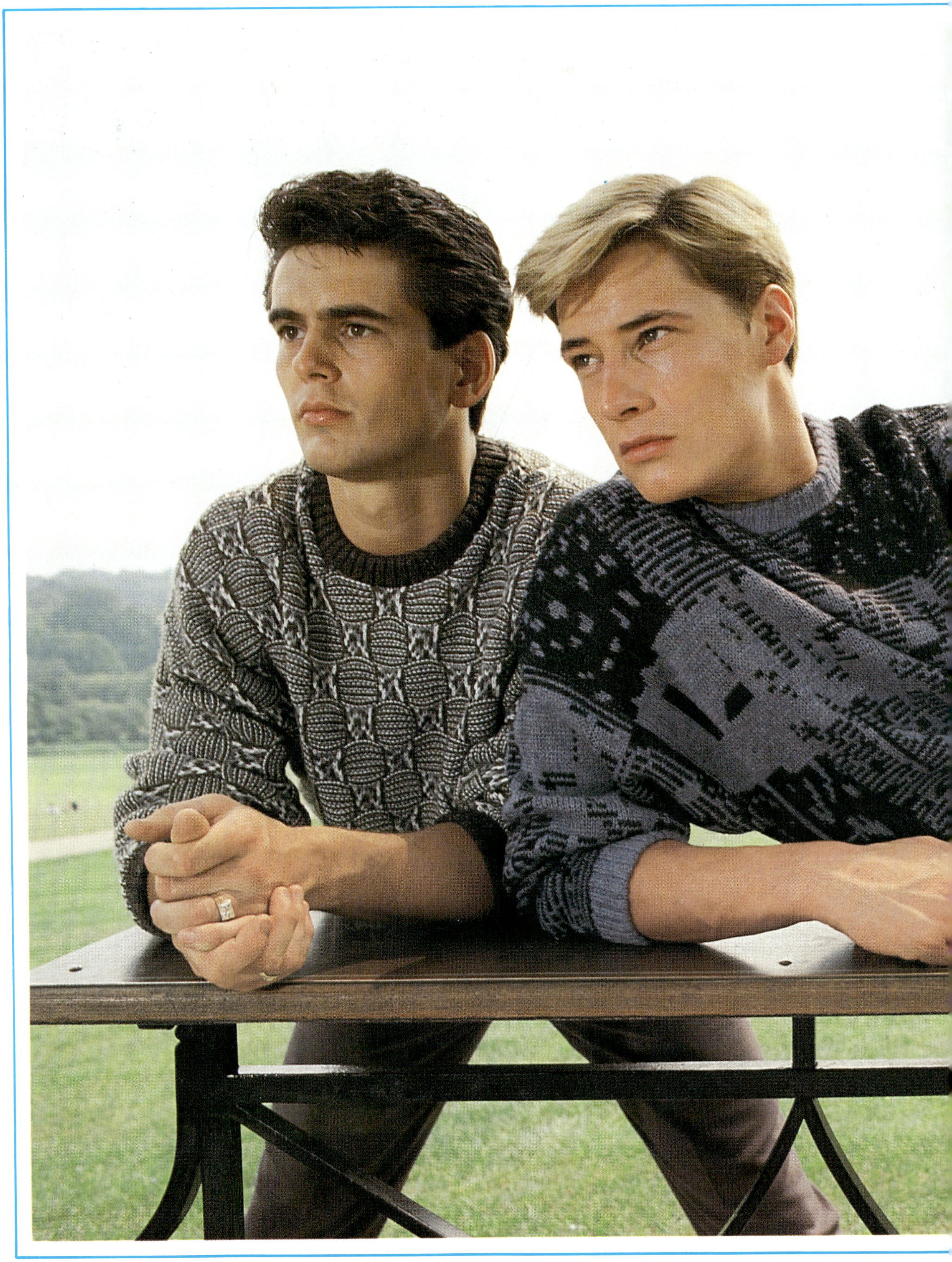

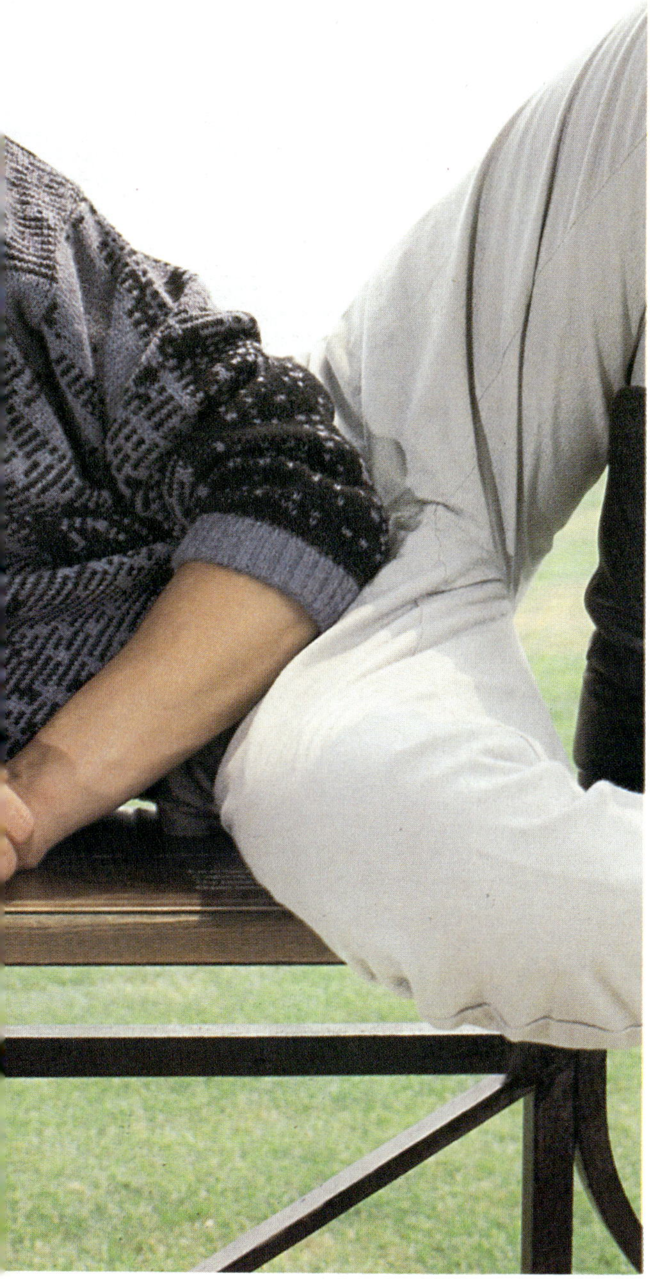

STYLE AND APPROACH

FASHION

In the professional field, fashion represents one of the major uses of male photography, and some of the most adventurous and innovative work can be seen on the pages of the glossy magazines. There are, however, different types of, and different uses for, fashion photography. The pictures taken for catalogue or advertising use, for instance, have a very different requirement than those taken for editorial fashion.

In mail order catalogue and much advertising photography, for example, it is vital that the garments are shown as clearly and accurately as possible. The color and texture of the fabric is a crucial element of such photographs and it is also important that they be seen in the best light, not creased or dishevelled for example. This inevitably means that the model is obliged to be quite static; the opportunity for movement and even, to a degree, gesture and expression, is quite limited. It is often necessary, for instance, to clip and peg clothes until they become smooth and crease-free. To adjust the fit, trousers are even guy-roped to the ground, giving the impression of a perfect crease and fall. In order to maximize the detail of the photographs, this type of shot is usually taken on a medium-format or even large-format camera, and lighting is kept deliberately soft and open to reveal the maximum amount of detail. When shooting in sunny locations, for example, a large white umbrella is often used to diffuse the sunlight and so eliminate hard, dense shadows.

Editorial fashion has a quite different purpose. Instead of selling a specific product, a good fashion photograph aims to create a style and mood. For this, stark, clear, detail might not be required. A fashion editor is much more concerned with the impression the clothes create than with revealing each stitch and fold of the garment and, to a large extent, the character and style of the model himself becomes a much more important factor. Whereas the catalogue art director is looking for a fairly bland Mr Everybody image, a magazine's art or fashion editor is quite likely to aim more for an aggressive and dominant personality.

The photographer too is allowed much more scope. Movement and harsh or atmospheric lighting are all part of his stock in trade; the use of a 35mm camera is often preferred, allowing as it does, a much quicker and freer mode of shooting, often with the aid of a motor drive. The choice of location too can be a vital element since it helps to create mood and, for this reason, very grand and sophisticated, calculatedly ambiguous, or mysterious settings are often used.

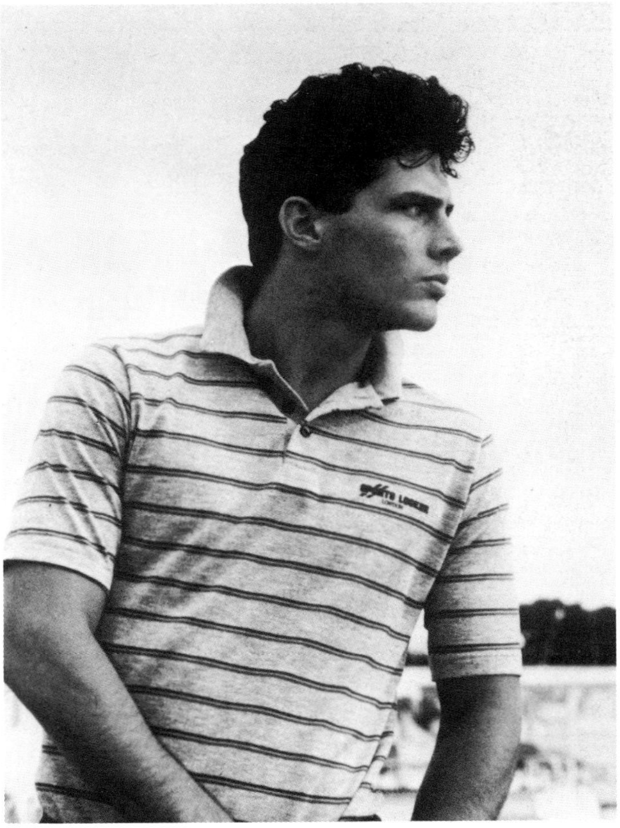

The two faces of fashion photography. In one, a typical catalogue or advertising picture, the main purpose is to show the garment being worn by the model. In the other picture, more of an editorial type of shot, the end product leans more towards style and mood.

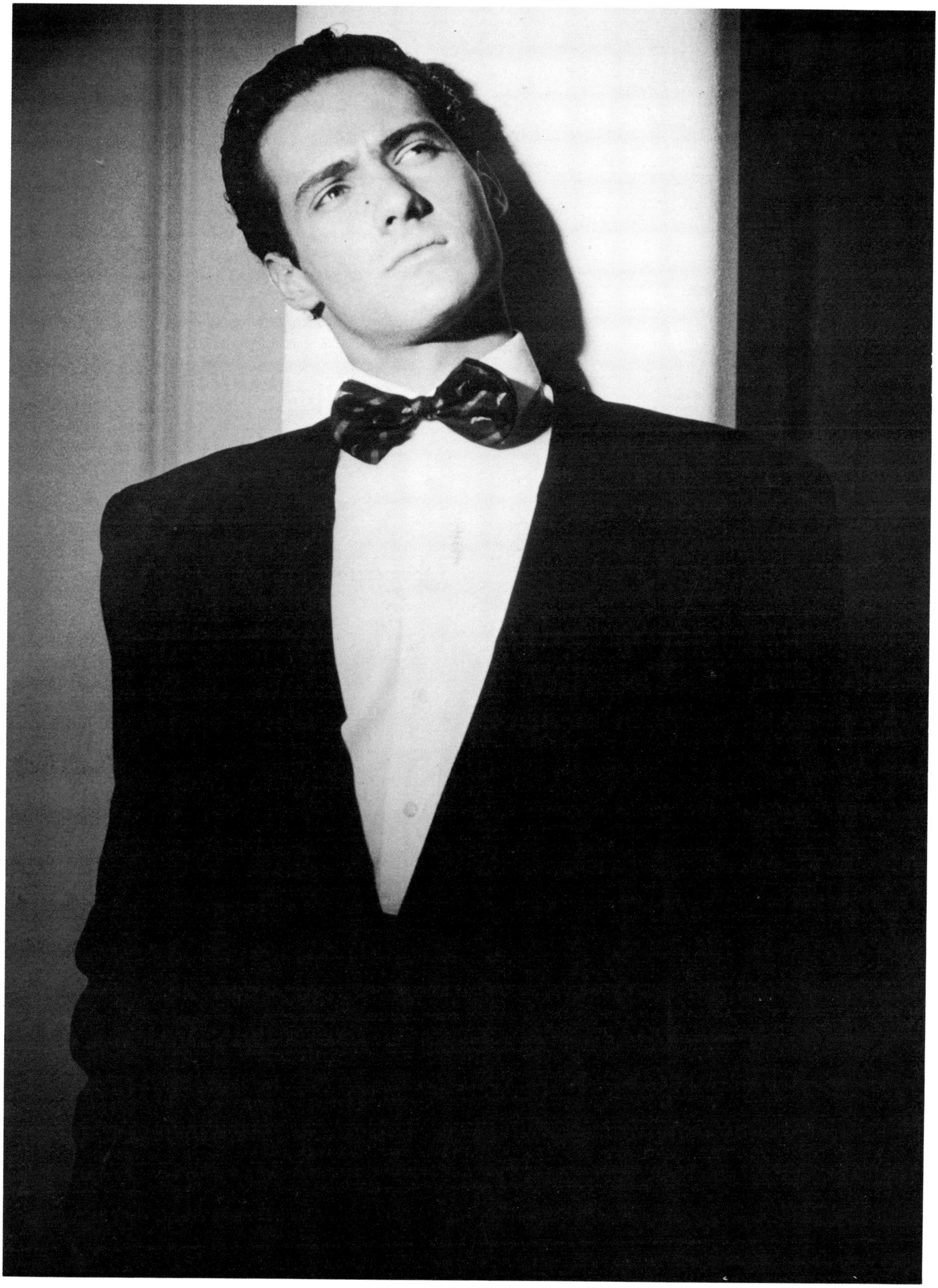

GLAMOUR

The role of the male model in glamour photography is, at first glance, more limited than that of the female, simply because female glamour dominates its male counterpart in the popular market. But times change and the attitudes to male photography are changing with them.

Although there is little evidence of the male model appearing in quite the same way, or as frequently as, say, the Page Three girl, or as models in the Pirelli calendar, male glamour photography is, nevertheless, flourishing and fine examples can be seen in many publications. The heyday of this particular genre might well be considered to have been during the peak of the Hollywood period, when the star cult and its following of fans and hero worshippers was at its greatest. In those nostalgic times, glamorous pictures of stars like Cary Grant and Rudolph Valentino were given exactly the same sort of treatment and interest by producers and photographers as the great female stars of the day. Realism was not wanted. The purpose of this type of picture was to uphold the illusion of sophistication and glamour which had been created on the big screen. To this end, much of the photography of this period was produced on large-format plate cameras, the models were heavily made up, the lighting was carefully and artfully arranged and the negatives skilfully retouched to eliminate skin texture and unseemly human flaws. These people were, afterall, godlike!

This approach to male glamour photography gradually gave way to more natural and less contrived images and the contemporary version of this type of picture is quite likely to show the subject with a day or two's growth of beard and a sweat-streaked face or body. Although the approach may be different, however, in practice the aim is still very much the same: to create and sustain the image which a particular star or his manager has designed, and the artifice of the photographer is used just as cunningly today as it was in the Hollywood era.

Today's glamour is of course by no means limited to film stars. Contemporary glamour tends to be more realistic in more ways than just the visual approach, and the subject of a male glamour picture today is just as, or even more, likely to be of a rock musician, a sportsman, an author or an artist.

The early, almost fantasy-like approach to male glamour photography, epitomized by Hollywood, has gradually, over the years, given way to today's more natural and less contrived images.

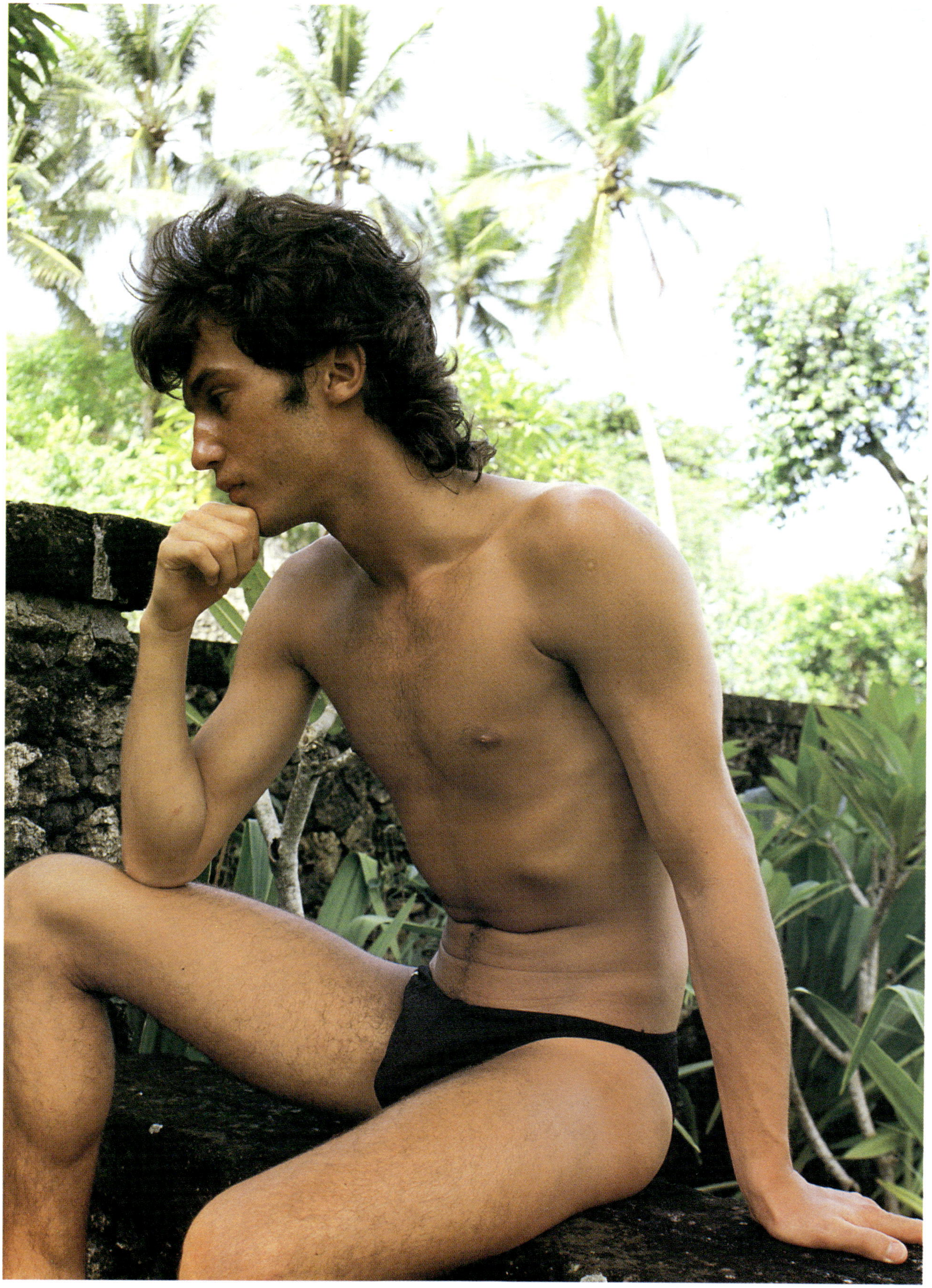

SPORT

Although it is fair to say that the world of fashion is largely female orientated, sport is very much a man's world, and sports photography largely reflects this. Professionally, it is quite a specialized field. Few sports photographers involve themselves in other subjects to any great degree and the opportunities for the non-specialist are quite restricted. This is largely because the facilities for photography at major sporting events are themselves quite limited and the opportunities for taking outstanding shots at such venues without an official pass are almost non-existent. There is even considerable specialization within sport. A photographer may, for example, shoot mainly tennis or golf and seldom or never cover events like football or athletics.

Sports photography falls into a number of categories, each with a very different set of problems and demands. Many sports require that the photographer has a good working knowledge of the event and, indeed, some demand that he is himself an active participant. Adventure sports, for example, such as mountaineering, hang gliding, surfing, sailing, sub aqua and free-fall parachuting mean that the photographer is exposed to the same risks as those performing.

The equipment needed for sports photography is also quite specialized. With adventure sports, for example, water- or weather-proof cameras and cases might be needed as well as remote control or special triggering devices. A motor drive is an almost obligatory accessory in most sports photography, as are very long-focus telephoto lenses. These also often need to be of wide maximum aperture to allow the photographer to shoot moving subjects in low light. For this reason, they are both heavy and bulky, as well as being extremely expensive.

One of the main reasons for both the appeal and effectiveness of a good sports picture is that it combines the excitement and drama of competition with the visual and aesthetic appeal of the male (and female) body when captured in graceful movement or straining to excel. It is the ability to combine these factors successfully which determines a good sports photographer. The essential techniques required to achieve this are the selection of a good viewpoint and the choice of the moment at which to expose.

The viewpoint determines the composition of the image and also establishes the opportunity for, and the nature of, the action, as at the start or finishing line of a sprint race, or a ground-level angle at a jump, for example. It is the moment at which the camera is fired, however, which is the crucial and decisive factor in creating an outstanding picture. It could be the moment as a weightlifter makes the final successful lift, with his entire effort mirrored in his expression; or it might be the fraction of a second that the ball leaves the boot of a soccer player, making a shot for goal. Whichever, it is the photographer's skill in anticipating and reacting instantaneously to such situations that creates the greatest sports pictures.

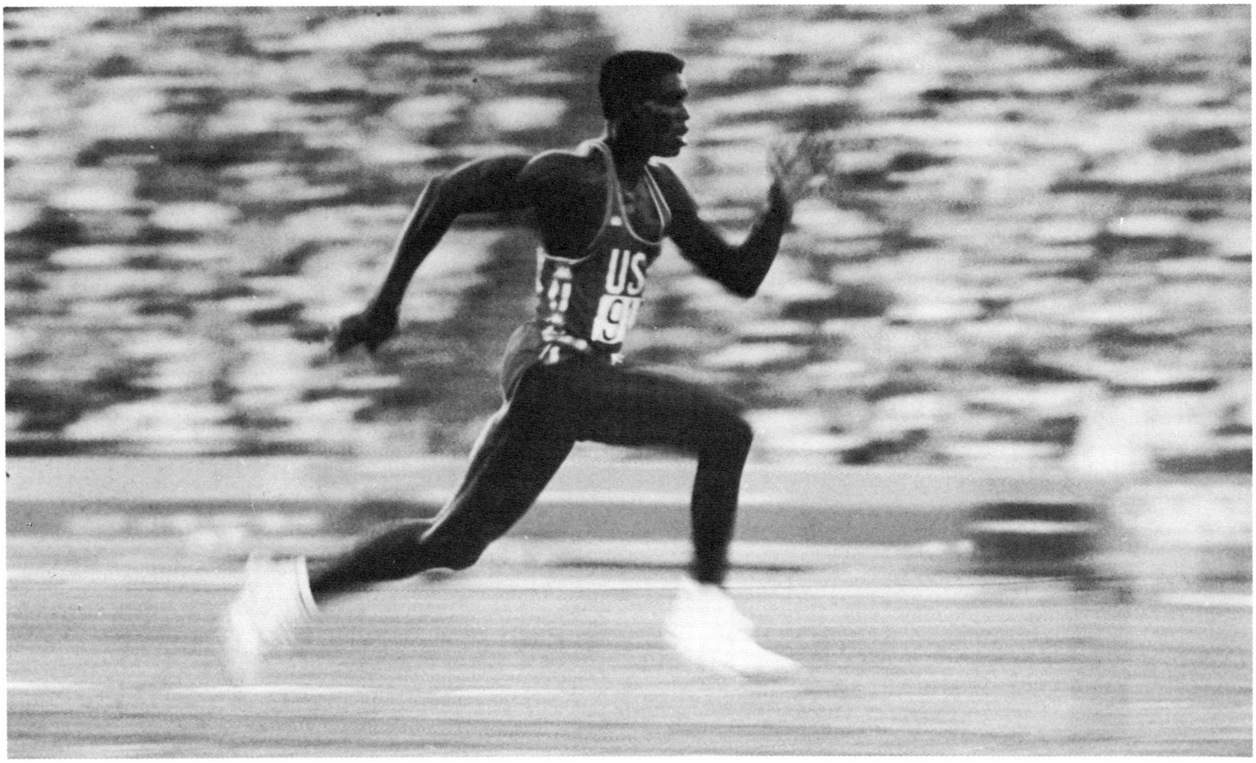

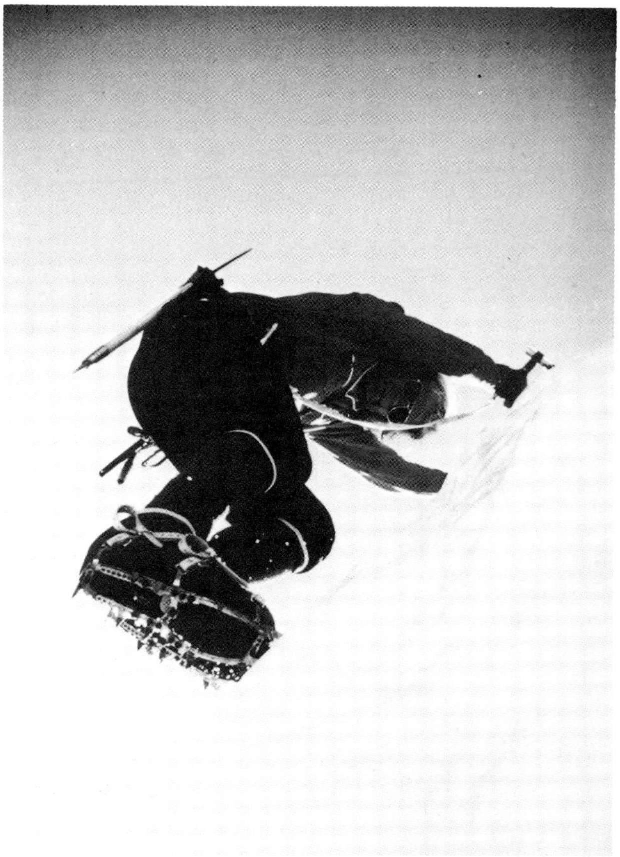

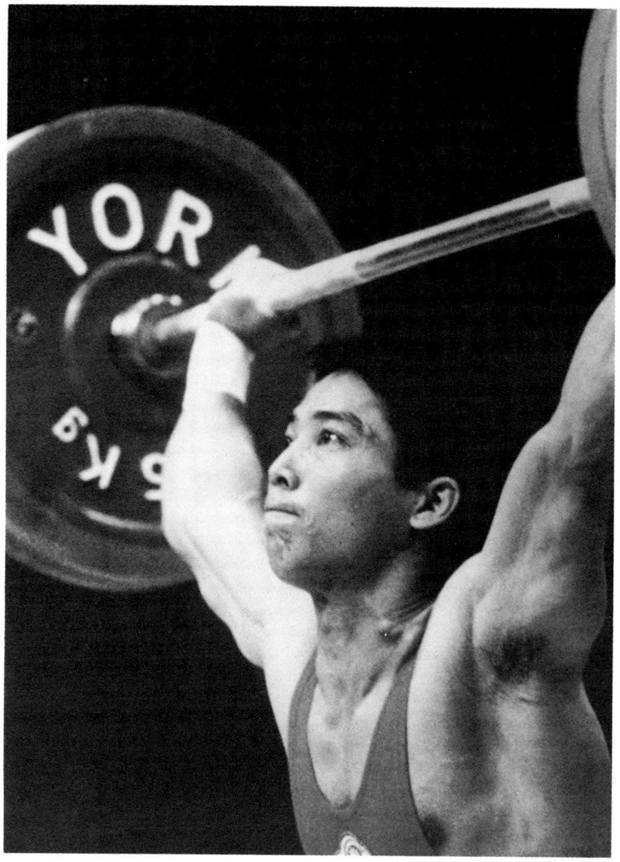

In some forms of sport photography, the photographer must also be a participant. As such, he must know as much about the sport itself as he does about camera techniques.

Viewpoint is everything in sport photography. This picture gains tremendous impact from the photographer being in a position to move in close and really fill the frame with his subject.

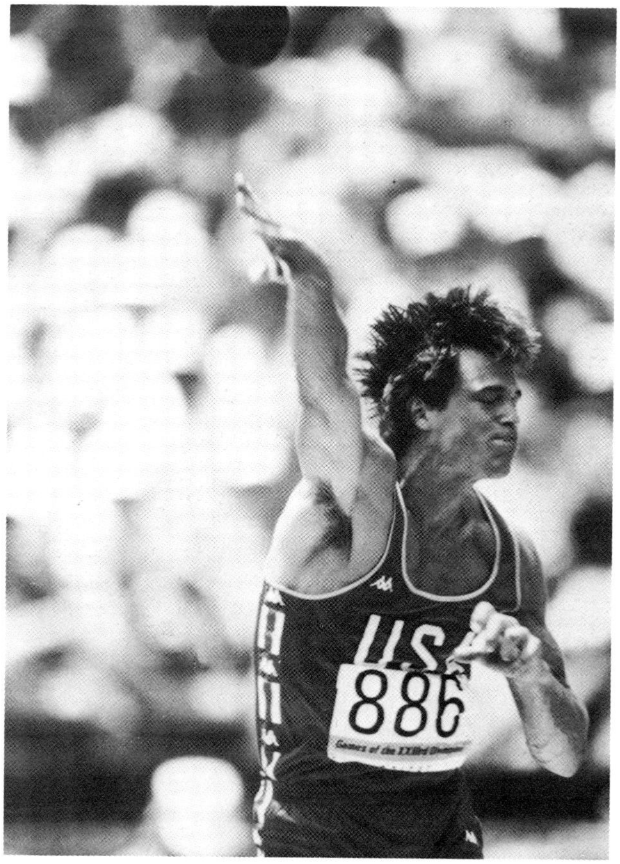

The use of a slow shutter speed and a panning action with the camera has led to a strong sense of movement in this shot.

A sports stadium can provide a messy and distracting background – something which can be cured by wide apertures and telephoto lenses, used to throw the problem well out of focus.

PORTRAIT

One of the first and most enthusiastic uses of photography was that of the portrait. Until its discovery, a likeness or memento of a person could be obtained only at great cost by the services of a painter or sculptor. Photography made the portrait a much more widely-available and accessible medium, leaving a permanent record of many more people of far wider social class and status than was possible before its invention.

The early portrait photographers were limited both by the inhibitions imposed by the painters' heritage and also that of the relatively crude equipment and techniques of the medium itself. But as methods improved and photographers became more inventive, so the art of the photographic portrait began to emerge in its own right.

There are essentially two types of portrait: those taken at the request of the sitter as a commission and those taken for the photographer's, or another person's own purposes. The difference is significant in that the former requires the photographer to make some attempt to please, which usually means flatter, the subject who is paying him; in the latter case, however, there is considerably less restriction upon the photographer's approach. Arnold Newman's portrait of Alfred Krupps, the German munitions tycoon, was calculated to make him appear sinister and even evil, and it was understandably not much appreciated by his subject.

A further distinction in the approach to portraiture is between the informal and naturally-lit subject where the result is, or appears to be, quite casual and uncontrived, and the formal studio picture where both the subject and the multi-source lighting is arranged and controlled with great care. Yusef Karsh is a classic example of the latter. He has made memorable, and often definitive, portraits of many of the great men of this century.

This approach is not widely used by many of today's portrait photographers, however, and even with studio pictures, the trend is to use natural light or electronic flash in a way which simulates daylight. Photographers such as Richard Avedon and Lord Snowdon have made this type of lighting very much a trademark of their work. In addition, whereas the more traditional portrait photographers would use a plain or softly-patterned background, this element, in a contemporary portrait, is often quite dominant. The environmental approach to portraiture, in which the setting or location is used to contribute to both the mood and composition of the image, as well as helping to establish the character and personality of the subject, is more widely-used today.

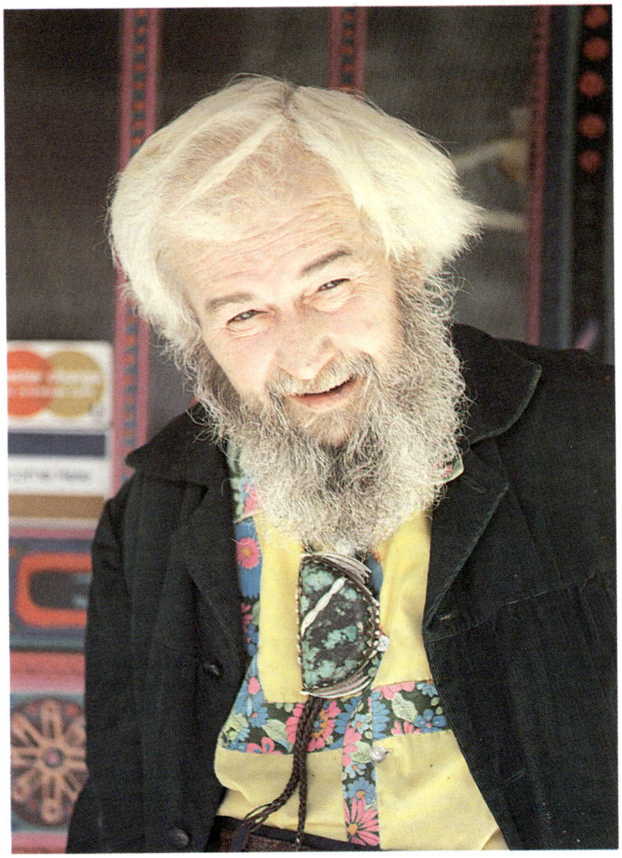

Good portraiture should put across something of the subject's character. It is up to the photographer to gain the sort of rapport with his model that is necessary to achieve this end.

Character in portraiture can also be put across by picturing your subject together with his day to day environment. The use of natural lighting is paticularly effective here. In all the pictures opposite, window light has been used to create a soft, atmospheric mood.

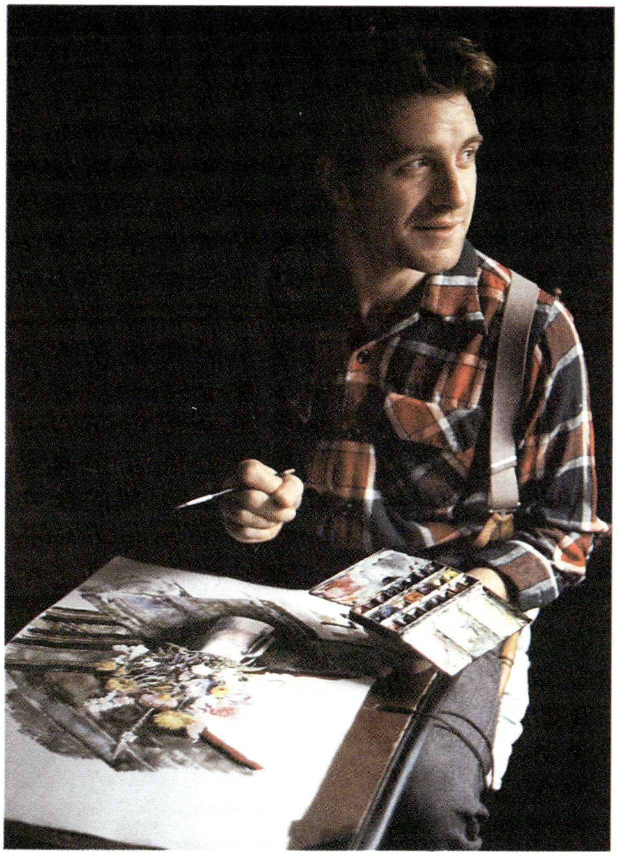

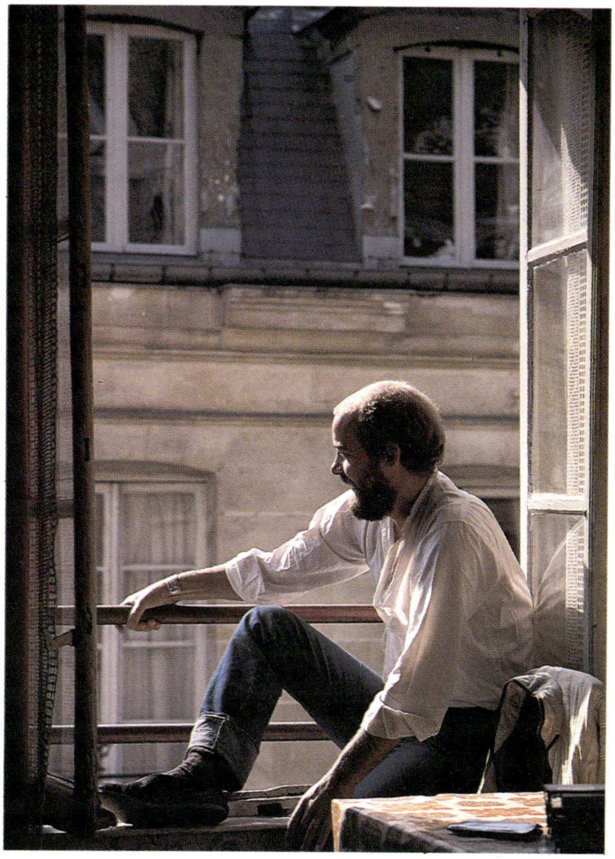

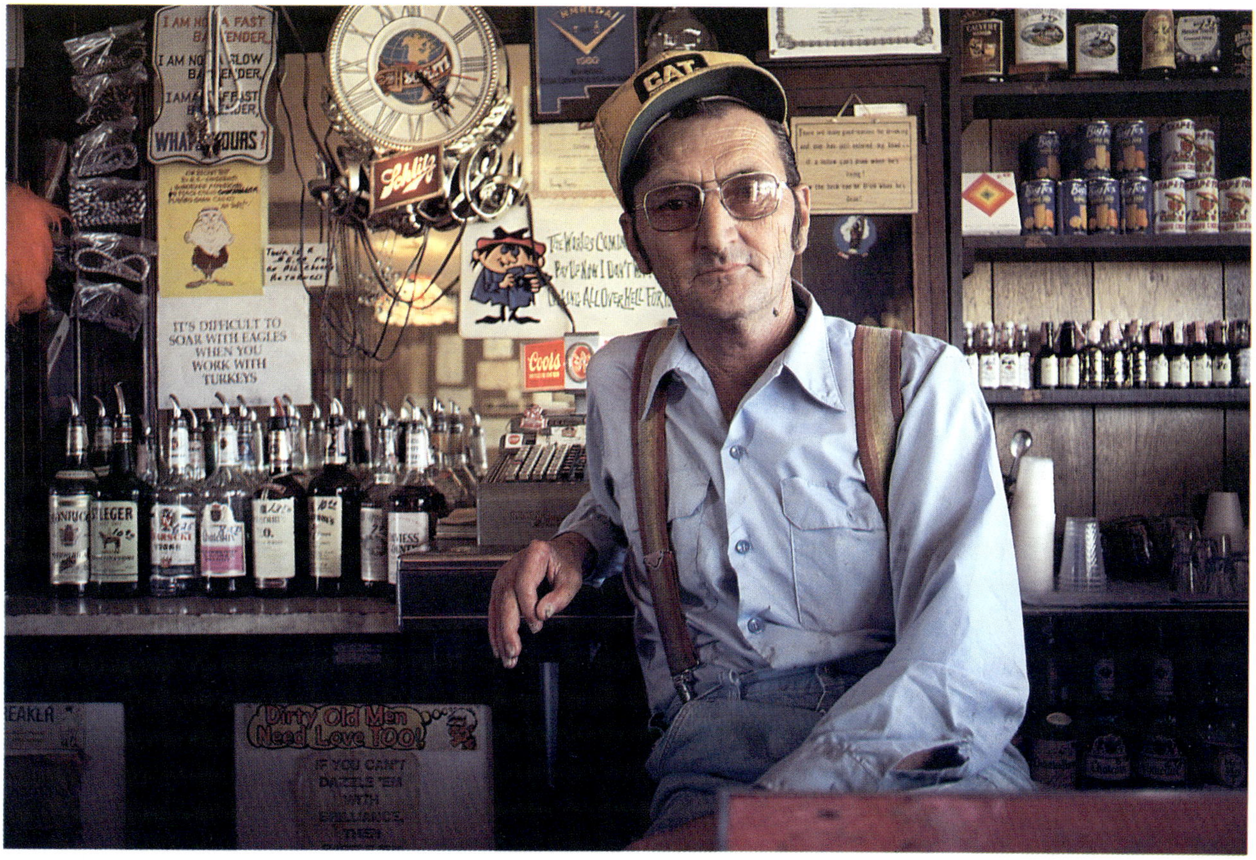
CAT
Schlitz
IT'S DIFFICULT TO
SOAR WITH EAGLES
WHEN YOU
WORK WITH
TURKEYS
Coors
Dirty Old Men
Need Love TOO!

THE NUDE

In classical art, the male model features almost as regularly as the female kind, so it is somewhat surprising, therefore, to find that the same is not true of photography. For the photographer who is taking pictures for his own satisfaction or personal expression, the male body offers equal, if not greater, opportunities for visual interpretation than does the female body.

In the early days of photography, the male nude enjoyed rather more popularity as a subject, perhaps because initially photography was more concerned with emulating classical art, and many leading photographers of the 19th and early 20th centuries used the male model as enthusiastically as the female. Indeed some photographers, like Von Gloeden, preferred the male nude to the virtual exclusion of the female.

As photography moved further away from the painter's art, so the male nude began to lose its appeal as a subject for photographers. One reason for this could be that the more realistic and natural images which resulted in this changing approach to photography were sometimes considered less socially acceptable. Photographs of the nude, both male and female, began to look rather less like art to the layman's eye and rather more like pictures of naked people, and to some, this effect was less acceptable with the male model than with the female.

This resulted in only a few photographers of note devoting much attention to the male nude and as a general rule those photographers who were interested primarily in the nude as a means of personal expression as opposed to commercial demands, invariably chose the female nude as their subject matter. The list of such photographers is indeed large. Among the contemporary photographers – names like Sam Haskins, David Bailey, John Swannell, Bob Carlos Clarke, David Hamilton, Jean Loupe Sieff, Harry Callahan and so on – little or no interest has been shown in the male nude.

This situation is beginning to change however, and more good, interpretive photography of the male nude is being seen these days. Photographers like Bruce Weber and Robert Mapplethorpe, having produced innovative and influential exhibitions and books, may well be heralding a renaissance of the male nude as a photographic subject.

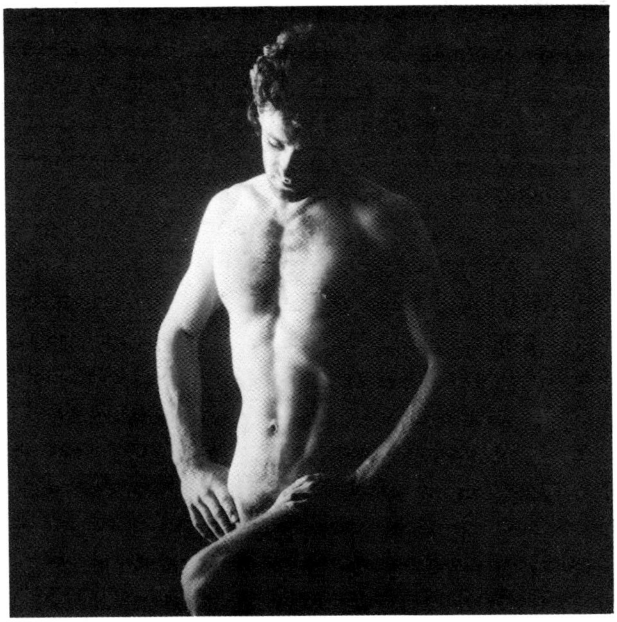

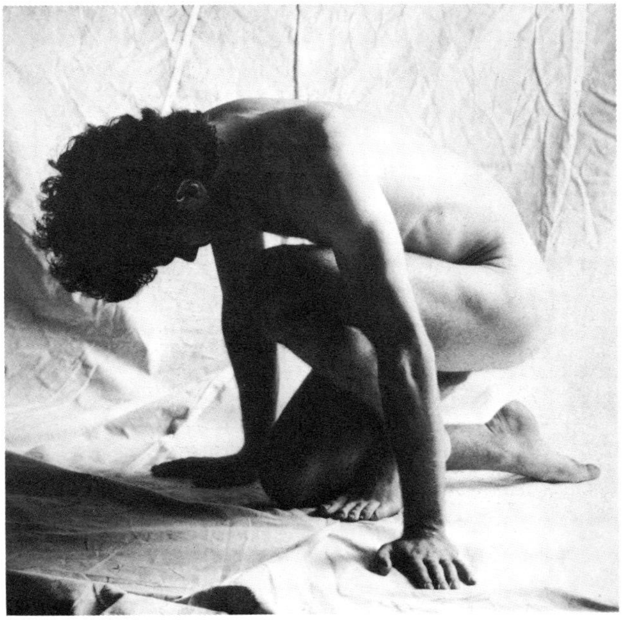

Despite the commercial popularity of the female form for glamour and nude photography, the male body can give photographers much more versatility in posing and lighting. The combination of those two factors in these three pictures works well primarily because the subject is a man.

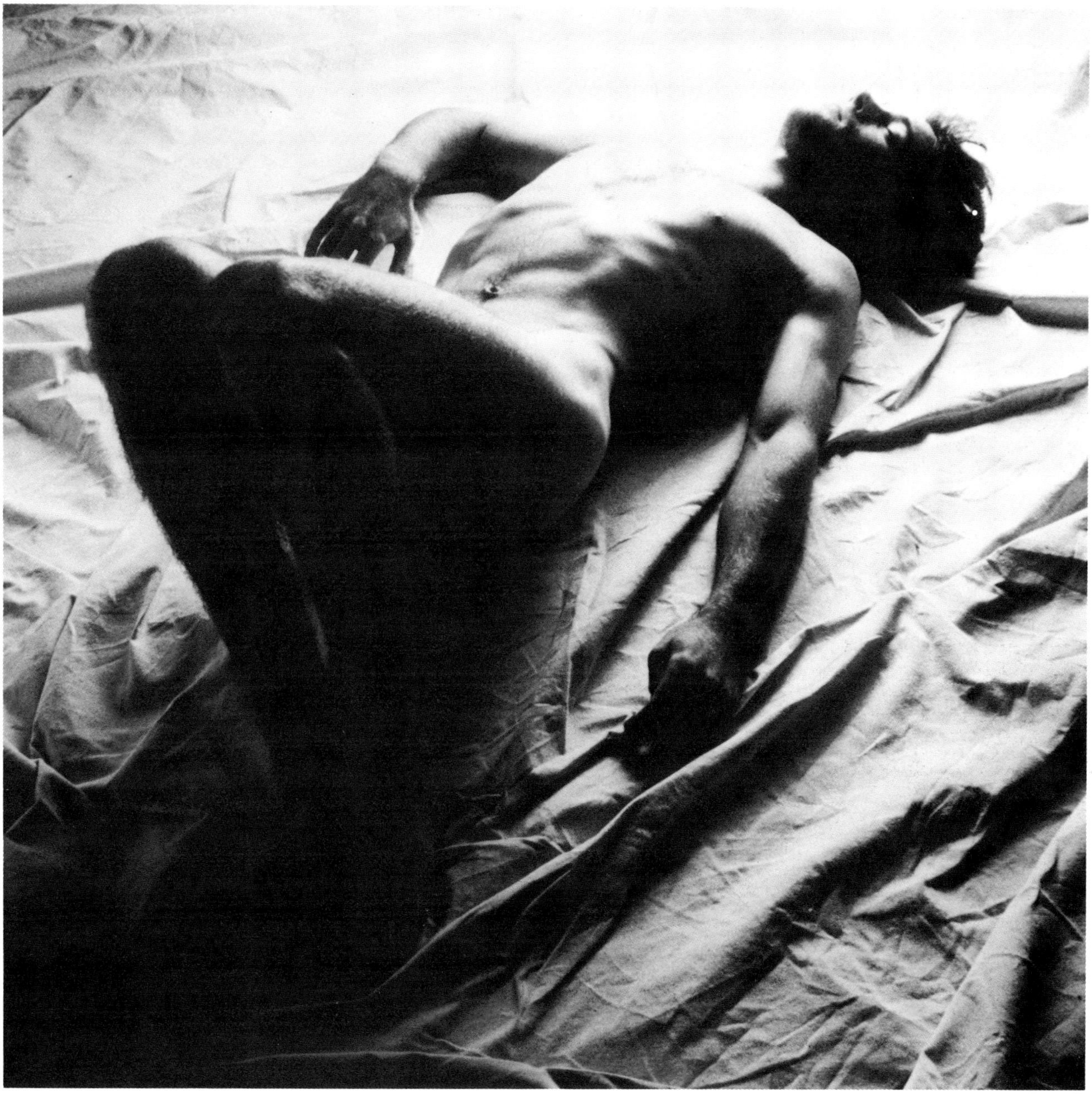

REPORTAGE

One of the most significant aspects of the advent of photography has been its ability to make the world and its people much more accessible to the vast majority of the world's population, most of whom seldom stray far from their roots. Since the day when a wet plate camera was first taken tentatively outside the studio with its cumbersome tent and accoutrements, photographers have enthusiastically and diligently recorded virtually every facet of human life and endeavour. In many ways the role of the reportage or documentary photographer has been the most useful and influential, since both education and information today is largely dependent on photographic images used by the media.

There are several fields in which the reportage photographer can work. Press photography, in which day-to-day events are recorded for the news sheets, can cover trivial events like a society or celebrity wedding to a catastrophe like a terrorist attack or a plane crash. Whatever the scale, or the importance, of the event, such work demands an almost ruthless and dedicated approach. Quite apart from any personal dangers which might exist, there is considerable competition between rival journals and their photographers. The ability to be in the right place at the right time and to be able to get the vital film back to the news desk, can be as important to a press photographer as his photographic skills. It has been said that there are just two important factors in press photography: f/8 and be there!

One field which is almost exclusively male is that of war. It requires a quite special person to be able to handle both the personal danger and the lack of involvement which is required of a war photographer. To be in the presence of dying, maimed and grief-stricken people, and to be able to concentrate your attention on cameras, lenses and composition, is by no means within the average photographer's capability. The truly great war photographers such as Don McCullin, Larry Burrows, Robert Capa and Phillip Jones Griffiths, are unique and will be assured a place in history, along with the events they have photographed. Although the ubiquitous television camera now keeps us up to date with the current horror, it is still the single, powerful, still photograph produced by people like these which captures our attention and last longest in our memories.

Documentary photography too has played a vital role in our understanding of mankind and the production of photographs and picture stories for the glossy magazines and books has been the major preoccupation of many of the greatest photographers. Men like Henri Cartier Bresson, Eugene Smith, Joseph Koudelka, William Klein and Robert Frank have created a collection of telling images which will say much more about life in our time in, say, two or three centuries, than the writings of academics and historians.

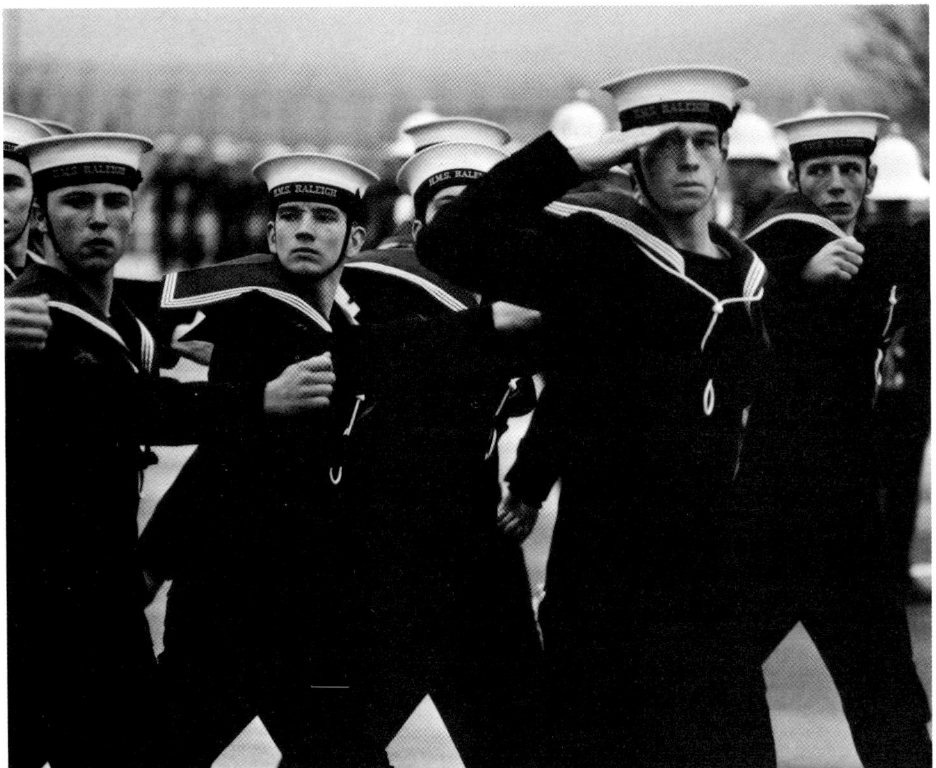

Reportage photography necessarily encompasses both sexes, but on certain types of assignment the subject matter is exclusively male – and the picture needs to emphasize gender as a matter of priority. The armed forces **(left)** *are almost exclusively male preserves, and some occupations* **(right)** *are closed to women for purely physical reasons. Many sports and games are by custom played only by men* **(opposite, top left)**. *In complete contrast, modern male street fashion deliberately questions traditional gender definitions* **(opposite, top right)**.

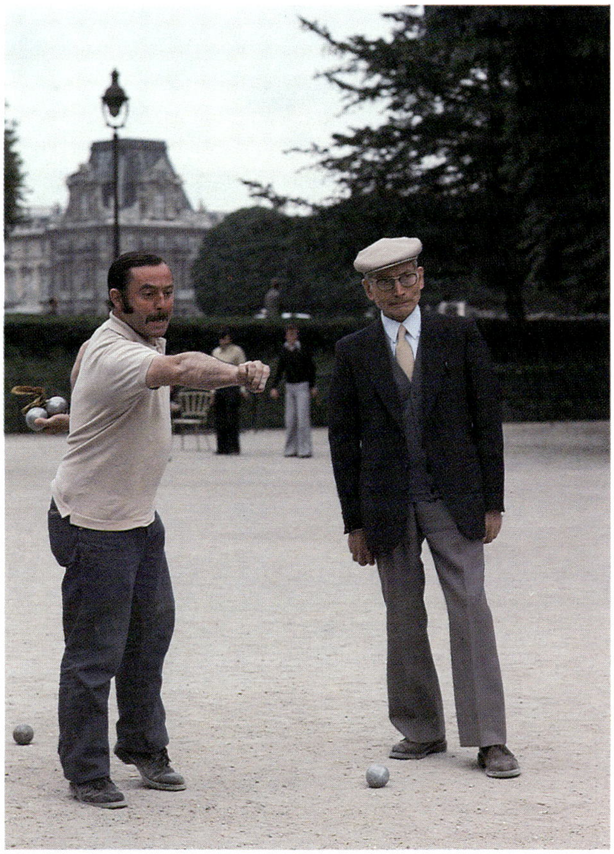

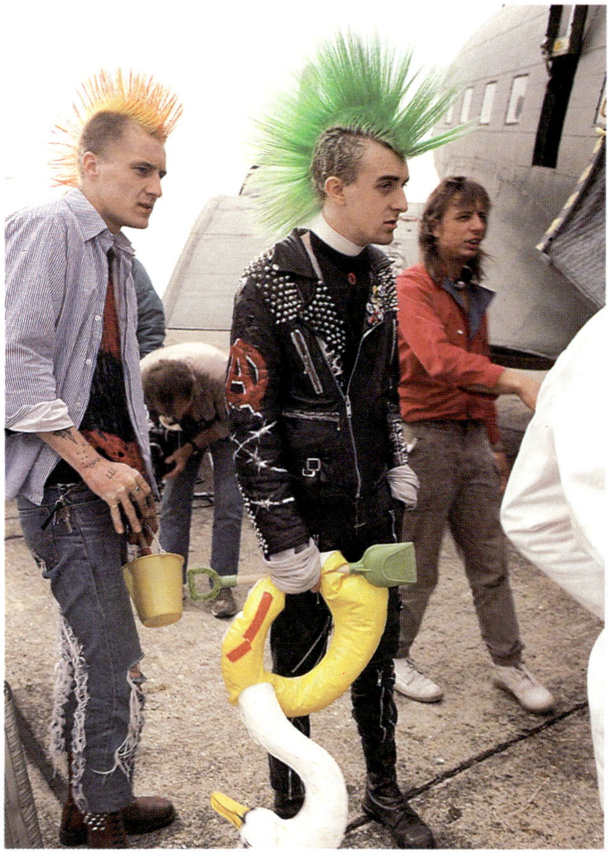

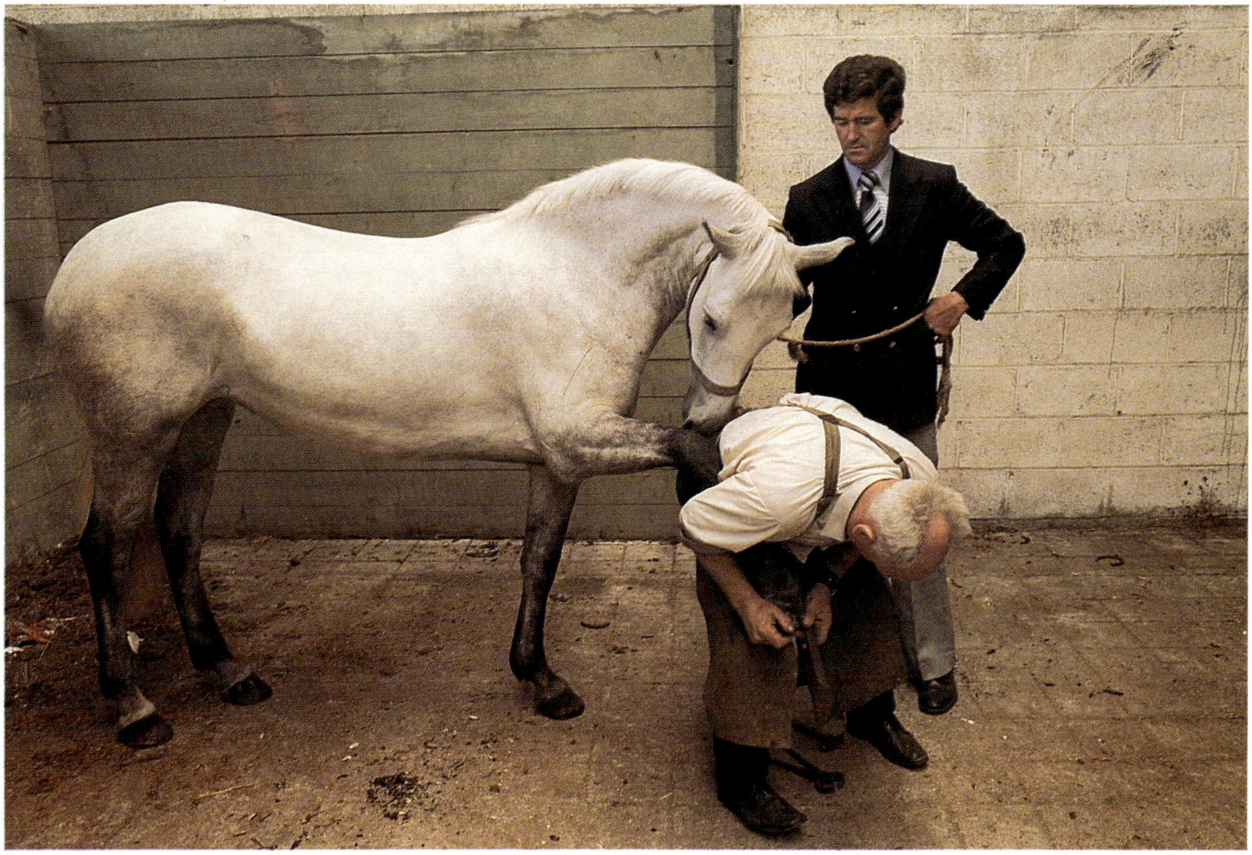

PUBLICITY

Whilst the camera has a reputation for not lying, most people now recognize that it can be persuaded to give perhaps a rather biased point of view. Indeed, its use as a means of propaganda has long been recognized as a vital element in image building and publicity, both for people and for products. It is said that the 1960s were the beginning of the 'Me' generation, and it could equally well be claimed that the 1980s saw the advent of the 'Image' generation.

In almost every walk of public and private life, people are increasingly conscious of their image, and the craft of the photographer plays a vital role in the creation and well-being of this asset. Some of the best photography of men is produced to this end, ranging from politicians and business tycoons to pop stars and media personalities. Selling yourself has become a major industry.

The photographs which the public see of this type give every appearance of being quite casual and natural, but this is seldom the case. Much care and attention goes into such a photographic session and a photographer who displays a skill in creating the right kind of images is very much in demand. Indeed, a great deal can be learned from looking at good publicity pictures: the choice of backgrounds and locations, together with clothes and props, as well as lighting and camera techniques, can be very helpful in giving you ideas for your own photographic sessions.

The work can be quite demanding and challenging, however, and quite apart from his photographic skills, it is also vital for such a photographer to get along well with people. It is not uncommon for a photographer to be informed quite curtly by 'a famous person' that he has just so many minutes to perform his miracles. Subservient acceptance of such demands is not only likely to produce poor results, but will also do little for his professional standing, although a display of temperament or a clash of wills will be equally counter-productive. It is necessary, therefore, for him to develop an easy but firm approach and even more important to be totally in control of his equipment and technique so that he can concentrate his full attention on the subject.

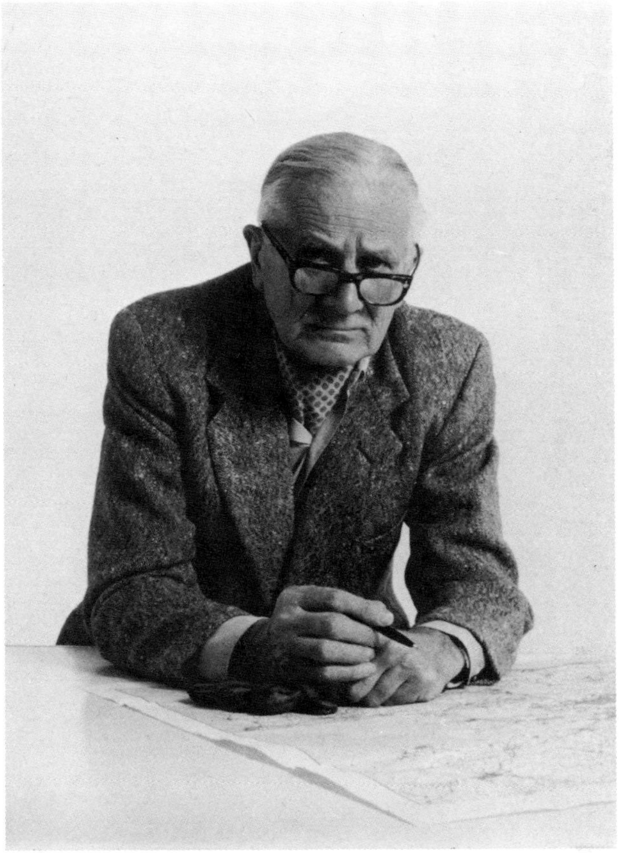

The point of a publicity picture is to sell your subject. One way to achieve that end is to picture him in connection with his work or a hobby.

The professional picture that appears to be a casual snapshot is rarely that. The photographer needs to exercise much care and attention over details .

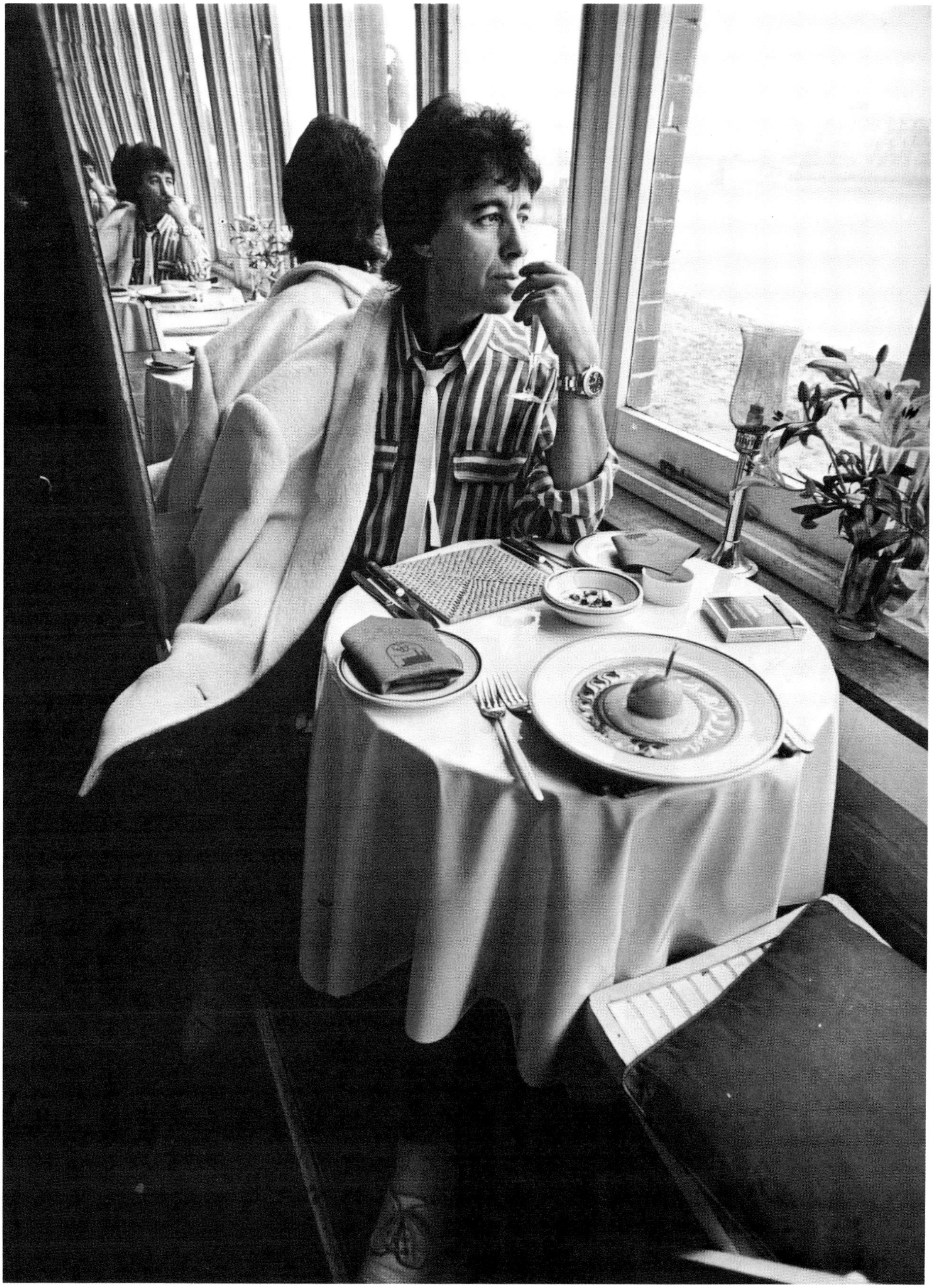

ADVERTISING

In the field of publicity, an image is created to sell a person. The advertising business, however, is usually involved in selling a product. The techniques involved are essentially the same as far as photography is concerned, with one important exception. The model, who is used to establish the image of a product, is usually creating a fictitious character. He is, in fact, a specialized type of actor. In fact, with professional modelling today, where the television commercial plays an ever-increasing role in advertising, the male model is often required to be an actor in the true sense.

A model casting session is a crucial stage in the preparation of a photographic session for a major advertising account. It is not at all unusual for literally dozens of models to be interviewed over a period of several days in order to find exactly the right person to create the role which will sell a particular product most effectively. The model agency directories and index cards cover every type of person from the current trendy teenagers and thirty-year-old thrusting young executive types, to bespectacled oldies for retirement plan ads. Whilst the requirement for male models for fashion falls into a fairly narrow and well-defined category, the same is not true of advertising photography, and there are agencies which specialise in finding even the most unlikely types of model, from tattooed punks to seven-feet-tall muscle men.

Unlike movie shots, the still photograph needs to be considerably exaggerated in order to have the required impact. It must be appreciated that whereas a film has a captive audience and can also rely upon movement and sound for its effect, a still photograph in a magazine advert or on a poster, has to literally stop people in their tracks, purely on the merits of its visual content. The skill of an advertising art director and photographer is in being able to distil the essential elements of a situation into something which can be recorded in a single, brief moment, and this often means striking a crucial balance between being well over the top and appearing believable.

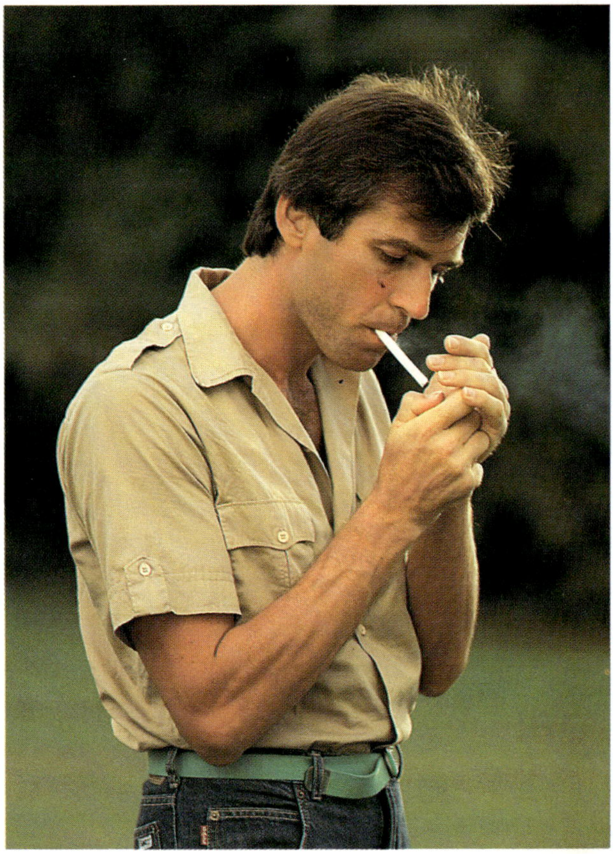

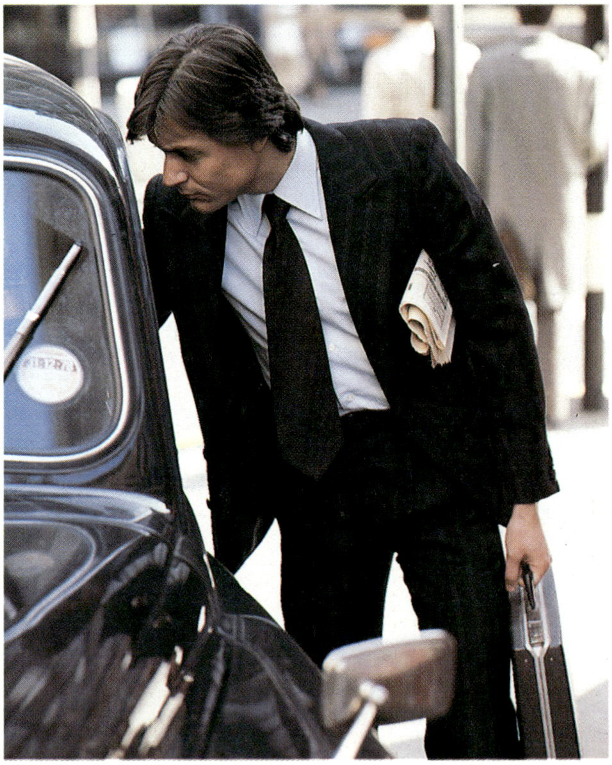

Advertising images of men are not confined to the promotion of visible products such as tobacco **(top left)** *or clothing* **(top right)**. *Often the product being sold cannot be depicted visually – for example business travel* **(near right)** *or consumer credit* **(far right)**. *In these instances, the advertising copy plays as important a role as the photograph itself.*

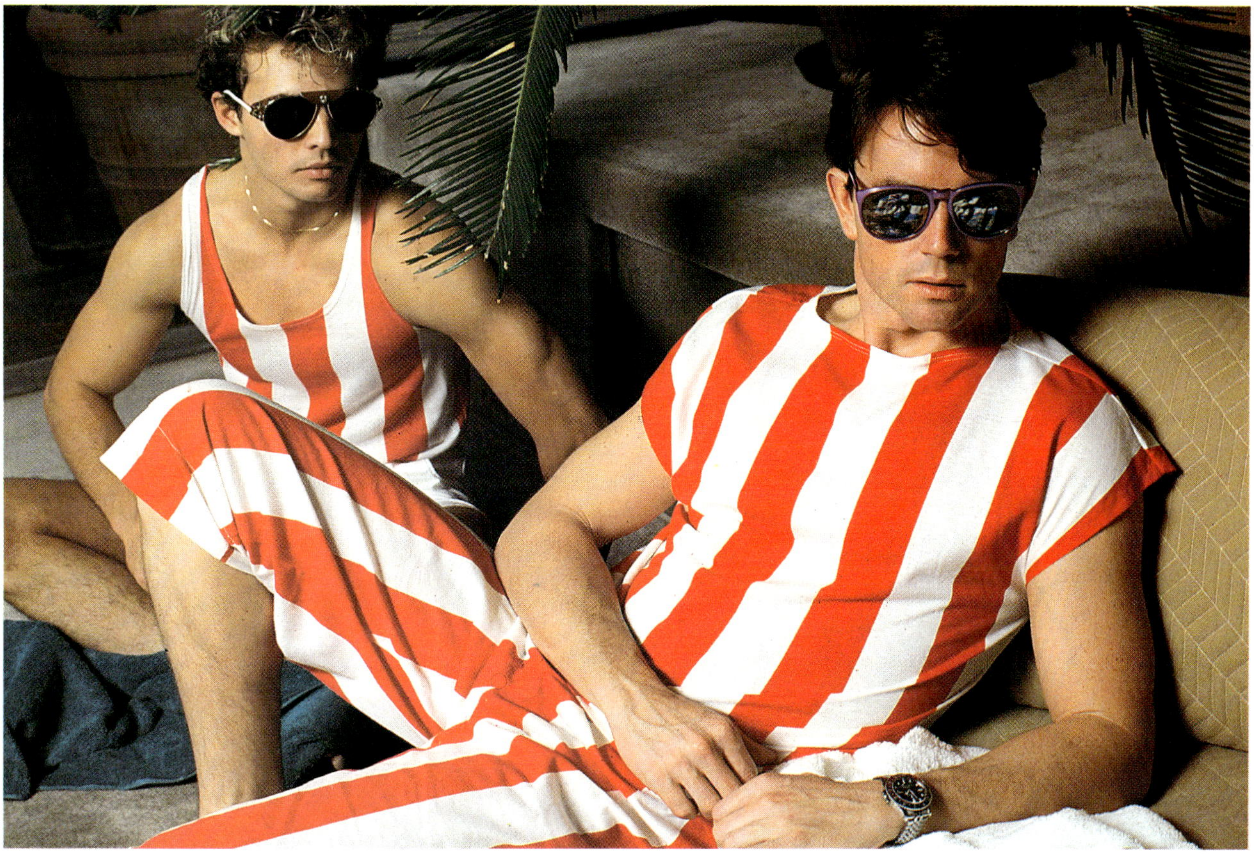

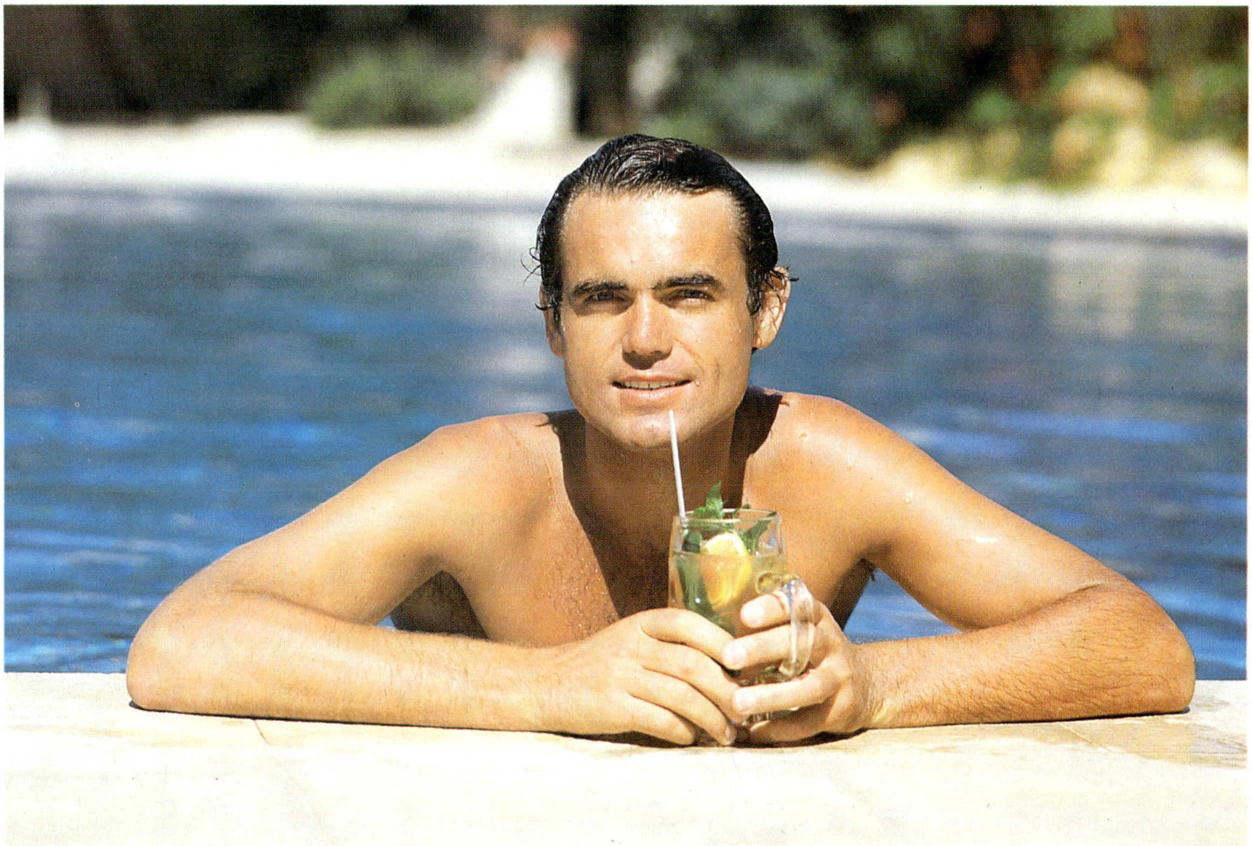

SOCIAL PHOTOGRAPHY

The mainstay of professional photography is much the same today as it was in the middle of the 19th Century: the social record, pictures taken of individuals, families and other groups as a personal memento. This started with the daguerreotype and then the carte de visite. The former was a fragile copper plate upon which the positive image was directly formed, making each one unique. They were usually kept in a small leather frame or wallet to protect their delicate surface. When the daguerreotype gave way to the more familiar negative/positive process, the carte de visite became the standard form of presentation for social photographs. Placed into a mount about 2½ × 4 inches, they became very popular in the 1860s.

Pictures of this type are a valuable social record, since they portray people from all walks of life in a way in which *they* wanted to be seen. Indeed, the archives of many of the great studios and photographers who did this work have become valued collections, both for their photographic merit and for their historical interest. Flattery of course was the essence of this type of picture and the techniques of soft focus and retouching were an important part of the photographer's skill and reputation. Today's photographers, on the other hand, tend to rely upon sympathetic lighting and a more natural, relaxed approach for their effect.

The single portrait is, however, only part of this type of work; the group photograph is another aspect that can have particular interest in the nostalgic sense. Whether it is a school group, a football or other team group or the members of a society, it can be fascinating to look back upon such pictures, even if you have no connection with the subjects. Some skill and a commanding manner is needed by the photographer to take successful group pictures, since it is vital that each person can be clearly seen, is looking towards the camera and has a pleasing expression. With a dozen or more people in the group, this can be something of a challenge. A well-known society photographer achieves success by giving a loud blast on a whistle at the crucial moment, apparently even when photographing Royalty.

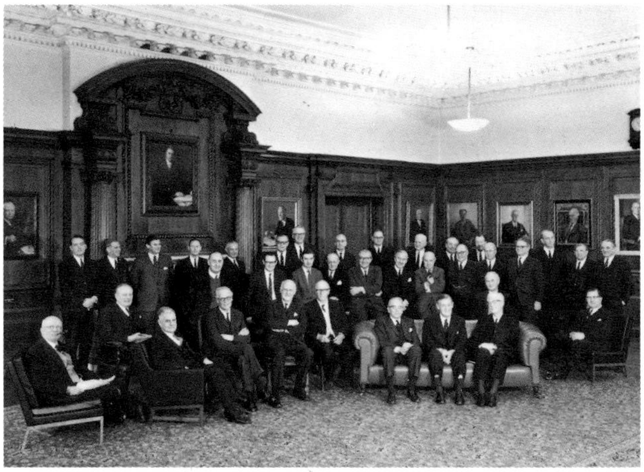

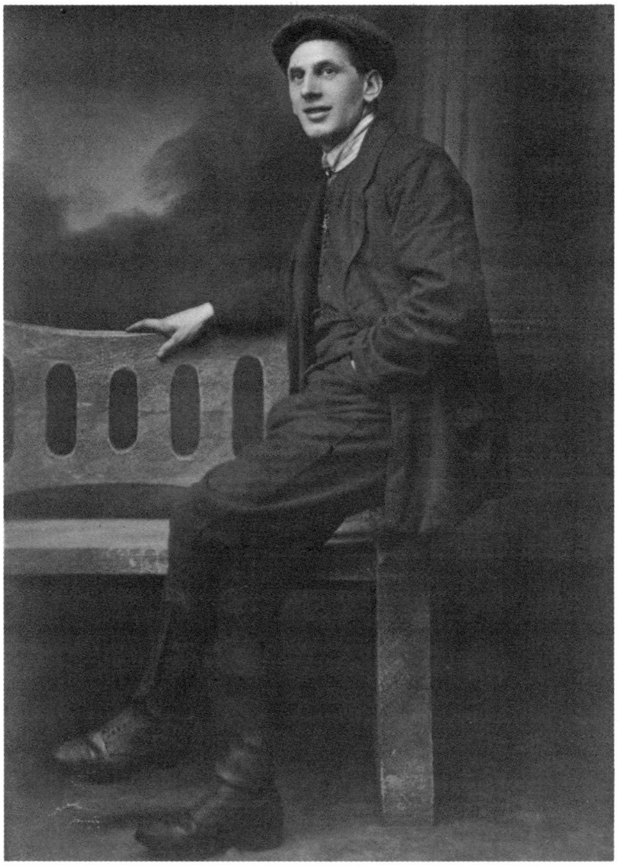

The social photographer's aim has always been to please the client – whether he is a miner in Sunday best **(above)** *or an eminent group of professionals* **(top)**. *In the past, extensive retouching would have smoothed the features of the social photographer's elder clients* **(right)** *but today a naturalistic approach is more common.*

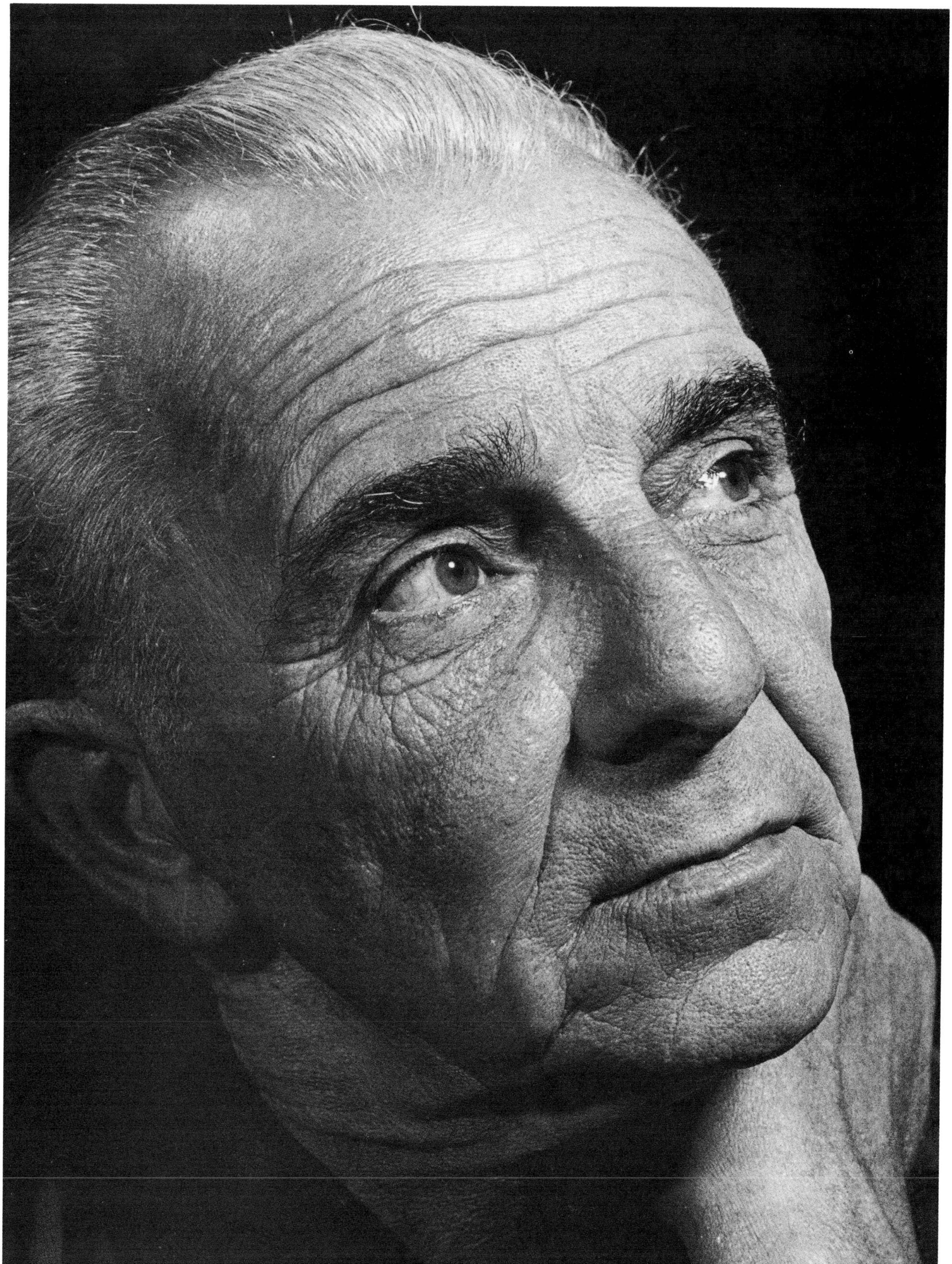

MUSIC AND THEATRE PHOTOGRAPHY

The stage is both a stimulating and challenging subject for photography. Outstanding performance pictures are by no means commonplace, but this is largely due to unavoidable restrictions, both in terms of lighting and viewpoints, which are imposed on a photographer working in this field. To some extent this can be overcome by pictures taken during rehearsals or at special photocalls, but these seldom have the impact and excitement of a real live performance in front of an audience.

Some subjects such as ballet are particularly difficult, not only in terms of the problem of capturing rapid movement under stage lighting conditions, but also of conveying the elegant and graceful qualities of that movement in a still image. Among the relatively few names that have excelled in this field are Barbara Morgan, E. O. Hoppé, Anthony Crickmay and Zoë Dominic; both Irving Penn and Richard Avedon have also taken memorable photographs of dancers such as Nureyev.

In complete contrast, an aspect of stage photography which offers particular potential for male photography is that of rock music. The flamboyant, colorful and invariably theatrically-presented productions offer dramatic and exciting opportunities for photography. A book of photographs and posters are an almost obligatory adjunct to the album and video which follows a concert tour by a major star or band, and the production of photographs of this type is an important part of the music business.

The common problem with all stage photography is that of lighting. Since it is a crucial element of the mood and design of the set, it follows that any form of additional lighting will detract, and it is usually necessary for the photographer to work with only the stage lighting. Because brightness levels, contrast and color quality of such lighting is constantly changing during a performance, it requires both skill and experience in terms of camera technique, composition and choice of viewpoint to produce outstanding pictures.

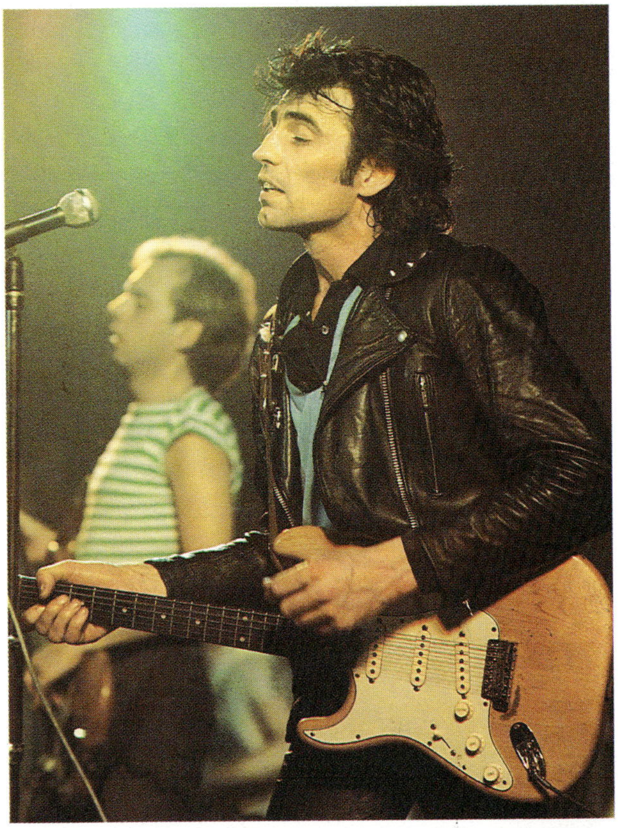

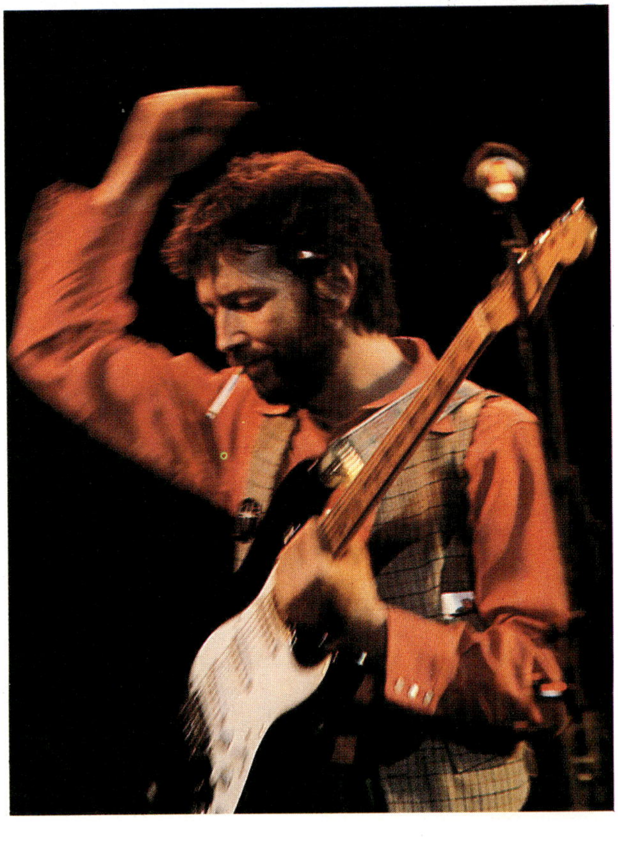

Rock concerts provide terrific potential for male photography, providing you keep a close watch on the ever-changing lighting. Try also to keep the subject as large as possible in the viewfinder, rather than losing him in a sea of blackness. Watch for flamboyant poses and unusual facial expressions.

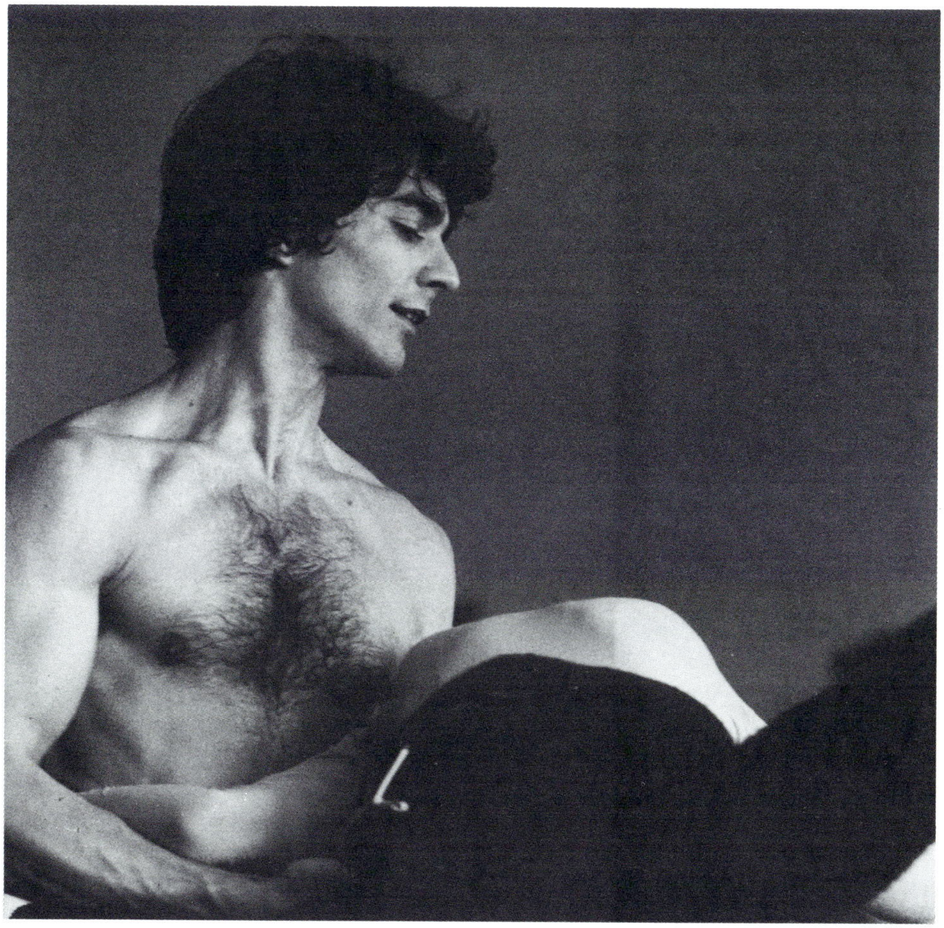

Shooting ballet is largely a matter of capturing the grace and movement in a single, still image, while keeping an eye on the way the stage lighting is falling on your subject.

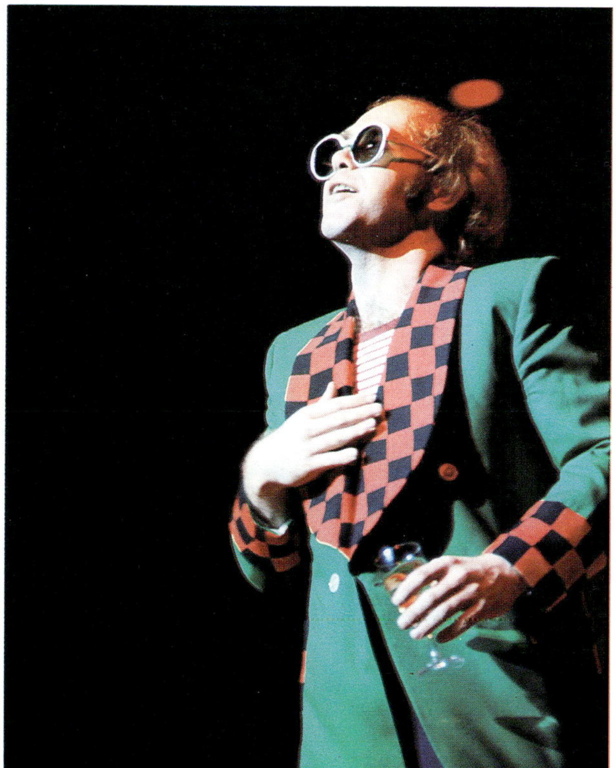

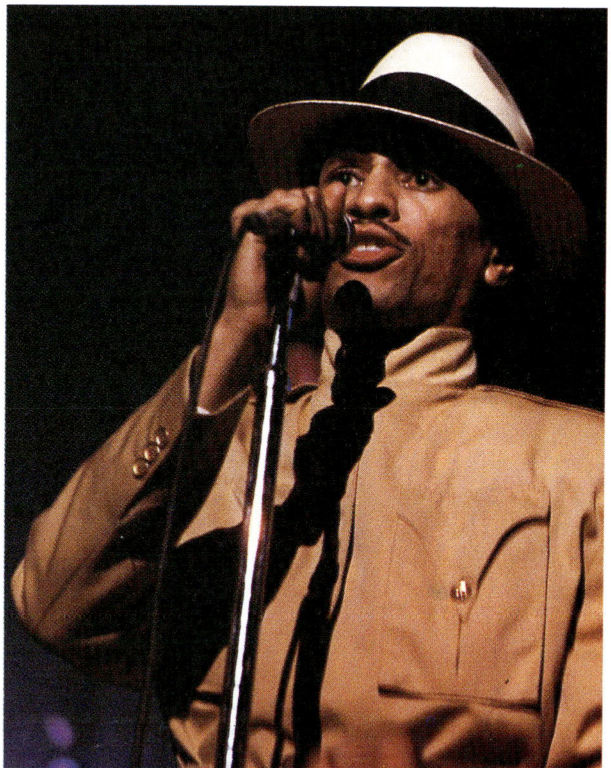

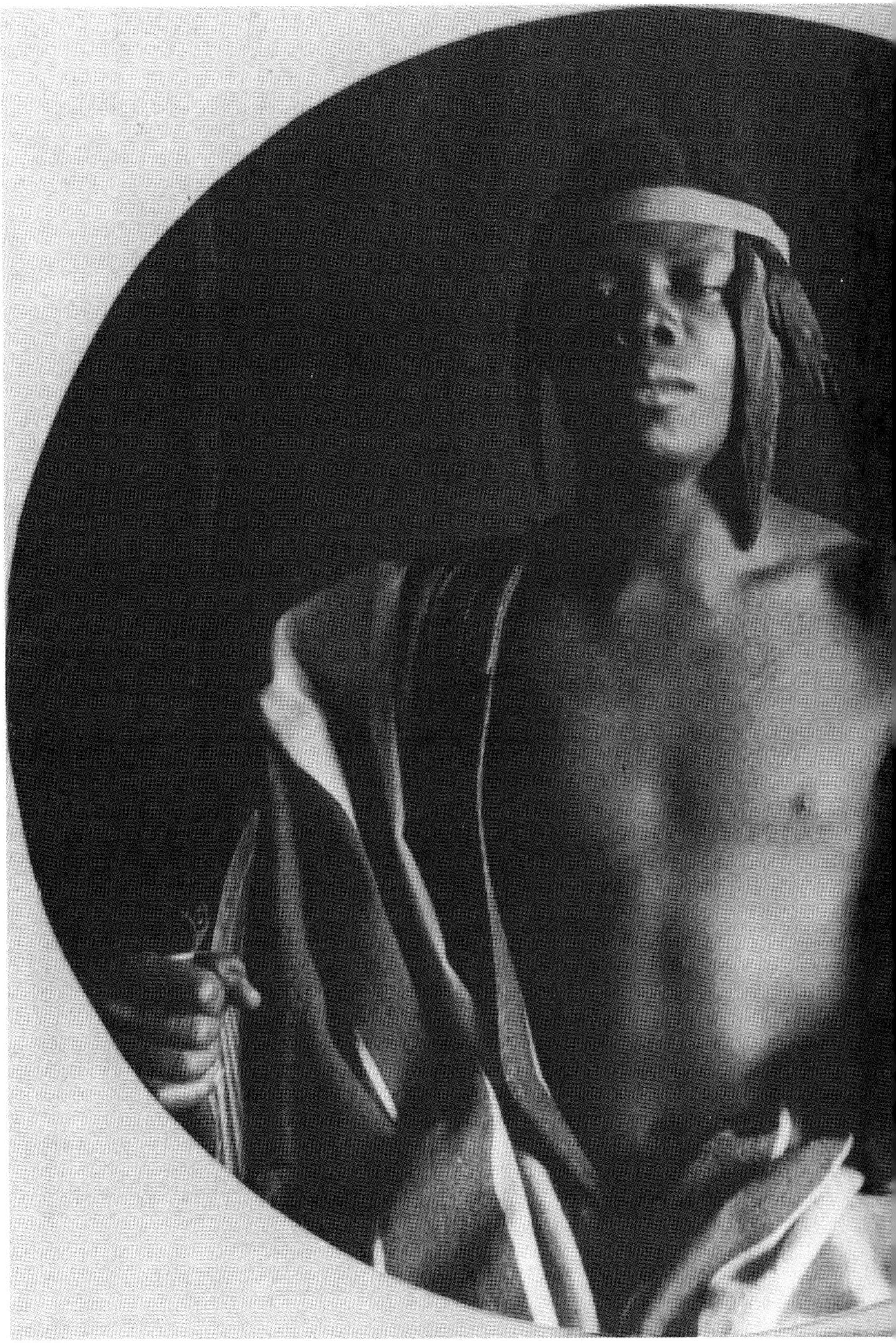

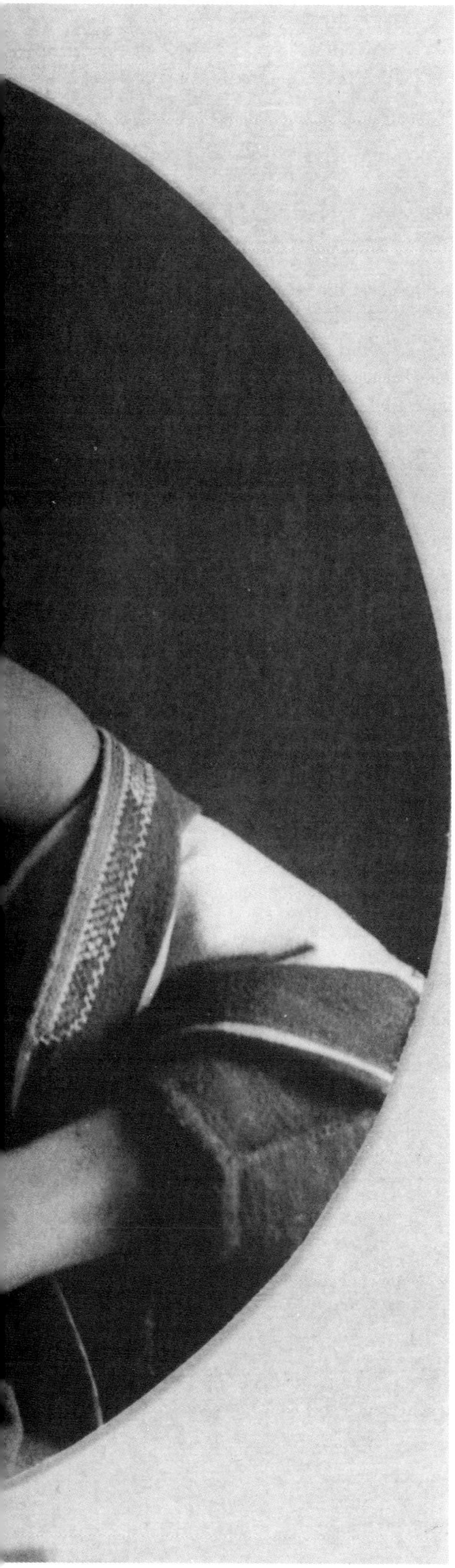

HISTORICAL PORTFOLIO

THE MALE IMAGE – YESTERDAY AND TODAY

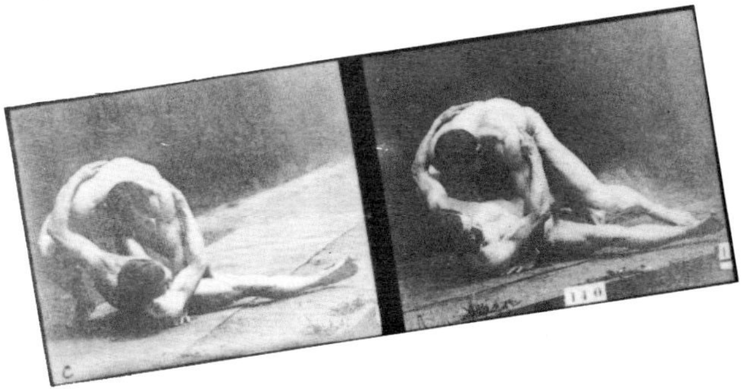

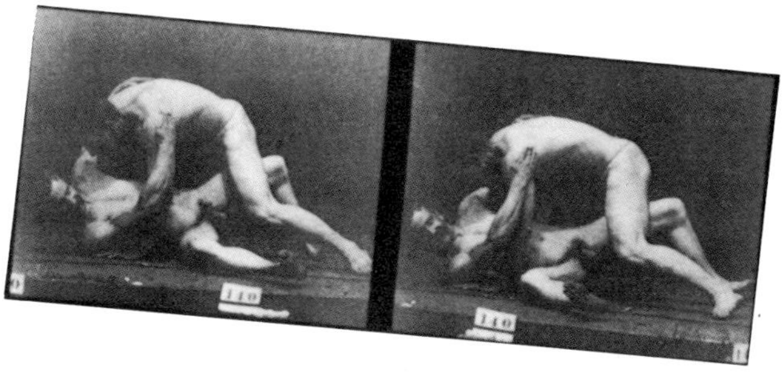

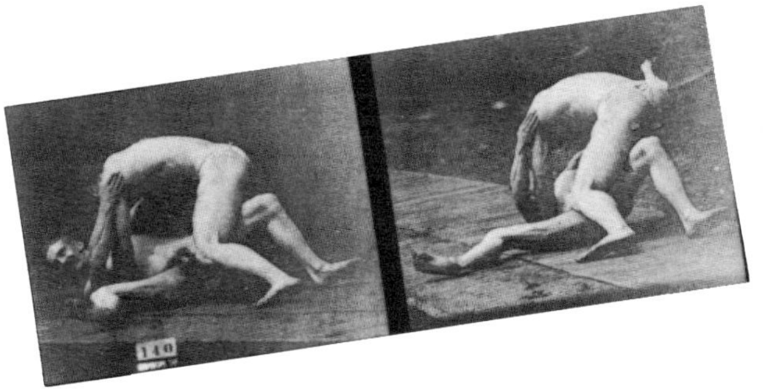

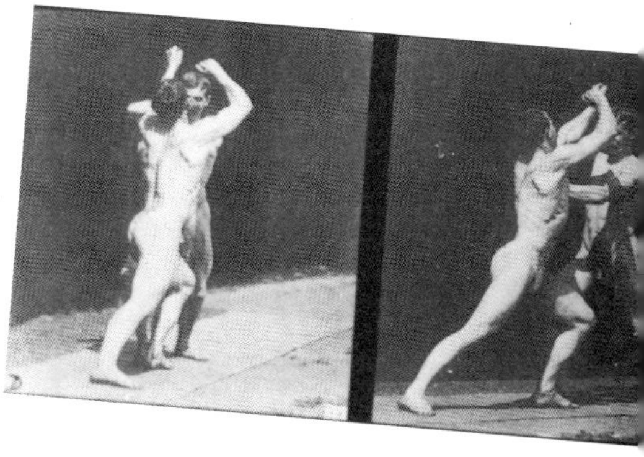

Two of the earliest applications of photography were portraiture and nude studies. Indeed, the daguerreotype process, invented by Louis Jacques Mandé Daguerre and announced for the first time in 1839 was, for many ordinary people, the first time they were able to afford a likeness of themselves and their friends or family. To a large extent the camera at this time began to take over from the medium of brush, paint and canvas. Hence the reaction from French painter Paul Delaroche: 'From today painting is dead.' Consequently many of the initial experiments in photography were in photographing the human form, and the male model enjoyed equal popularity with the female for this purpose. For this reason, it is easy to understand why the approach to photography in the early part of the 19th Century was influenced by paintings, and also why many of the early photographers were either practising or frustrated artists.

David Octavius Hill and Robert Adamson are good examples of this. The former was a painter living in Edinburgh who had exhibited at the Royal Academy and, in 1843, he was given a huge commission to paint an enormous canvas containing the portraits of nearly 500 dignitaries of the Church of Scotland. In order to cope with this undertaking, he decided to use photography as an aid. To this end, he became involved with a young engineer, Robert Adamson, who had already experimented with the calotype process and had begun to practice as a commercial photographer a few months before they joined forces. It was a partnership which epitomizes photography, a blend of both artistic and technical skill. Hill was by all accounts an indifferent painter, but his perceptive eye, coupled with the mastery of the process which Adamson soon acquired, gave rise to a series of outstanding portraits and character studies.

Oscar Gustave Rejlander is another painter who turned successfully to photography. Born in 1813, he exhibited his first print in 1855. This was a combination of many different negatives, a technique which was sometimes used to emulate the expansive and elaborate compositions of the painter/artist. His best known work is a combination of epic proportions. Thirty different negatives were combined to create an image which he called ***The Two Ways of Life***. However, he also produced many powerful, straightforward portraits and figure studies, some of which were made for artists' reference. He was commissioned to produce photographic illustrations for Charles Darwin's ***The Expression of the Emotions in Man and Animals***. He also experimented with studio lighting, using controlled daylight in an indoor setting, achieved by using black screens and tunnels to eliminate unwanted light from the subject.

Whereas most of the work of the early photographers was of necessity rather static, portraits and nudes being treated very much in the same way as a

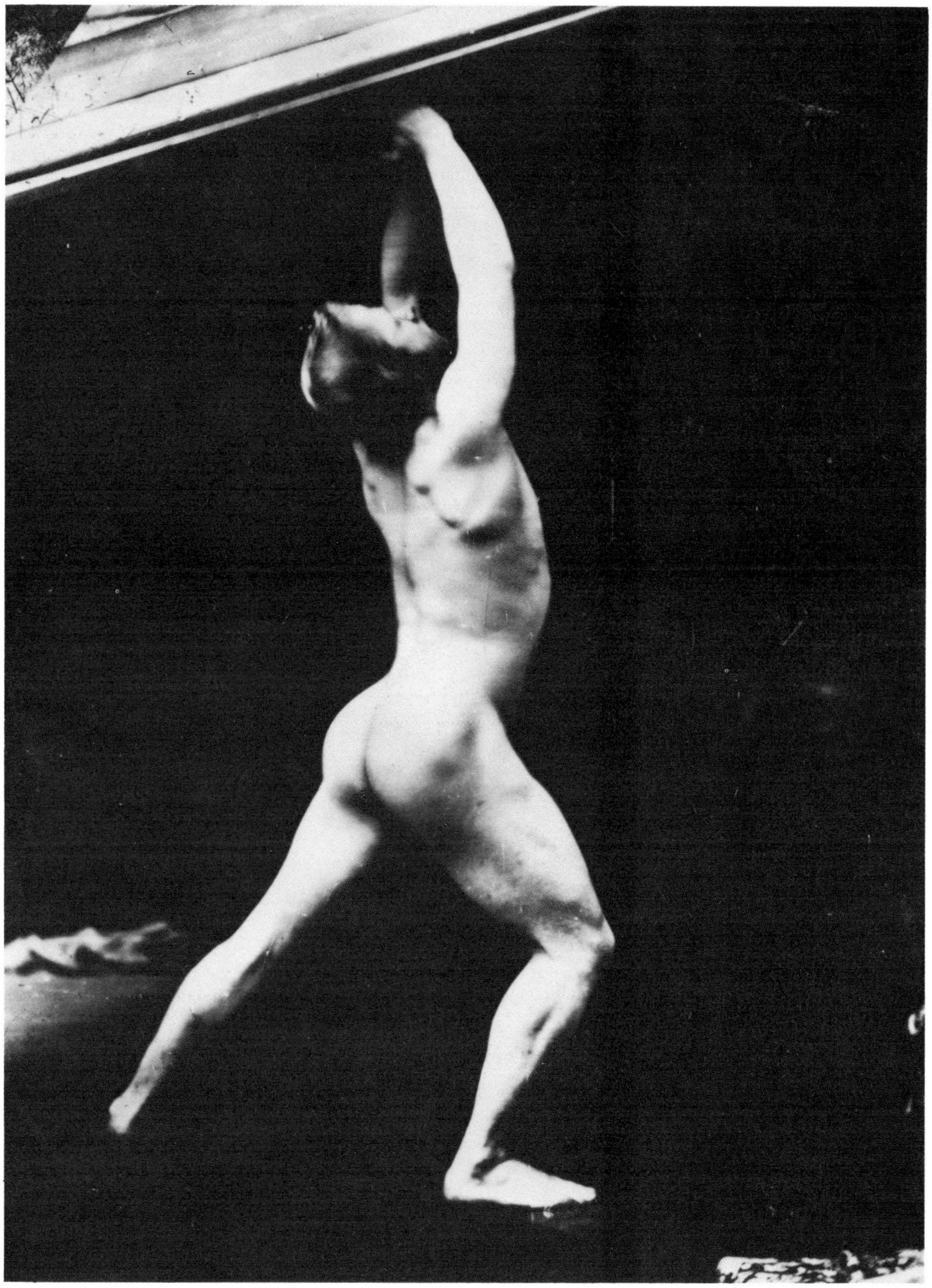

Many early male nudes were sold as 'Studies for Artists' – ostensibly for the benefit of starving painters who could not afford to pay life models. However, the number of such studies sold suggests that in the nineteenth century paintings and sculpture were many times more popular than today. This example is by O. G. Rejlander.

Eadweard Muybridge took many thousands of pictures of the human body in motion (see page 32). These sequential images are from a series entitled Men Wrestling.

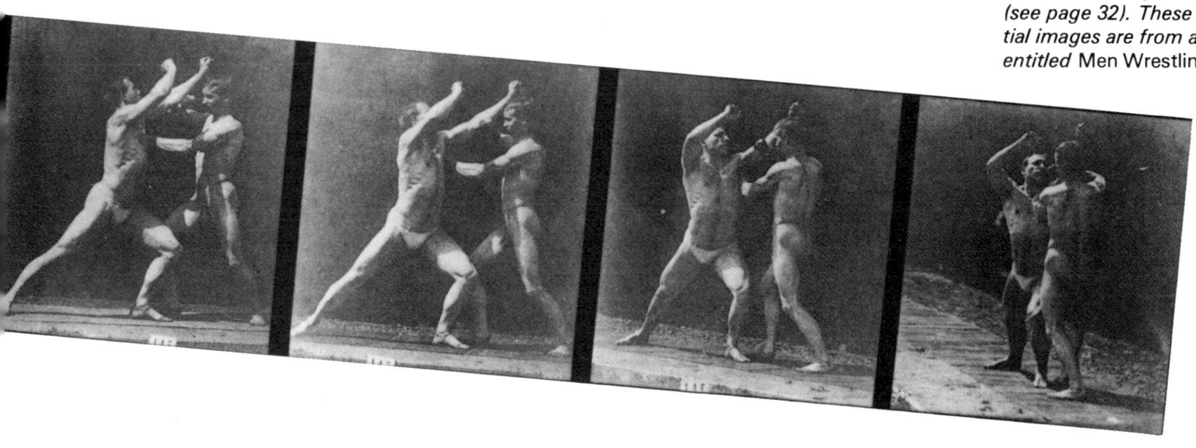

still life subject, the photography of Eadweard Muybridge was very much concerned with movement. He was born in England in 1830 and was first employed in the family business of papermaking. In 1851, he moved to America where he learned the craft of photography from a New York portraitist using the daguerreotype process, Silas Sellick. Muybridge's first pictures were of the Western States under the pseudonym Helios, but his greatest interest developed as a result of the question, 'Do all four legs of a galloping horse leave the ground together?' The answer – 'yes!' – was discovered by setting up a sequence of twenty-four cameras, each triggered by a thread stretched across the animal's path. This was followed by many other experiments in both animal and human movement as well as conventional portrait and nude photography. Some of the latter, it is claimed, has influenced the work of the painter Francis Bacon.

Fred Holland Day was a wealthy Bostonian, born into a rich family in 1864. His father was a leather merchant, he benefited from independent means and was able to indulge his aesthetic interests, which included painting. In partnership with a friend, Professor Copeland, he became a publisher and included in the work he published were the sketches of Aubrey Beardsley. He was also a personal friend of such personalities as William Morris and Oscar Wilde. His interest in art eventually led him to photography and he applied himself to this new medium with considerable enthusiasm. He was considered something of an eccentric and, often dressed in flowing Turkish robes, he was frequently seen wandering the countryside with his camera and models, creating romantic and often mythologically inspired pictures. His work was often controversial. Like most other photographers of this period, he was very much concerned with the acceptance of photography on the same intellectual and aesthetic level as painting and with similar status. Although not a particularly religious person, he decided to advance his cause by embarking on a very ambitious project – to illustrate the last days of Christ. He cast himself in the title role, subjecting himself to a long period of starvation and growing his hair in readiness for the photography. Suitable locations were explored in the environs of Boston and props and clothes were made with scrupulous attention to detail. The photographs, which took three months to complete, were given critical acclaim. Tragically, in 1904, most of Holland Day's photographs were destroyed in a fire and few examples of his considerable output survived.

At the turn of the century, dramatic improvements began to take place in both cameras and photographic materials. The introduction of the rollfilm and the Box Brownie not only meant that photography was accessible to many more people than before, but it

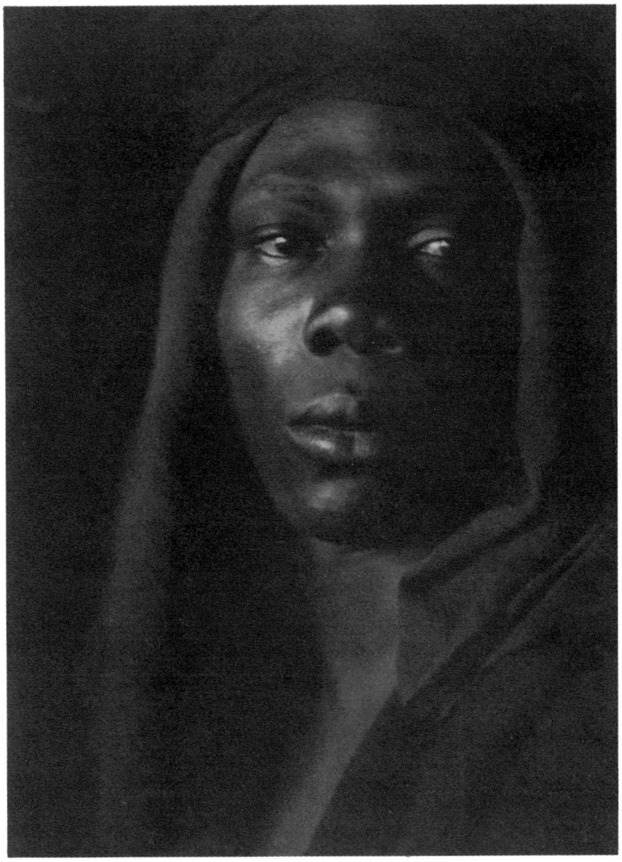

Though best remembered for his eccentric behaviour, and his series of self-portraits in the role of Christ, Fred Holland Day left behind him a wealth of superb images of men. His work is now highly sought after. Left: Ebony, *1899. Right:* Negro with Hat. *Below:* Leung Foo.

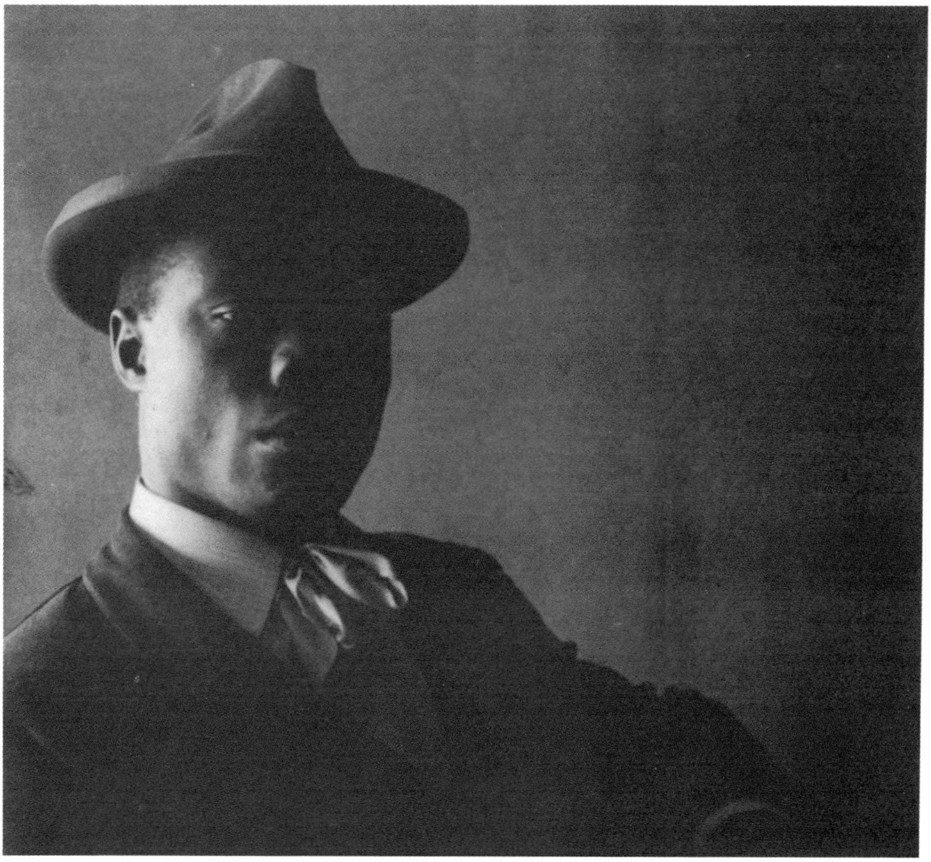

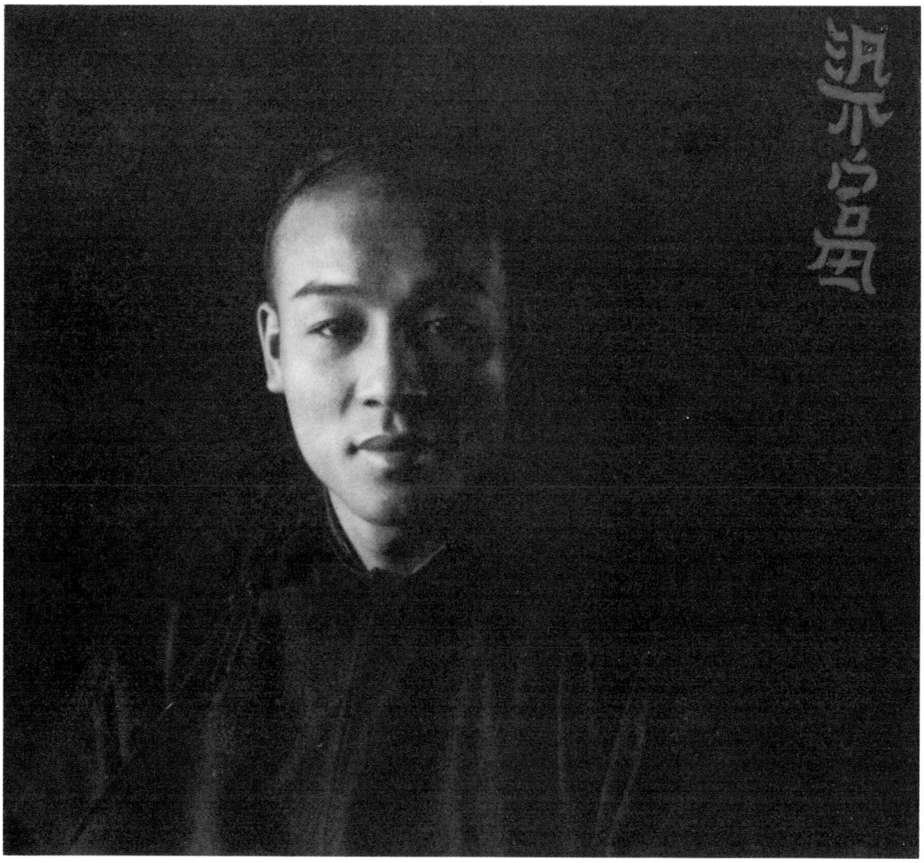

also allowed the camera to be used in a much less restrained and formal way. The preoccupation with emulating the work of painters, which had so far obsessed photographers, started to give way to a more 'photographic' approach, and one way in which this materialized was with the birth of reportage or documentary photography.

Dr Eric Saloman was undoubtedly one of the pioneers in this new style of photography. Born in Berlin in 1896, he was the son of a banker. After a variety of jobs and the survival of the First World War as a prisoner for four years, he eventually took up photography as a career in 1927. Unlike the cumbersome plate cameras of the earlier photographers, Dr Saloman used a small Ermanox camera, using tiny glass plates of 4.5 × 6 cm with, for those times, a very fast f/2 lens. This allowed him to take pictures in poor light, photographing with only available light in such places as courtrooms and at official receptions. He frequently took candid and unposed pictures of many important figures of his time including Neville Chamberlain, Ramsey MacDonald and Albert Einstein. He developed a technique which allowed him to shoot without flash in situations where other methods would not have been permissible.

To many people Henri Cartier-Bresson epitomizes the straightforward, uncontrived approach to photography, where the quality of the image is dependent purely on the photographer's perception and his skill in timing and composition. Born in France in 1908, he has for over fifty years produced a consistent flow of memorable and powerful pictures, many of which are considered to be among the best ever taken of the human situation. His serious involvement with photography began in 1930, immediately making the newly-introduced format, 35mm, and camera, the Leica, his trademark. He has travelled all over the world and photographed a tremendous variety of people and situations, from famous personalities to peasants and prostitutes. He works almost exclusively in black and white, believing that the element of color detracts from the impact of his images. He is very concerned with retaining his anonymity, rarely allowing himself to be photographed. His approach to photography is the ultimate in low profile, carrying usually only a camera body with a standard lens in his coat pocket. Insisting that his pictures are not cropped and are processed and printed by someone else ensures that their impact and effectiveness is not in any way the result of technical contrivance and control, but solely that of his own unique vision.

One area in which photojournalism has become a powerful tool and also in which photography of the male predominates, is that of war photography. This type of work requires a special breed of both person and photographer, able to be present and witness the unspeakable horrors of conflict without actually

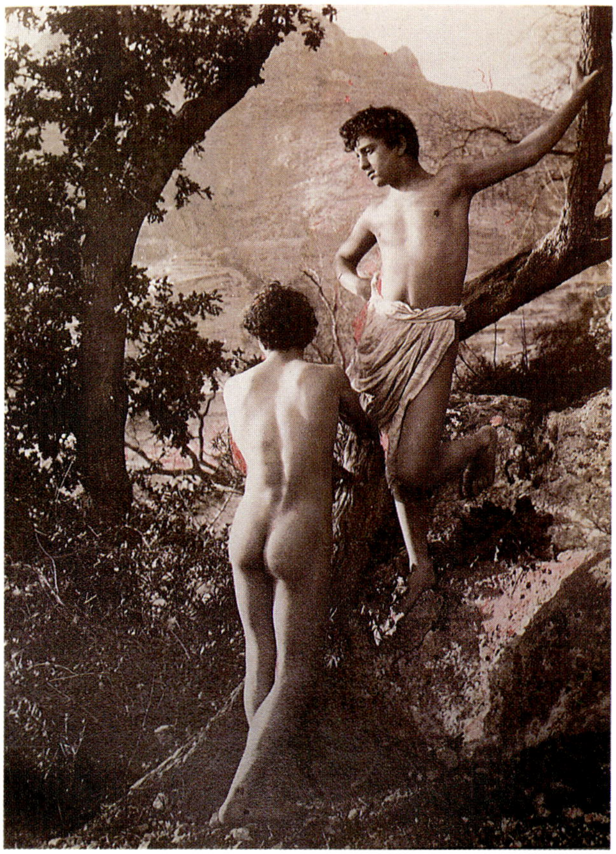

Baron Wilhelm von Gloeden was an expatriate German who took up residence in the Mediterranean town of Taormina in the hope of cure for his consumption. The disease left him, but he stayed on the island indulging a new-found passion: photography of the local men and boys. He was prolific, producing most of his output between 1900 and 1914. Stylistically, his images are remarkably straightforward, and lack the soft-focus romanticism that was popular at the time.

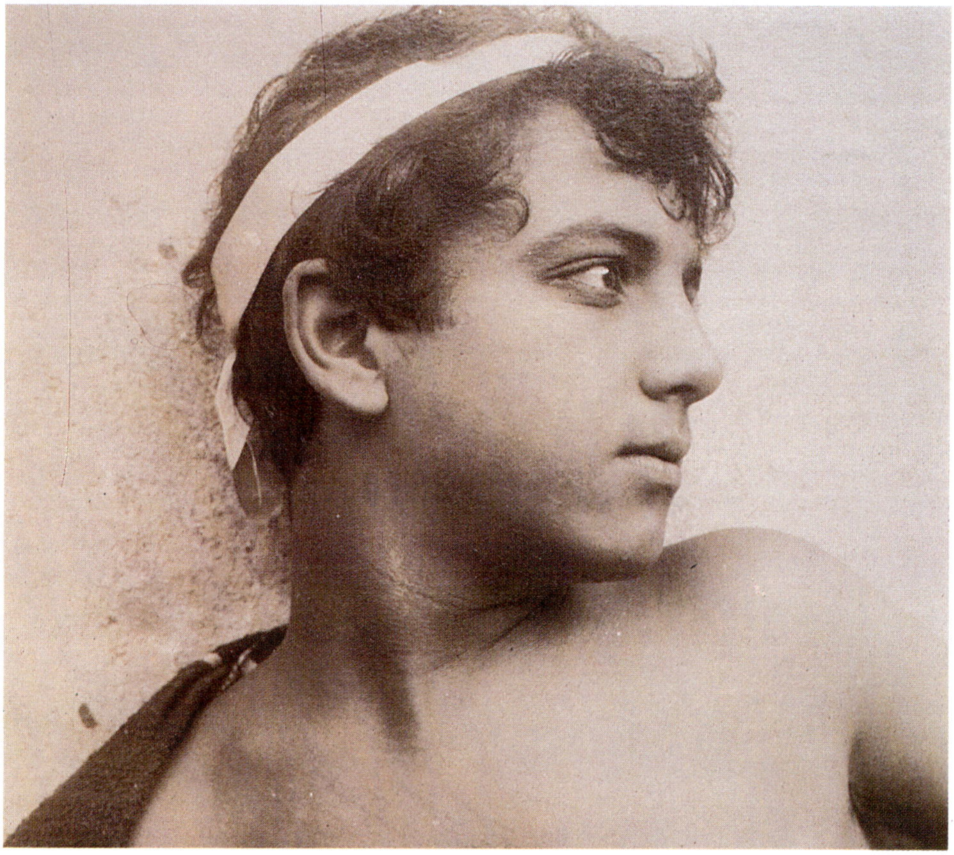

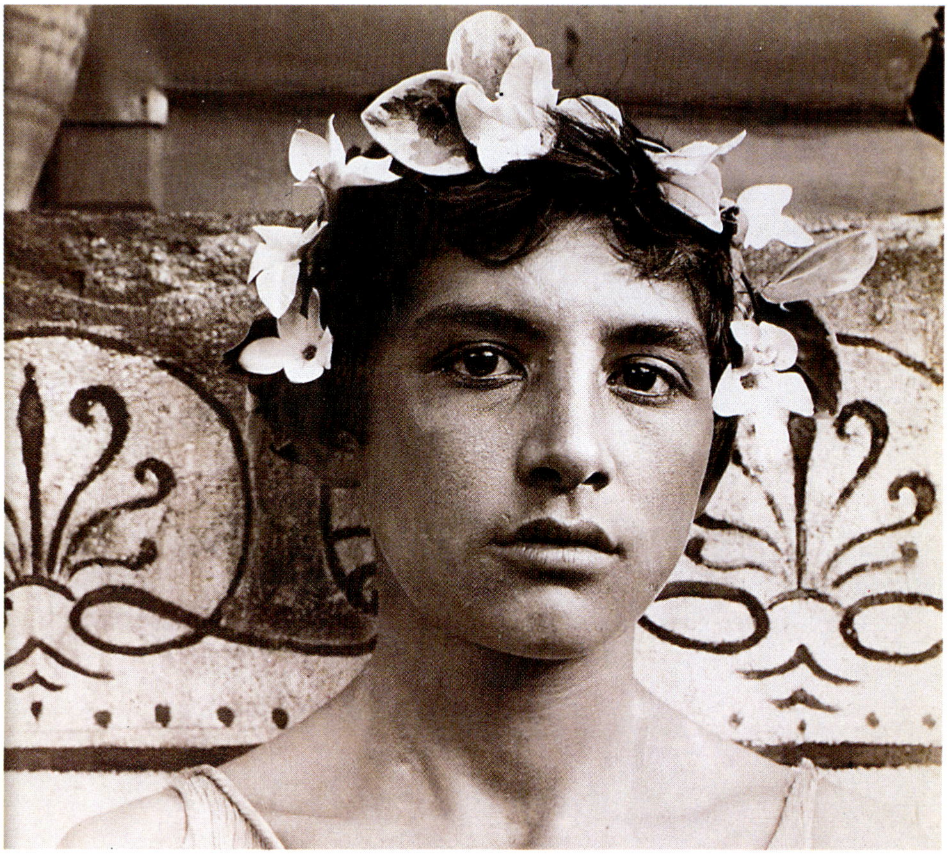

becoming a part of them. One such photographer was Robert Capa, born in Budapest in 1913. He was a US citizen but educated in Berlin, where he began his career as a photographer's assistant in 1931, moving to Paris when the Nazis took power in 1933. He photographed the Spanish Civil War, during which he made one of the most memorable war pictures of all time, that of a Spanish soldier, frozen in mid-air with his arms outstretched at the moment a bullet takes his life. He also photographed the Japanese invasion of China, World War Two in Europe for ***Life*** magazine and the early days of Israeli independence. Along with Cartier-Bresson, he became a founder member of Magnum, but in 1954 he was tragically killed by a landmine while working on an assignment in Indo China.

Portrait photography too was dramatically affected by the new realistic approach to the medium as boldly-lit and often hard and decidedly unromantic images began to replace the diffused, sentimental images of the earlier exponents of the genre. Richard Avedon emerged as a master of the studio portrait. Born in 1923 in New York, he started his career as a messenger for a photographic business at the age of seventeen, leaving to join the marines where he studied photography. After leaving the service, he continued his studies under Alexey Brodovitch and subsequently became a staff photographer, first with ***Harpers Bazaar*** magazine and later for ***Vogue***. Although his main preoccupation for these publications was that of fashion photography, he produced a continuing series of powerful and dramatic portraits, invariably in black and white. Much of his best work of this type has been published in his books ***Observations*** and ***Nothing Personal***. His studio portraits are lit with electronic flash, often creating a quite harsh effect and sometimes using a wide-angle lens and close viewpoint to emphasize the realistic and uncompromising quality of his pictures.

The sea and those who sail it have been recurring themes that allowed men to be pictured in a world that is traditionally their own. Here, you will find no coy approaches to male photography. The action and the environment are, and always have been, the dominating factors. That theme is epitomized here by two pictures, taken by F. J. Mortimer and titled Empire's Watchdogs **(below right)** *and* The Relief Boat **(below)**. *The third picture, titled* Port au Prince **(right)**, *is by Max J. Shapiro.*

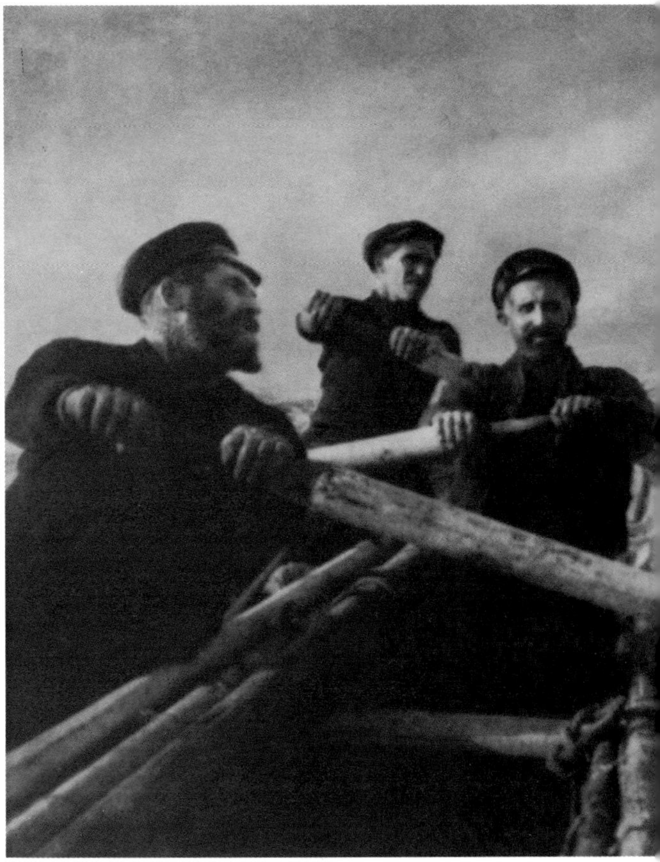

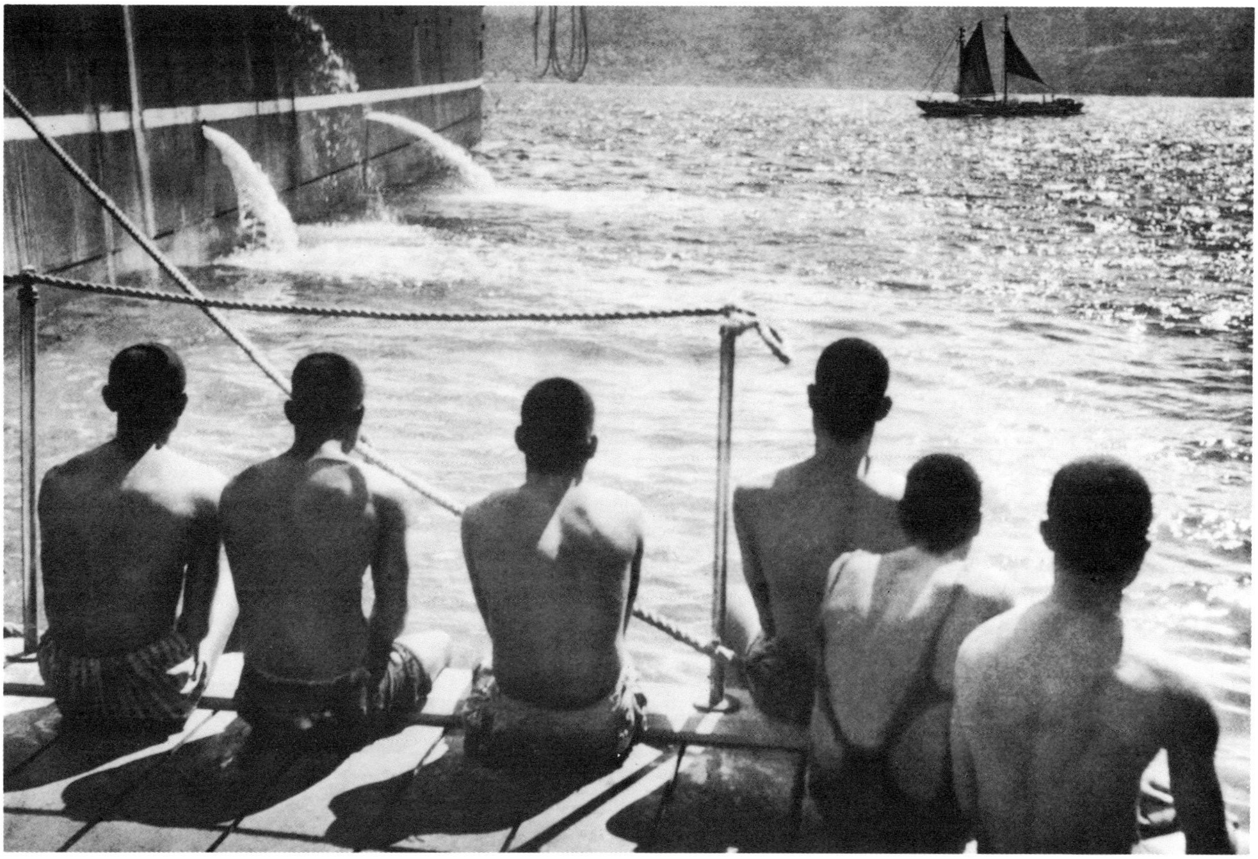

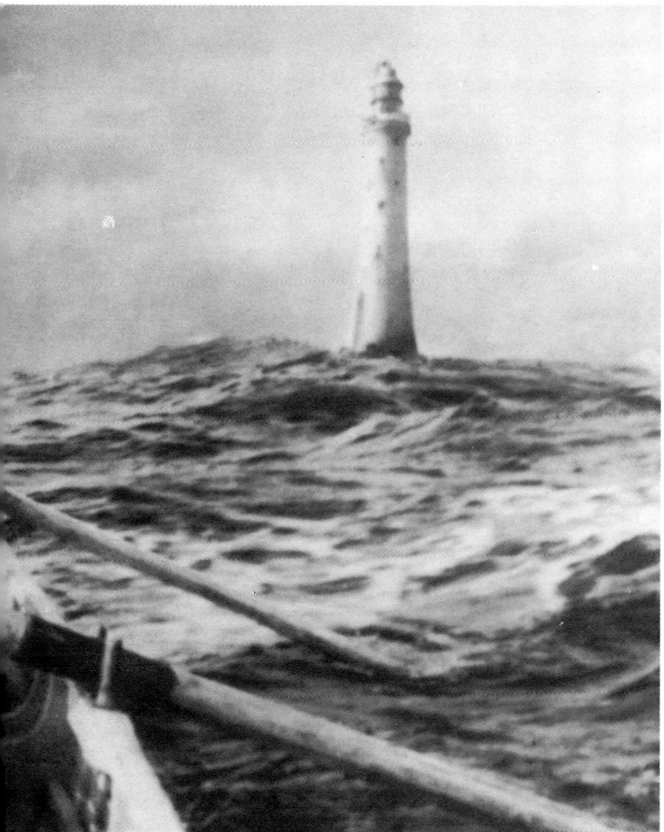

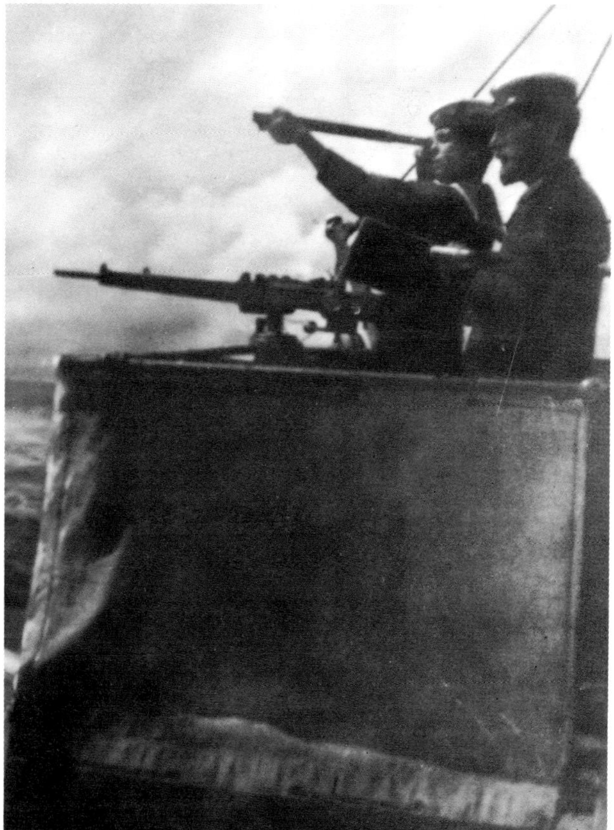

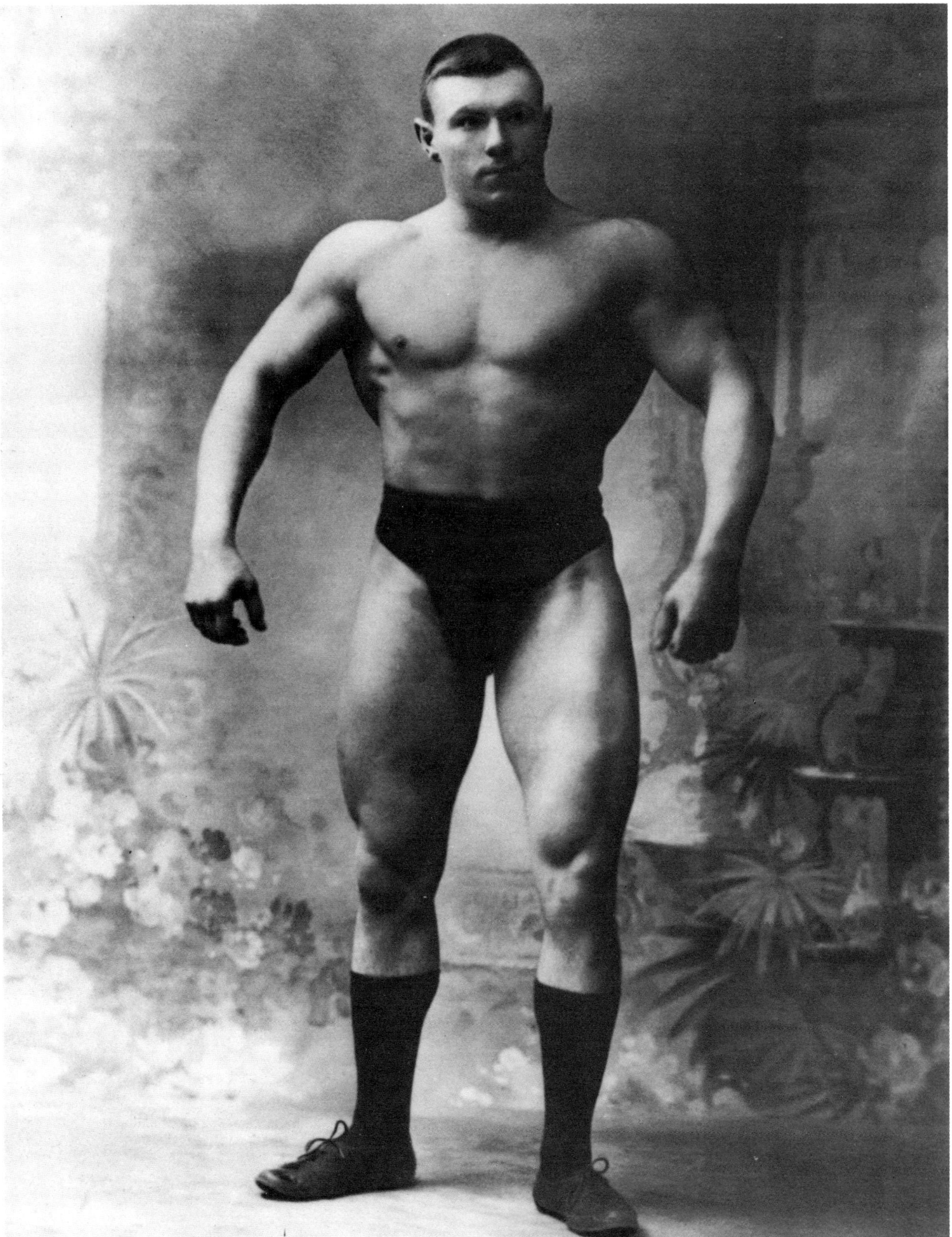

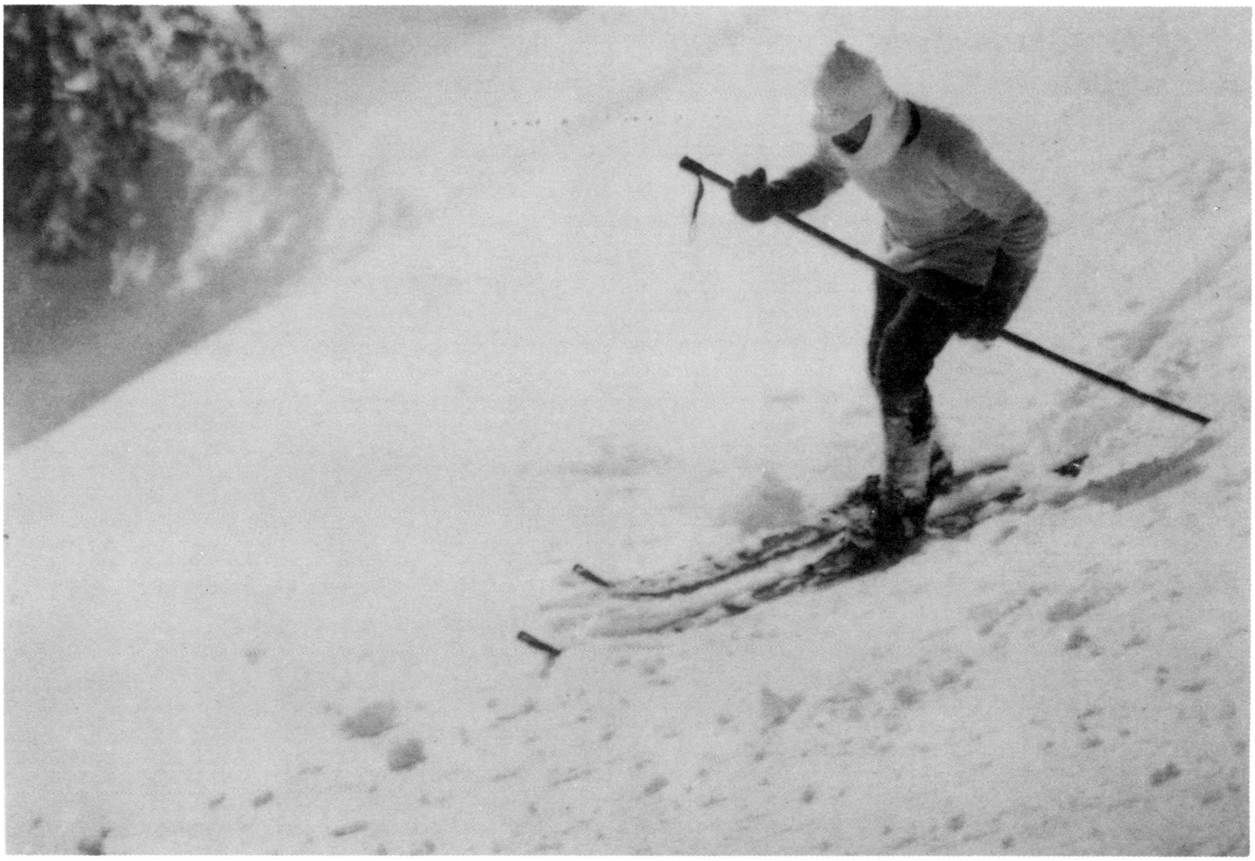

Sport has always been a popular theme for photographers, though limitations of early materials and equipment meant that images such as The Combat *by W. G. Hill had to be posed as tableaux by motionless models. Straight portraits of sporting personalities – such as* Hackenschmidt, The Russian Champion Wrestler, *by Paul Martin – were more common. Eventually, though, faster plates and shutters made possible true action pictures, such as Ward Muir's* Alpine Ski Runner.

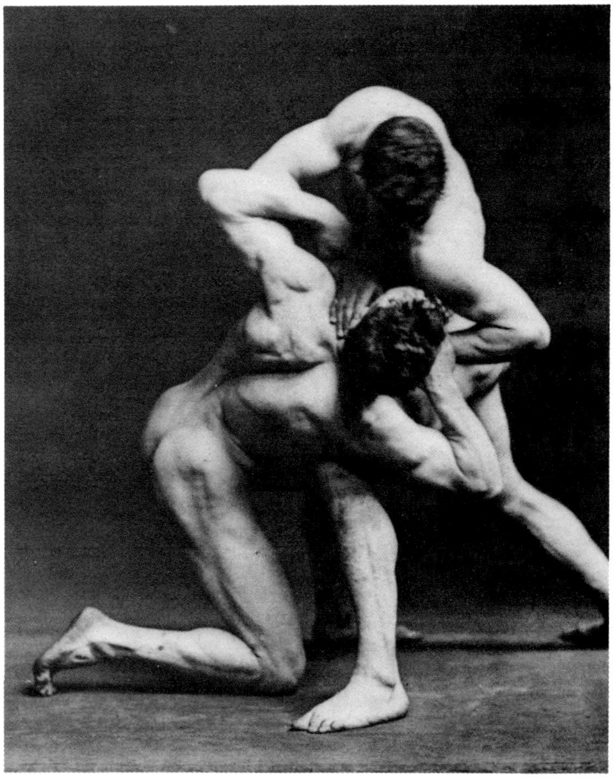

Portraiture has been the mainstay of many photographic businesses since the moment when a practical method was found of making the relatively short exposures needed to capture human subjects. Stylistically, formal photographic portraits have tended to follow in the traditions of painting, as exemplified by Samuel Bairne's picture The Lord Mayor. *When photography gained momentum as an art-form, though, portraiture gradually discarded painterly conventions: the other images shown here have a uniquely photographic quality that owes little to paint and canvas.*

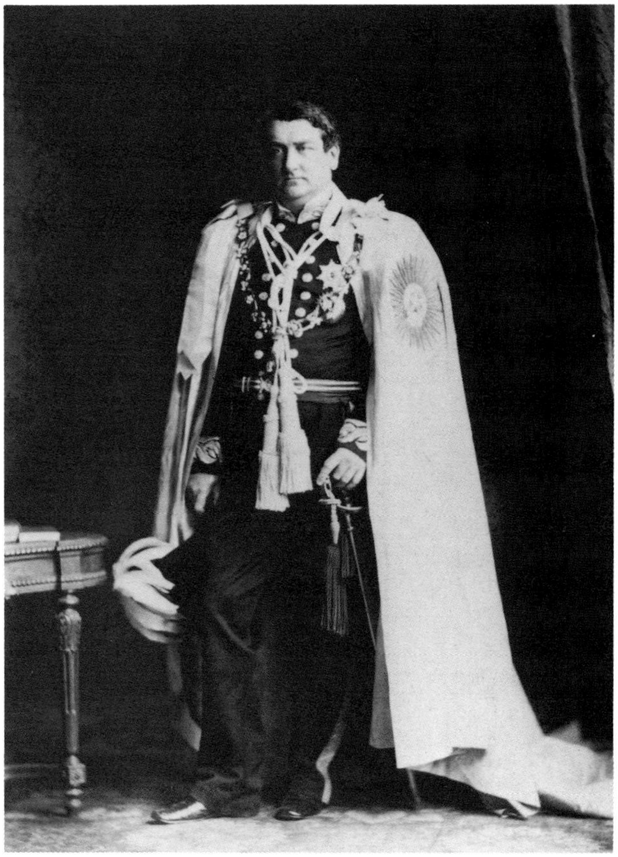

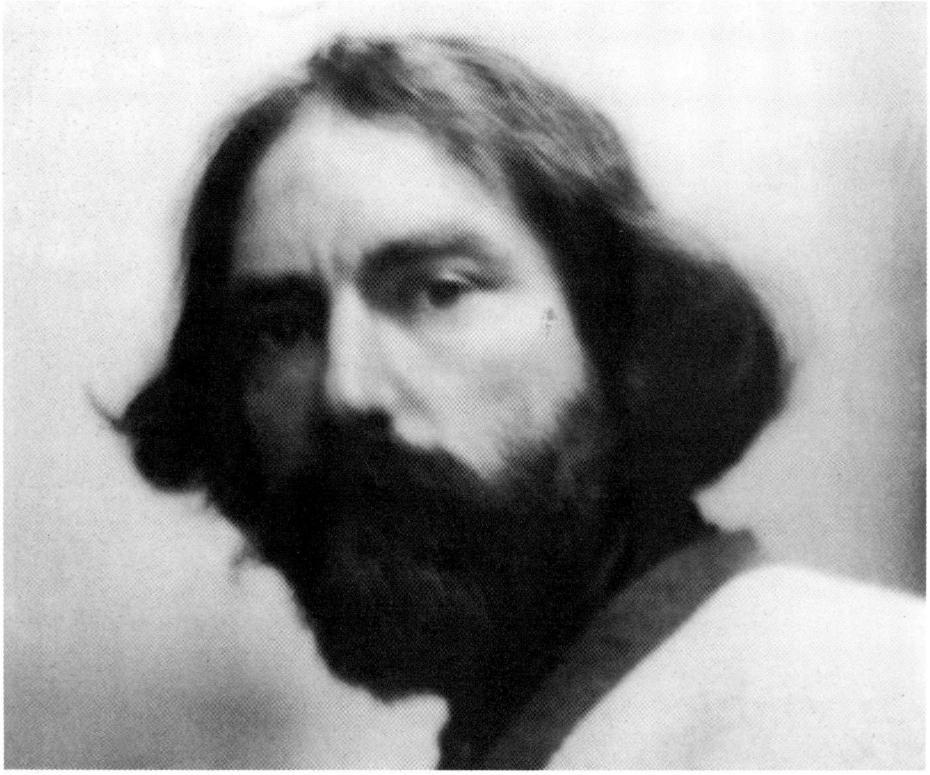

Left: Augustus John *by Malcolm Arbuthnot.*
Right: Aubrey Beardsley *by Frederick Evans.*

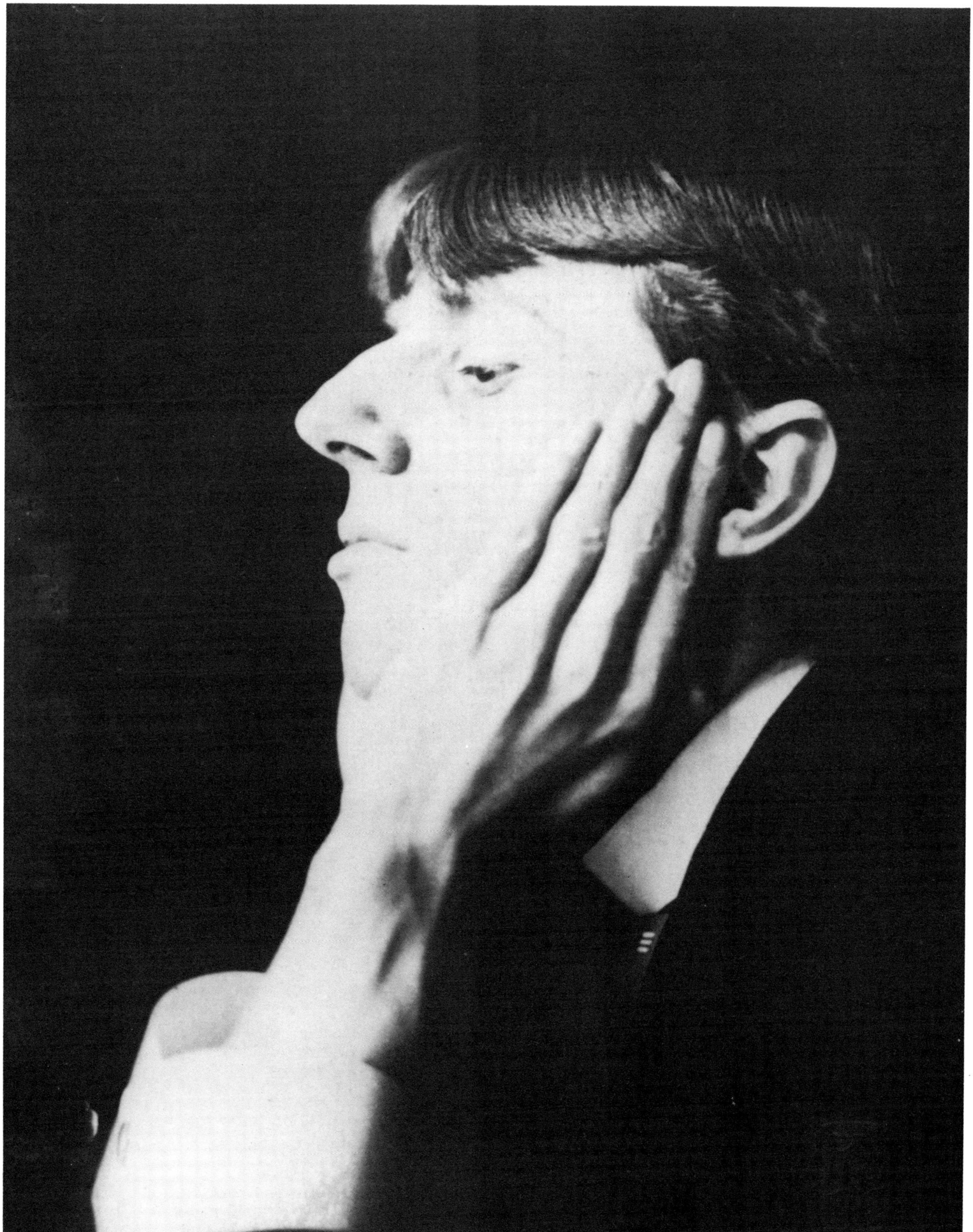

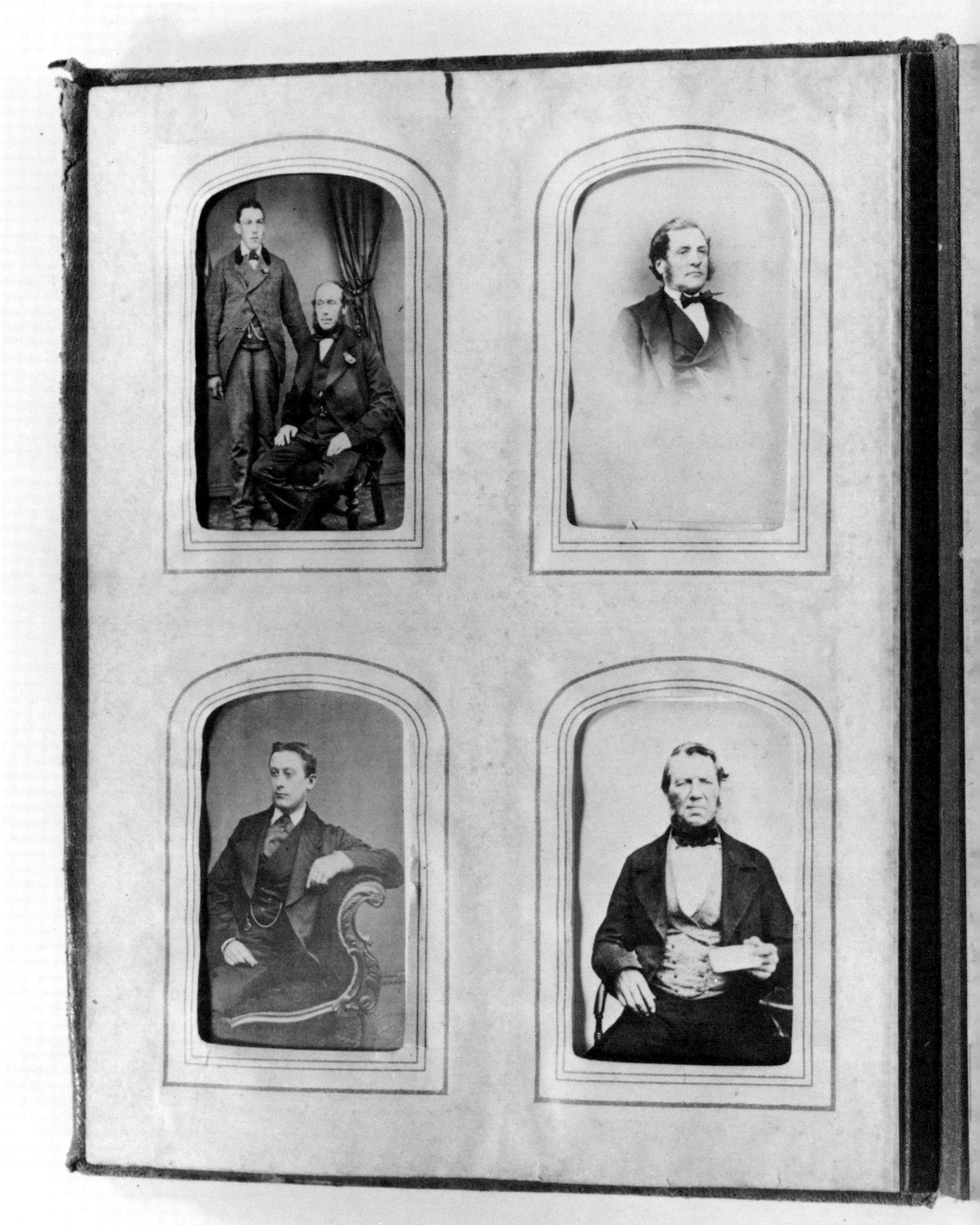

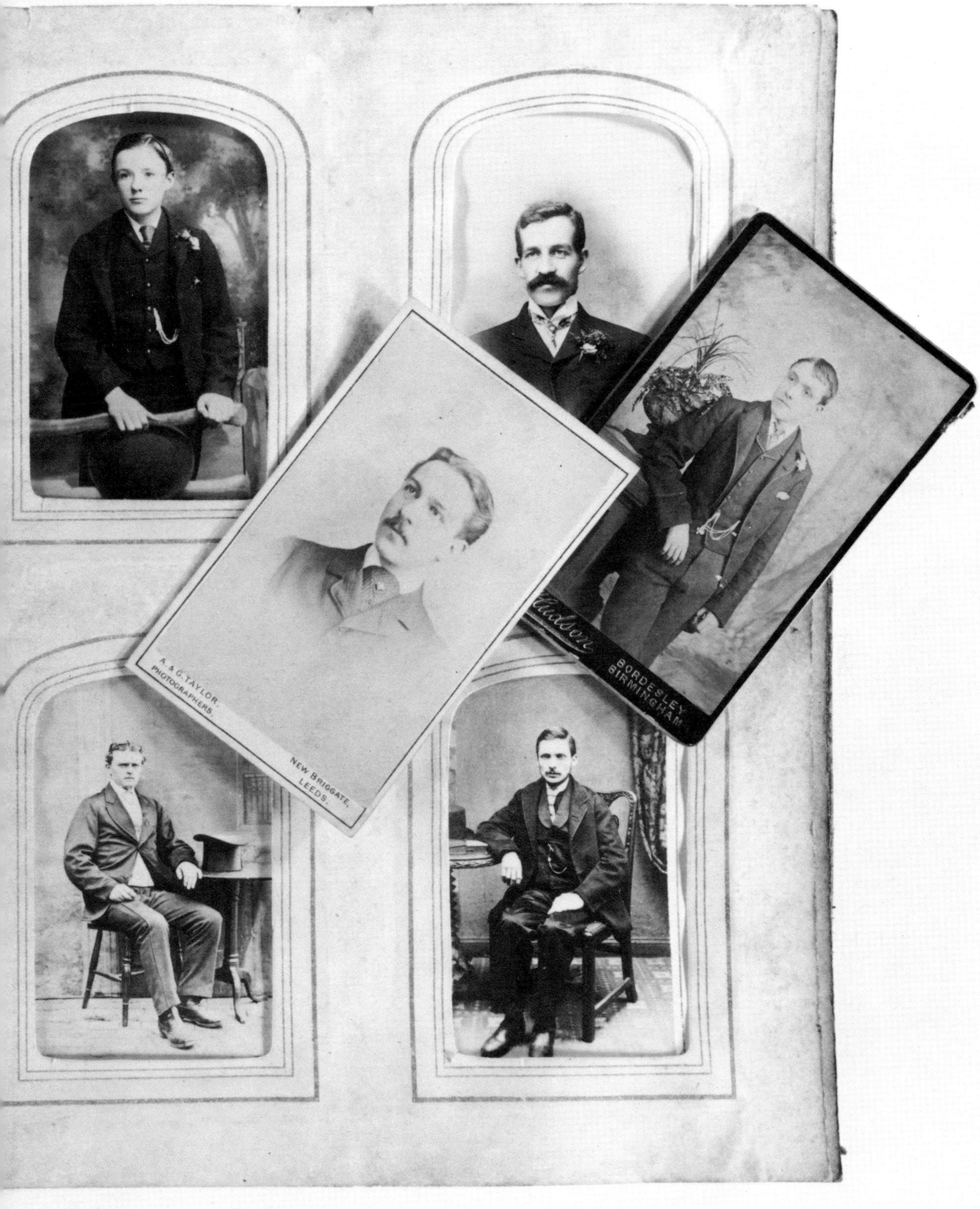

A. & G. TAYLOR,
PHOTOGRAPHERS.
NEW BRIGGATE,
LEEDS.
BORDESLEY,
BIRMINGHAM.

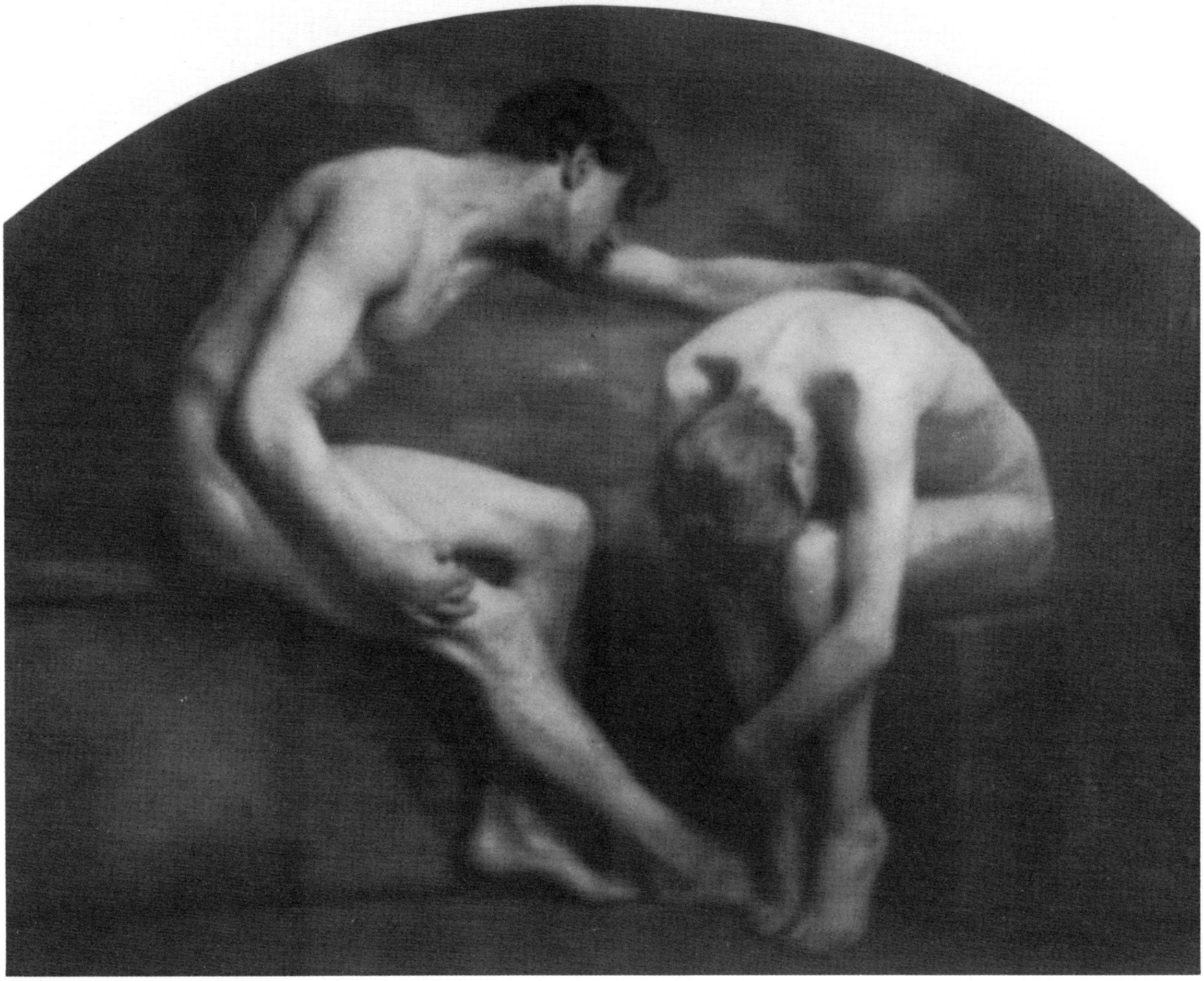

Cartes-de-visite **(previous page)** *were small, cardboard-mounted portraits produced inexpensively and in abundance and in the 1850s and 60s often used by the subject as a visiting card – hence the name. Suddenly portraiture, previously the prerogative of rich men, became a reality for the masses.*

The male nude has always been seen differently by different types of photographer. On one side, there is the classical approach, showing the nude as little more than an exercise in shape and form, light and shade. But in Victorian times, a different approach was popularized with a more sentimental look at the subject, resulting in a fantasy-like image, destined to become the glamour photography of today. Here we see an early example of each genre: the classical approach in a study by Bowyer Mewburn **(above)** *and the romantic side from Fred Holland Day* **(right)**.

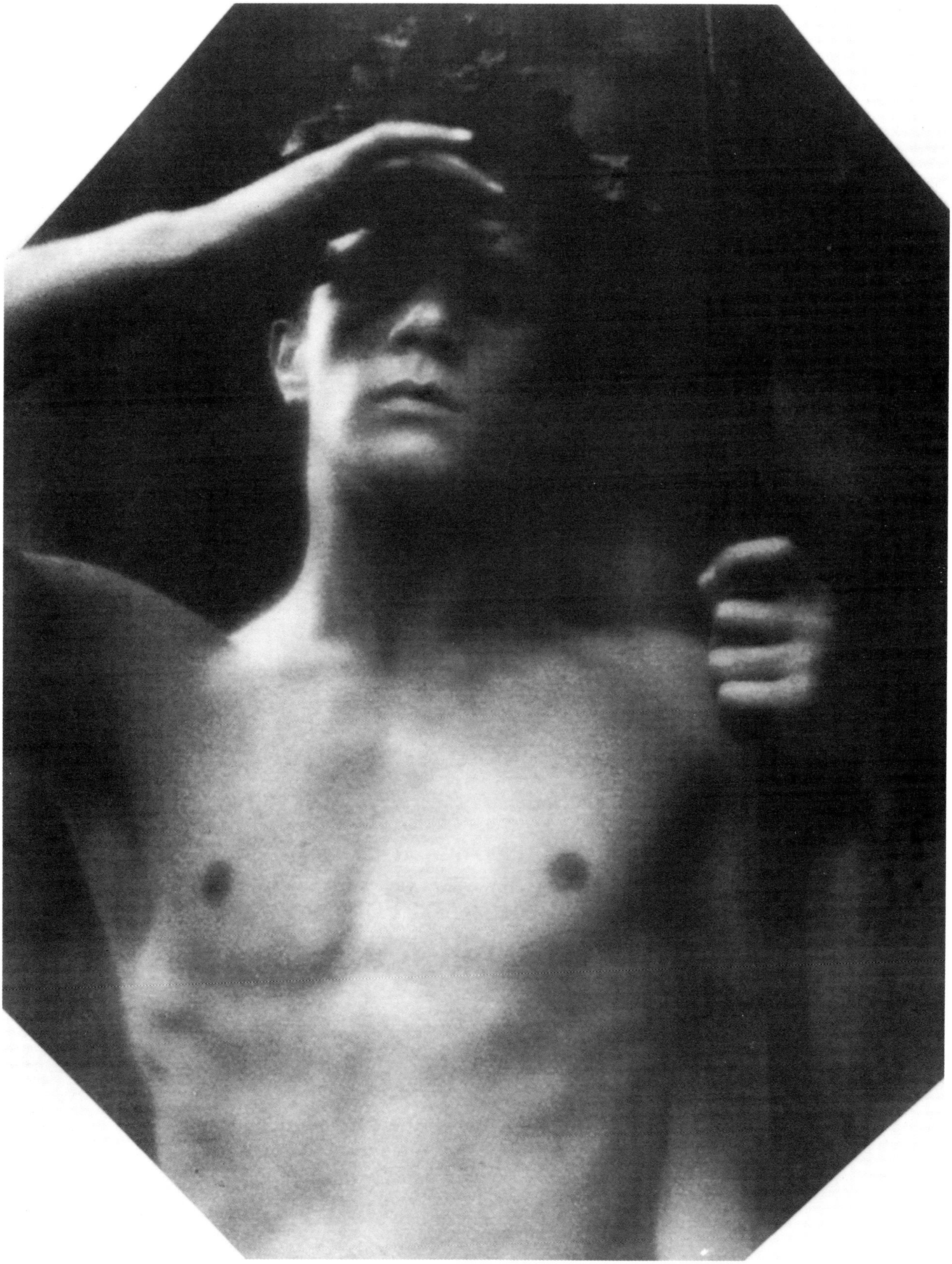

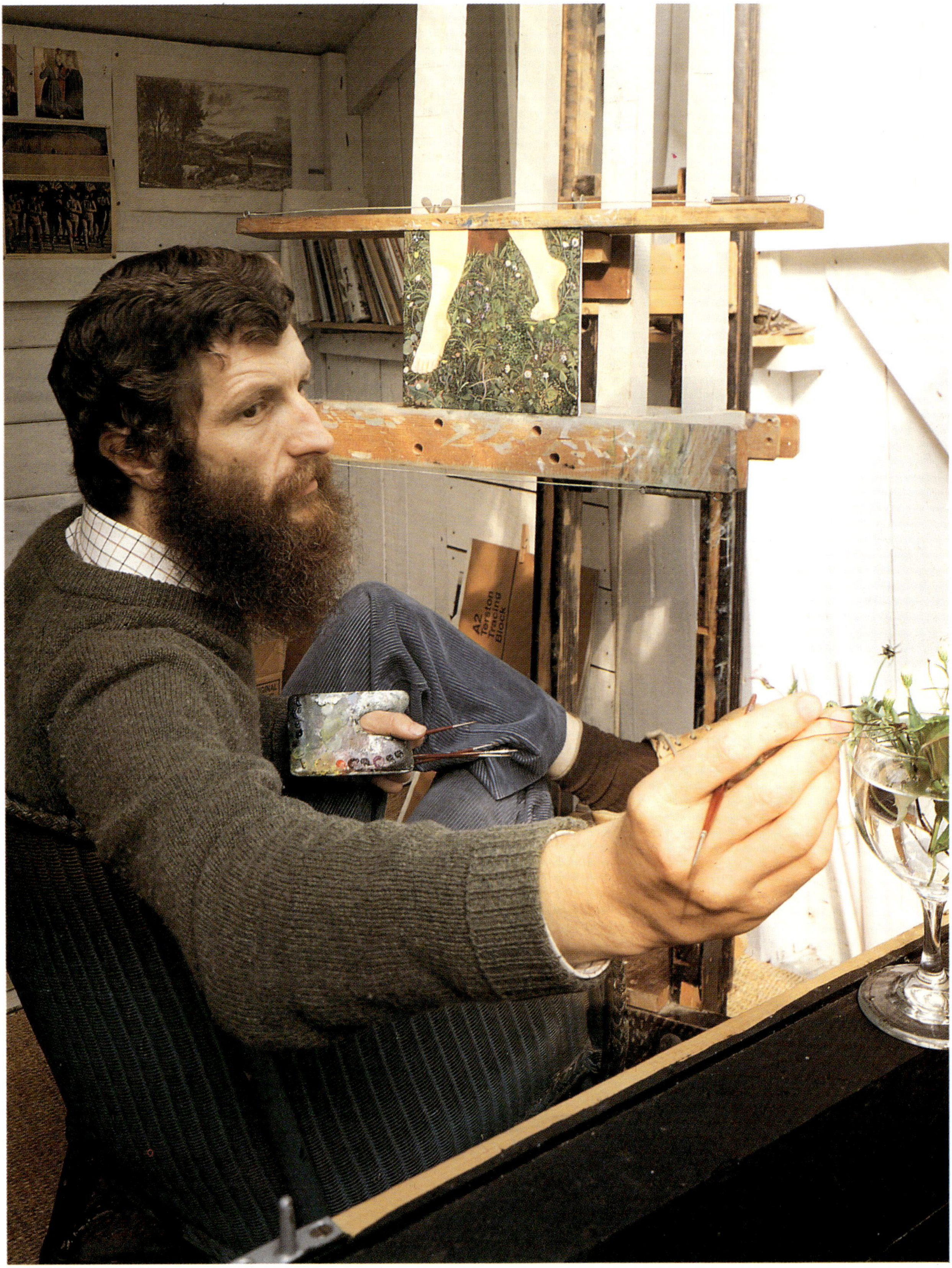
A2
Terston
Tracing
Block

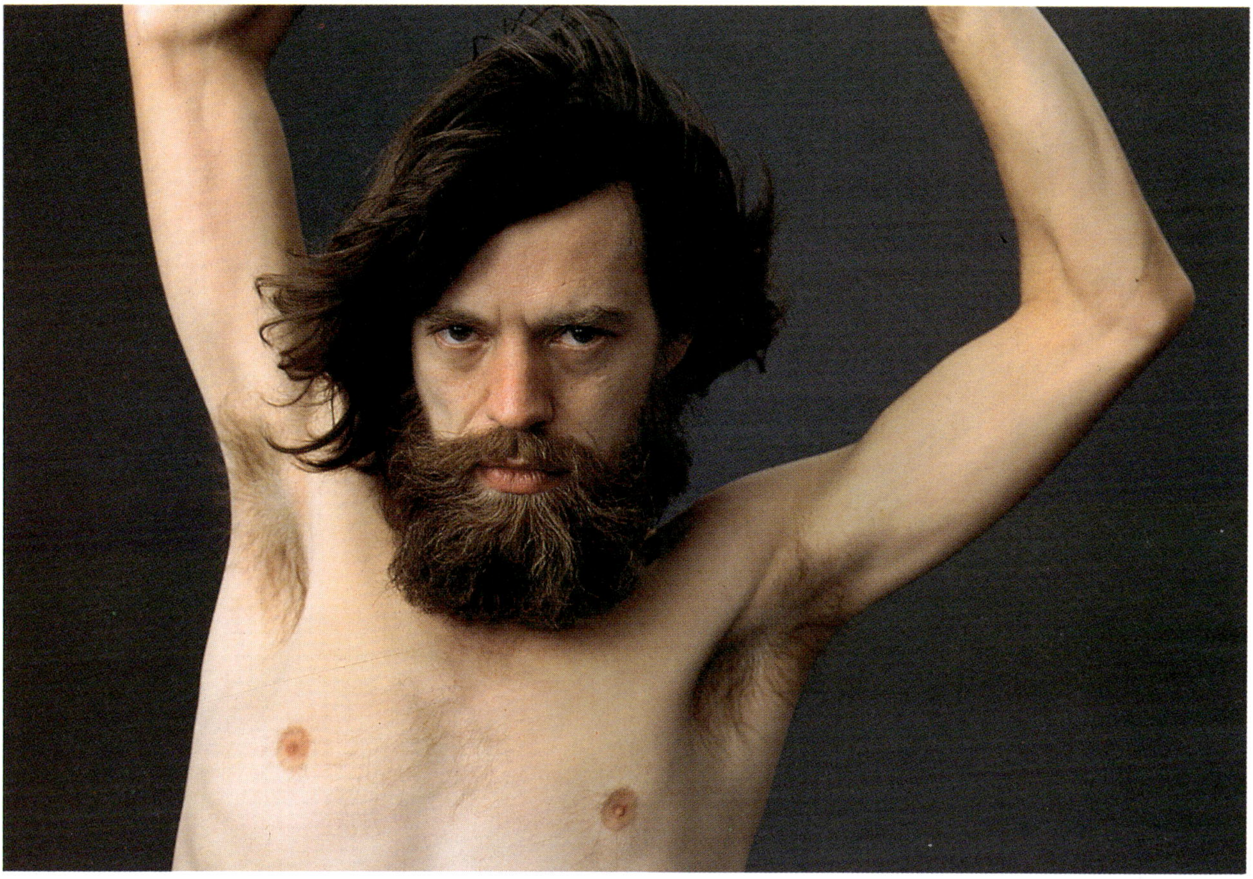

Today's photographers are very much a product of all that has gone before. In their pictures, you can see the influences of the past, coupled with new ideas and the technology now available to make those ideas work. Here are two examples of the modern approach to male photography. In the picture of artist Kit Williams **(left)**, *photographer Michael Freeman has shown us, not only the man, but something of his life and art as well. In the second picture, of rock star Mick Jagger* **(above)**, *photographer Annie Leibovitz has taken a man with a strong character of his own and moulded onto it her own unique way of seeing her subject. The result is a picture that is at once different and intensely compelling.*

Despite color being so readily available today, many modern photographers still prefer to work in black and white. Nick Scott is a commercial photographer whose clients often demand color but who, when he is shooting for himself, will always choose to work in mono. Scott's pictures are a study in casual detail. At first glance, they look almost like snapshots, as though they were taken candidly. A deeper study of pictures like these reveals much more than that, though. His attention to detail, his careful organization of the light available in any location, the way his subject blends with his surroundings and the way those surroundings complement the study, all add up to a powerful composition of shapes and tones that prove Scott to be a modern master of mono photography.

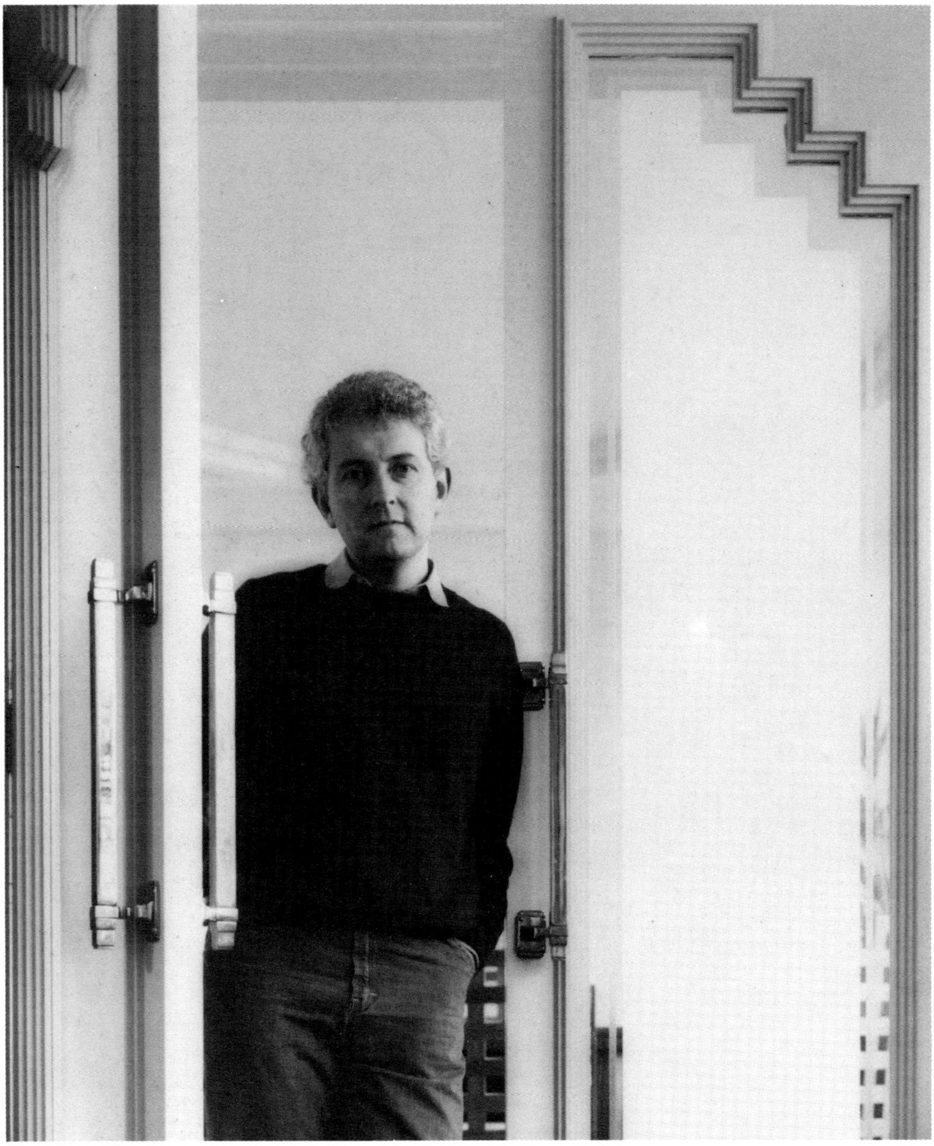

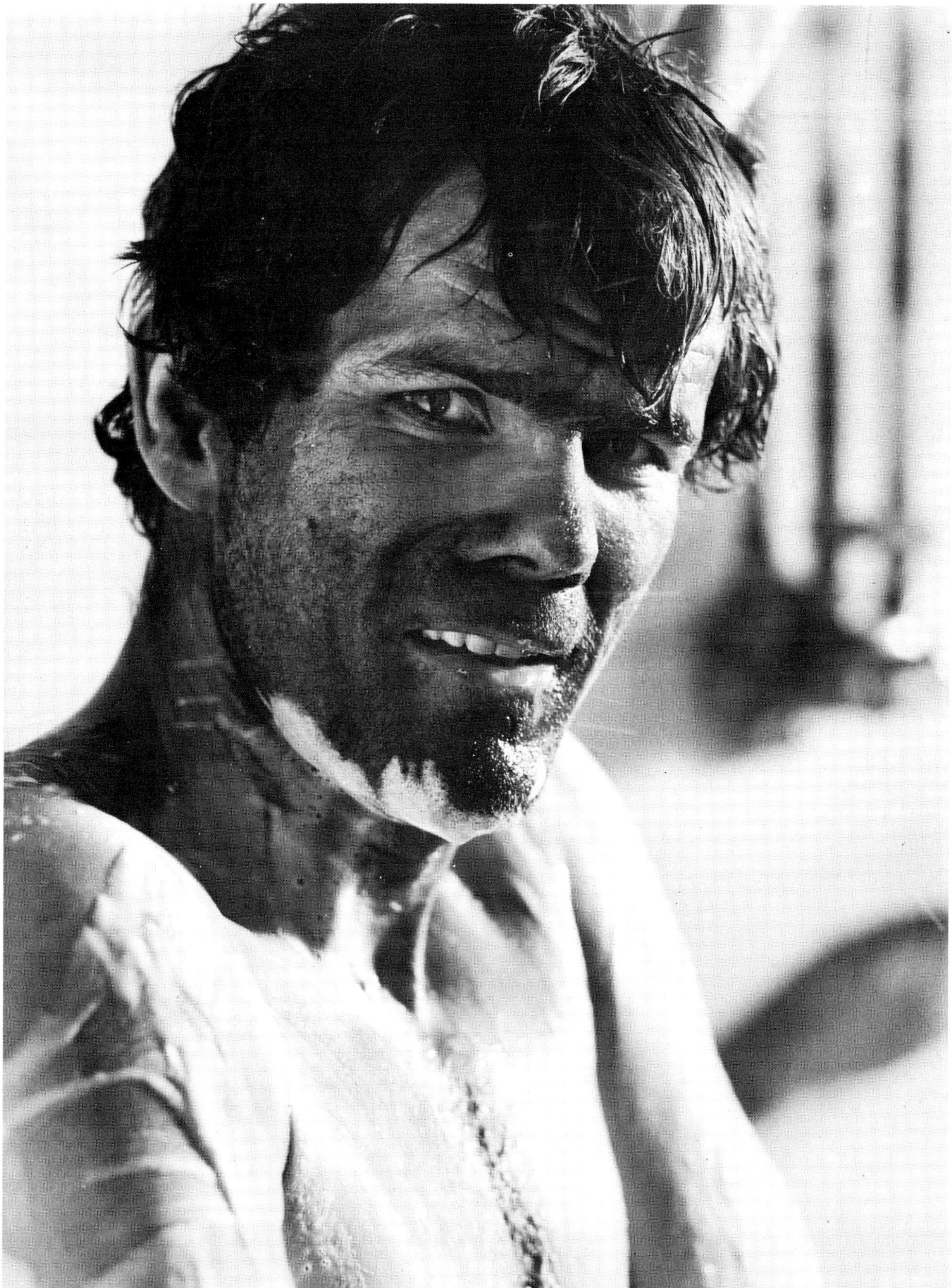

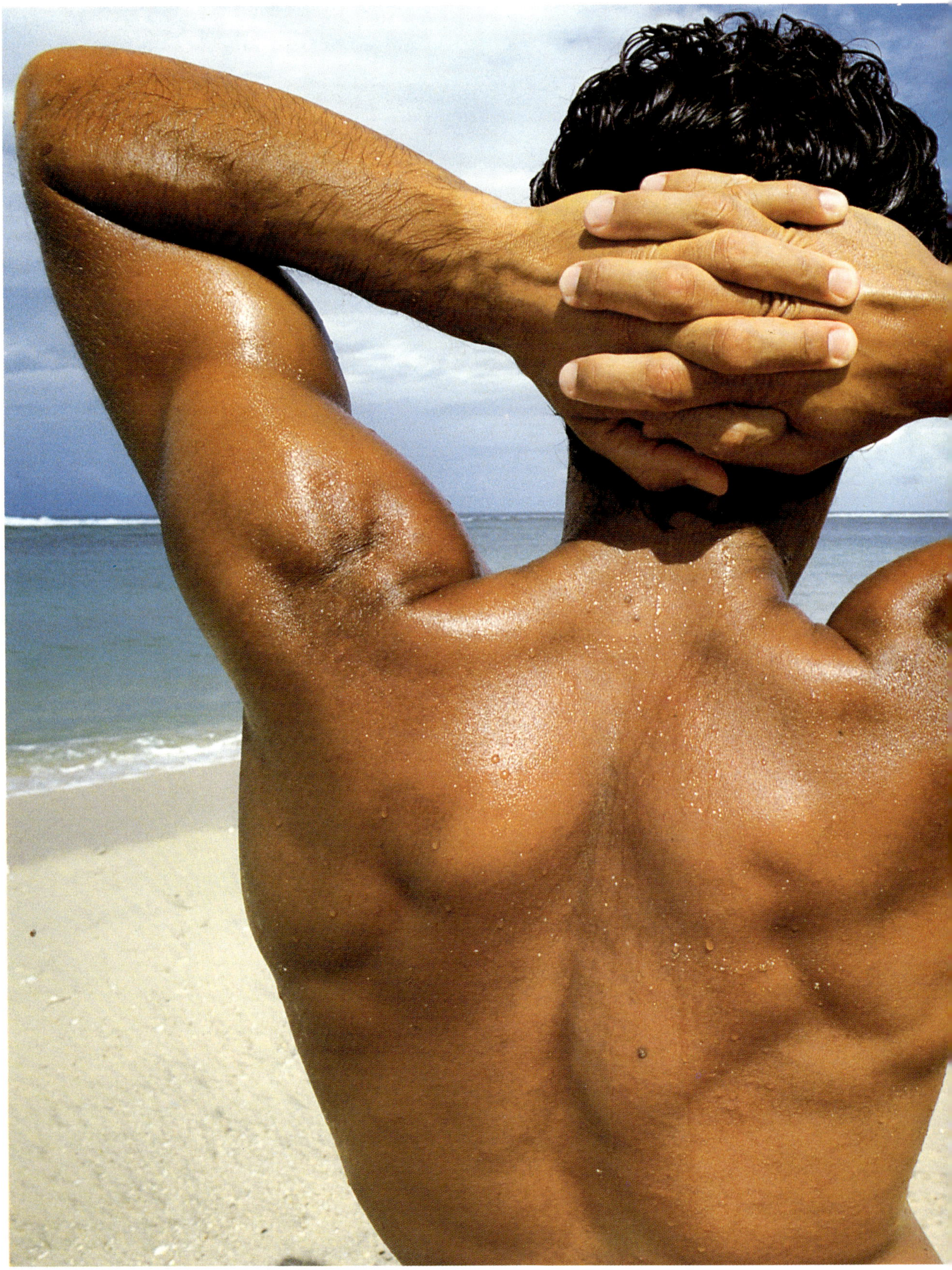

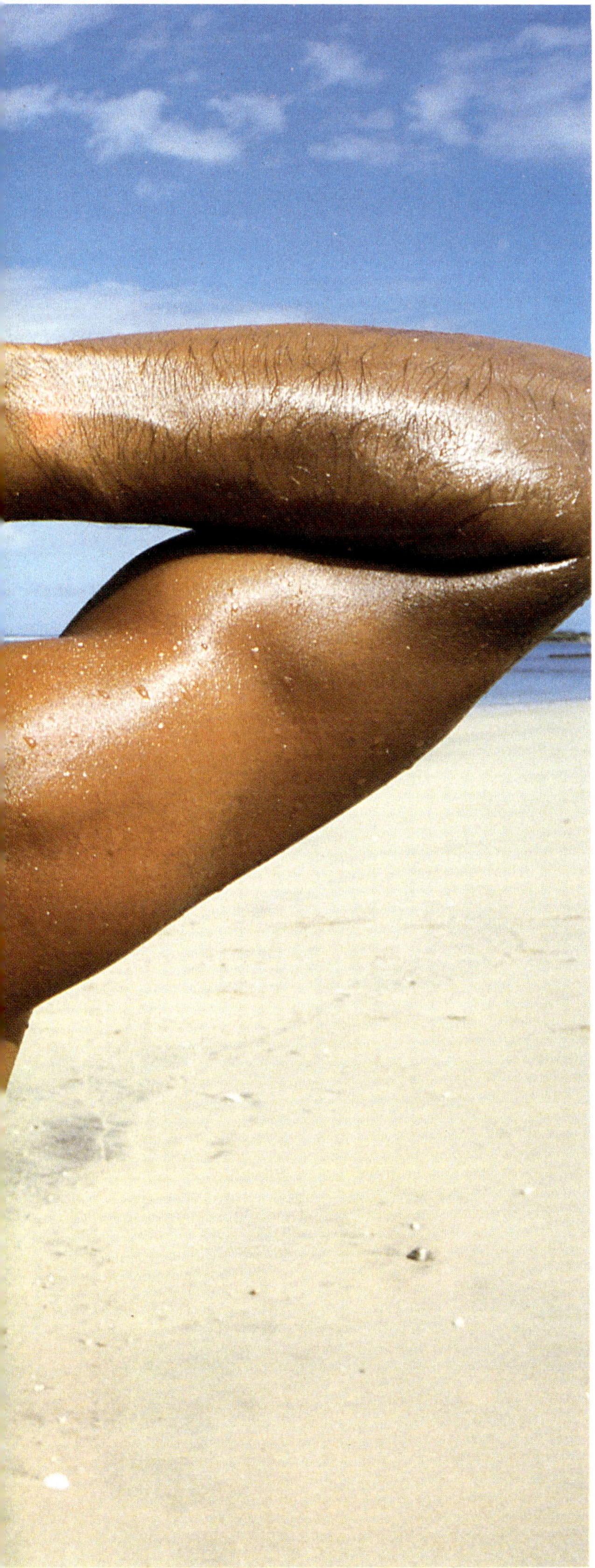

CHOOSING AND POSING THE MODEL

FINDING A MODEL

Obviously the first step in any photographic session is to find a suitable model. Your choice will largely be dictated by the particular type and purpose of shot you have in mind. The concept of being photogenic is unfortunately not as straightforward as it might be: a person who appears to be extremely good-looking on a purely visual or social level, may not appear so in front of the camera. This is not necessarily because of any inherent difference between what you see and what the camera sees, but more that any tension or inhibition which the camera induces is likely to change the appearance and behaviour of your model adversely. For this reason the character of your model can be as, if not more, important than appearance, and it will certainly help if your model is, by nature, both relaxed and at least a little extrovert. This is particularly important if you are not very experienced and perhaps less than sure with your camera and equipment.

There are also, of course, physical characteristics to consider. For a portrait session, you should choose somebody who has interesting or assertive features and an expressive and mobile face; for a nude shot, choose a man who has a reasonably-muscled body and avoid a very pale skin. The camera has the habit of accentuating undesirable qualities and it is as well to bear this in mind when choosing your model. A pale, thin face will tend to appear even more so, and the suspicion of a paunch, for instance, can look positively obese in a photograph. Skin is also an important consideration. Blemishes, five o'clock shadow and even nicotine-stained fingers will all be much more noticeable in a photograph. Do not overlook the possibility of using some make up, however. The subtle use of a little tinted foundation, for example, can make all the difference, particularly with fairly close-up pictures.

Don't fall into the trap of only considering the obvious type of person and face for your pictures. The ruggedly good-looking Mr Right image which the media like to project is not necessarily the best type of model when it is a question of taking interesting and strong pictures of a more interpretive nature.

Where to find your model? Well obviously the first place to look is among your friends and associates. This will give you the advantage of already having a good rapport, and any possibility of camera shyness or inhibition will be greatly reduced. This is certainly a good idea if you are a beginner, since your friends are likely to be more tolerant and understanding of any uncertainty you show and errors you might make.

Approaching a stranger can, for many people, be quite daunting, but on occasions you may see someone who you feel would help to produce some good pictures. If you feel that you might not be able to articulate your proposal easily, it is far better to find an intermediary to make a request on your behalf. It is a good idea to have a business card printed which you can give to a prospective model. This will not only establish your credentials and present a business-like appearance, but will also allow your subject to consider the proposal and telephone you at a later time avoiding any embarrassment that might be caused by a refusal. It is also very helpful to have a small portfolio of your work available to show potential models. This will usually help to gain their interest and convince them of your abilities.

Another method of finding models is through institutions and associations. For nude pictures, for example, you could approach a local art college which uses models for the life class. Obviously you will have to be prepared to offer a fee, but this is usually quite low in comparison with professional model fees. Another possible source for nude or body shot models could be a gym or a weight-training club. If you offer copies of the photographs you take, there should be little difficulty in finding willing models.

Professional model agencies are of course the most obvious sources of subjects. Unfortunately model fees are quite high and, for personal work, may be hard to justify, although the advantage of working with experienced models can be considerable for many types of picture, particularly if you are inexperienced. Most model agencies, however, are keen to find photographers to do what are known as test shots. These are pictures taken either of new and less-experienced models to help them to build a portfolio, or to find suitable pictures for the model directory or index cards, or of well-established models who simply want to update their portfolios.

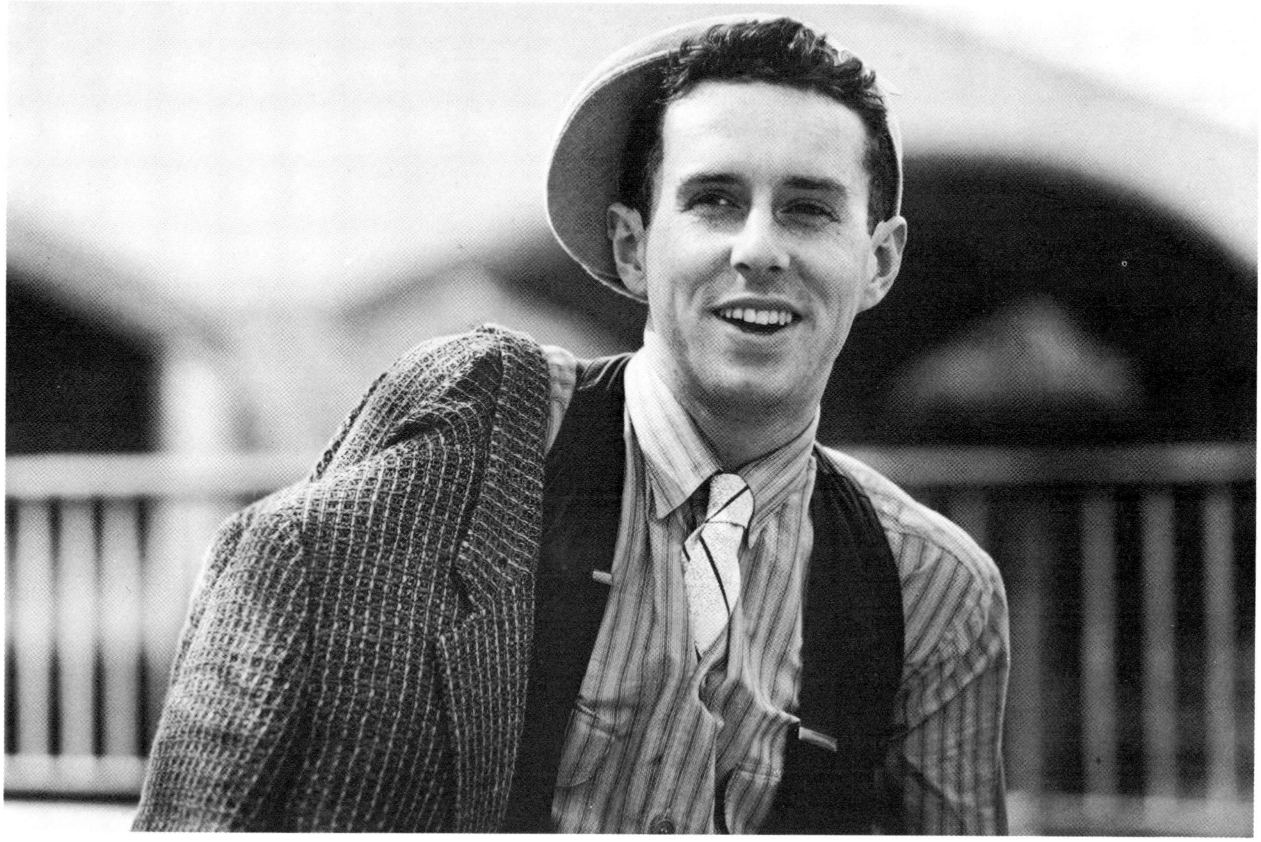

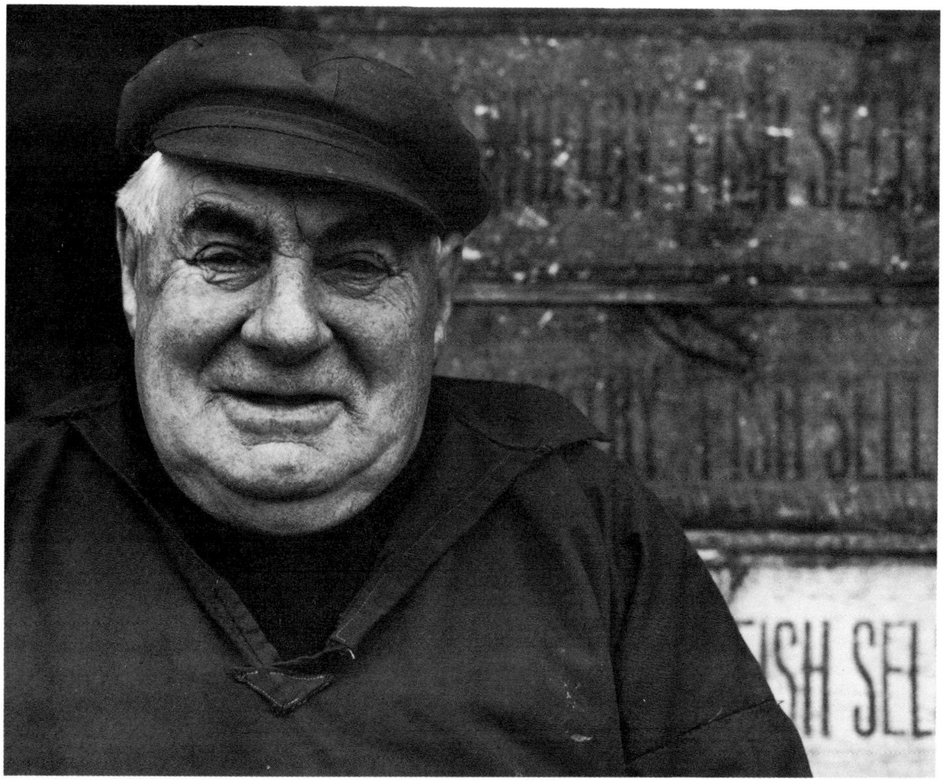

If you are taking pictures for publication, choice of model may be dictated by the client, who often specifies the age, height, build and coloring required **(above)**. *If the pictures are for your own interest, though, there are no such restrictions. In complete contrast to the often bland features of professional male fashion models, the lines on the face of this old man* **(left)** *are like a map of a lifetime's experience.*

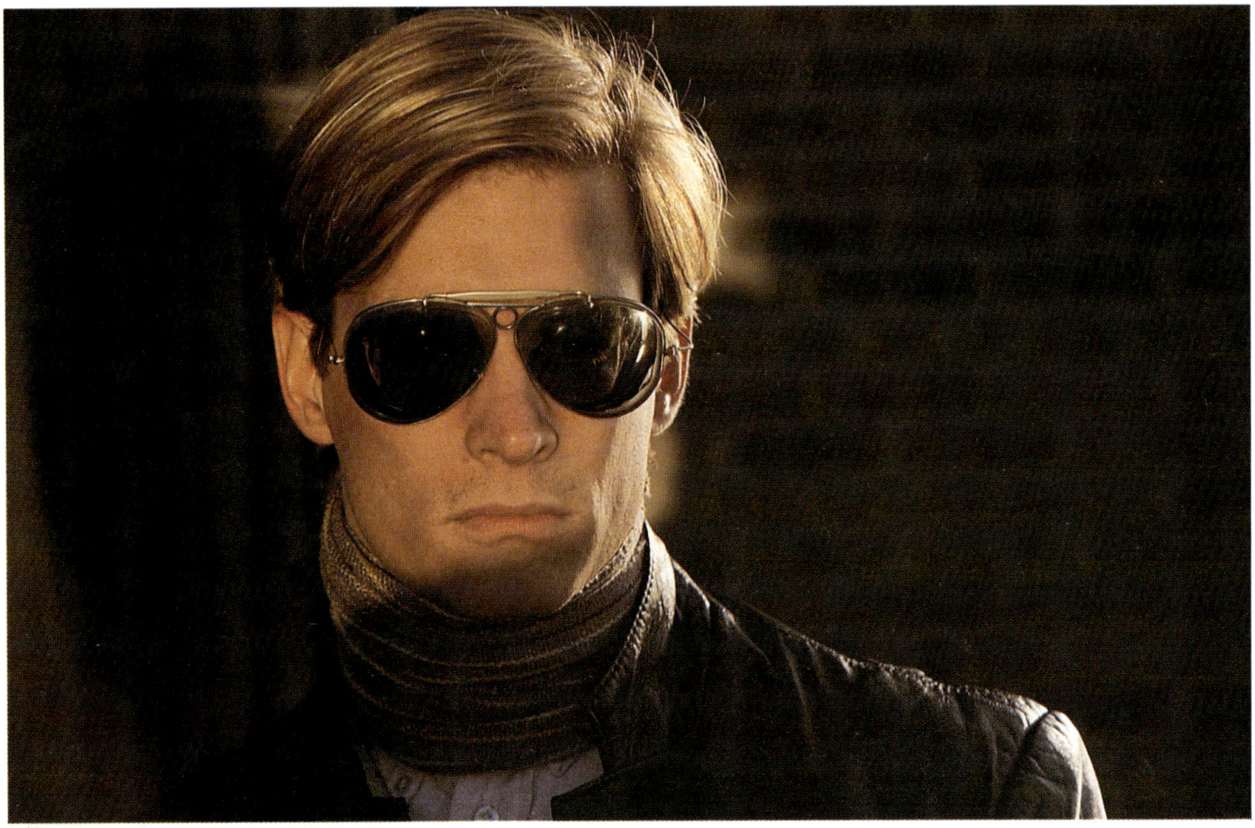

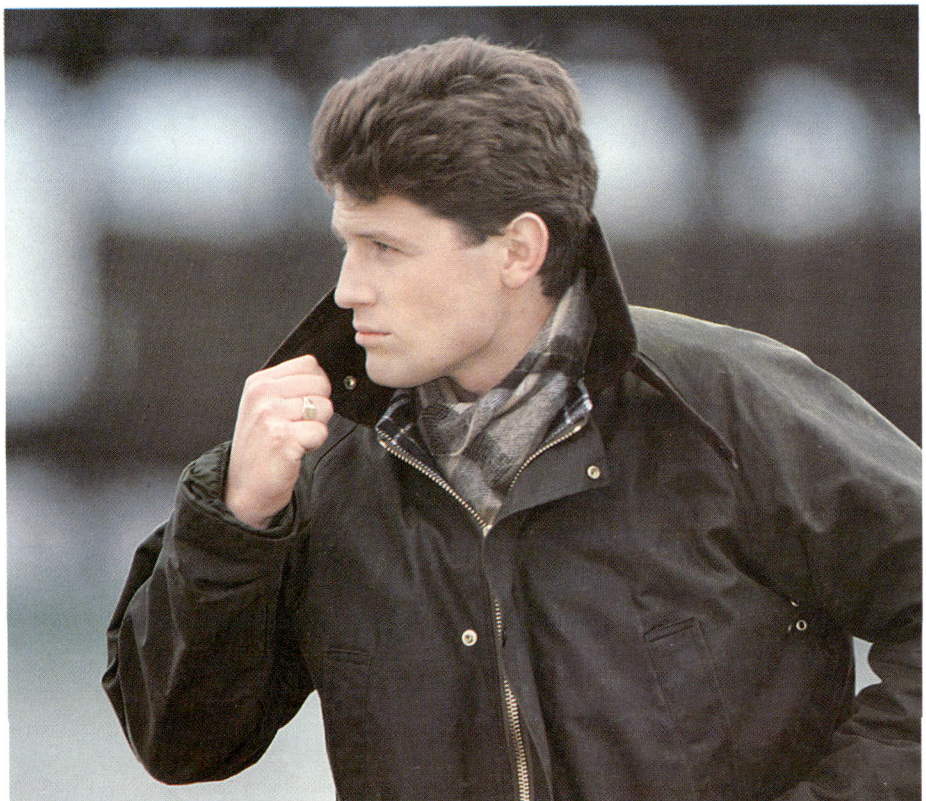

A good, strong face **(above and left)** *is an essential when you anticipate shooting close-up poses like these. Look for a model with character, rather than one who merely has what is accepted as traditional good looks.*

Friends and associates often make good models, but when the pose and overall effect calls for something a little more off-beat, as in this example **(right)**, *then a professional model is an invaluable aid to your creativity.*

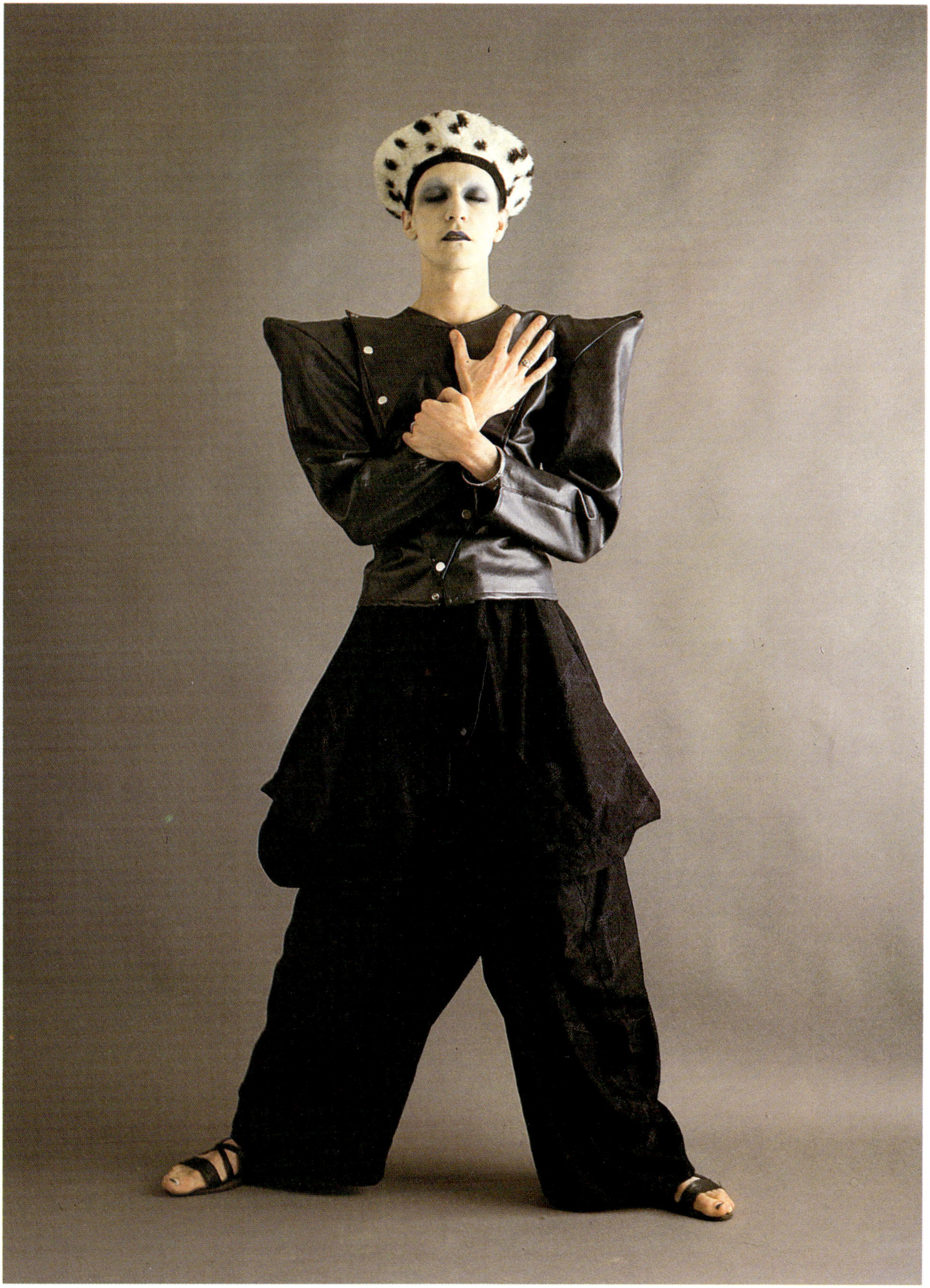

DIRECTING THE MODEL

Two of the most important factors in working with and directing a model successfully are to create a good rapport and to have a clear idea of what you want to achieve. To a large extent they are interdependent, since if the model senses that you are not quite sure of what you are doing, it will be virtually impossible to create a good working relationship.

It is a good idea to write yourself a brief, outlining the ideas that you have for particular pictures, what you will need in the way of props or accessories and notes on what particular type of lighting you might use or any special camera techniques that might be employed effectively. You might also make a few rough sketches to indicate framing and composition. These preparations will not only help you to organize your session but will also enable you to explain to your model what you want to achieve. He in turn will be able to make suggestions and develop ideas which will help considerably in creating a good rapport.

It is also vital to be well-prepared in terms of equipment. Make sure that cameras, lenses, accessories and film are ready to hand and, if you are working in the studio, that lights and background are set up ready for the first shot. You should also ensure that the working conditions are comfortable. There should be somewhere for the model to change and you should ensure that the studio is warm, particularly if you are shooting nudes. Make sure there is some coffee or other refreshment on hand, and it can also help to have some background music available while you are shooting.

Even with a professional model, it is important to give them confidence in what they are doing; with an inexperienced model, it is crucial. For this reason it is helpful to keep up a constant flow of conversation, making encouraging comments about how well the session is going, even when its not going too well! Nothing undermines a good rapport more than allowing an awkward silence to develop.

When you want to put your model into a particular pose, it is best to explain what you want and to allow them to fall into it in their own way rather than to attempt to direct them limb by limb. This can not only be rather inhibiting for the model but will also tend to create a very self-conscious and unrelaxed pose. If a particular idea is not working too well, it is better to abandon it and maybe return to it later. To persist in dogged pursuit can easily have a negative effect. Remember that the picture will only work if both you and the model feel that it looks right and feels good, and any uncertainty or awkwardness on either part is bound to result in a disappointing picture.

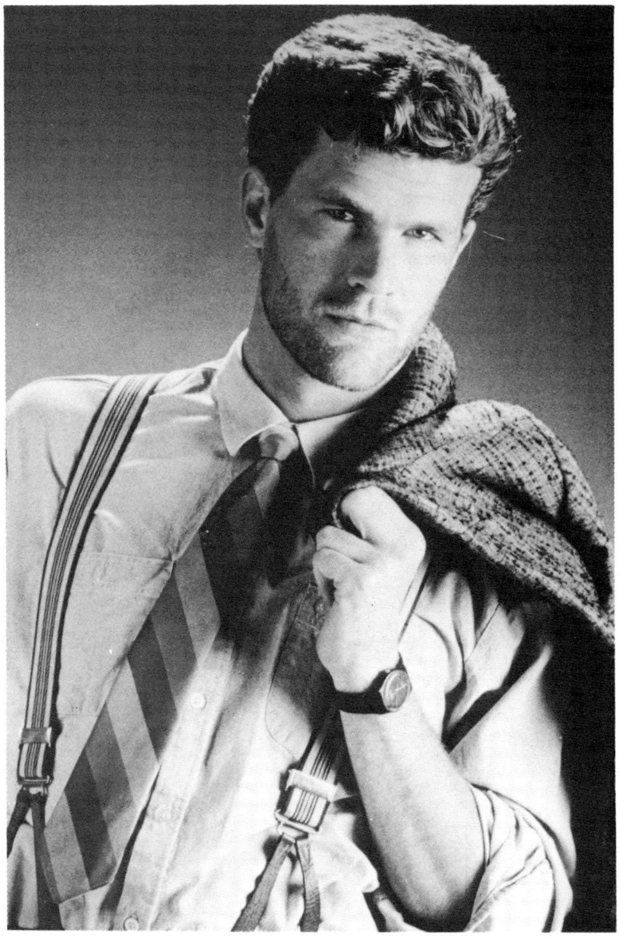

Try to keep a good, friendly atmosphere going during the shooting session. The relaxed expression in this shot is the result of the photographer's rapport with his model.

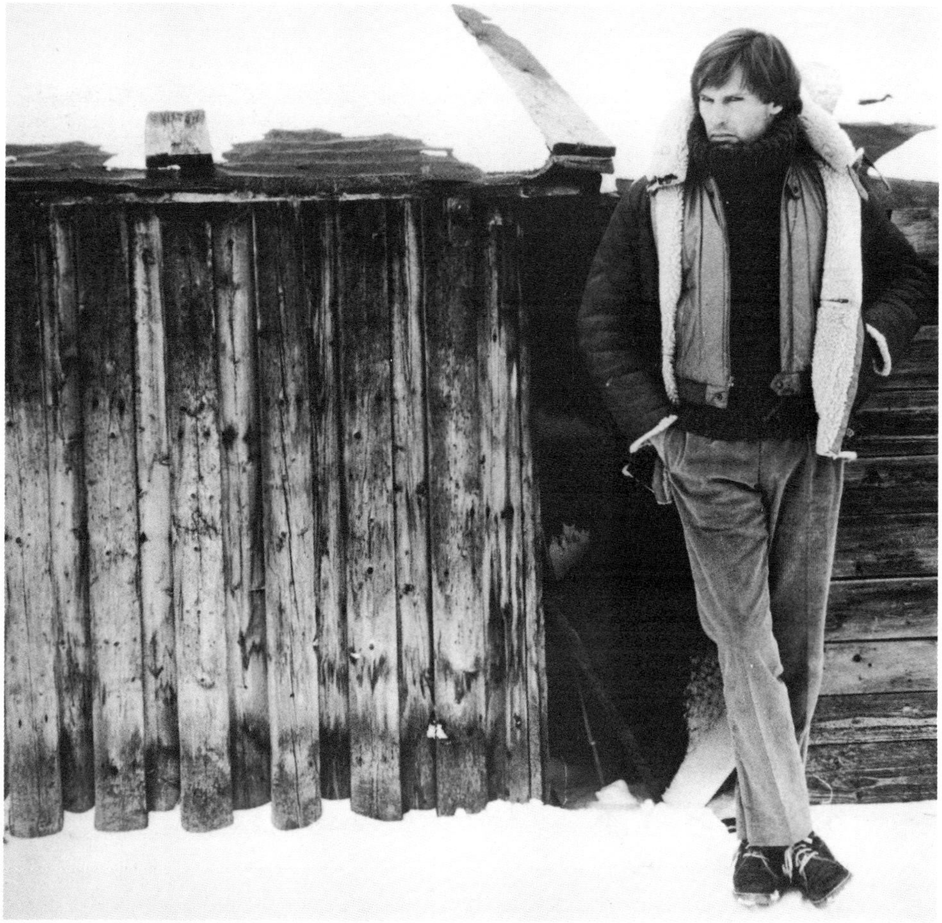

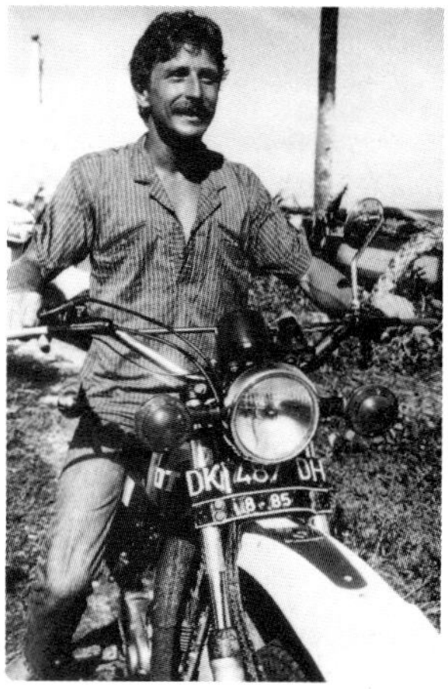

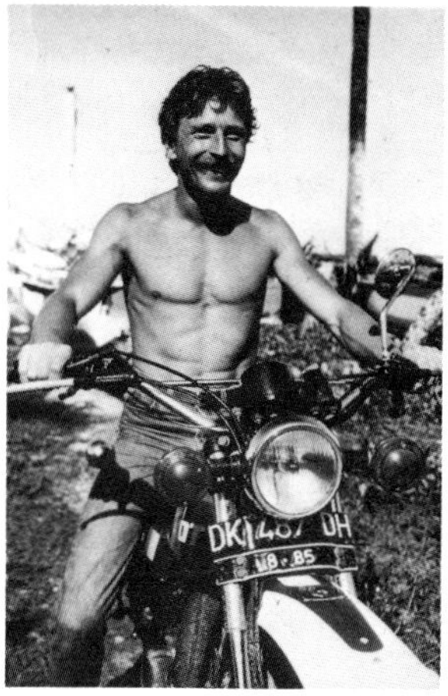

Sometimes small variations on the same pose can make all the difference to a picture, so change the details as the session progresses.

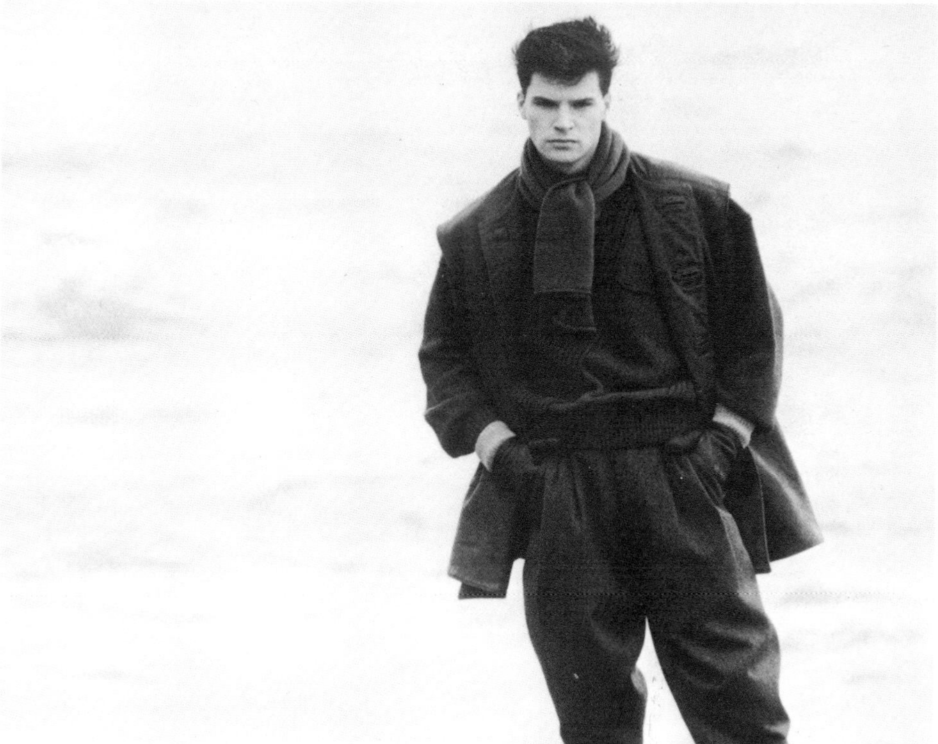

The expression on a face can set the mood for the picture **(left and above left)**. *Explaining to your model the effect you are after before you start to shoot will invariably result in better pictures.*

CHOOSING CLOTHES

One valuable aspect of model photography is that you have much more control over your subject than in many other fields. With landscape pictures, for instance, beyond choosing a viewpoint and deciding at which moment to make the exposure, you are largely governed by the whims of nature. With portrait, fashion and nude work, you can select most of the elements to be included in the image. For this reason it is vital to consider every aspect of a picture very carefully and clothes are of course a major element of most male pictures.

The mood and nature of a photograph can be established by the choice of clothes. Even with a portrait, a crisp white shirt with perhaps cuff-links and a smart tie could be used to create a quite formal or sophisticated mood, whereas a denim shirt or a sweater would have a completely opposite effect, even if the other elements of the picture were the same. When planning a session, it is a good idea to discuss the clothes with your model in advance, perhaps even to the extent of having a wardrobe check. This gives you the opportunity to choose precisely the right clothes for a specific shot and in many cases you might see a particular garment which could give you an idea for a photograph, perhaps suggesting a background or a setting.

Texture can be an important element, particularly with black and white photography; it can add both interest and impact to a picture to use clothes made of rough denim and leather, for example, for this reason. You must also consider the clothes in connection with the background and surroundings of the picture. As a general rule, it is best to select clothes which create a degree of separation between the model and the background, rather than choosing a tone or a color that is too similar. An exception to this is when you are aiming for a tonal or color effect. For instance, in a low-key picture, it is vital that all the tones are at the darker end of the scale and the choice of, say, a white shirt could completely destroy the effect. You should also be wary of clothes with a particularly bold color or pattern, as this can easily dominate the image and be too assertive, detracting attention from the model and even possibily creating an imbalance in the composition.

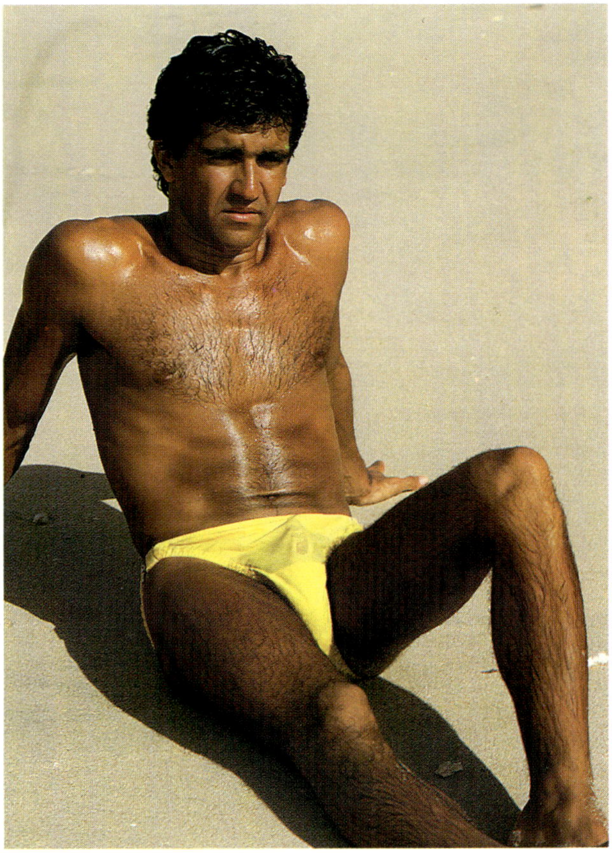

Clothes can be used for different effects. Here, the bright yellow of the model's trunks makes a key point in the picture's composition, contrasting well with the muted tones of his body and the background.

The way your model dresses can help to separate him from, or blend him with the background. Dressed in red, he will seem to advance over other, cooler colors like blue or green. Add texture with leather clothing and it will contrast well with the smooth lines of a plain background.

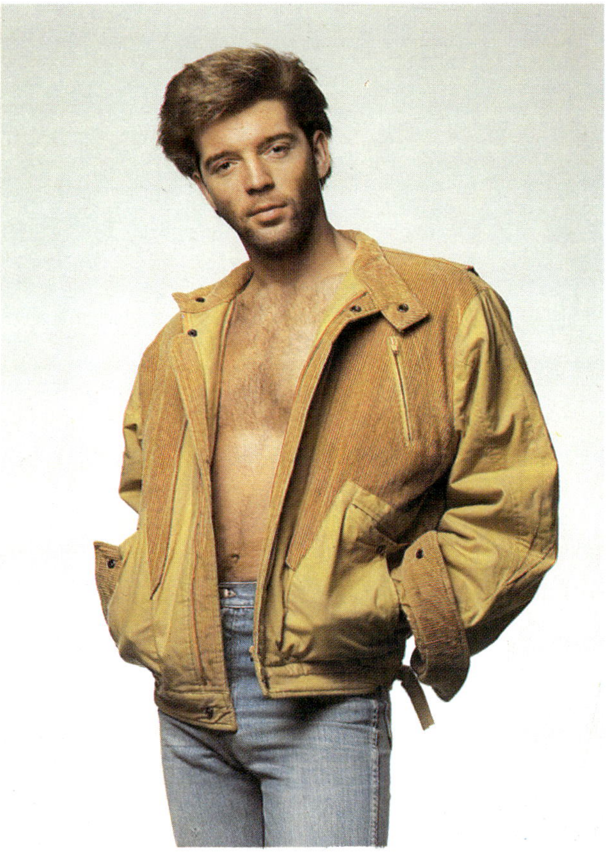

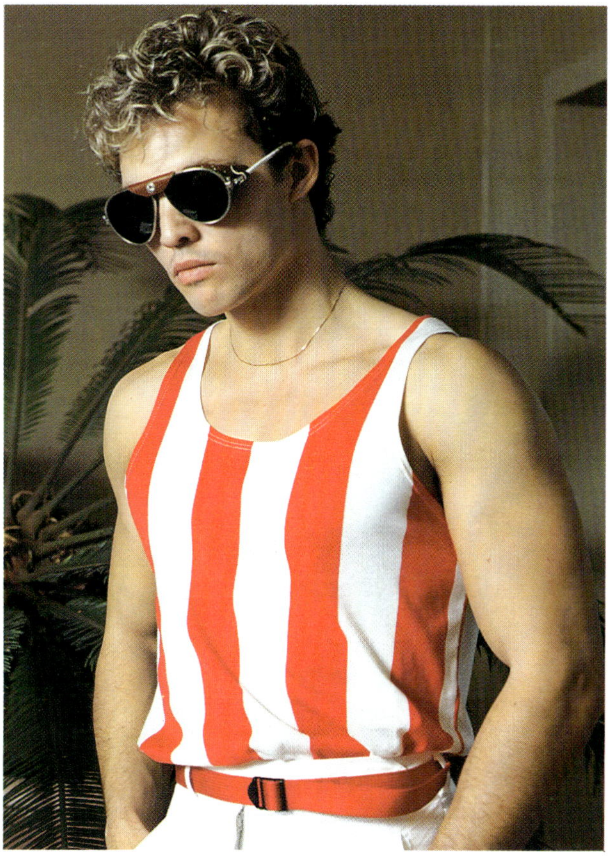

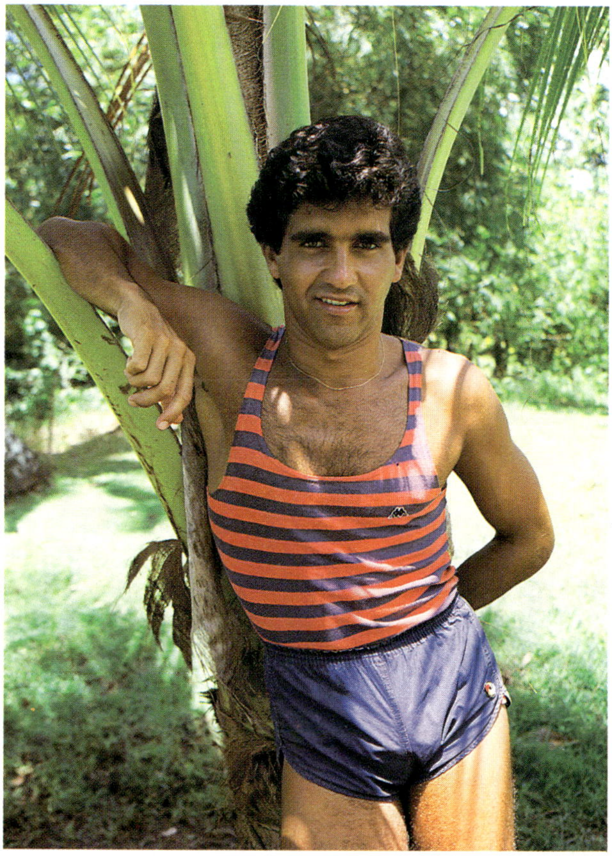

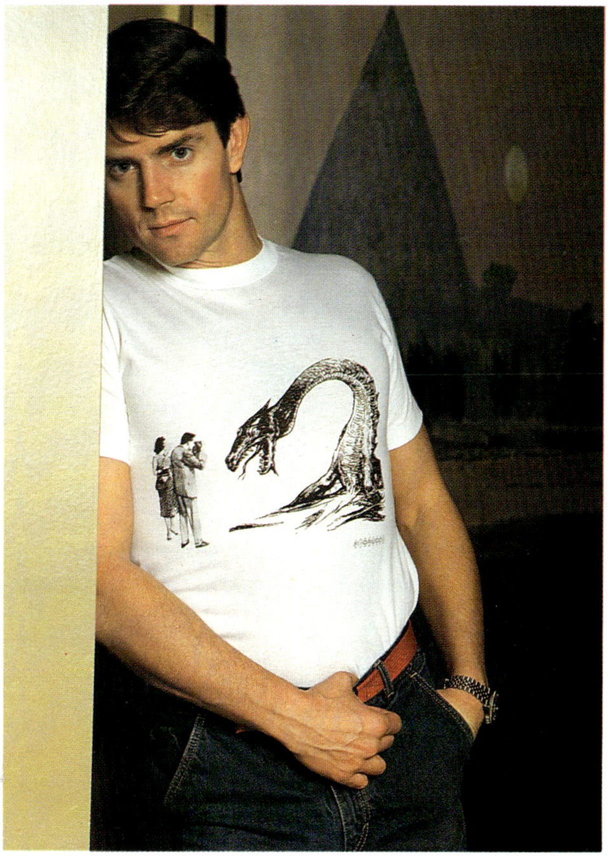

USING PROPS

Props can be an important element of choice in a picture since they help to create a mood, as well as adding interest and providing an additional ingredient to the composition. A prop can be literally anything you add to the picture from a chair or similar piece of furniture, to a cigarette or a pair of spectacles. Even with a portrait, a suitably-chosen prop can be a valuable addition to the picture. Models often find it difficult to know what to do with their hands, and something like a cigarette or a glass can encourage them to adopt a more relaxed and natural pose.

With three-quarter-length and full-length shots, props can often be used to allow the model to adopt a wider range of body positions than would be possible unaided because just standing can easily produce a rather stiff and unrelaxed appearance. Professional studios usually have a selection of useful items that can be called upon as required, but most homes can provide a number of useful props of this type: chairs, sofas, small tables, even items like a step ladder or a bicycle can, in some circumstances, add just that extra ingredient which makes the difference.

In male photography, sports items can be both appropriate and useful, particularly for body shots in the studio, since it is usually best for this type of picture if the muscles are slightly tensed, and holding or using items like a dumb-bell or squash racket can make this appear more natural. In outdoor locations, there are many more opportunities for finding and using this type of prop: surf and sail boards, golf clubs, even a motor cycle or a car can be used.

In outdoor locations, a prop does not necessarily have to be a specially-imported item. There are often natural features that can be used effectively as an aid to the picture. A park bench or a rustic fence or gate, for example, are ideal when shooting full-length, to provide both support and additional interest. When exploring the possibilities of a location, you should develop the habit of looking for objects that can be used in this way as well as just looking for backgrounds and settings.

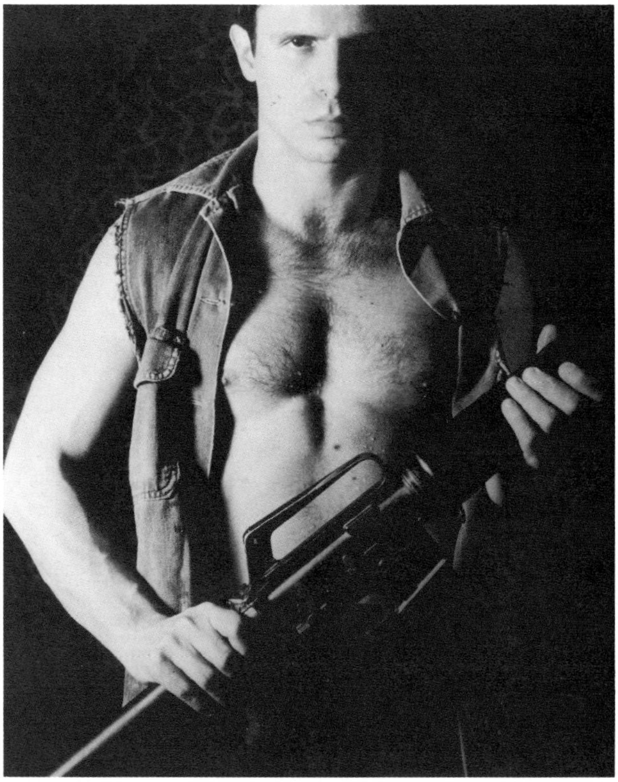

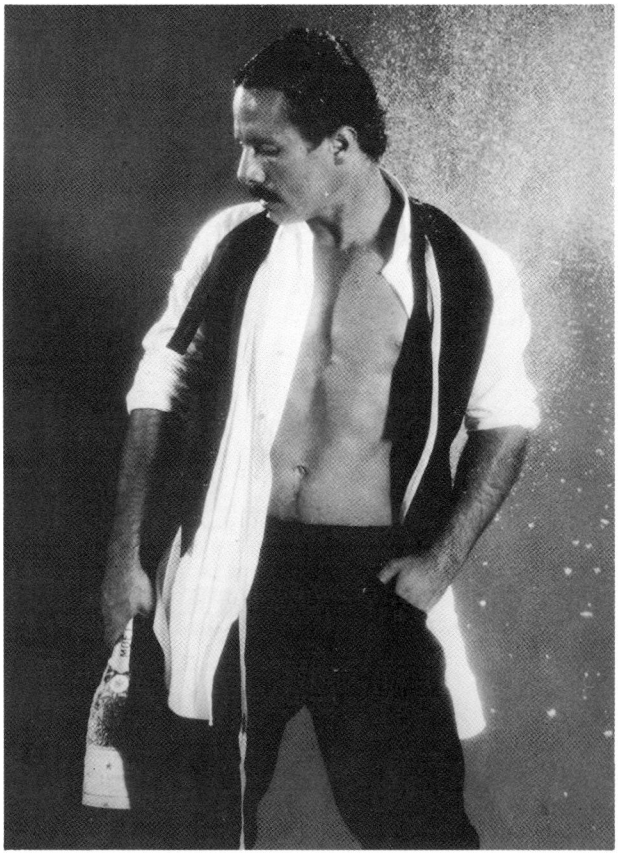

Props can be used to dictate body positions, especially in three-quarter-length and full-length poses. Notice how handling the gun **(top)** *has brought the model naturally into a fairly aggressive stance, whereas the very different way the bottle is being held* **(bottom)** *has led the model into a different, far more relaxed way of standing.*

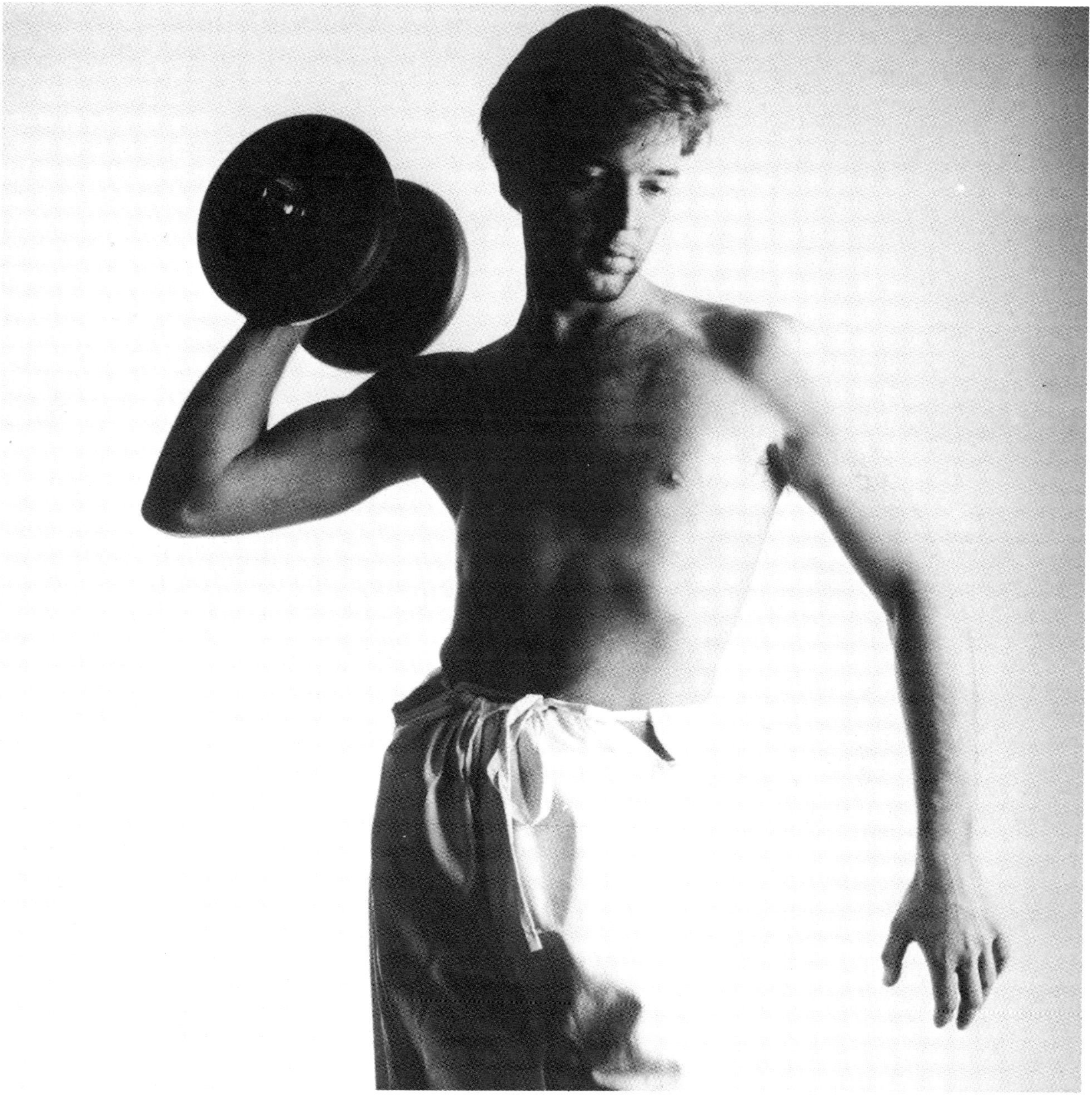

Sports items make natural props for this type of photography, giving the model a relevant reason for tensing his muscles.

HEAD AND SHOULDER SHOTS

The criteria for any sort of pose, with the exception of action and possibly abstract shots, are that the model should be comfortable and feel natural. This is as important for a head and shoulders shot as for any other, and sitting upright on a chair or stool is seldom likely to be either natural or comfortable. Leaning slightly forward with the model's weight supported lightly on an arm is often a good way of creating a good position. This can be arranged by seating the model on a low-backed chair, placed the wrong way round to the camera, the model using the back of the chair as a support for an arm or an elbow. Another method is to position a small stool near the chair upon which he is seated; placing his foot on this, will raise his knee to a convenient height for support.

As a general rule, it is best to avoid posing your model so that his shoulders are square onto the camera, because this tends to create a static and uninteresting appearance, making the composition too symmetrical. For most pictures, it is usually better to angle the shoulders so that one is much nearer the camera than the other, although you must be careful not to shoot from too close a viewpoint, as this could cause an exaggerated perspective effect in this position. In fact, for most head and shoulders portraits, it is preferable to use a long-focus lens and shoot from a more distant viewpoint. It is also preferable, in most cases, to seat your model so that the camera is a foot or so above his eye level. With the majority of faces this will be the most flattering angle from which to shoot, and again with this consideration, it is often best to pose the model so that the camera sees a three-quarter view, rather than full face.

It should be remembered, however, that these are only generalizations and should not be adhered to rigidly, since the effect you want to create, combined with the features of a particular model, will ultimately dictate the best angle. A higher than eye-level viewpoint will emphasize the eyes and make the face appear to taper more towards the chin, whereas a lower than eye-level viewpoint will make the model's jaw more prominent and make the nose appear shorter. Apart from considerations of appearance, the viewpoint will also affect the nature of the picture. A low angle shot will create a more aggressive and assertive mood, whereas a higher viewpoint will lead to a more passive look.

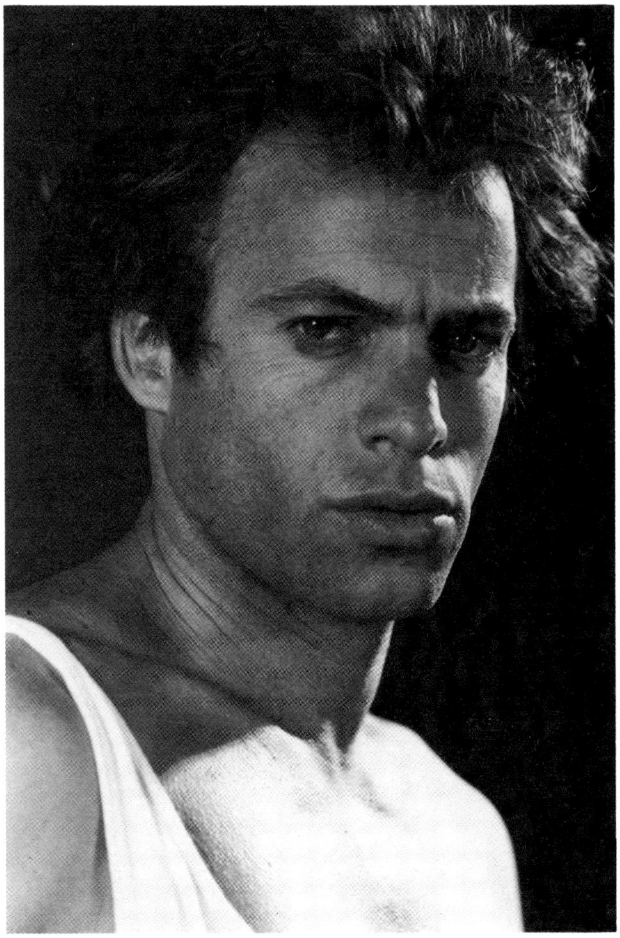

Straight, square-on to the camera poses are best avoided. Turning the shoulders slightly **(above)** *will give your picture more impact.*

When positioning a shoulder in this way, take care to avoid distortion. The use of a medium-telephoto lens will help to keep everything in the right perspective.

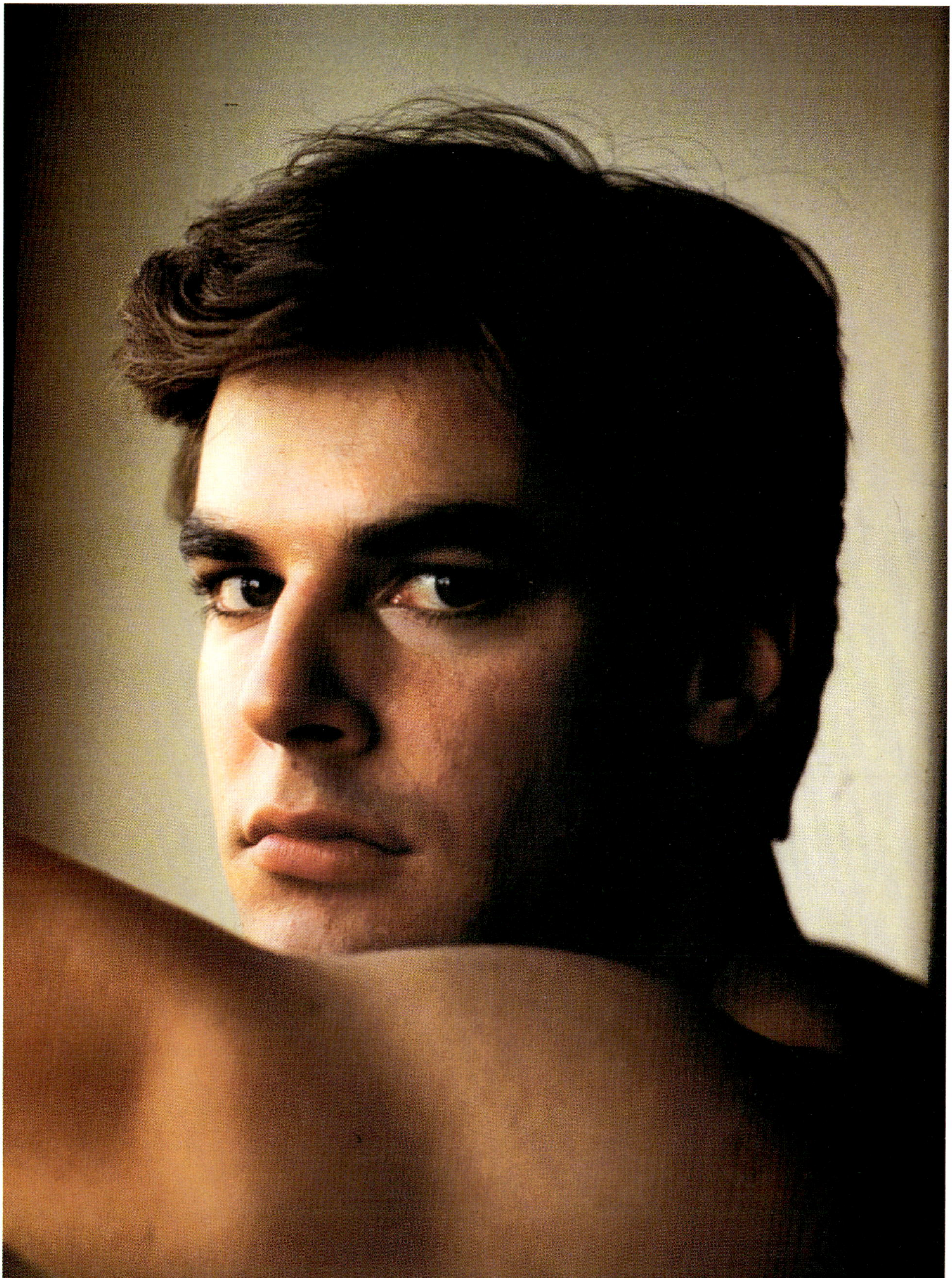

FULL LENGTH PICTURES

Full-length and three-quarter-length poses provide a different set of problems for both model and photographer, particularly in the studio. The main difficulty is that simply standing still will invariably look plain, uninteresting and very static, so it is necessary to inject some feeling of movement or shape into the body to produce an effective composition. Props can be helpful in this respect, since they can either provide a support for the model to lean upon or hold in some way to vary the shape and angle of his body, or for him to actually use to create a sense of action or movement. Experienced models develop the knack of achieving this effect simply by simulated movement. Twisting the body and moving arms and legs, even within the confines of a studio background, can create the illusion of genuine movement and action, but it is easy for such techniques to look unconvincing, particularly if the model, or the photographer, lacks experience.

Even with a head and shoulders shot, knowing what to do with arms and hands can be a problem for the model and with a full-length shot, the difficulty is multiplied. The best solution is to find some genuine piece of movement or action for the model to use and this is much easier to do on location than in the studio. Outdoors, you can use walls, fences, gates, benches or trees for the model to lean against. A full-length shot would look much more natural and relaxed with the model leaning back against a tree, for instance, with his hands in his pockets, rather than just standing passively. In addition there is much more scope for genuine movement outdoors than within the confines of the studio. You can actually get your model to walk or run towards the camera, for example, and shoot as he does so. A useful tip here, incidentally, is to prefocus at a predetermined spot and make your exposure when he reaches it; you'll find it much easier than trying to alter focus accurately as he moves closer to the camera.

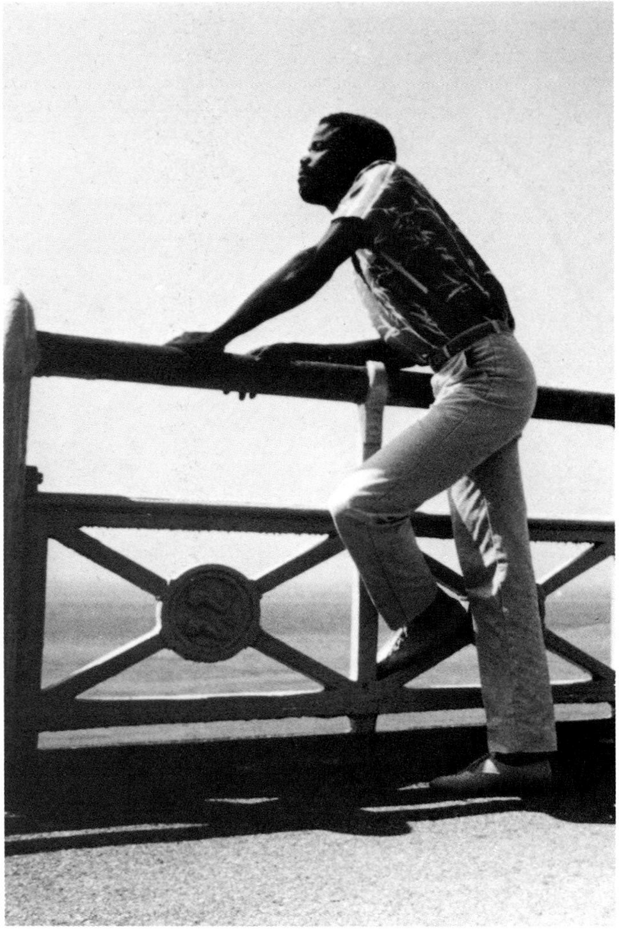

This balustrade made an ideal prop for a full-length picture, because it provided natural supports for the model's arms and feet.

Full length pictures are easiest if the model has a prop to hold, or something to lean against. Without props, many models find it difficult to strike relaxed poses. Here the photographer got his model to run towards the camera, and the activity solved the problem.

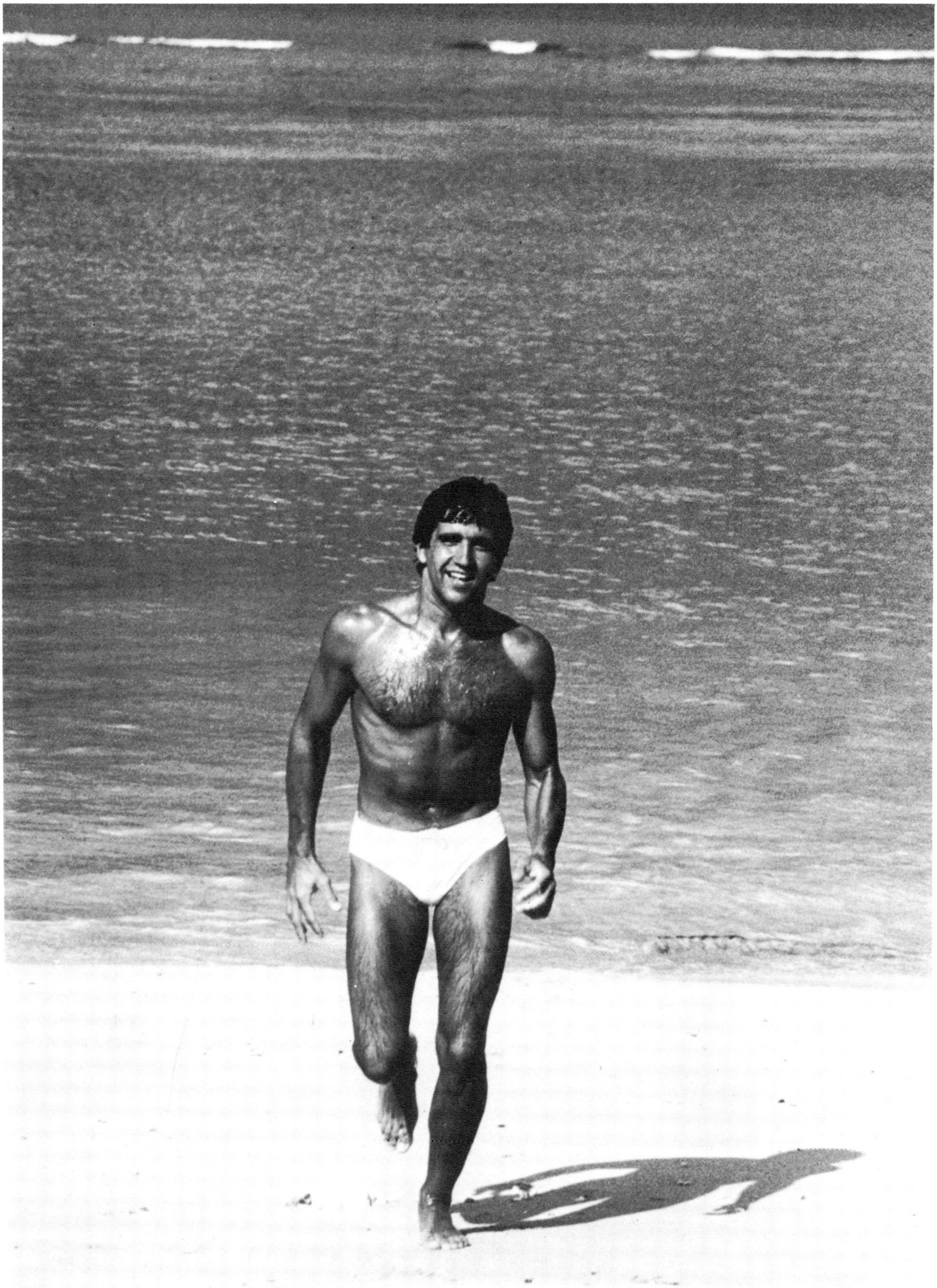

MORE THAN ONE MODEL

Photographing two or more models together offers much more scope for interesting composition, but it also presents some new problems. A head and shoulders portrait is relatively simple in terms of posing with just one model, but with two or more, some thought is needed to arrive at the best positions for each. With a double portrait it is usually best if the two heads are at slightly different levels. One solution is to place one model on a chair or stool and either stand or kneel the other just behind and above. It is important to position them so that the two heads are as near to the same distance from the camera as possible, otherwise you will have difficulty obtaining equally sharp focus in both faces. Even so, you will find the need to use quite a small aperture to ensure adequate depth of field.

With three or more models in a portrait, you will probably find it necessary to place one more at yet another level. Since your aim is simply to achieve a pleasing balance between the faces and to avoid the picture becoming too symmetrical, it can often help if one or more of the heads is in profile, with others at three-quarter or full-face. This will add a further element of interest and balance to the arrangement. The direction of the eyes will also affect the picture, and you should aim to have the models looking in a similar direction, rather than allowing them to diverge. Alternatively, these poses work well if one of the models is looking towards one or more of the others.

With three-quarter and full-length shots, unless it is important for both models to be standing, as in a fashion picture for example, it is also preferable if their heads are not exactly on the same level. This can be arranged most easily by having one of the models lean or sit on a suitable support. If this is not possible, then a more interesting arrangement can be achieved by placing one of the models closer to the camera. But be sure that you use a small enough aperture to ensure that both record equally sharp.

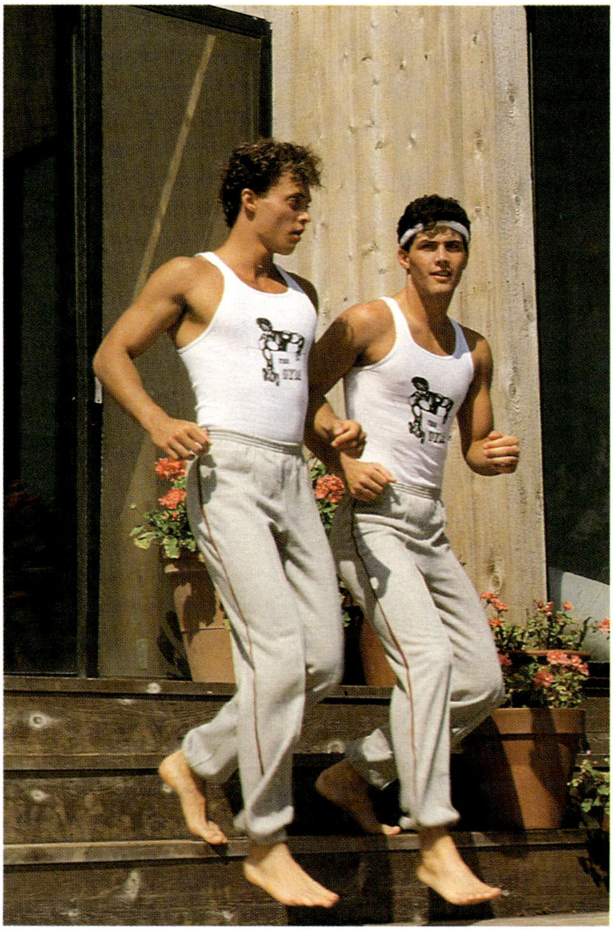

When using more than one model, position them at different head heights for better composition, and keep them in the same plane to maintain sharp focus on each. Use of a small aperture will help in this direction.

Working with three models leads to more pleasing results if you group them in a triangular shape. Notice how the positions of the models in this picture create a series of triangles – one of the most powerful shapes in picture composition.

Avoid the symmetrical look by asking one of your models to turn slightly, rather than having them both straight-on to the camera.

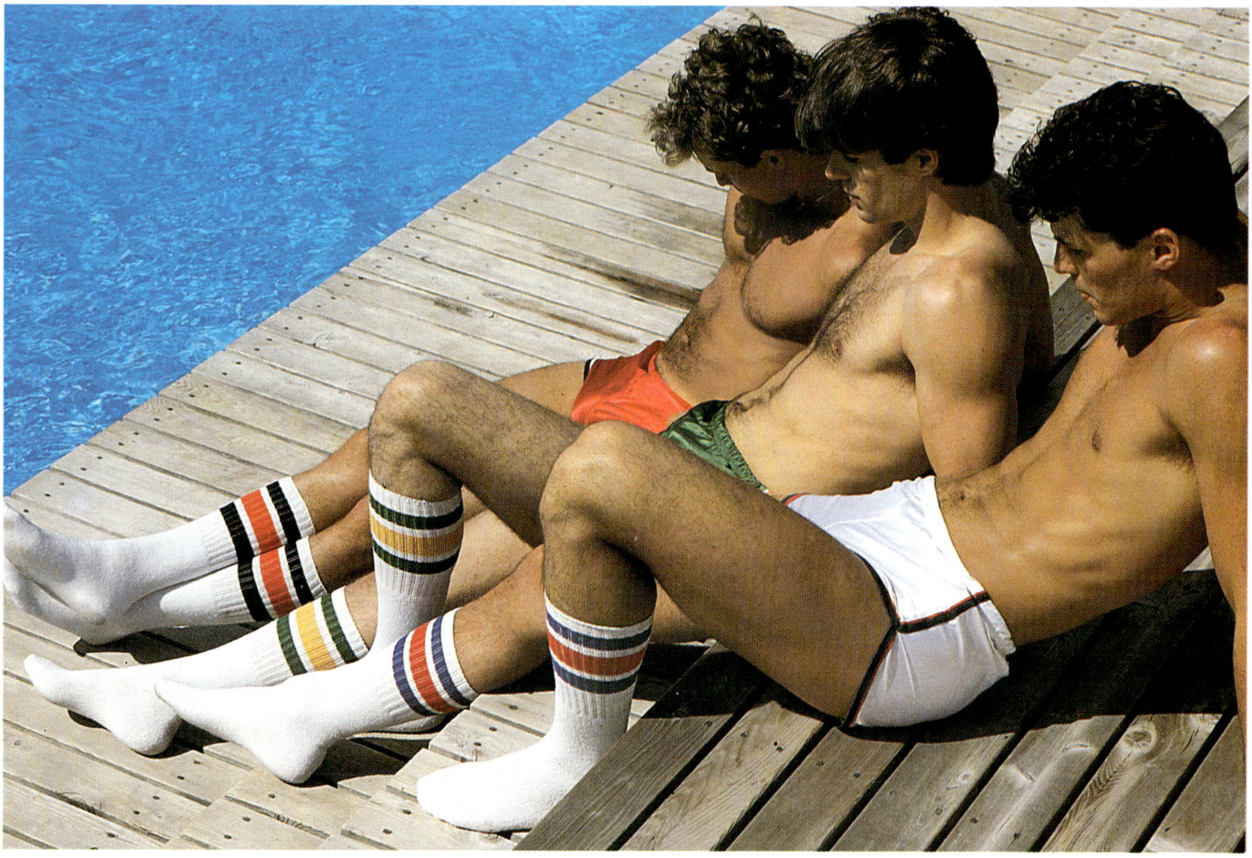

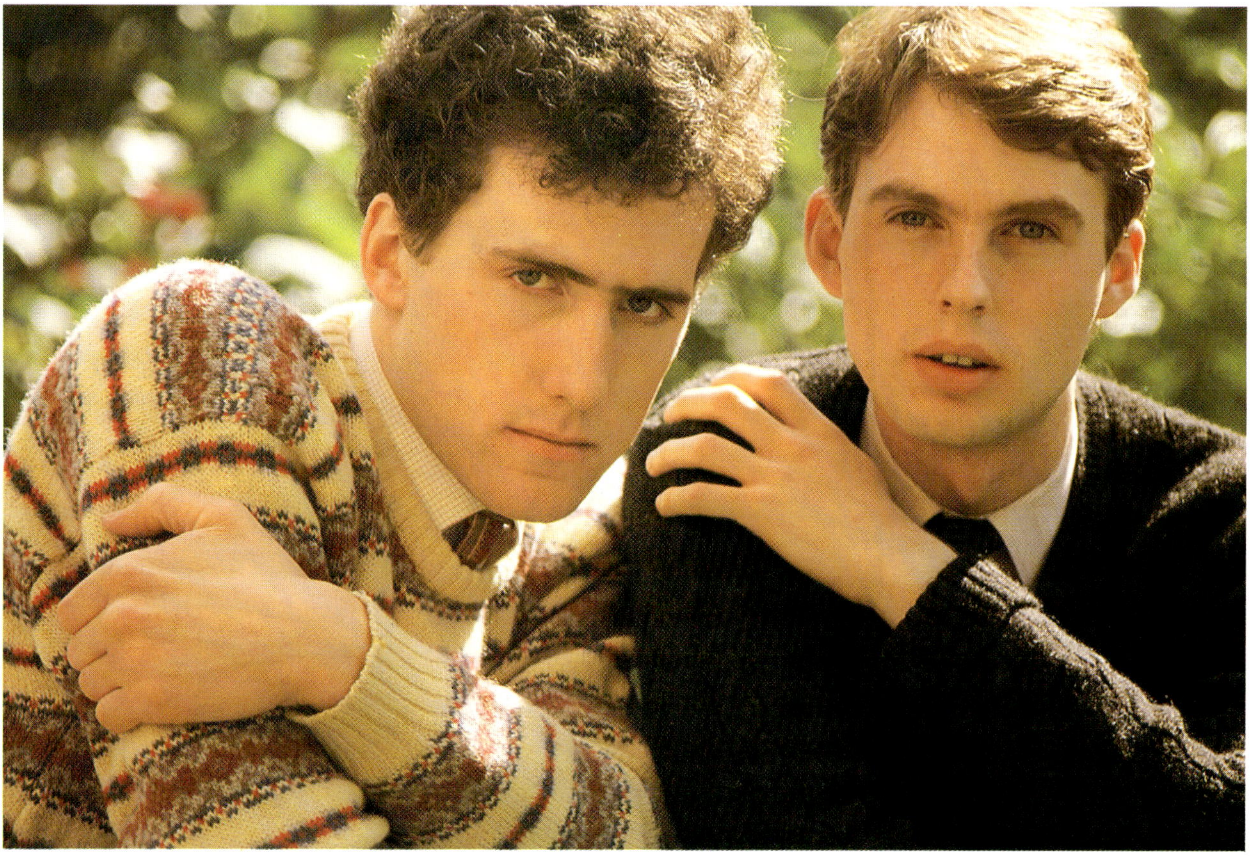

TAKING BEEFCAKE PHOTOGRAPHS

The basic techniques of taking pin-up or beefcake photographs of a male model are essentially the same as those with a girl. Obviously the main concern is for the model to appear as attractive and appealing as possible, and both the pose and the lighting must be arranged to create the most flattering effect. Although not completely obligatory, a reasonable and judicious amount of bare skin is generally considered to be an important feature. However, as with female glamour shots, the all-revealing, full-frontal type of approach can lose more in terms of subtlety and taste than it might gain in initial impact. A casually unbuttoned shirt, revealing a glimpse of healthy torso, can look more effective than a bare-chested shot.

Skin quality is a vital element in pictures of this type and a tanned face and body can make a tremendous difference to the appeal of the model, whether shooting in black and white or color. It helps to use a little oil to impart a subtle sheen to the skin and this will enhance the effect of a tan. When shooting in color, it will also help to use a correction filter, such as a Wratten 81A or 81B to make the skin appear a richer and warmer tone. The skin quality can also be enhanced by the choice of clothes and props. A blue denim shirt, for example, or white swim trunks will provide a tonal and color contrast to the skin, accentuating its effect. The background or setting of the shot should also be considered with this factor in mind, and it is important not to allow the background to become distracting. As a general rule, such pictures are most effective when quite tightly framed, placing maximum emphasis on the model's face and expression.

Eye contact is an important factor with this type of picture and although it is possible to shoot good beefcake pictures without having the model looking towards the camera, there is no doubt that both the impact and the sexual appeal of a photograph can be emphasized when the model's eyes appear to be looking straight at the viewer. This can be achieved by asking the model to look directly into the lens, rather than just towards the camera.

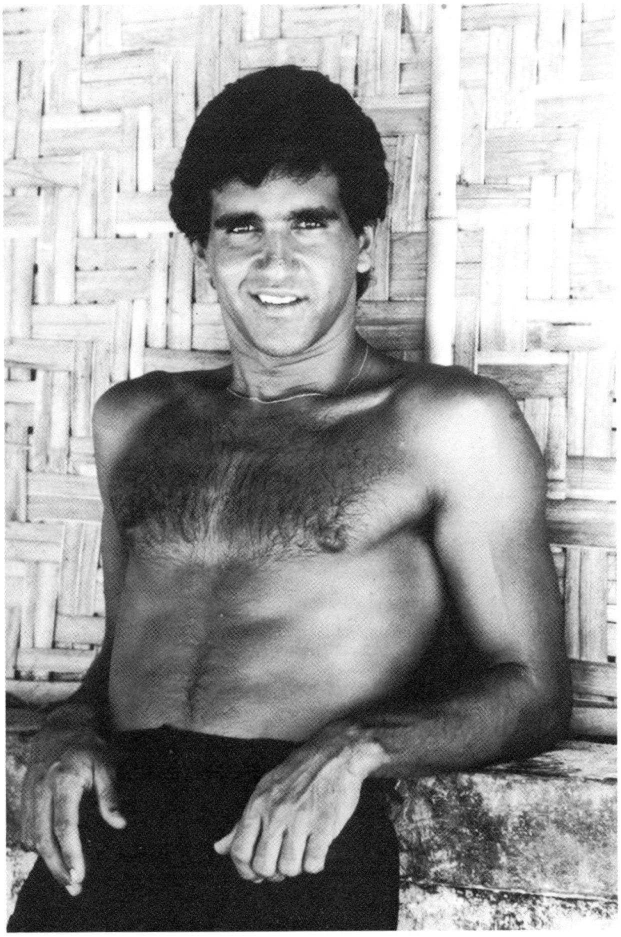

The model's expression plays a role that is important – perhaps even more important – than the sheer area of skin revealed. In this image eye contact with the camera suggests frankness and intimacy – both essential elements of beefcake pictures.

Skin texture plays another role in beefcake pictures – here the careful use of lighting brings out the tone and texture of the model's body.

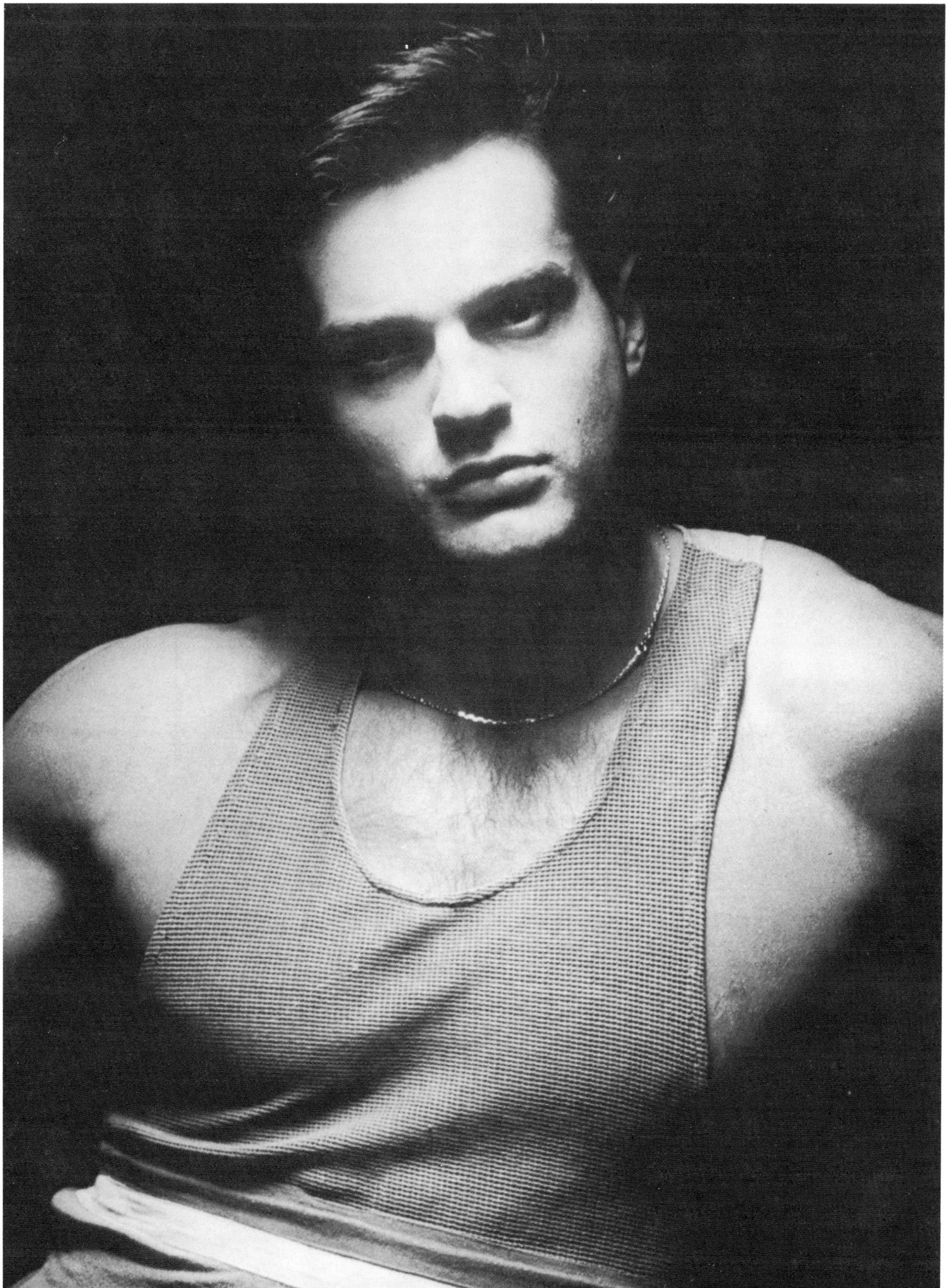

ABSTRACT NUDES

To a large extent the male body lends itself more readily to the techniques of abstract nude photography than that of a woman. This is because such pictures depend largely upon those visual elements of the subject which can be most effectively exploited in a photographic image, such as texture, form and shape. To a degree this can be more easily achieved with a man's body.

There are a variety of ways in which a subject can be abstracted. The most elementary is to simply depersonalize the model by eliminating the face. This can be achieved either by having the model turn his head away from the camera, or by framing the picture more tightly and cropping the head completely. Obviously this will only introduce a limited degree of abstraction but in many cases it will be sufficient to change the nature of the photograph from one which is essentially a picture of a person, to one in which the viewer's attention is directed more to the qualities of the image itself than to the subject.

Very tight framing can be used to create a much stronger degree of abstracting. It is, in fact, possible by this means to create pictures in which the subject is hard to identify at all, and the image simply becomes an arrangement of tones and shapes. This effect can be achieved either by the use of very close viewpoints, or with the aid of a telephoto lens; each method has its advantages. Close viewpoints can also create an unfamiliar and exaggerated perspective, and this too can be used to heighten the effect of abstraction, although it is important to appreciate that exaggerated perspective can create an unattractive and distorted appearance if allowed to occur in an accidental or uncontrolled way. Another problem that arises from the use of close viewpoints is the way depth of field becomes more limited at close-focusing distances, and a small aperture will be needed to ensure that the image is adequately sharp from the nearest to furthest details.

A long-focus lens offers the advantage of framing the image quite tightly from a more distant, and often more convenient, viewpoint. In addition, the problems of exaggerated perspective are eliminated. With a very long-focus lens, the impression of depth and perspective can, in fact, be greatly reduced, and this too can be used as a means of creating a degree of abstraction. The problem with depth of field also exists with a long focus lens and it will be necessary to use a small aperture if you want the image to be equally sharp all over. Alternatively, it is also possible to use a shallow depth of field as a further means of abstraction, and a long-focus lens, combined with a wide aperture, will enable you to focus sharply on a particular area of the body, leaving closer and more distant details as a vague blur.

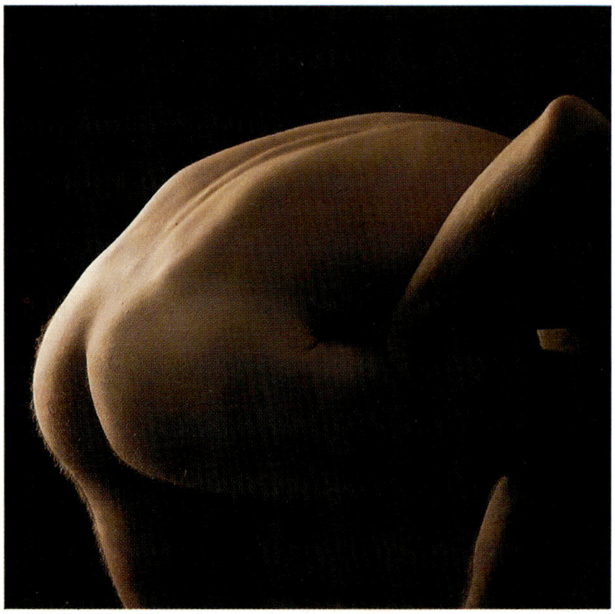

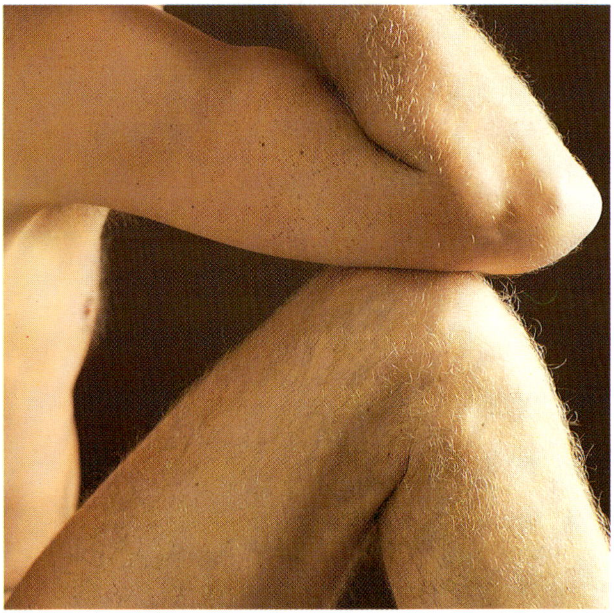

Tight cropping on the subject, turning body and limbs into little more than shapes, is another way of tackling this particular type of work. Depending on viewpoint, the pattern can be strongly angular **(above)** *or composed of smoother, flowing lines* **(right)**.

Abstract nude photography, as opposed to beefcake pictures, means making the subject more anonymous. One way to achieve this is to simply eliminate the face in some way **(left)**.

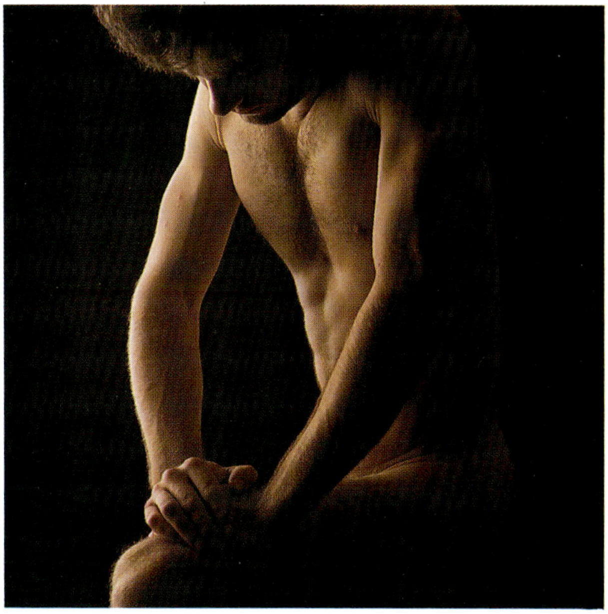

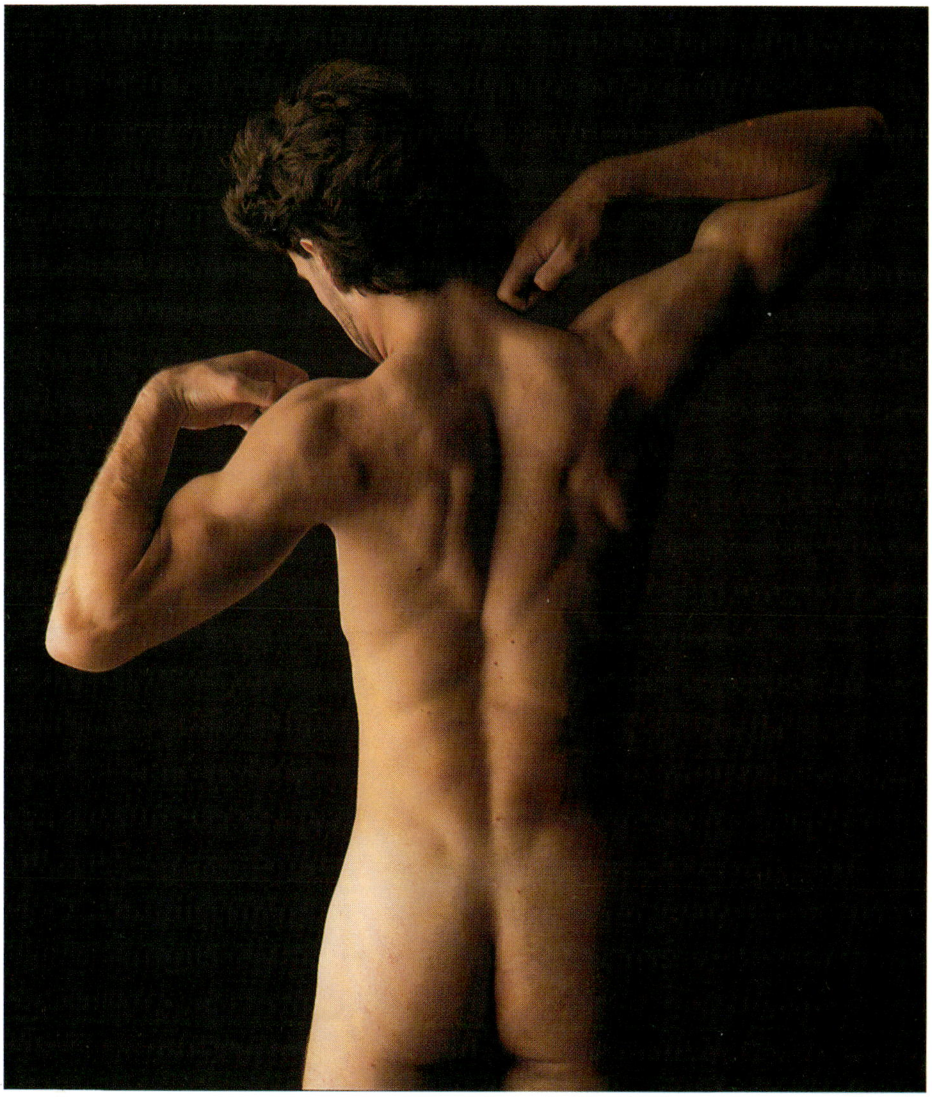

Close viewpoints like the one above can lead to a narrow depth of field, requiring small apertures to keep the focus sharp from the front to the back of image.

EXPLOITING ATHLETICISM

One of the features of male photography, which can be exploited more fully than when working with a female model, is the more muscular and athletic qualities of the subject. Although athletic abilities are just as relevant when photographing a woman, the emphasis is generally more on graceful movement, whereas when photographing a male model, it is possible to adopt a harder and more aggressive approach with both posing and lighting.

Ideally for this type of picture, it is best to choose a model who is genuinely quite athletic, perhaps someone who works out regularly or does weight training. However, unless you are taking pictures for a particular purpose or effect – such as for a muscle-building magazine – it is best to avoid someone who is too developed, since the tendency of the camera to exaggerate physical characteristics can create aesthetically unattractive results.

There are a number of ways of approaching this type of shot. In the studio, it might be best to aim for quite tightly-framed, even abstract images unless you have a large amount of space. In this way, you can focus the attention on particular parts of the body and the model can tense his muscles, moving to create a variety of shapes and effects without the need to show precisely what he is doing. Once you include more of the model, it will obviously be necessary to have some appropriate props or a setting which can be used to create a convincing scenario. Even something quite simple such as dumb-bells or a punch bag could be used in a small studio to allow the model to become genuinely involved in an action, rather than simply posing.

A gymnasium is, of course, an ideal indoor location, but you will need to be careful about the choice of viewpoints and how you frame the picture, since backgrounds and equipment in this type of setting can be distracting. Shooting outdoors, you have much more scope. All sorts of outdoor sports can be used to create interesting and dramatic body shapes and the opportunity for the model to move more freely. You will, on the other hand, have much less control over lighting, and when choosing camera angles and viewpoints, the effect of the light must also be taken into account in addition to considerations of the background and composition.

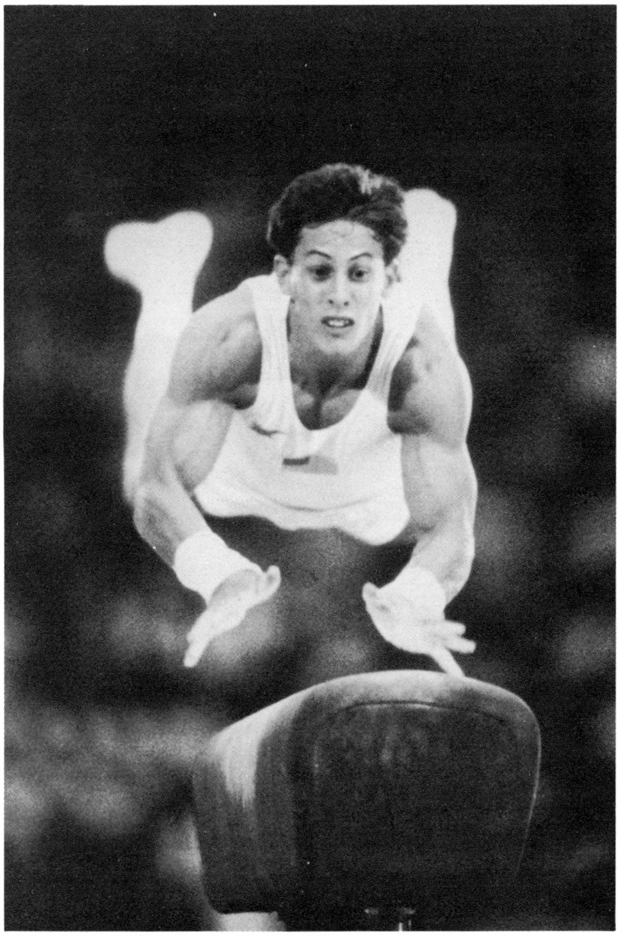

The sports stadium makes a natural setting for photographing athletes in action, but technique must be honed to perfection, choosing a shutter speed that will stop the action and yet still allow for adequate exposure under artificial light.

Outdoors, you have more scope for movement, so allow your model to move more freely as you shoot.

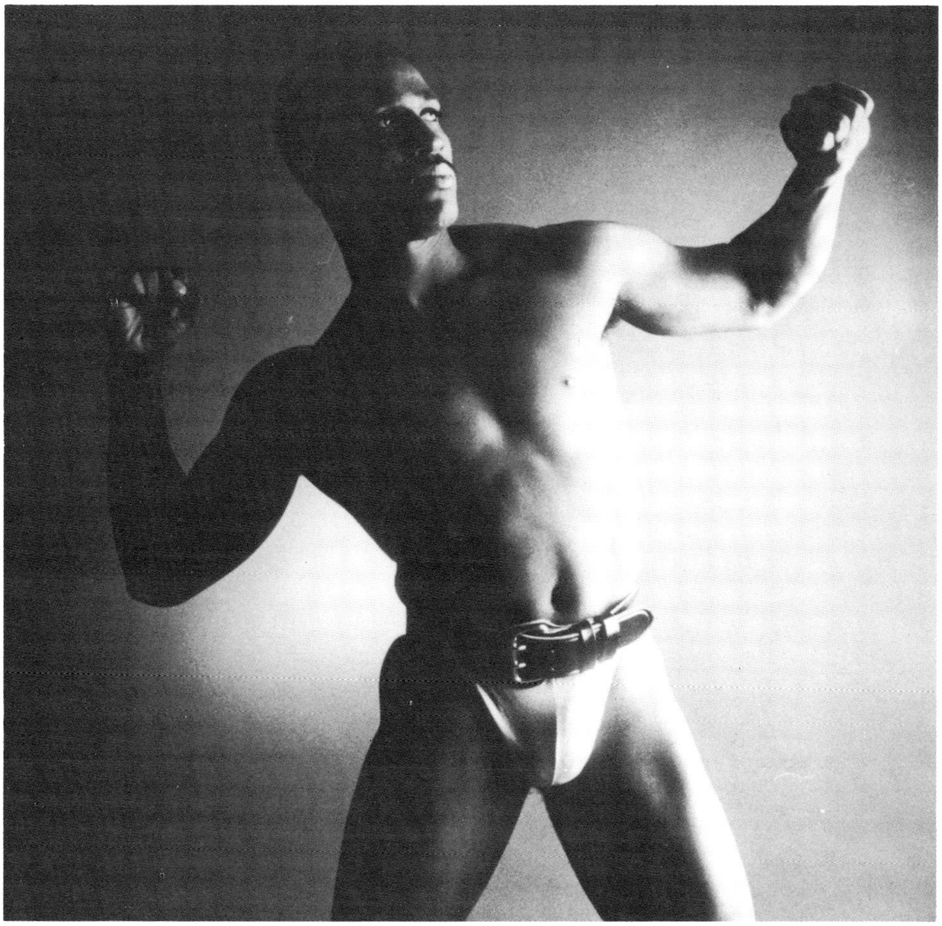

Athleticism can be far better employed with male models than with women **(left)**. *This is just one area in which male models are more versatile than their female counterparts.*

If you're going to exploit athleticism to the full, you must start with a model who is naturally athletic **(below)**.

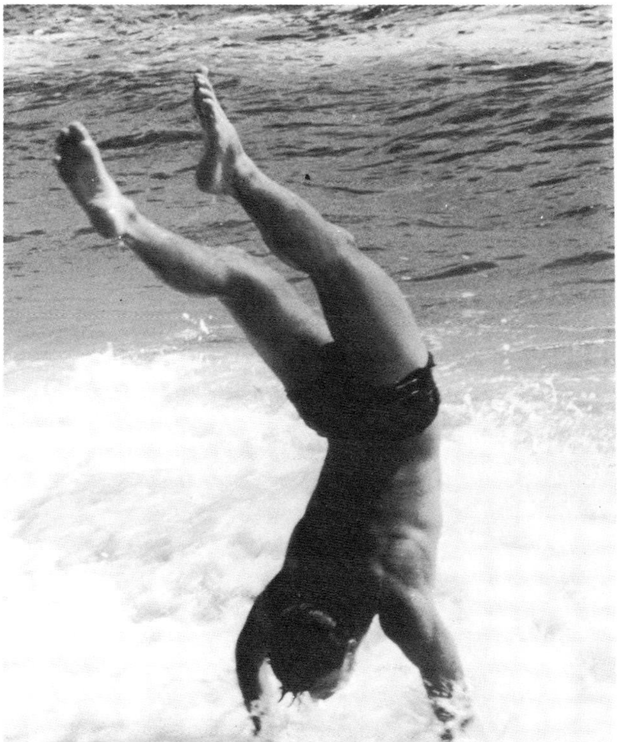

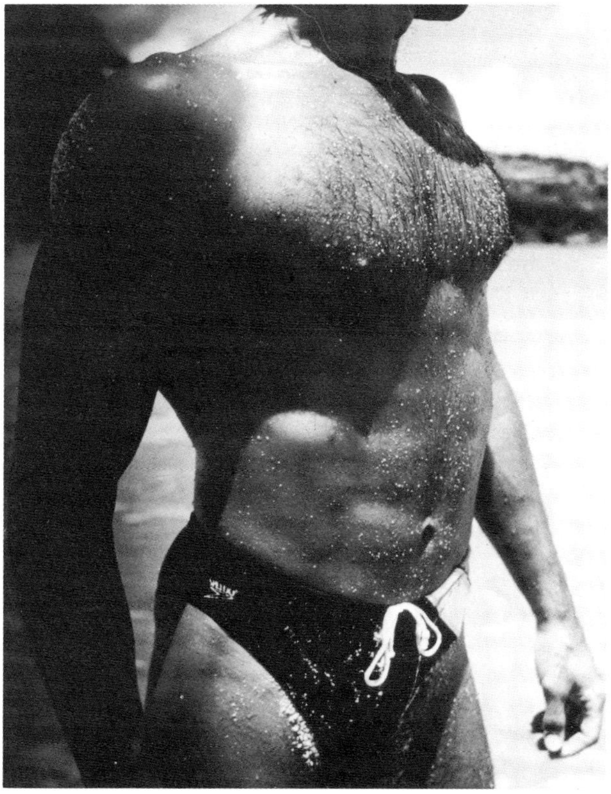

CREATING EROTIC IMAGES

To a large extent eroticism, like beauty, is in the eye of the beholder. What might appear to one person as a sensual and arousing picture, may well to another seem banal or tasteless. This is one aspect of photography in which it is difficult, or even impossible, to be completely objective; your approach to this type of subject will be guided largely by your own taste and feelings. There are, however, some basic guidelines which can help to establish a mode of working and to decide which aspects of the subject should be emphasized.

It should be appreciated that eroticism is mostly in the mind, and it depends more upon mood and fantasy than it does on stark reality. For this reason, a sense of eroticism can be more readily evoked in an image which leaves something to the imagination; a frankly pornographic picture may, in some circumstances and to some people, be sexually arousing, but not at all erotic.

A degree of mystery and ambiguity is often an effective way of evoking the right mood and response in the viewer, and it can be achieved in a variety of ways. Composition is perhaps the most basic way of creating the effect. By careful choice of viewpoint and selective framing, it is possible to simply give a glimpse of the model, his body, or of a situation. This allows the sexual aspect of the image to be implied rather than clearly demonstrated, and the viewer is able to read much more into it than would be possible to illustrate. Lighting too can be used in this way. Low-key or shadowy effects can be used to lose or subdue some of the detail in the image and to quite literally shroud it in a little mystery. Indeed, shadows can play a significant role in this type of picture.

Texture can be an important element in creating an erotic quality. The camera has the ability to record the subtlety of surfaces in a way which invites a tactile response from the viewer as well as a purely visual one, and this can heighten the sensual quality of a photograph. Lighting which emphasizes textures such as skin and fabric can be an effective technique, but in addition, it is possible to emphasize the effect by combining different or contrasting textures. In this way, both are accentuated, like droplets of water on skin, for instance, or leather against skin. Juxtapositions like this can create powerful images.

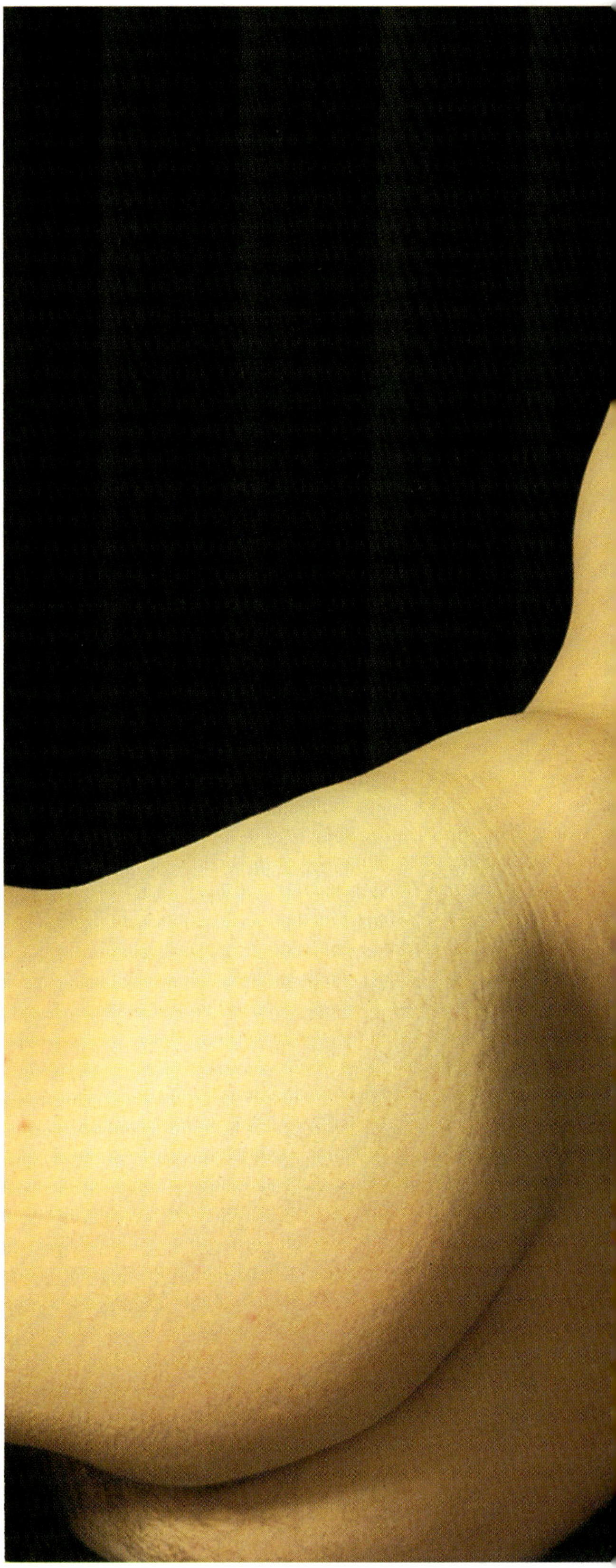

Eroticism is hard to define and what is meaningful to one person can often be meaningless to another. An air of mystery, soft focus techniques, low lighting to create shadowy effects . . . all are ingredients of the erotic.

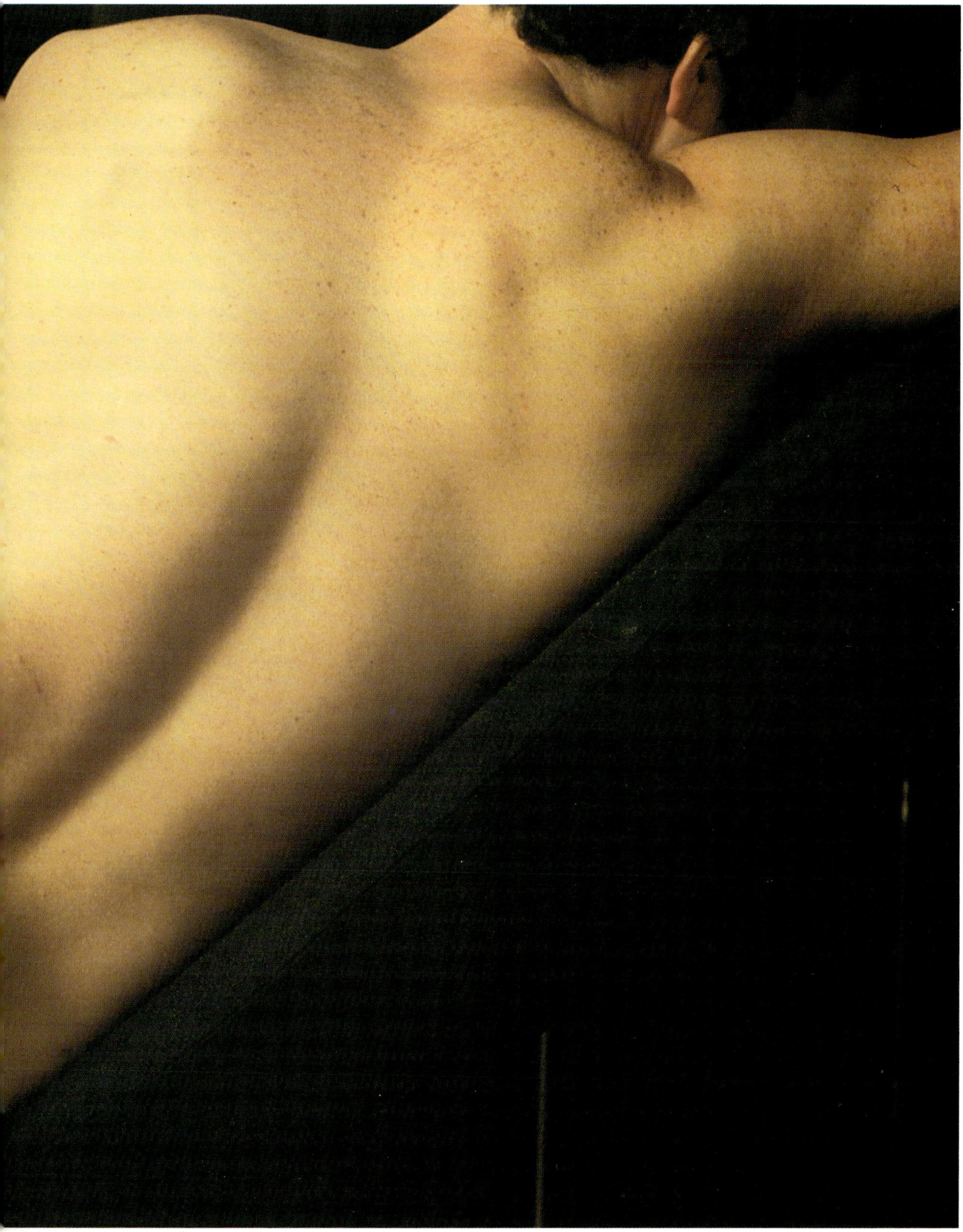

SHOOTING A MODEL PORTFOLIO

One of the things which the keen photographer of the male is likely to be asked to do is to take photographs for a model's, or prospective model's portfolio. This is an essential requirement for a model, since it provides a sort of shop window for potential clients and can help to give some idea, not only of how well a particular model photographs, but also to show the range of character and styles which he can project. In fact, most model agencies will want to see at least a selection of photographs of a newcomer to the profession before they are prepared to start representing him. Even experienced and well established models like to periodically update their portfolios and the opportunity to experiment and maybe try out a new image can be more easily done during a special test session than whilst actually on an assignment.

Variety is the essence of such a session and ideally it should be planned to incorporate both studio and location shots, as well as head and shoulders and full-length pictures. In addition, most models will want to be photographed in a variety of clothes, casual as well as smart or sophisticated, and in many cases a good body shot is an asset. This could be in swimwear, for example. There is also a considerable potential for what is known as 'spare part' modelling. If a model has particularly good hands, teeth, hair or even eyes, he will want close-up shots to emphasize these points since models are often booked just for this particular feature. The same applies to any particular skills, such as waterskiing or windsurfing.

It is best to shoot in both black and white and color, as each have their particular uses. Color prints can look very effective in the portfolio and will show off a good tan in, say, a swimwear shot, but they may be prohibitively expensive for use as an index card or a mailing shot. Quite often the model directories or head sheets are printed only in black and white. Whatever the choice, you should ensure that the prints are well made and carefully finished to remove any blemishes or dust spots. Good presentation is vital, both for your own reputation and to create the best impression for the model himself.

A professional model will use pictures to present himself, both in the form of a portfolio and in the model cards seen here. Shooting with this in mind, you need to illustrate plainly and clearly your model's potential, the type of work he undertakes and other details that will be of interest to future clients.

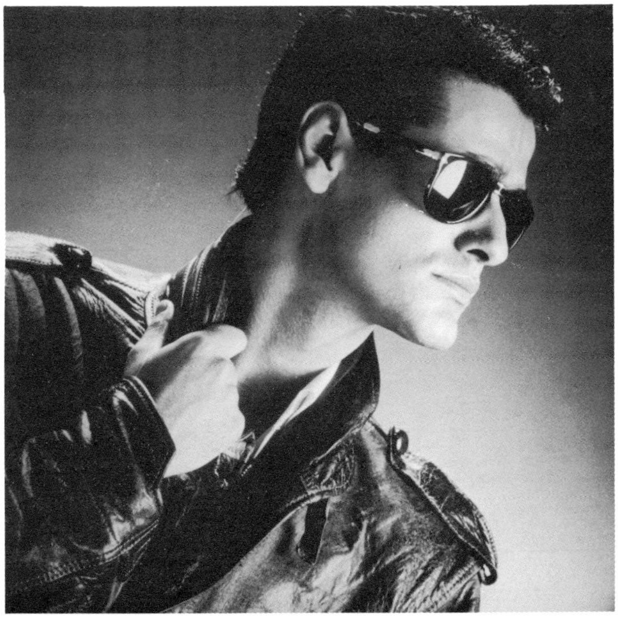

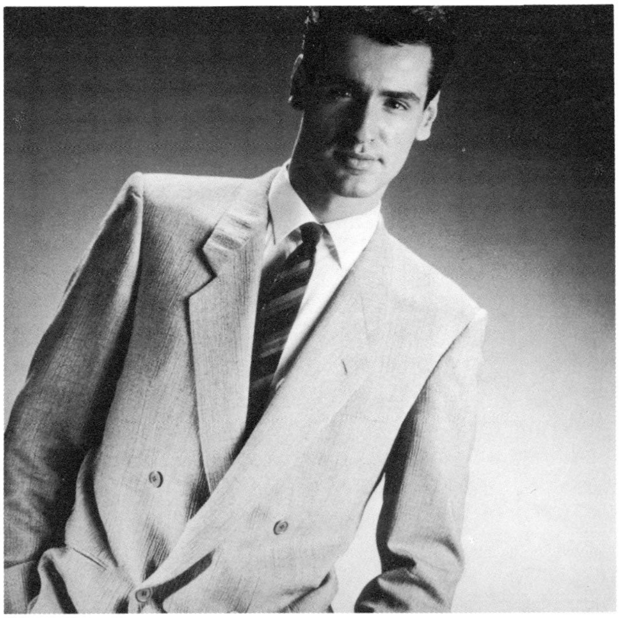

DARREN AVERY

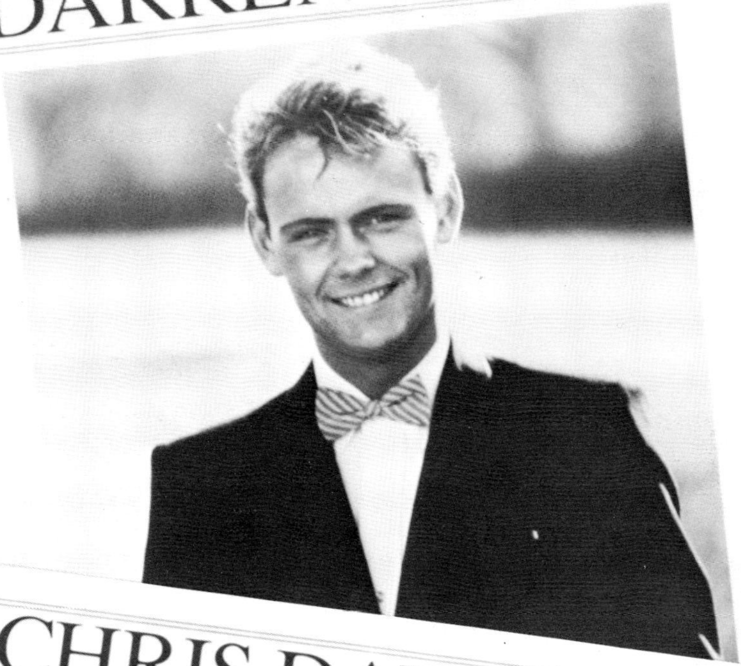

CHRIS DAVIDSON

Height 6'1½"/1.84 Chest 40/1.02 Waist 32/81 Inside leg 32/81 Outside leg 42/1.07 Collar 15½/39-40 Suit 40/1.02 Shoes 9½/44 Gloves 9 Hair: Lt Brown Eyes: Blue/Green
WINDSURFING/WATER SKI/ALL SPORTS

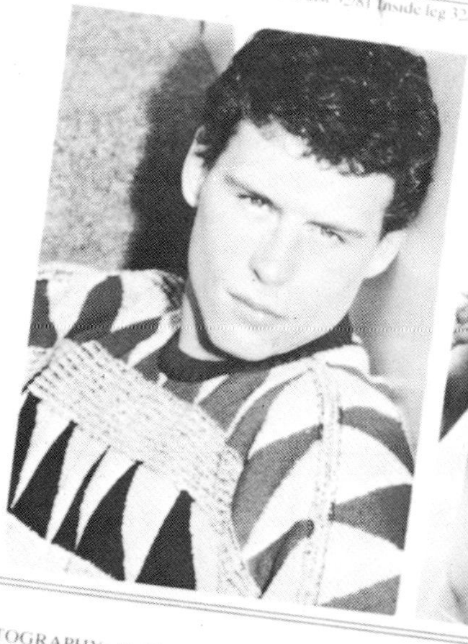

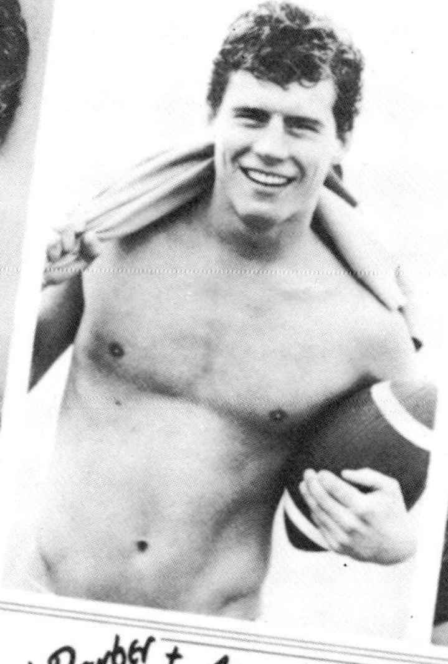

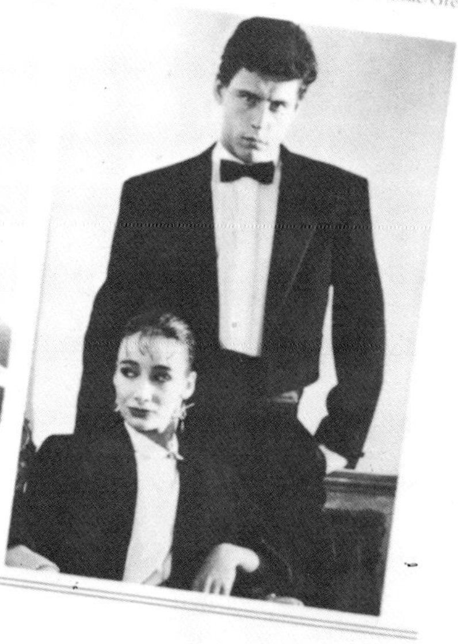

PHOTOGRAPHY AND SHOWS: 01-935 3329
01-486 0830
01-935 4132

Gil Barber + Associates
Model & Television Agency
Suite 10 38 Wigmore Street London W1
Tlx 21879 TELEX G attn GBA

TELEVISION: 01-486 0839
24 HR ANSWERING SERVICE: 01-935 3329

a MICHAEL BARNES b JOACHIM FREDERICK c JOACHIM FREDERICK FOR GIANNI VERSACE d JOACHIM FREDERICK FOR GIANNI VERSACE

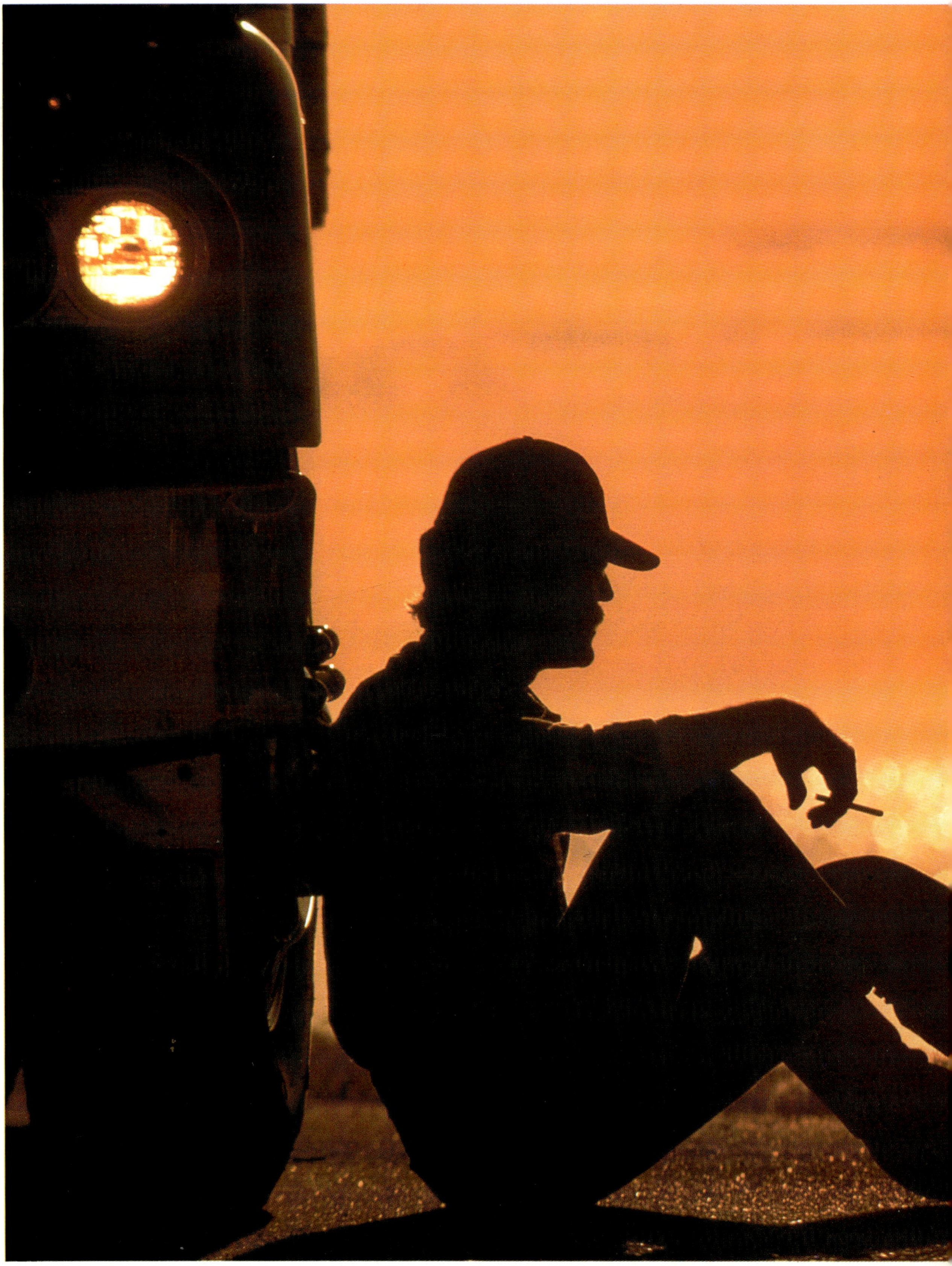

USING LOCATIONS

PLANNING A SESSION

Good planning is vital for any photographic session and particularly so when working on location, since to overlook even a small detail can seriously disrupt your photography. It is a good idea to write a check list of everything you need to take with you, from cameras and equipment, to a roll of tape or a screwdriver. This can be taped inside your camera bag and each item checked off just before you leave.

With regard to equipment, it is advisable always to carry a spare camera body, as you can be sure that any mishaps or breakdowns are bound to occur miles from home. It is also essential to carry a stock of spare batteries for dependent items like automatic cameras, flash guns and exposure meters. An ample supply of film will avoid the frustration of running low before you have completed the session and a selection of filters should be considered as a standard item of equipment. A light-tight bag for exposed film is very useful – the black plastic envelopes in photographic paper boxes are ideal – as is a marking pen to label what you have shot and to identify any rolls which might need to be clip-tested or push processed.

If you are using lighting equipment, spare bulbs and fuses are vital, as well as either adaptors or spare plugs in case an alien socket is encountered. An extra long extension cord is also important, as you will invariably find that the best place for the lighting is precisely where there is no convenient socket. Even with outdoor shots, one or two large, white reflectors are recommended to help control lighting quality and contrast. These can be the type made of fabric, supported on collapsible frames, or simply large sheets of white cardboard or polystyrene. Using flash, it is helpful to take an extra-long synchronization cord or a slave cell for situations when you might wish to position a flash some distance from the camera. A roll of adhesive tape is invaluable for fixing and securing lights and accessories in difficult places, and when shooting fashion pictures, a selection of clips and pegs for adjusting the fall and fit of garments can be invaluable.

Don't forget to make some provision for a little comfort and refreshment for both your model and yourself if it is to be full-day session and particularly if it is to be an outdoor location. A lack of thought in this direction can cause a session to end prematurely. Last, but by no means least, make sure that you have planned exactly what you intend to do. Jot down the ideas you have had for each shot, plus any props or particular clothes that will be needed. If any pictures involve special techniques, make a note of these too. It is surprising how easy it can be to lose track or direction in the heat of the moment and a written list will allow you to make constant references, avoiding a lull or lack of momentum developing during the session.

If you are taking pictures some distance from home, you will need to anticipate every eventuality, both photographic and otherwise. For example, these four apparently similar pictures were shot on three different lenses: a 28mm wide-angle, and telephoto lenses with focal lengths of 105mm and 200mm. Additionally the photographer used a blue filter over the lens to darken the flesh tones and give the model a more ruddy complexion. Without adequate planning, these vital accessories would have been left behind in the studio.

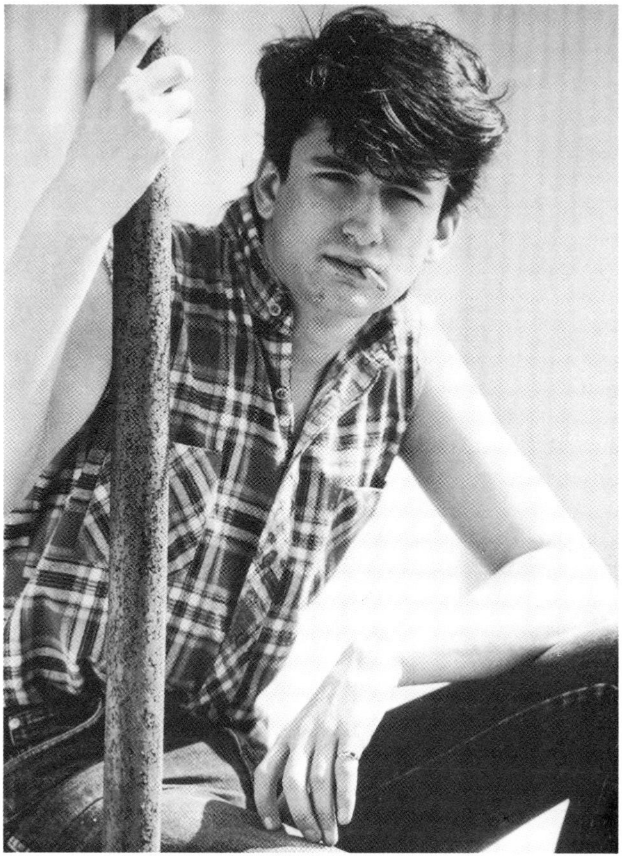
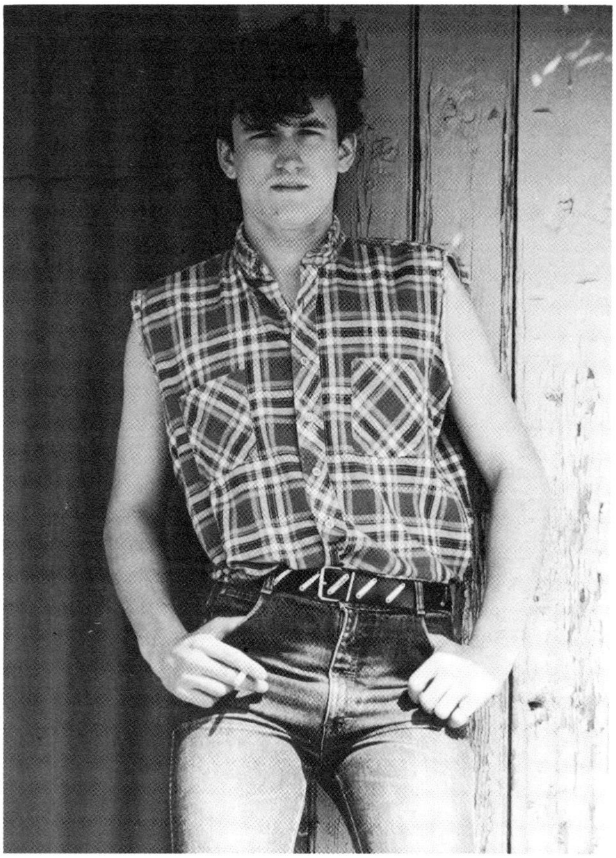
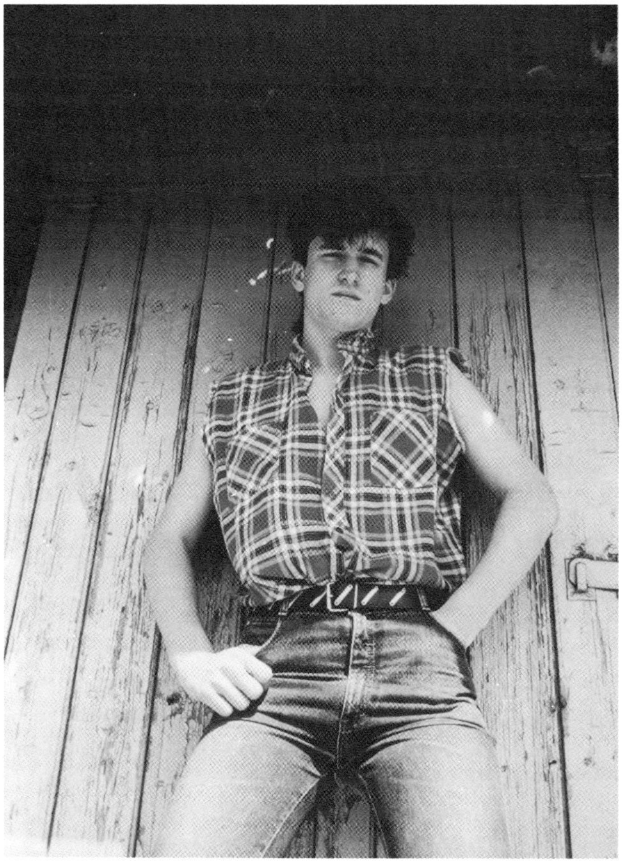
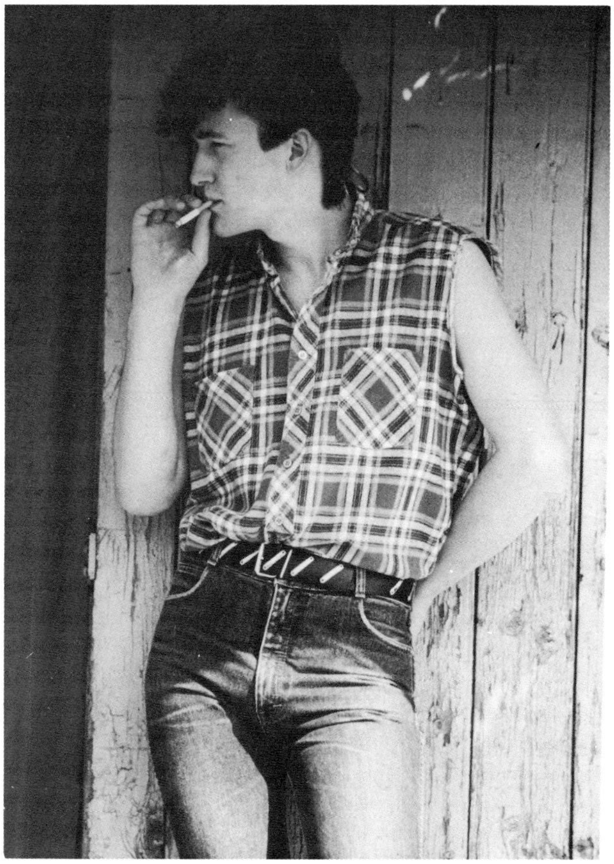

CHOOSING A LOCATION

Where models are involved, it is vital to know exactly where you are going for a session and precisely what pictures you intend to take, particularly when working with professional models, since any aimlessness or wasted time can be very expensive. Choosing a good location is the best way of ensuring a relaxed and productive session, but what are the factors to consider?

An easy mistake is to be swayed by an impressive or picturesque landscape or setting. It is quite possible to discover, having decided on such a location, that there is, in fact, only one picture there. As a general rule, it is more important to look for a location that has a number of interesting corners and aspects rather than a single dramatic view, particularly if you intend to spend several hours there. Many of the shots you will be taking will only need quite small areas of background and a location where these can be varied easily will be much more stimulating and productive.

It is a good idea to visit your intended location a day or so before the session if possible, and to take a camera along. This allows you to fully explore all the possibilities in terms of camera angles, viewpoints and backgrounds, and get a clear idea of the pictorial potential. If you are using daylight indoors, or at an outdoor location, don't forget to consider lighting angles. Make a mental note of where the sun will be at a particular time of day. If you plan to use lighting equipment, make a note of where the mains sockets are and their type.

With an outdoor location, make sure that you have good access with a car. If you have to take a lot of clothes as well as cameras and accessories, a long walk will be a nuisance, and a car can also be a useful base from which to work, providing a secure place for the model to change and leave his gear. It is also worth ensuring that you have selected a place which will allow a degree of privacy, as a crowd of onlookers can be rather off-putting, particularly if your model is inexperienced.

If you are planning a session lasting several days away from your base, it can be well worth while to select a hotel in terms of its photographic potential as well as its accommodation. Even if it is more expensive, a hotel with good interiors and perhaps a garden or pool, will allow you to take a lot of shots more quickly and with greater comfort and convenience than if you have to travel out for every location each day. It can also be a useful source of accessories and props, like loungers and sun umbrellas. Most managers will allow you to borrow such items for a short period if you explain your reasons.

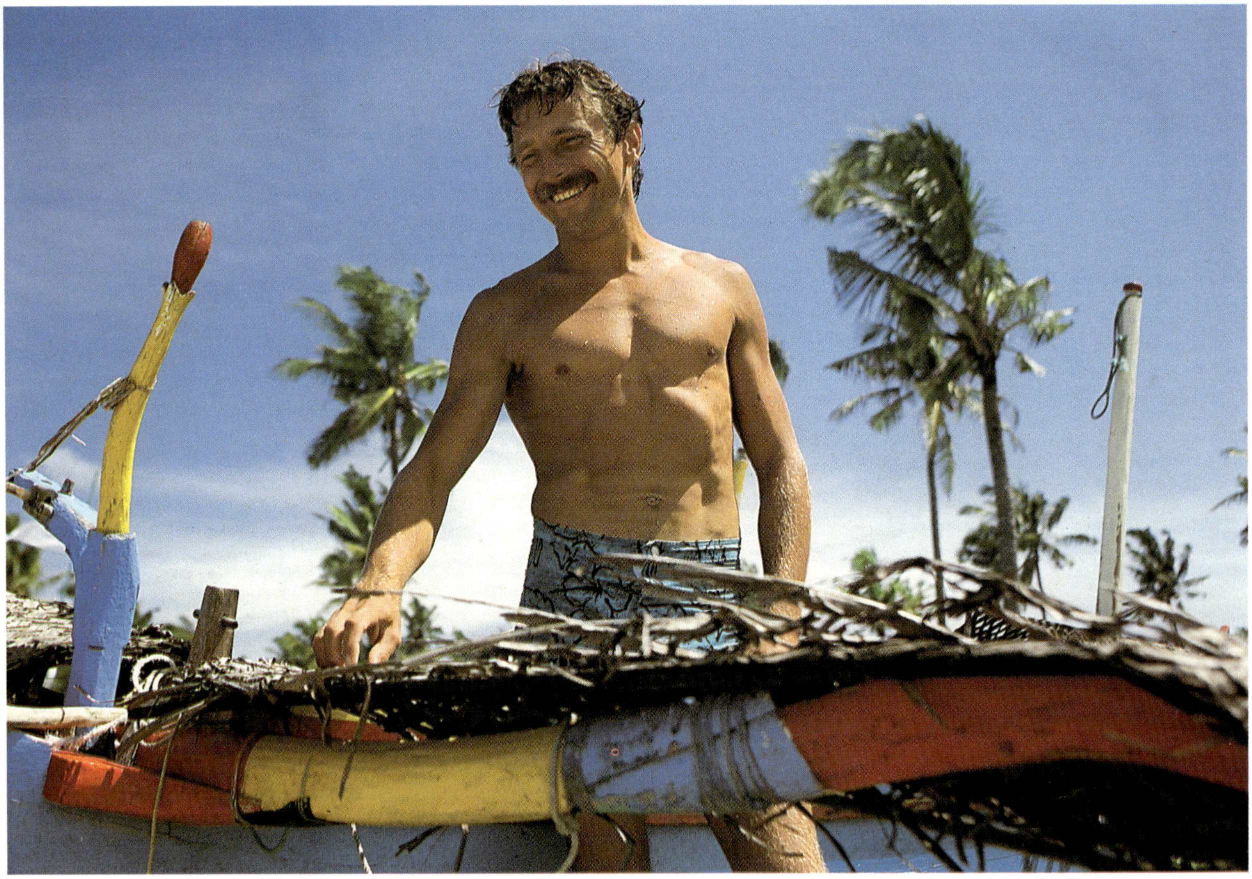

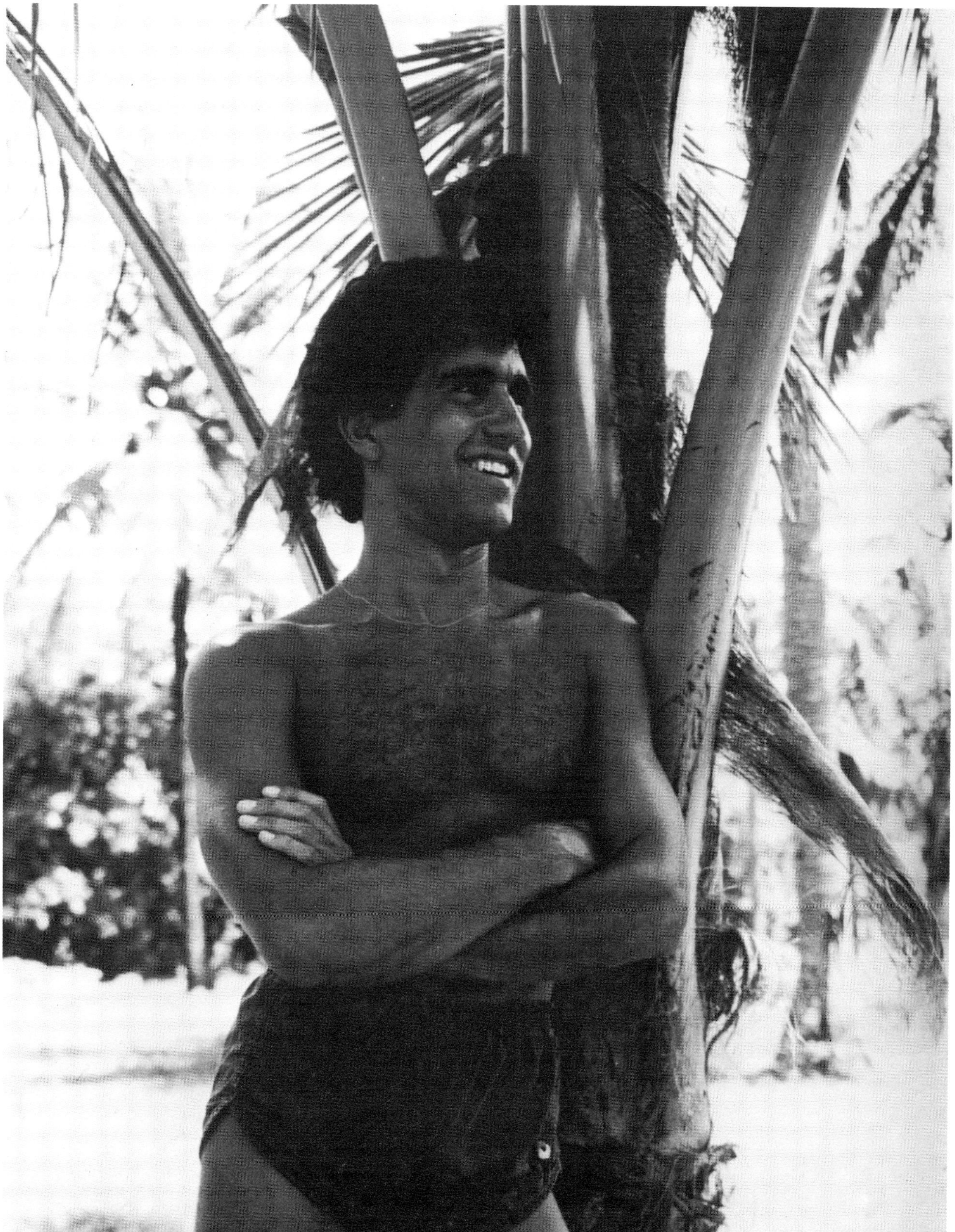

BEACH AND SEA PHOTOGRAPHY

The beach is a popular location for many types of photography and for a number of good reasons. Firstly, the light is often particularly good. The open sky and light, reflective surroundings create a pleasing and flattering quality, and the space also makes it possible to shoot from a variety of viewpoints to alter the angle and direction of the light. The openness also means that it is always possible to find plain, uncluttered backgrounds when needed.

Naturally, it is the water and the sand which are the most obvious physical and visual attractions, and for male photography in particular, the opportunity for athletic activity as well. The seaside environment also makes it an ideal setting for nude and body shots if only for the reason that it provides a rationale. Nude pictures in particular can easily look contrived or banal when photographed in a setting where the model would normally be fully clothed.

When choosing a beach location, it helps considerably if you can find somewhere that has access to showers and other creature comforts. A full day's photography on the beach can become arduous if there is no opportunity for the model to freshen up and remove accumulated sand and salt water from time to time. You must also remember to take extra care of your equipment, since both sand and salt water can be lethal to cameras and other accessories. It is best to keep each item inside a sealed plastic bag inside the camera case while not in use and to carefully remove every trace of sand and moisture before replacing it.

Although the light can be especially good for photography on the beach, it is important to take some precautions. Firstly, when shooting in color it is usually necessary to use a UV or Skylight filter because there is a strong presence of Ultra Violet light by the sea and this can cause a blue cast in color shots. In fact it is often preferable to use a warm-tinted color correction filter such as a Wratten 81A or 81B. This will help to make skin tones more attractive and to emphasize the effects of a tan. One exception to this is early in the morning or late in the afternoon when the sunlight has a naturally warmer quality.

Exposure calculation needs to be made with care because the light surroundings and large amount of reflected and scattered light can easily mislead the meter into believing conditions to be brighter than they really are, causing underexposure. The best method is to take close-up readings from the model, ensuring that the meter is not influenced by the bright surroundings. Another method which can be used with a separate hand meter is to take an incident light reading.

Action shots on the beach and in the sea are an obvious subject and a good opportunity to experiment with both frozen movements, using a fast shutter speed, as well as blur, using a slower shutter speed. When shooting with your model in the water, it is a good idea to use a telephoto lens. This will allow you to shoot from a more distant viewpoint and avoid the risk of sea water being splashed onto the camera. If you have an underwater or weatherproof camera it is a good opportunity to get some really dramatic close-up and water-level shots. This type of camera is also ideal for photographing subjects like surfing and sailboarding.

It is possible to make good use of both sand and water with nude and body shots, the strong textural quality of the elements used to enhance skin quality. The effect of water on oiled skin, for example, can produce very strong images as can sand on skin. In addition, the beach offers many other possibilities for this type of juxtaposition. Rocks and driftwood or weathered fishing boats all have great potential as props or backgrounds for close-up or even abstract pictures. Of course there are many more useful objects and beach impedimenta which can be used in this way: beach chairs and tents, as well as sun shades, sailing boats, surf boards and so on. All add color and interest to the composition as well as providing an aid to posing.

Don't overlook the beautiful characteristics of late afternoon sunlight. Its warm, mellow quality can be particularly advantageous for nude and body shots, and it is worth-while planning your day so that you don't run out of steam before this occurs. In addition, with an east- or west-facing beach, there is the possibility of sunsets or sunrises over the water, which can be used to create very moody pictures. Exposure for this type of picture needs to be considered carefully as the setting which records the colors of the sunset most effectively will leave foreground details underexposed. One solution is to simply allow your model to become silhouetted against the sky or sea.

The best way of obtaining detail in both your model and the sunset background is to use fill-in flash. For this, you must first calculate the exposure for the background. Let's say this is 1/60 second at f/8. Next you must calculate the exposure for the flash, according to its distance from the subject. Say this is f/11. All that is needed now is to reset the shutter speed to 1/30 second to compensate for the smaller aperture. This will maintain the correct exposure for the background but the change of shutter speed will not affect the flash exposure. In practice, you may find it preferable to vary the exposures a little by bracketing. The effect of a sunset can often be made more dramatic by slightly underexposing and it is best also to slightly underexpose the flash exposure as the correct flash exposure can create a rather artificial appearance.

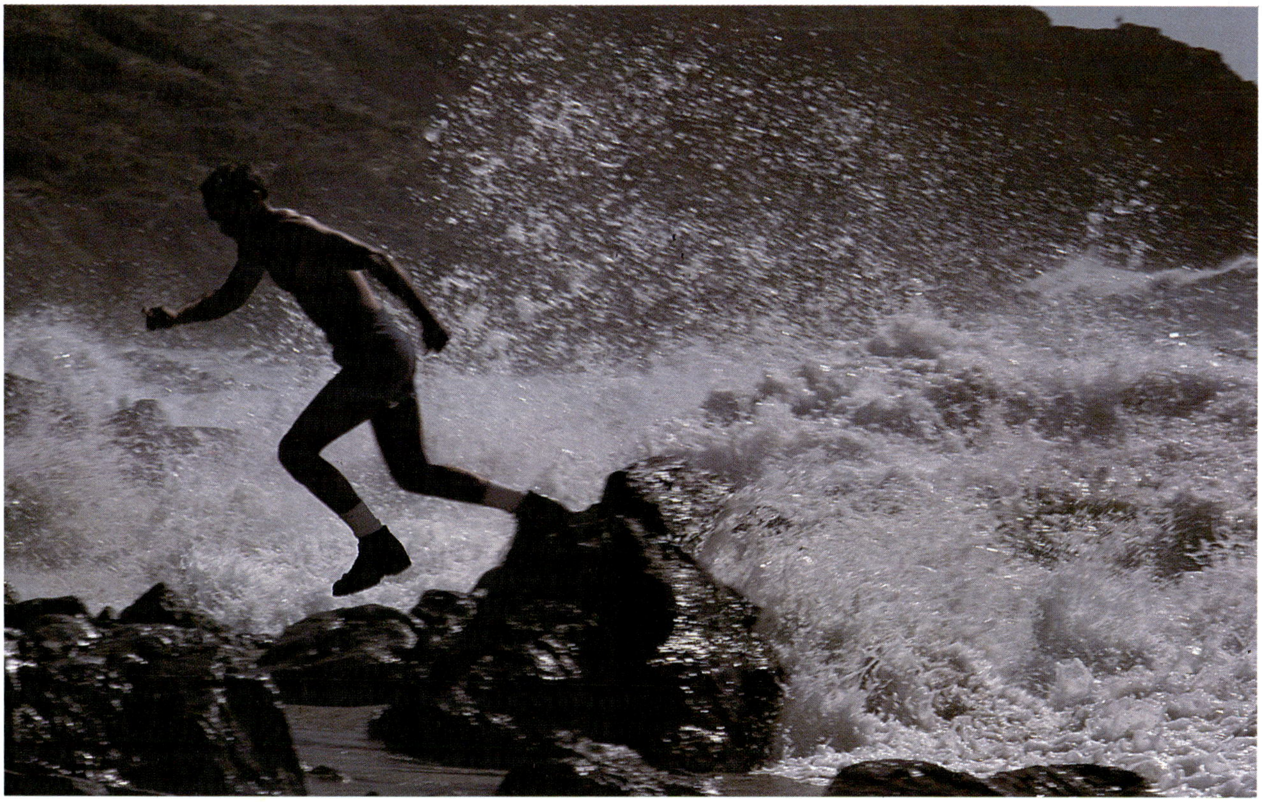

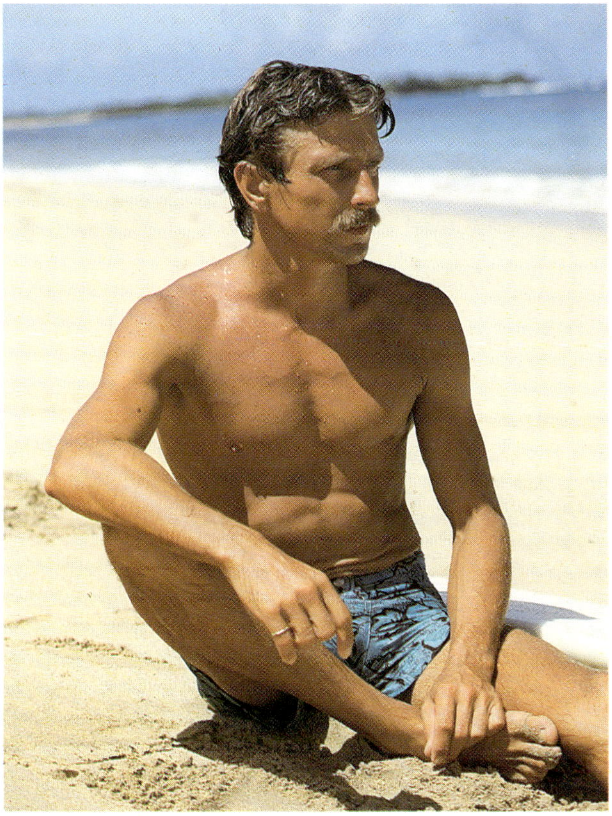

A location like this calls for movement in your model. Matching the pose to the environment in this way gives your pictures more strength and vitality.

Exposures need to be carefully measured on the beach, since the sand reflects the sun and gives your camera the impression that the light is brighter than it really is. In such locations, take your meter reading from the model himself, exposing for correct skin tones.

BEACH AND SEA PHOTOGRAPHY

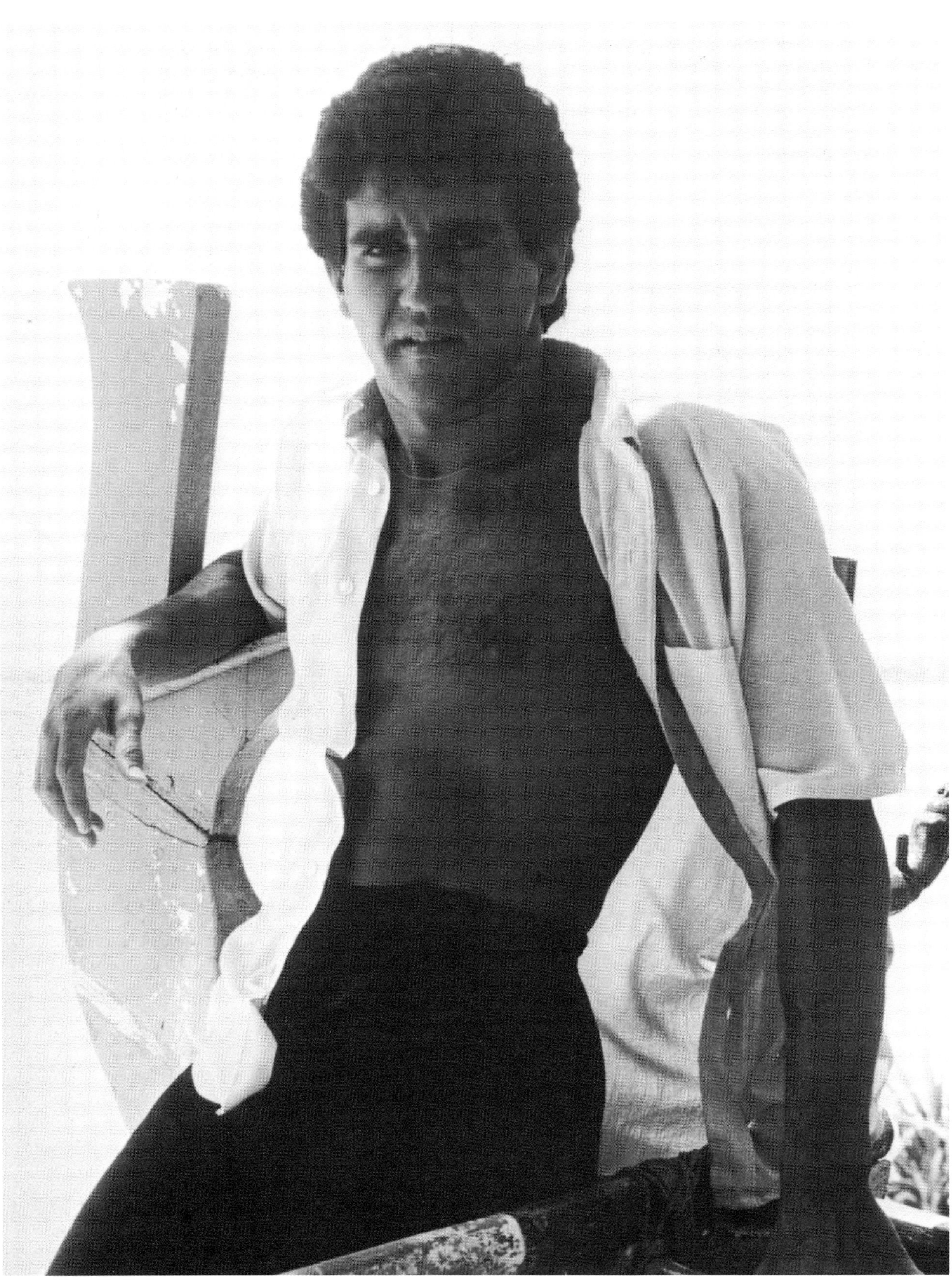

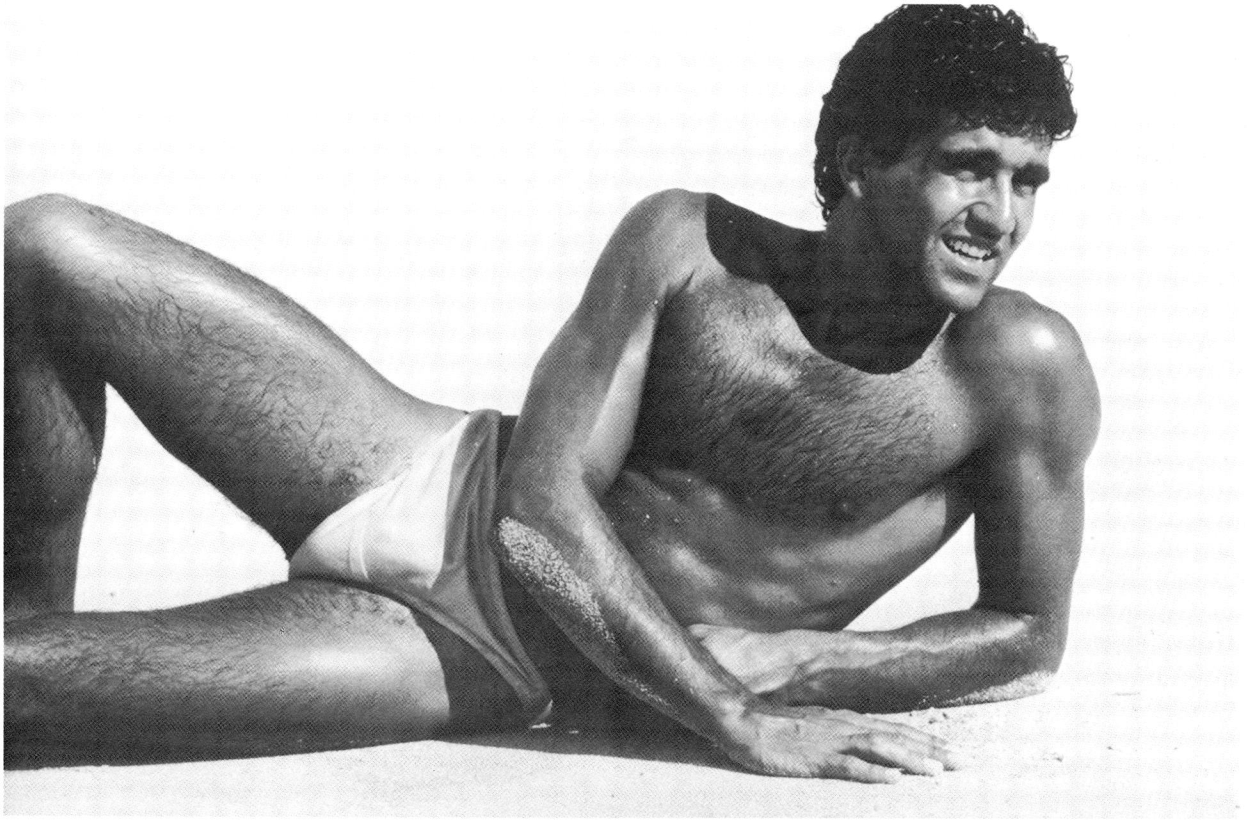

The sand dunes make a good, natural reflector, enhancing skin tones when shooting body shots on the beach **(above)**.

The bright light of a beach can sometimes make your model squint in the sunlight. Shooting against the light or in open shade helps prevent this problem **(left)**.

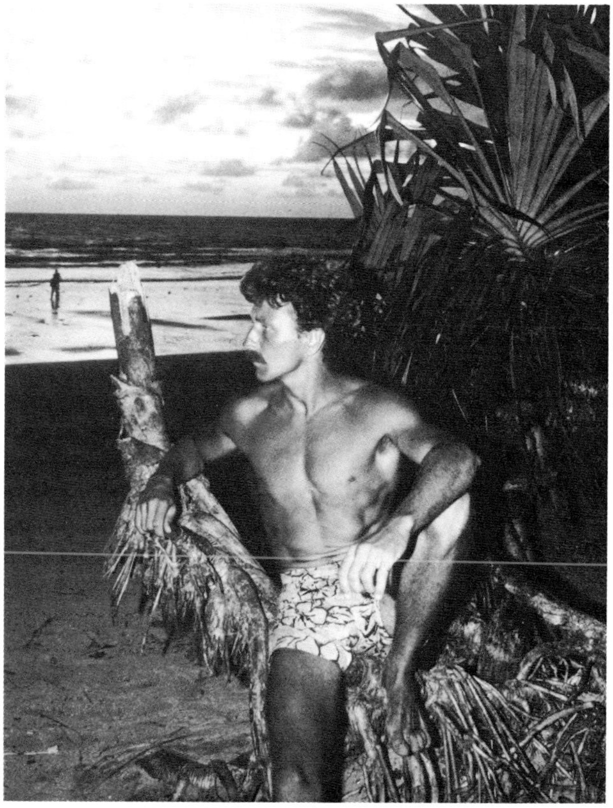

Use flash to light your model as the sun goes down, balancing exposures so that your lens will also record detail in the sky behind.

USING THE LANDSCAPE

The countryside offers the easiest and most accessible location for male photography, and if fairly anonymous backgrounds are required – such as with a portrait – then almost anywhere will do. However, an interesting landscape can also be used in a much more dominant way, offering considerable potential for strong and interesting compositions.

One way in which this can be achieved is to allow the model to become part of the overall composition rather than simply as subject and background. This usually involves accepting a smaller and less tightly-framed image of your model, but with careful composition, he can still be made the main focus of attention, and the approach can make it easier to create moody and atmospheric images. When working this way, look initially at the scene purely in terms of the landscape, making an allowance mentally for the addition of your model, rather like looking for a picture with a hole in it. It is important to ensure that the image is well-balanced and the model placed in the most effective position so that the landscape does not compete for attention or become a distraction. The choice of viewpoint and the way you frame the picture are the most effective means of achieving this.

The lighting is a vital element in this type of picture, since you not only have to consider it in terms of how it affects your model, but also its effect on the landscape itself. The distribution of highlights and shadows will be a dominant element of the composition. The sky too can be an important aspect of the landscape, and it can often be effective to emphasize the sky by the use of filters to make it more dramatic or a richer color. Polarizing or graduated filters are invaluable for this purpose when shooting in color, white contrast filters such as a red or orange can make a blue sky a much more dramatic tone when shooting in black and white.

Don't only consider the landscape in terms of a wide, sweeping view however, since quite close-up details like trees, rocks and other natural formations can also be used as elements of a composition, introducing visual qualities like texture and pattern into the image.

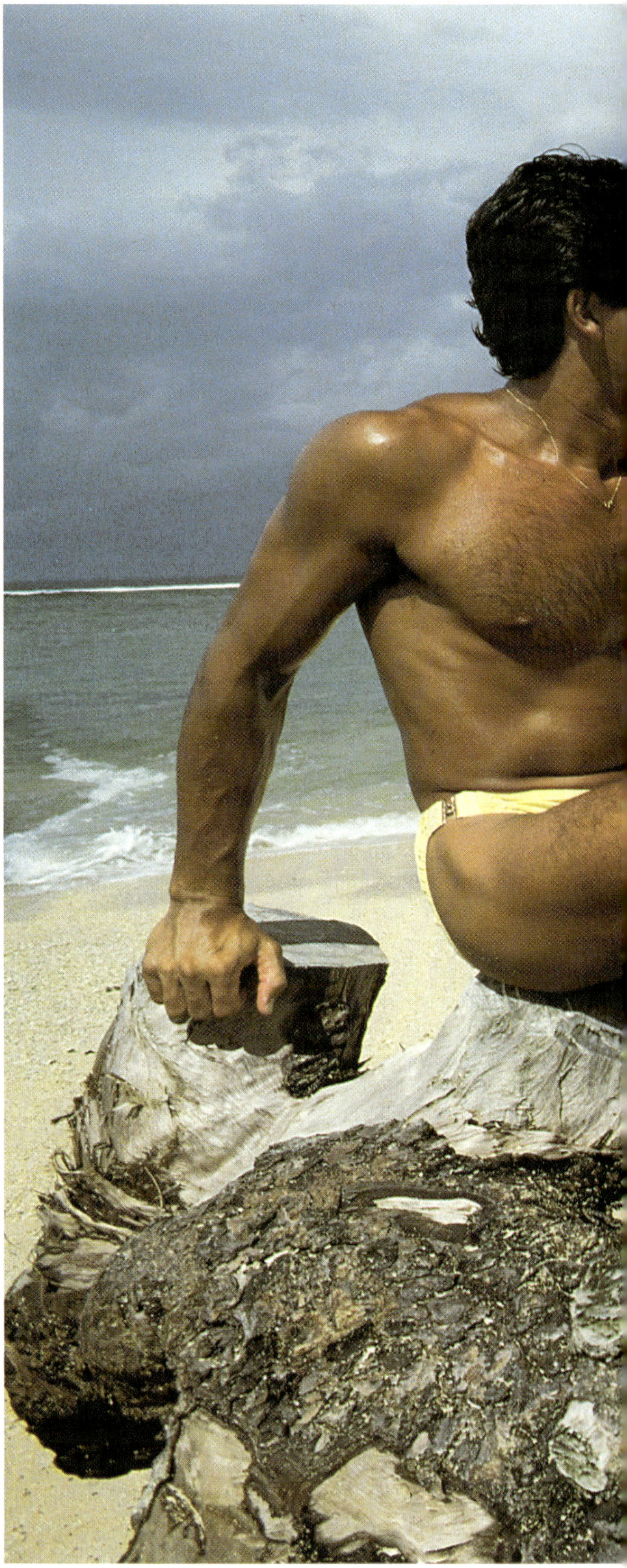

Your model doesn't have to be the key point of the whole picture. Sometimes he might be used as just one, much smaller element in what is essentially a landscape study.

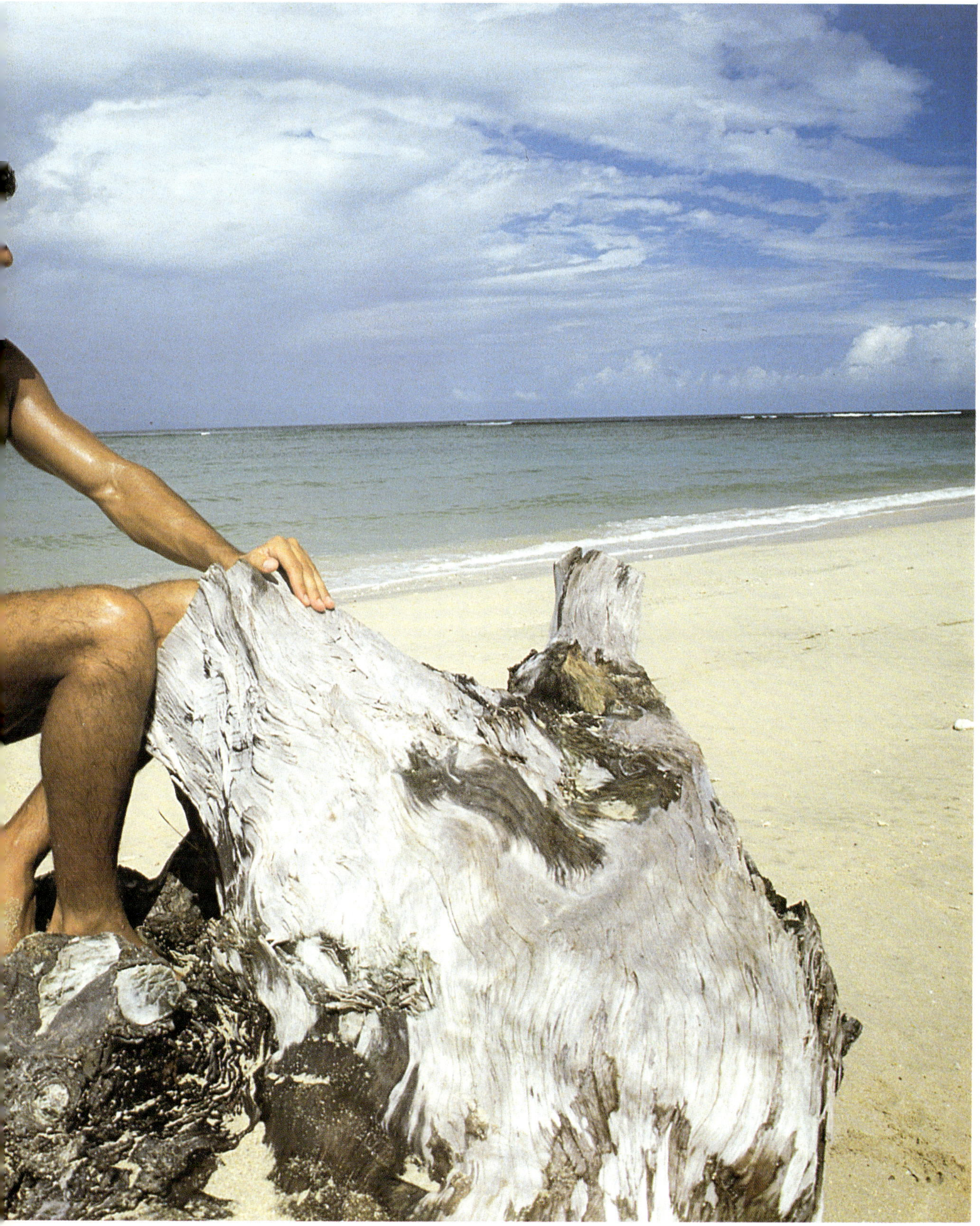

THE URBAN SETTING

The urban environment offers many location possibilities; the straight lines and angular shapes of buildings can offer an interesting variation of mood and composition to pictures taken in a landscape or beach setting. Fashion photographers make frequent use of architectural settings for their pictures since this type of background provides an effective contrast in terms of shapes, colors and textures to the model and the clothes, as well as making an appropriate setting.

Pictures of this type offer considerable scope for making use of the effects of perspective; using a wide-angle lens will allow you to create strong lines within the image. When photographing a model, for example, with the view down a street or with the facade of a building in the background, a wide-angle lens will enable you to take a quite close-up viewpoint of the model, while including a large area of background, creating bold lines which converge dramatically into the distance. This technique will increase the impression of depth and distance in the image. A long-focus lens, on the other hand, will appear to compress perspective, making a distant background appear much larger and closer to the model. This will, in turn, diminish the impression of depth and distance.

Even with closer, more tightly-framed pictures, streets and buildings can make effective locations. Quite simple things like doorways, steps, railings and windows can be useful and provide interesting elements of composition with their bold shapes and textures, creating an uncluttered, contrasting background. An effective way of using such features is to create a frame around the image of the model. This can help to focus the attention on him and make a stronger composition.

Lighting can be an important factor with pictures of this type, since dense shadows and extremes of contrast can be created, particularly on a sunny day and in narrow streets. As a general rule, it is best to avoid including both extremes within the image. Either choose viewpoints and position your model in such a way that the shadows are very small, or shoot so that the picture area is entirely in shadow and calculate the exposure accordingly. This aspect of urban photography makes it a good choice of location on a cloudy or overcast day.

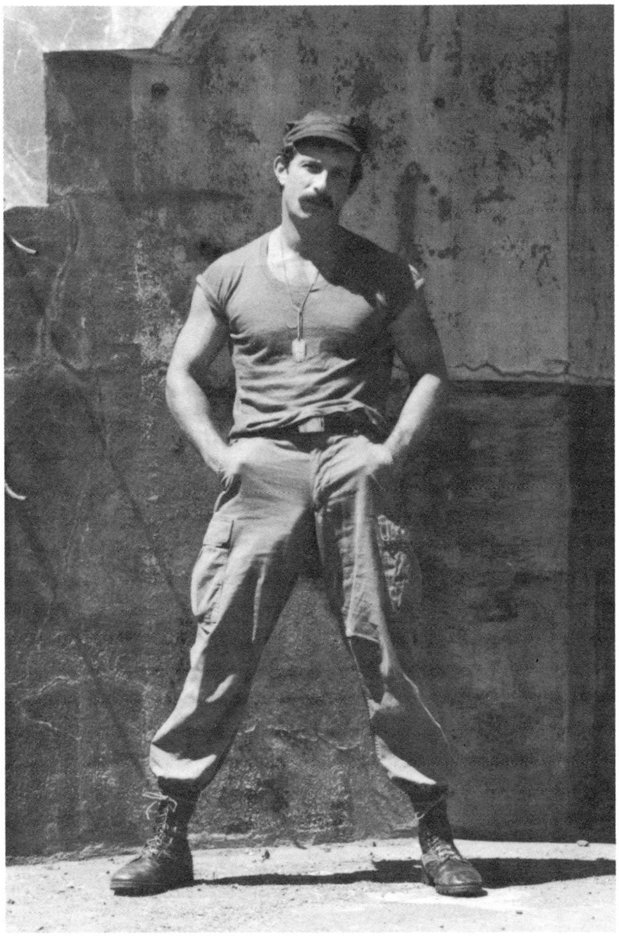

Decaying city walls provide a background that does not intrude, yet has enough texture and pattern to be interesting.

Look for patterns among the buildings and other structures that make up the urban environment **(opposite top left and right)**. *They can be used to give your pictures a structure and geometry that is lacking in images made in rural locations. Rooftops* **(opposite)** *offer seclusion and privacy, and have one other big advantage: the sky as a backdrop.*

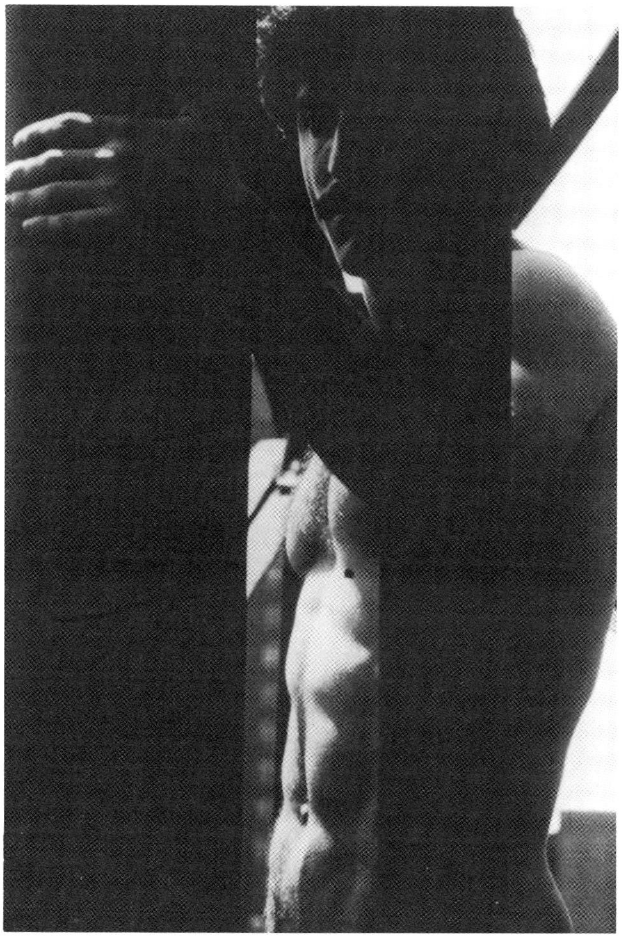

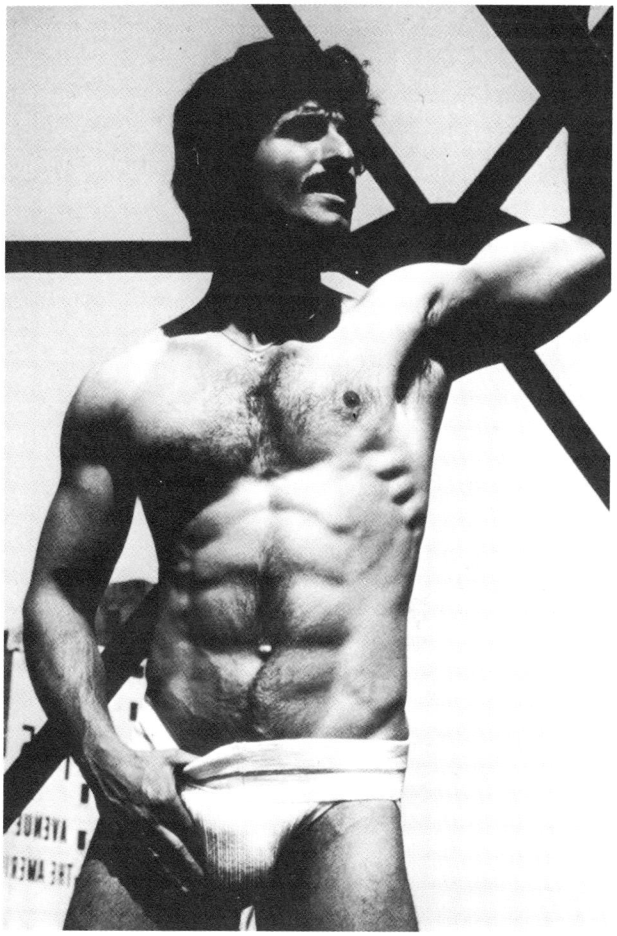
AVENUE

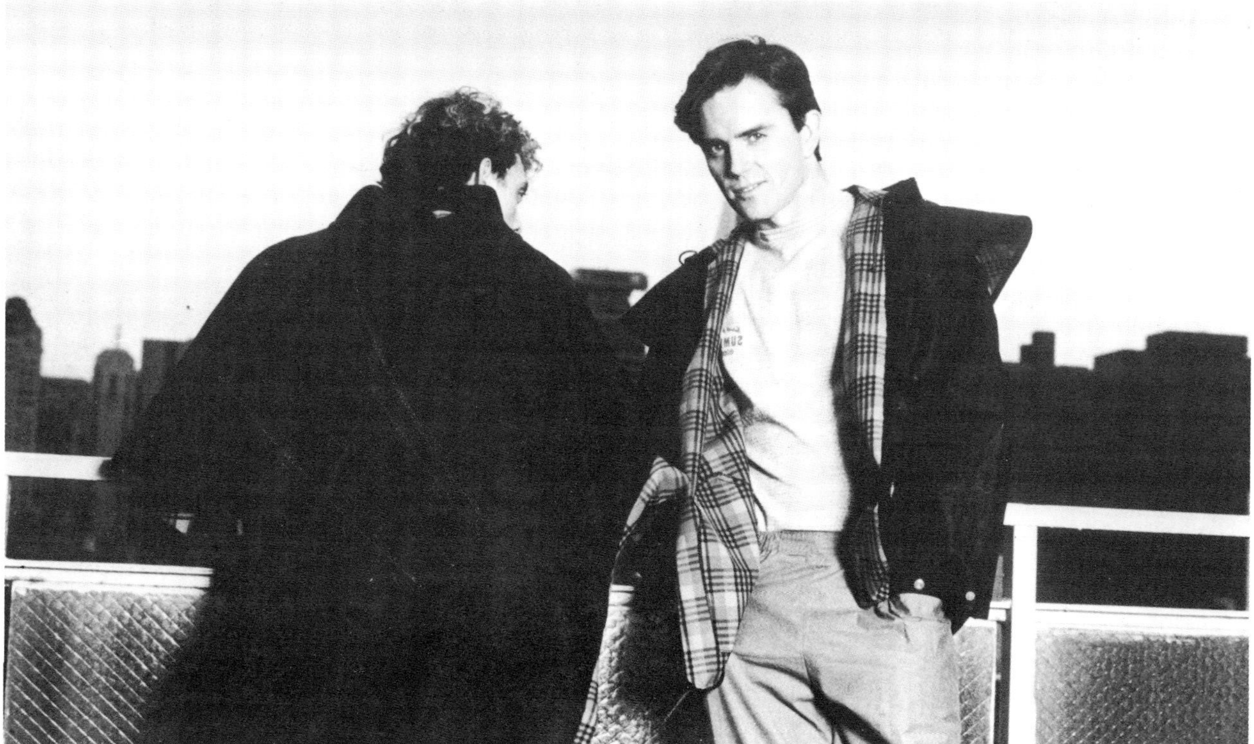

SHOOTING IN SUNLIGHT

When shooting out of doors, most people prefer the idea of a sunny day and indeed there are many situations, such as on the beach, in which sunshine can be an essential element of the photograph. However, bright unobscured sunlight can present technical problems and some care is needed to produce the best results.

Photographic film can successfully record only a limited brightness range and in sunlight this limit can quite easily be exceeded. When this occurs, the result will be to lose detail in either, or both, the highlight and shadow areas of the image and unless you can learn to anticipate and control the problem, harshly lit, poor quality pictures will result. Unfortunately, it can be misleading to judge this visually since our eyes are very much more accommodating to extremes of brightness than the film we use, and what appears quite satisfactory visually often results in a disappointing photograph. Experience is the best tutor, but it will help you judge the way the image will record by viewing the subject through half-closed eyes.

One of the best ways to control the contrast or brightness range created by sunlight is in the choice of viewpoint and the way the model is positioned. Since it will not be possible to record detail in both the lightest and darkest areas of a sunlit subject, it is best to ensure that you angle both the camera and the model in such a way that he is either predominantly in shadow and expose accordingly, allowing the small areas of highlight to be overexposed, or to choose a viewpoint which ensures that the shadows are small and unobtrusive and then to calculate the exposure for the lighter tones.

Another means of control is in the choice of surroundings. If these are essentially dark in tone, then there will be a little reflected light, but when your model is placed in a light-toned setting, on a beach for example or near a whitewashed wall, then a considerable amount of the sunlight will be reflected back into the shadow areas, reducing the contrast and creating detail in the darker tones. Using direct sunlight has a number of positive advantages. It can be used to emphasize skin texture and to create bold relief within the subject and of course it will enhance the effect of suntanned and wet or oiled skin. But there are situations where it will not be an advantage, and on a sunny day it can sometimes be preferable to position your model in an area of open shade – under a tree, for instance, or beside a wall. This will often give a more satisfactory and flattering light, with a close-up portrait, for instance, where the presence of dense, and sharply-defined, shadows would be too intrusive and the emphasis of skin texture unattractive. It is also important to appreciate when shooting in color that open shade can create a blue cast, since much of the light you are using will be reflected from the blue sky. It is therefore necessary to use a warm color-balancing filter such as a Wratten 81A or 81B to offset this.

Another method of finding a softer and less directional light on a bright, sunny day is to shoot into the sun by placing your model with his back to it and aiming the camera towards it. In this way, the model is virtually in his own shadow. An added advantage is that the backlighting created by this technique can create a pleasing and sometimes dramatic rim of light around his outline. This can be an effective way of creating a good separation between your subject and the background, but you must be careful when assessing exposure, as a reading taken in the normal way will indicate less exposure than you actually need. The best method is to take a close-up reading from the subject, ensuring that the meter is not influenced by the strong highlights created by the backlighting. The same warm filters will also be needed to avoid the blue cast since you are still, in effect, shooting in open shade.

It is also possible to control the brightness range when shooting in direct sunlight by artificial means. A large white reflector, made of cardboard, polystyrene or fabric stretched over a frame, can be placed close to your model on the shadow side and angled so that the light from the sun is directed into the unlit areas. This can considerably reduce the contrast and add detail to the darker tones of the subject.

It is also possible to use a small flashgun for a similar purpose. The method is to take an exposure reading for the subject in the normal way, making no allowance for the dark shadows created by the sunlight. Let's assume that this gives you an exposure of 1/125 second at f/8. It is necessary to calculate the exposure for the flashgun according to its distance from the subject, say this requires an aperture of f/5.6 for the correct exposure. If you were to give the correct flash exposure, however, this would eliminate the shadows completely and create a flat and artificial effect, so it is best to underexpose the flash by about two stops. Therefore your should set the aperture to f/11 and reset the shutter speed to 1/60 second to compensate for the smaller aperture.

Direct, bright sunlight can create harsh contrasts. One way round the problem is to photograph your model in open shade, lit by reflected sunlight.

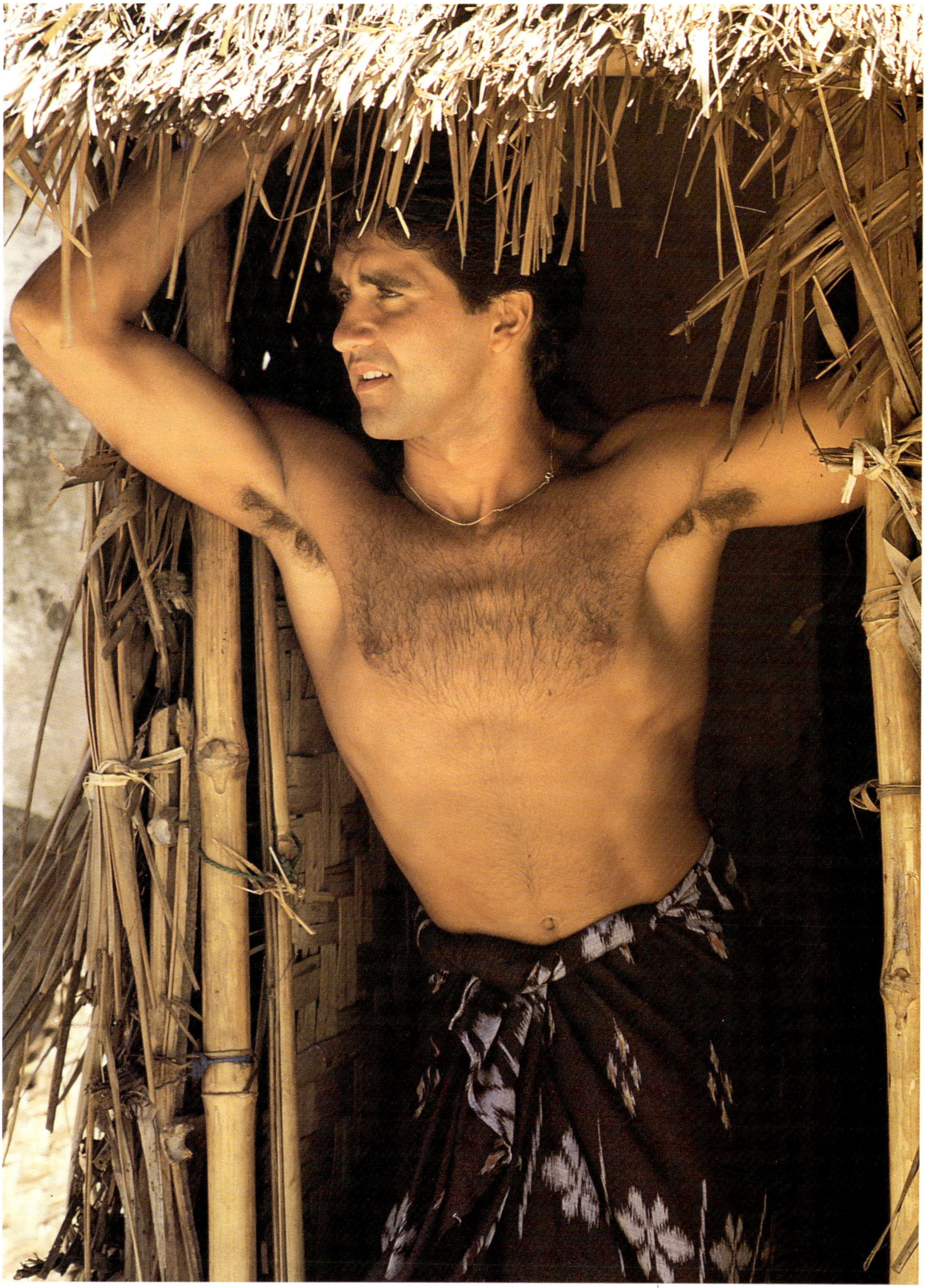

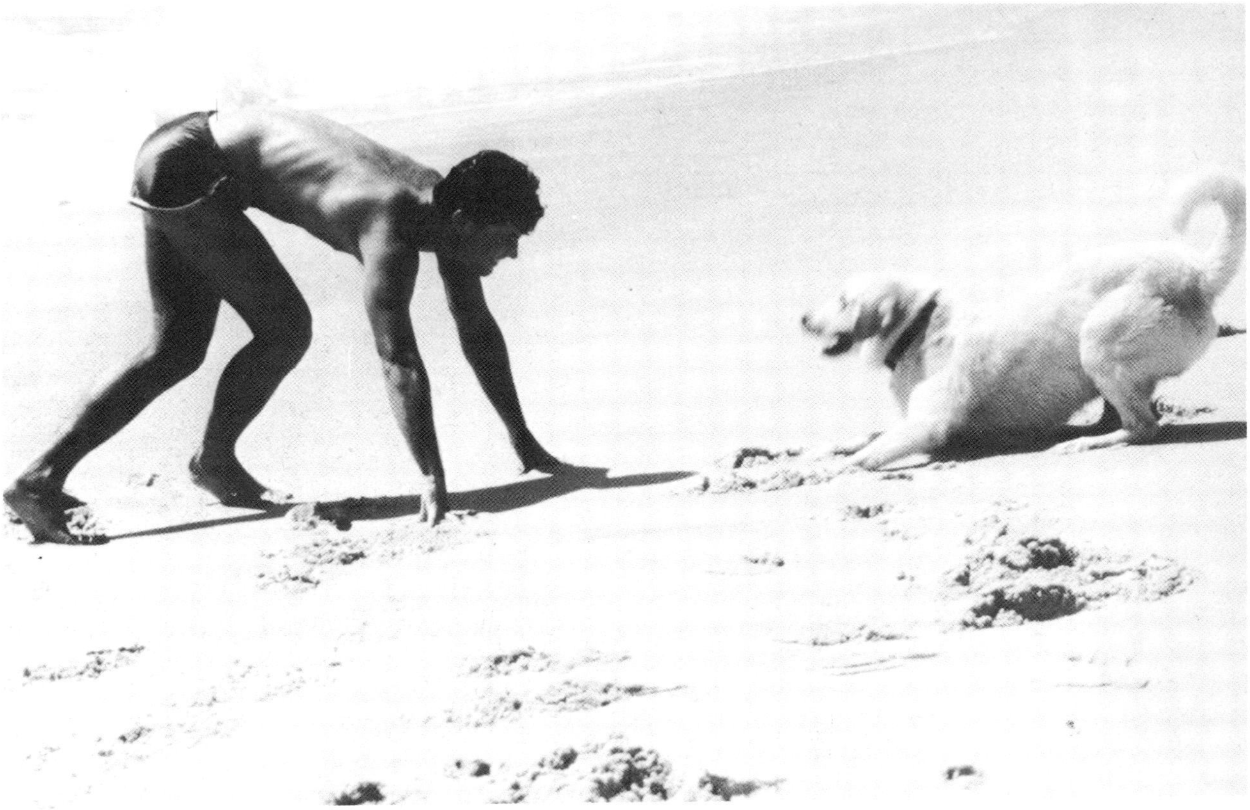

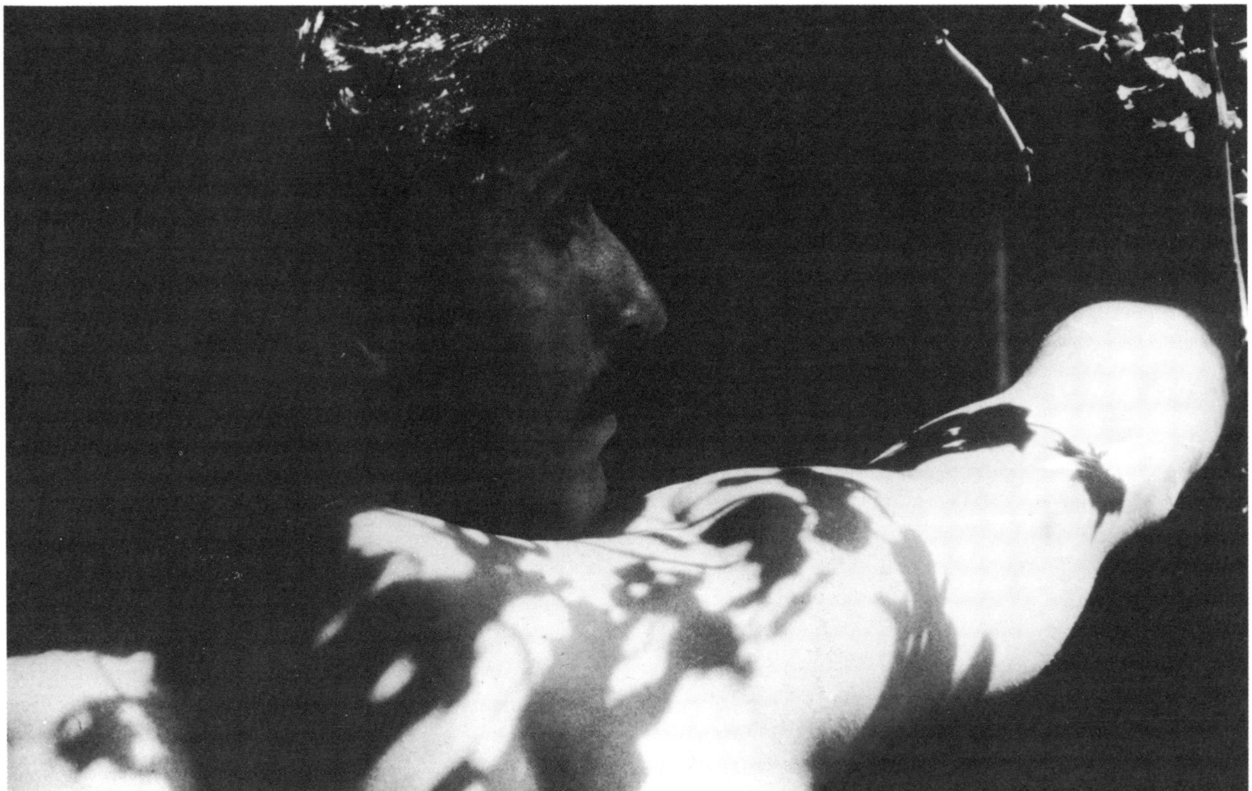

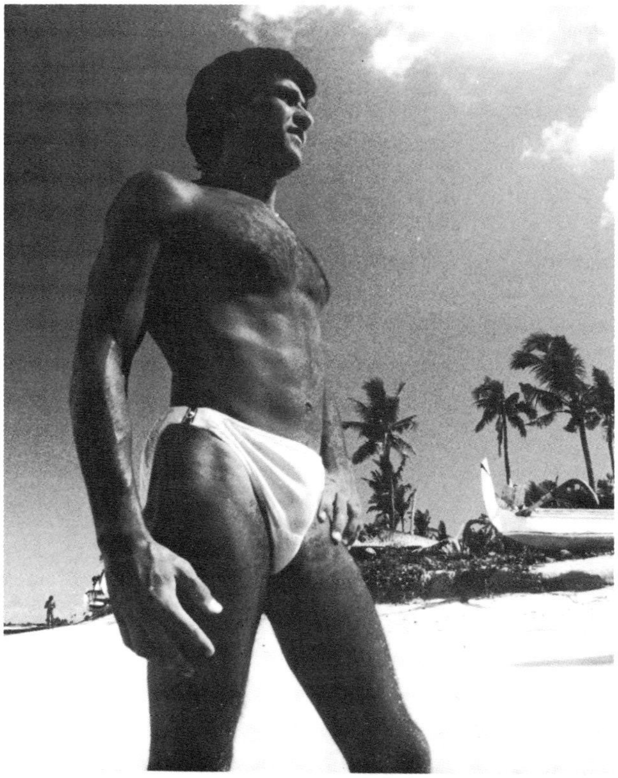

Skies can often record too light in bright, sunlit pictures. The use of a polarizing filter will help to darken them without affecting the skin tones of your model.

Your film can't cope with too wide a range of light levels **(opposite, top)**. *Here, the exposure has been calculated for the model's skin tones and the sand has consequently recorded lighter than normal.*

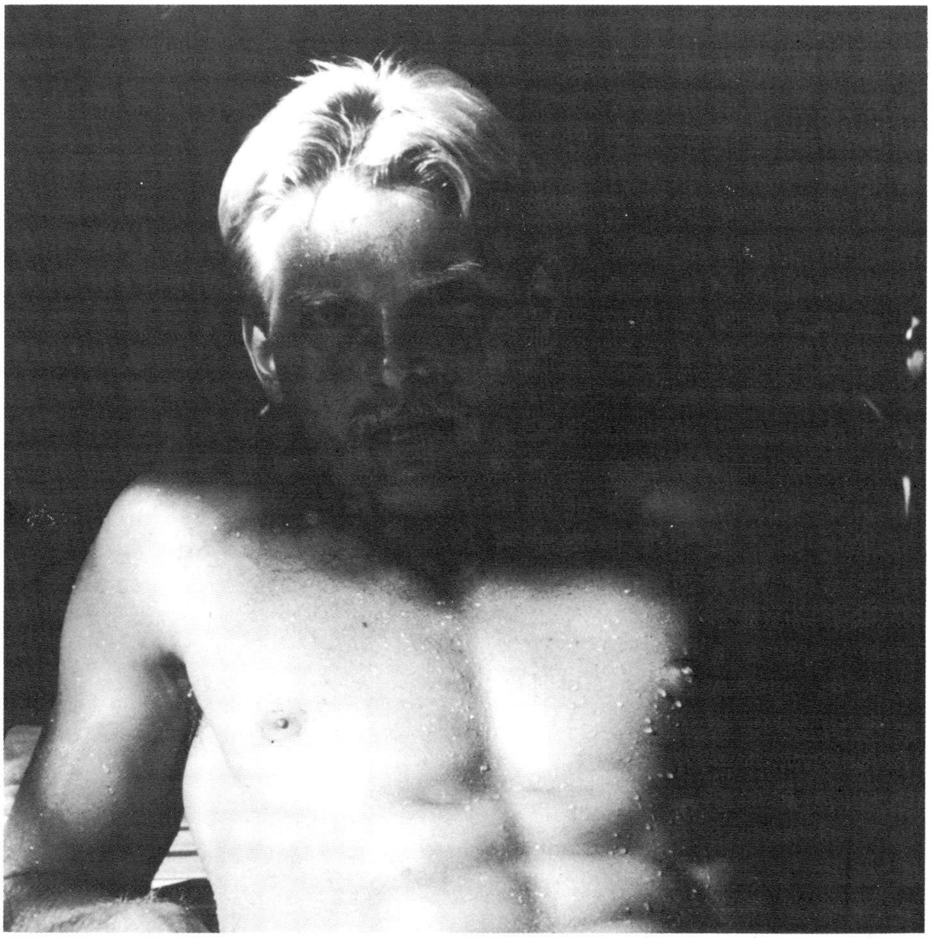

The difference in light levels between highlights and shadows can also be used on the model himself. Here an abstract effect has been created by exposing for the body, the model's face falling into shadow **(right)**. *The shadows of leaves in the picture opposite have been used to dapple the model's body with an interesting pattern of light and shade.*

SHOOTING ON DULL DAYS

In some respects a cloudy or overcast day can be preferable to bright sunshine. There are no problems with dense shadows and you can shoot from a variety of angles without any drastic effect on the nature and direction of the lighting. In addition, it is easier for the model to move around more freely since the softer, and less directional, light of a cloudy day will be less likely to create unattractive effects. Remember, however, that some subjects and locations, such as the sea or beach, for instance, simply cry out for a sunny day as much for the atmosphere as for the quality of the light.

There are two main difficulties associated with a dull day. One is that the image contrast can be *too* low and the other is that the light can excessively create what is known as a 'top' effect. With a portrait, for example, it can easily produce rather unpleasant shadows under the eyes. In such situations, it is possible to avoid this by placing your model so that the directly overhead light is shaded from him, under a tree perhaps or in a doorway. If this is not possible, then you can also avoid the effect by ensuring that your model angles his head slightly so the shadows are not created.

Insufficient contrast can also be overcome by selecting the elements of your picture to deliberately increase the brightness range of the subject. You might find a very light or dark tone or detail in the setting to act as a background, like a white wall or a deeply shaded doorway. Your choice of clothes and props for the model can also be used in this way. A white shirt will make a considerable difference to a picture with mainly middle and dark tones, and in the same way, a dark jacket or black accessory or prop would increase the tonal range of the image in the other direction.

When shooting in color, the same effect can be achieved by introducing bright, bold tones into the image. In fact, considerable impact can be obtained by having just one area of strong, saturated color in a picture which is otherwise quite dull and grey. It is vital, however, that this is within the main centre of interest of the image, something your model wears, for instance, as it could simply be distracting.

It is important to understand that Ultra Violet light can also have a strong presence on an overcast day, and the use of a warm-tinted filter such as a Wratten 81A will be needed to prevent a blue cast when shooting in color and to improve the quality of skin tones.

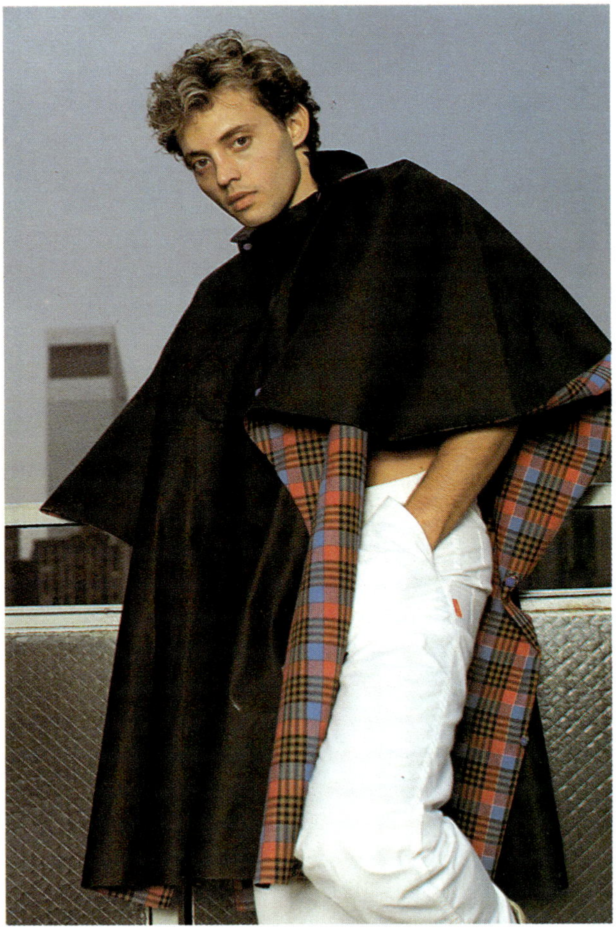

Dull lighting can sometimes lead to extra-low contrast **(above)**. *Such conditions can lend a mood of their own to the picture, but the addition of one white area – in this case, the models trousers – can help to lift the picture into something a little more special.*

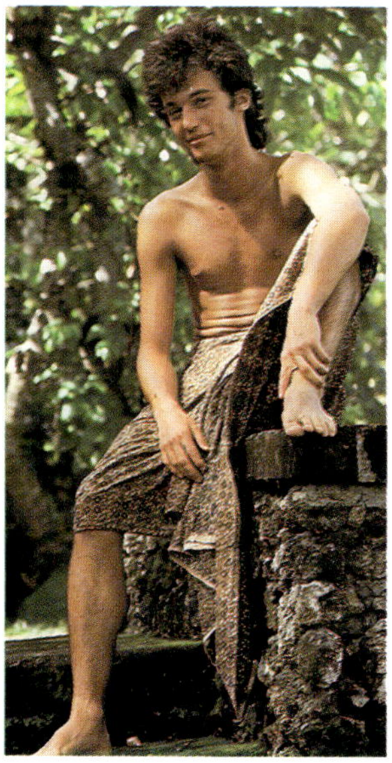

The combination of a sky that is lightly overcast and a model positioned in the shade of, say, a few trees, leads to pleasant lighting with a range of tones modern film emulsions handle to perfection.

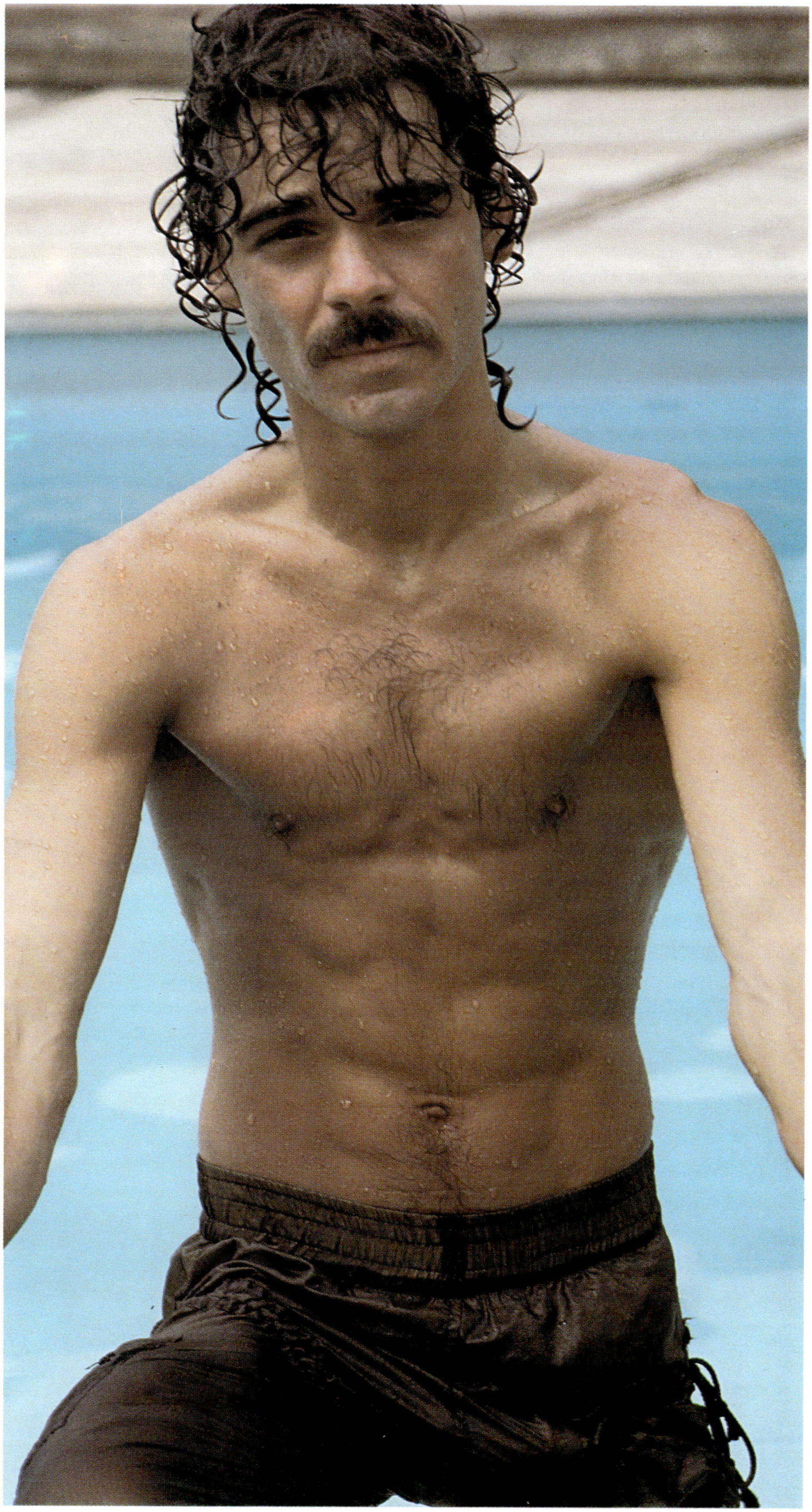

A subject like this could not easily be photographed in bright sunlight because the film could not cope with both the skin tones and the texture of the water. The lower contrast of a slightly duller day, however, solves the problem.

CONTROLLING THE BACKGROUND

The term background rather implies something less important than the subject. This is not the case with photography, as every element of a picture should be considered and selected carefully. The background can have a positive effect on the nature and quality of a photograph. In many cases ill-considered or distracting backgrounds are the cause of disappointing pictures.

In its most basic role, the background provides a contrasting tone or detail to the main point of interest, the model. In this type of photography, it is vital that the model is clearly defined and well separated from the background, and there are a variety of ways in which this can be done. The most straightforward way of achieving your aim is to ensure that the background provides either a tonal or color contrast to the model or the clothes he is wearing. If he is wearing a light-toned suit, for instance, he could be positioned in front of a dark wall, while a model with a rich, brown tan could be photographed against a blue sea when shooting in color.

Lighting can also be used to create contrast. A brightly-lit area of a scene could be used as the background to a dark-toned subject and a model wearing, say, a white T-shirt could be positioned against an area of deep shadow. Back lighting, when shooting into the sun, can also be used effectively for this purpose since it can create a rim of light around the model's face or body, lifting him out of the background.

Sometimes it is not possible to avoid a fussy and distracting background no matter where you position your model of camera. In that instance, it might be possible to control matters by means of focus. The range of sharp focus in front of and beyond the subject varies according to the aperture you select. This zone is known as depth of field and it increases as the aperture is made smaller. Consequently, if you ensure that there is as much distance as possible between your model and the background and select a wide aperture, the model will appear in sharp focus but the background details will record as an out-of-focus blur, subduing details and creating a smooth tone. This effect can be greatly increased by using a telephoto lens as it has an effectively narrower depth of field.

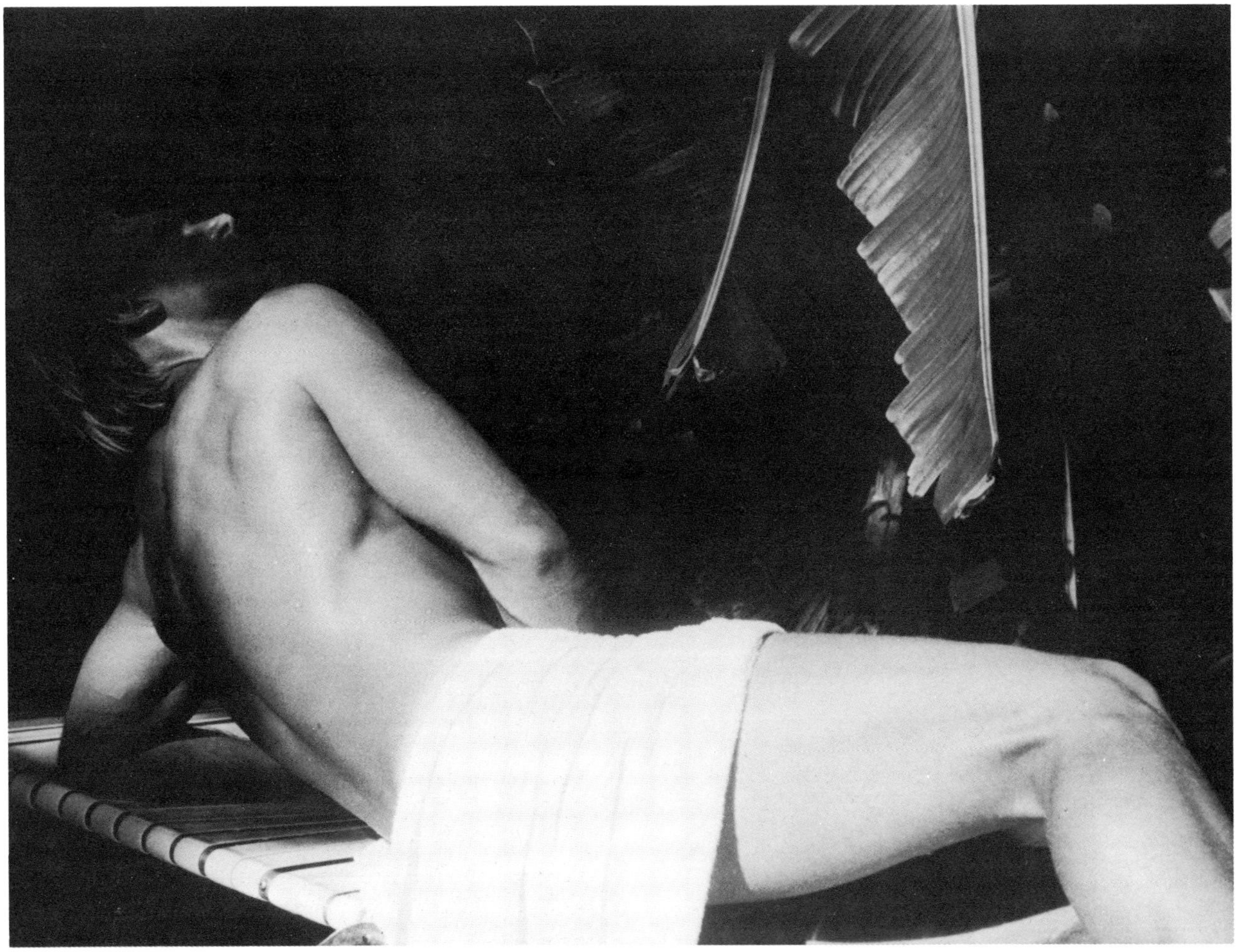

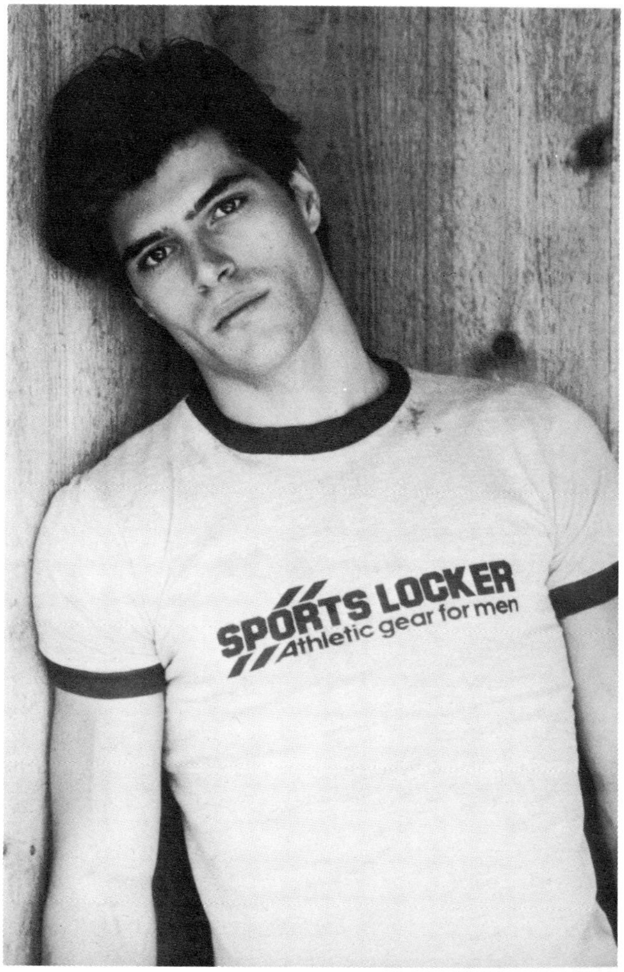

Tones and colors help to separate your model from his background, so make sure he wears clothing that either contrasts with or complements, the background, depending on the final effect at which you are aiming.

Different methods can be used to separate your model from the background or integrate him with it. Here, lighting has been used to highlight the model, keeping the background in a more subdued shadow.

If the far background of this picture had been sharp, it would have been too dominant in the composition. Using a wide aperture for a shallow depth of field, thus rendering the distant details slightly out of focus, keeps the background in its place.

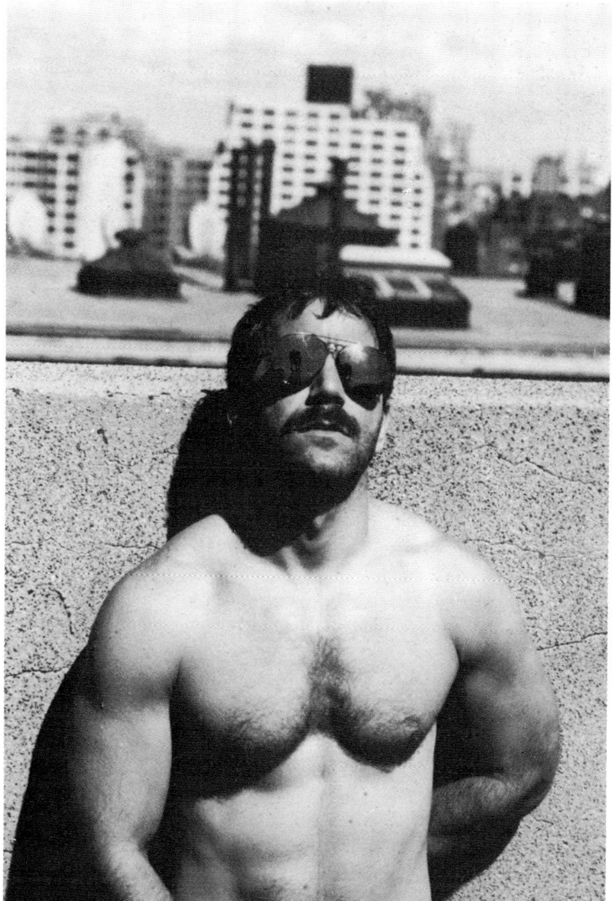

USING THE FOREGROUND

When photographing a model, the subject is essentially on two planes only: those of the subject and the background, with nothing between the camera and the model. However, the inclusion of foreground interest can add considerably to the effect of a picture and when choosing a viewpoint and positioning your model, you should also consider this possibility.

One advantage is that foreground interest can increase the impression of depth in a picture because it emphasizes the effect of perspective. The closer an object is to the camera, the larger it appears to be in relation to more distant details. It is this quality which is mainly responsible for creating the illusion of three dimensions in a two-dimensional image. This effect will be considerably enhanced by using a wide-angle lens, because it allows both close and distant objects to be included within the camera's field of view. A very wide-angle lens such as a 20mm with a 35mm camera can be used to distort dramatically the effect of perspective and to create bold and unusual effects.

The inclusion of foreground details can also add considerably to both the interest of the picture and to the composition. In some circumstances, the perspective effect created by the foreground can be used to lead the viewer's eye into the picture, adding impact to the image, while in other situations, foreground details can be used as a frame around the image helping to contain and concentrate the attention. A good example of this is when shooting through a doorway or with the overhanging branch of a tree between the camera and the model.

Depth of field can be an important factor with shots of this type. If you want both the model and the foreground to be sharp, then it will be necessary to use a very small aperture. The use of a wide-angle lens will make this easier as it has an effectively greater depth of field. It is by no means always necessary to have the foreground interest sharp, however, and it can be effective in some circumstances to choose a viewpoint and select an aperture so that the foreground details are deliberately blurred. This can be particularly striking when shooting in color, as a colorful foreground – flowers for instance – can create a soft blend of hues when thrown well out of focus. You can achieve that by ensuring that there is some distance between the model and the foreground, focusing on the model and using a wide aperture. The effect will be further enhanced by use of a telephoto lens.

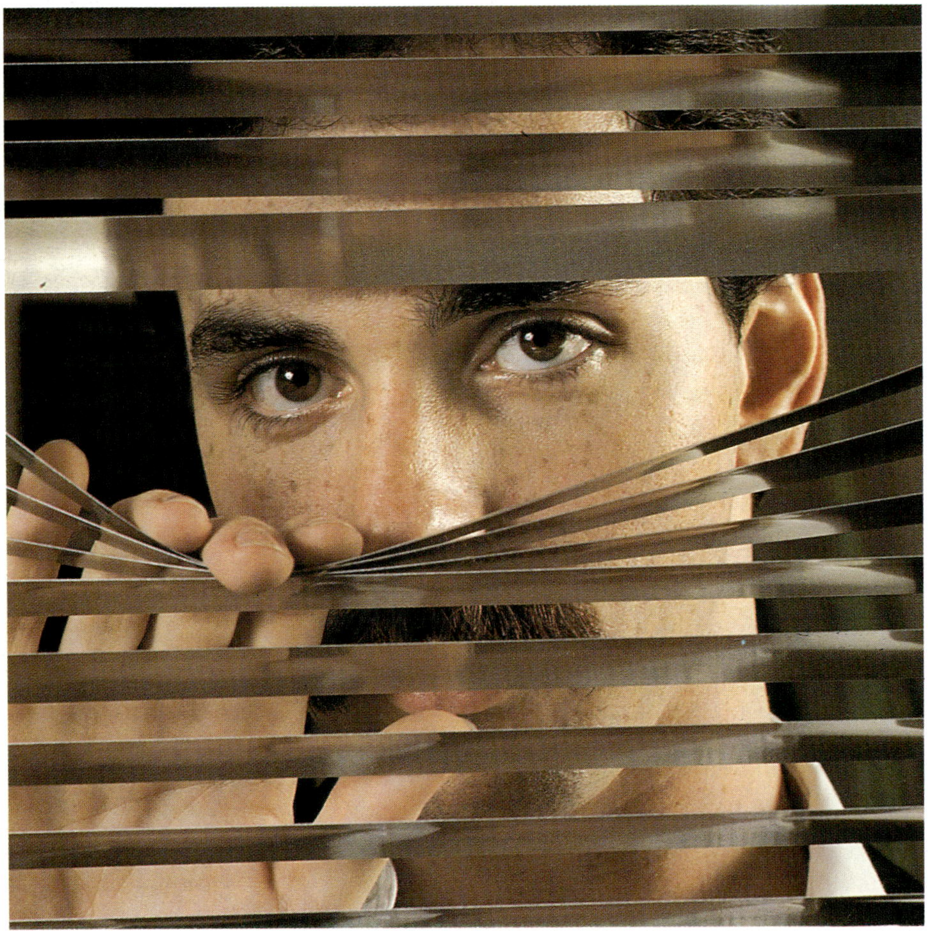

Sometimes the foreground can be used as part of the picture itself – a raison d'être *without which the shot* **(left)** *would have little point. In a picture such as this one, small apertures to keep foreground and model equally sharp are an important consideration.*

Using a larger aperture on the camera lens reduces depth of field, in this case throwing the foreground out of focus **(right)**. *In pictures like this, always focus on the model, rather than on objects between him and the camera.*

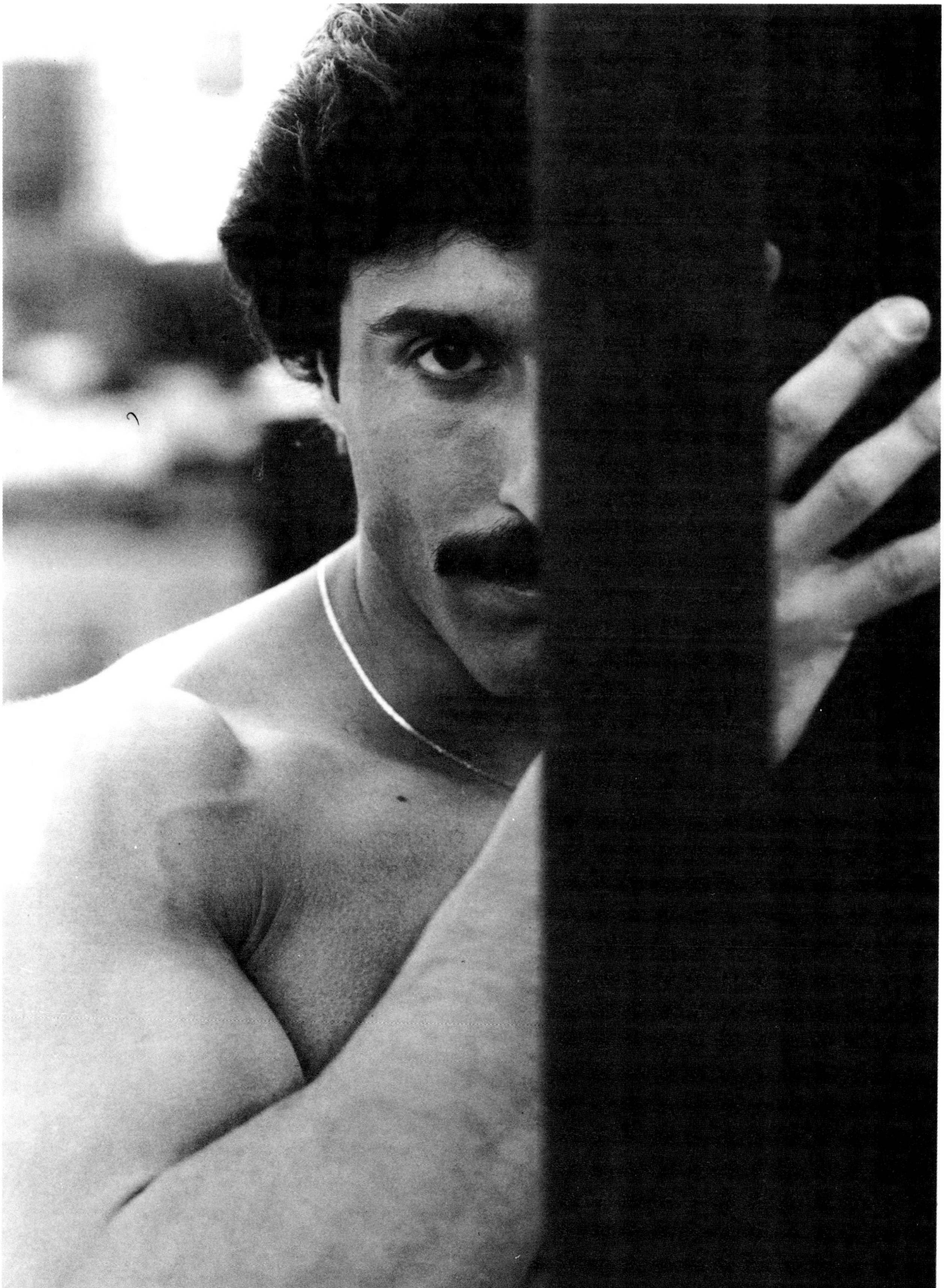

USING DAYLIGHT INDOORS

Daylight need not only be considered in terms of outdoor photography. It is equally ideal for indoor pictures, providing there is a good window or skylight. Indeed, some portrait and fashion photographers have designed their studios to enable them to use daylight for a large proportion of their work. The main drawbacks are that it is of course less easy to control than artificial light and not as bright as it is when shooting outdoors. On the other hand, it can be used to create soft and natural effects and is particularly suitable for portrait and nude work.

Because the light source itself, the window, is in a fixed position, it is necessary to control the angle and direction of the lighting by altering the position of the model and the camera relative to it. If the window is parallel to a line drawn between the camera and the model, it will create strong side-lighting with one side of the model brightly lit and the opposite side in shadow, producing pronounced modelling in the model's face or body. However, as the model is turned to face the window and the camera position moved in line with him, the lighting will become more frontal, creating smaller shadows and less modelling.

The quality of the light will depend on both the weather and the location of the window. Traditionally artists prefer a north-facing window because it offers a more constant light quality and (in the northern hemisphere) will not be exposed to direct sunlight. It is relatively simple to control the light quality by draping a diffusing medium, such as white translucent nylon or even tracing paper over the window. Because window light is mainly reflected from the sky, it usually has a higher color temperature than that for which the film is balanced and will tend to create a blue cast. For this reason, it is usually necessary to use a color correction filter such as a Wratten 81A to offset the effect.

Because window light creates a relatively small source compared to shooting outdoors, it tends to produce a greater brightness range and a more contrasty image, making shadows appear more dense. For this reason, it will often be necessary to use a reflector to reduce the brightness range and to add detail to the shadow areas. A large sheet of white-painted hardboard, cardboard or polystyrene is ideal and can be positioned by propping against a chair, close to the model on the shadow side to reflect some light back into these areas. A tripod is another very useful accessory for daylight indoor photography, as you will need to use longer exposures than when shooting outdoors. A tripod will also reduce the risk of camera shake, as well as making it easier to frame and focus the camera precisely.

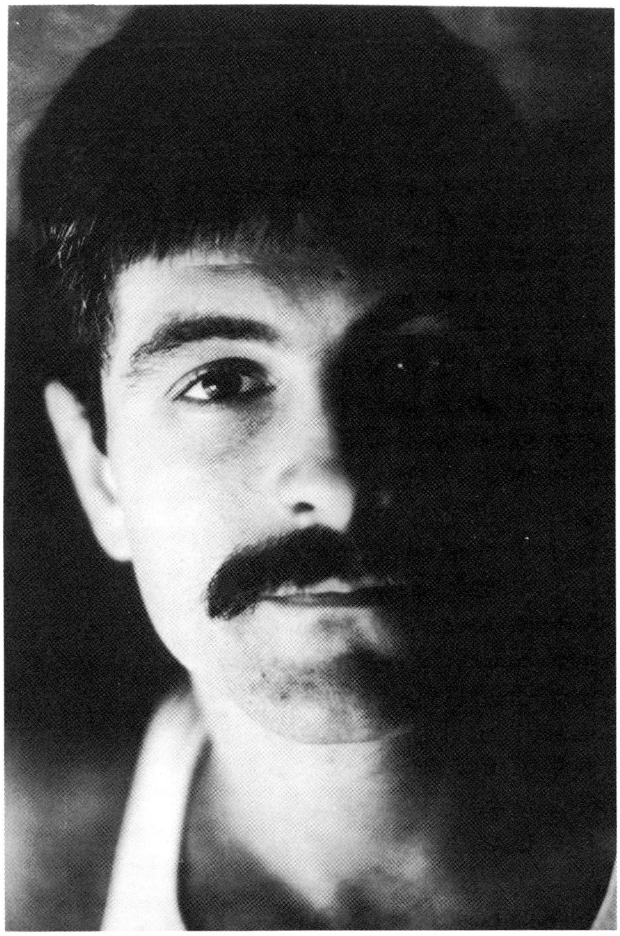

Direct light, preferably from a north-facing window, will throw soft, natural illumination onto your subject. Positioning him to the side of the window lights one part of the face allowing the other to fall into shadow.

Position your model in the right way and direct light from a window can also be used to add highlights to hair and body. A reflector helps to fill in the shadow areas and so gives a better balance to the lighting.

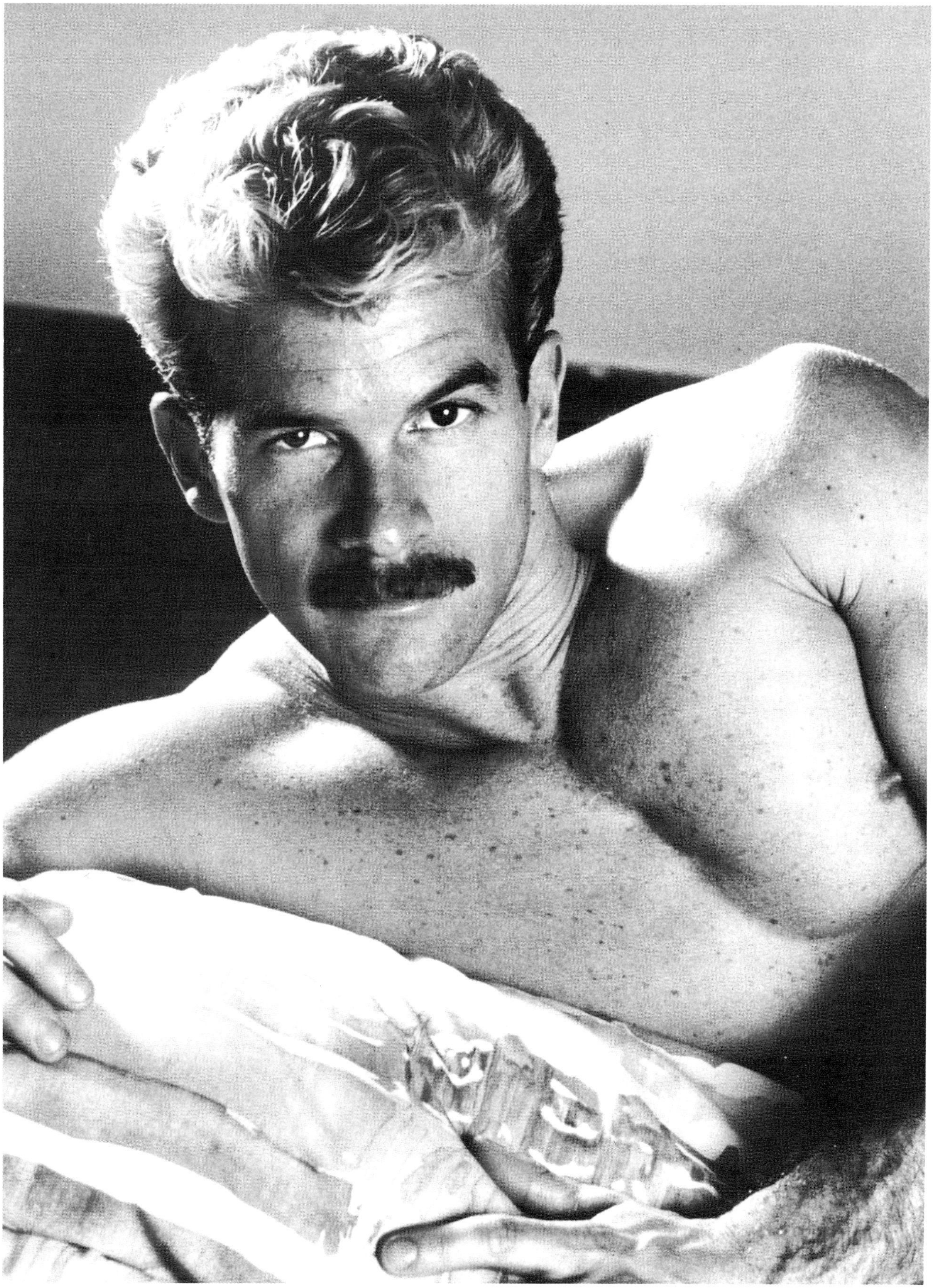

USING ROOM SETTINGS

With many indoor pictures, just a simple or plain background is all that is needed. However, a good location can also be used to create more interesting and elaborate pictures. The interior of a room can often be used most effectively as a part of the composition. Grand or interesting interiors are often used by fashion photographers to create more moody and evocative images. In addition, just a small corner or a piece of furniture in a room can often add to the effect of a picture either as a more interesting background, as a prop, or as an aid to posing.

The main difficulty with this type of picture is the risk of the picture becoming too cluttered or distracting and care in choice of viewpoint, the framing and composition of the image is needed to avoid this. As a general rule, the less you put into a picture, the more effective it is likely to be, and you must be discriminating. Study the image through the viewfinder carefully and become aware of any objects which do not contribute to its effect. The use of a tripod will help you to concentrate more on the content of your picture as well as allowing you to leave your camera set up, framed and focused whilst you make adjustments to the background or lighting.

In many cases, you will simply be able to remove an offending item such as a picture on the wall or an ornament; in other instances, you may have to change the position of the camera or the model. It is not only physical objects you need to be aware of, though. Bright highlights on furniture or ornaments can also be very distracting, and if you are using a multiple lighting set-up, these must be watched carefully.

It is also important that the model is separated from the background quite clearly, since it is easy for him to be overwhelmed, particularly in an ornately-decorated room. You should position him and/or choose a viewpoint which enables him to be juxtaposed against a plain or contrasting tone within the scene; in front of some plain drapes, for instance, or an area of shadow. If you are using artificial lighting, you can also arrange this to obtain good separation between subject and background, by using backlighting or rim-lighting, for instance. Focusing too can be used to subdue an obtrusive background. It is by no means always necessary to have the setting in sharp focus, and by using a wide aperture you can keep it slightly soft, which will help to emphasize the sharply-focused model.

The less you put into a picture, the more effective it often is. This is especially true of room settings, where so many domestic elements can prove a distraction, rather than an advantage. Study the image through the viewfinder carefully before you shoot and remove anything which does not contribute directly to the picture's purpose.

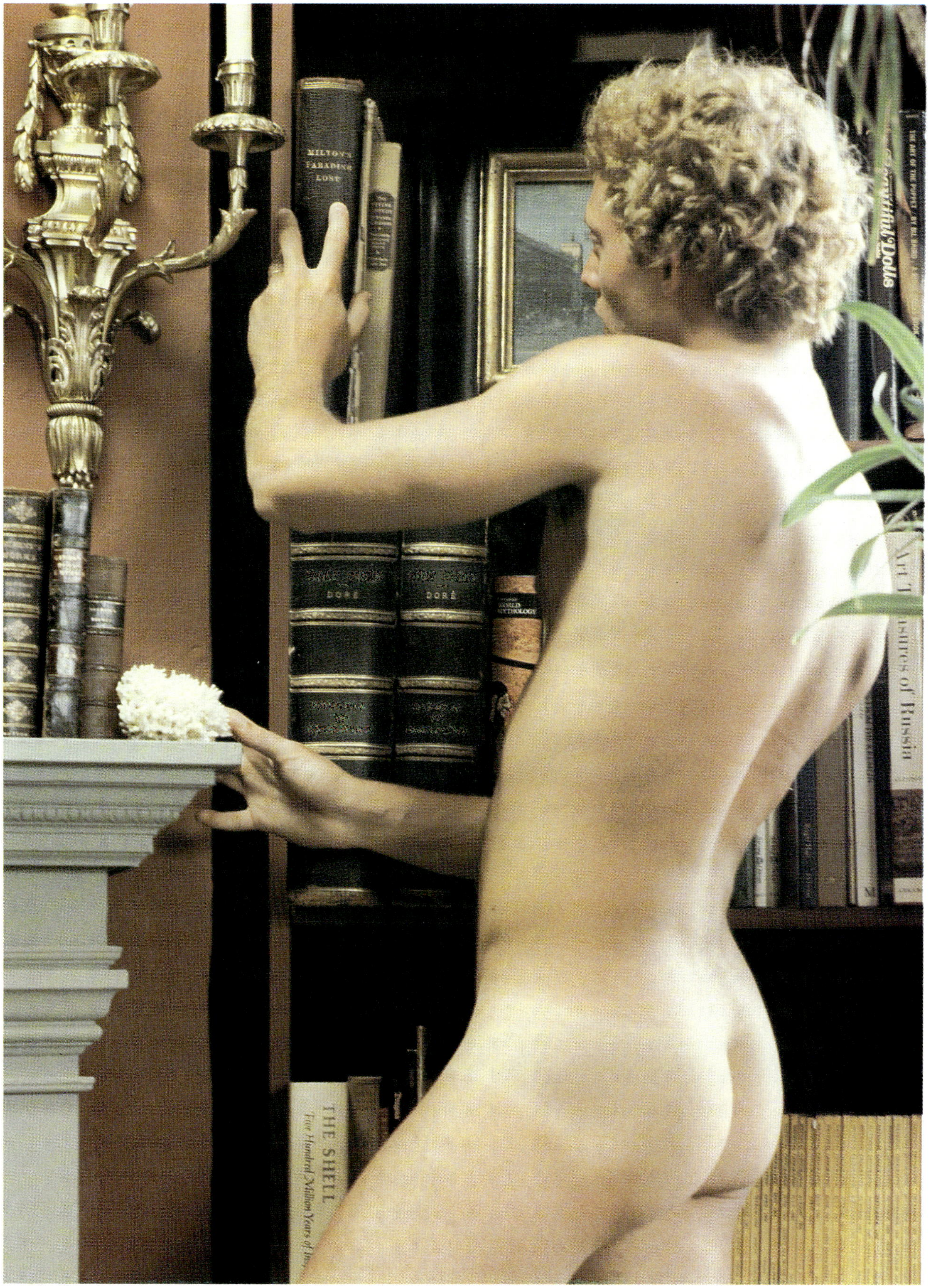
MILTON'S PARADISE LOST
DORÉ
DORÉ
WORLD MYTHOLOGY
THE SHELL

USING INDOOR LOCATIONS

In addition to room interiors, there are also other types of indoor locations which can be useful for male photography and which can present some different photographic problems. A gymnasium offers an interesting setting and also provides an opportunity for action pictures; other similar locations include squash courts, indoor pools and a dance or rehearsal studio.

The main difficulty with such locations is that the overall area is much greater than an ordinary domestic room and this can be a problem with lighting. You may be able to shoot with daylight, through a large window or skylight or by available light, but with a moving subject, the difficulty will be in ensuring a fast enough shutter speed to freeze the action. This can usually be overcome by the use of fast film and wide-aperture lenses.

If you do intend to use artificial lighting such as flash, then a problem can arise in illuminating both the foreground model and the more distant background adequately. Using direct flash from the camera position will result in a well-lit model, but with the background underexposed, recording as a much darker tone with little or no detail. One solution is to bounce the light of the flash from a white wall or ceiling. This will diffuse it, creating a softer and more even light. There will of course be a substantial loss in the level of light from the flashgun, as much of it will be absorbed and scattered by the reflective surface. Consequently you will need to use a powerful gun to cover all but the smallest areas. The additional exposure can be calculated by measuring the distance from the gun to the ceiling, or wall, and from there to the model, the correct aperture found by dividing this total into the guide number of the flashgun and opening up one stop extra to allow for the absorption.

If there is not a suitable white wall or ceiling for this purpose, or if the flashgun has insufficient power, then it is possible to combine a flash exposure with a slower shutter speed. In this way the model in the foreground will be lit by the flash, but the longer exposure will also allow the background lighting to record adequately. This technique cannot be used if the resulting shutter speed is slower than that needed to freeze movement, since although the flash exposure will freeze movement within the model, in the areas where he is moving against the background, his movement will record as a halo of blur. Although this can be used creatively and for effect, it will simply look odd if allowed to occur accidentally.

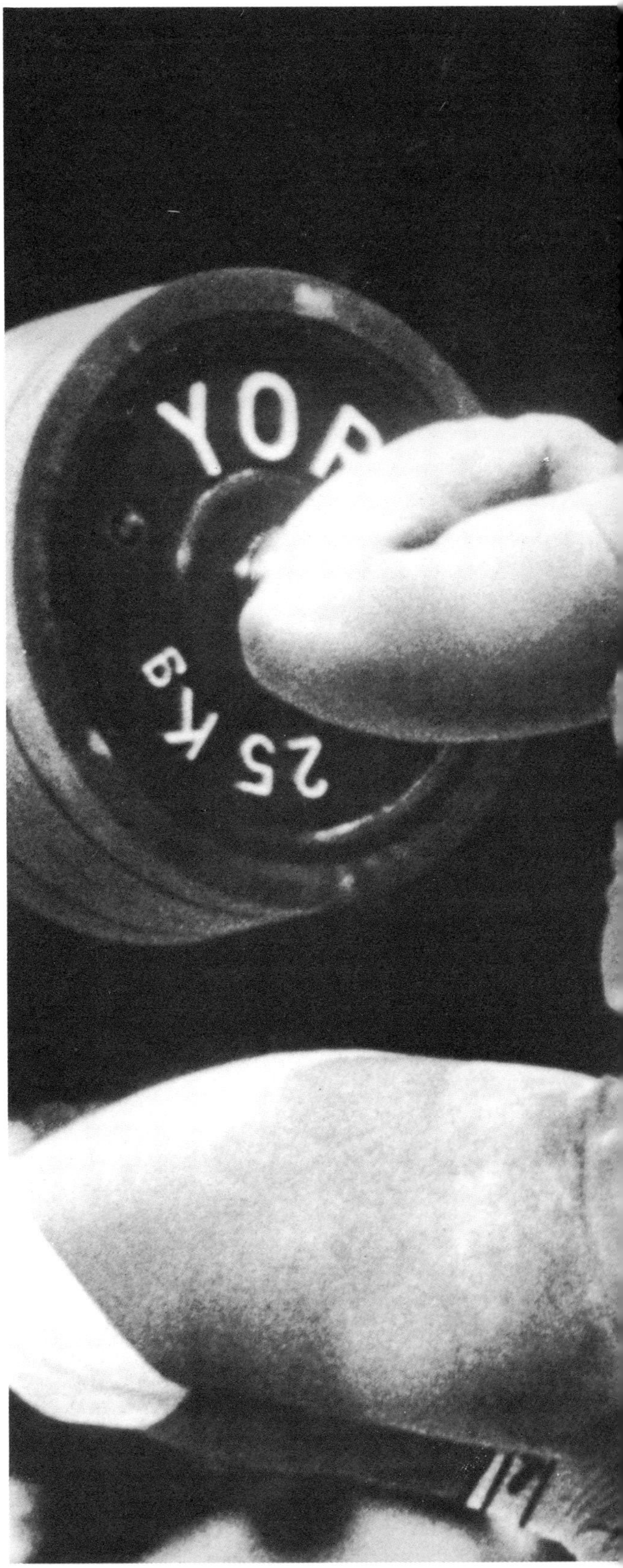

The light level in a sports stadium is invariably low. For this picture the photographer used ISO 400 film to compensate for the low light, and prolonged development to boost film speed still further.

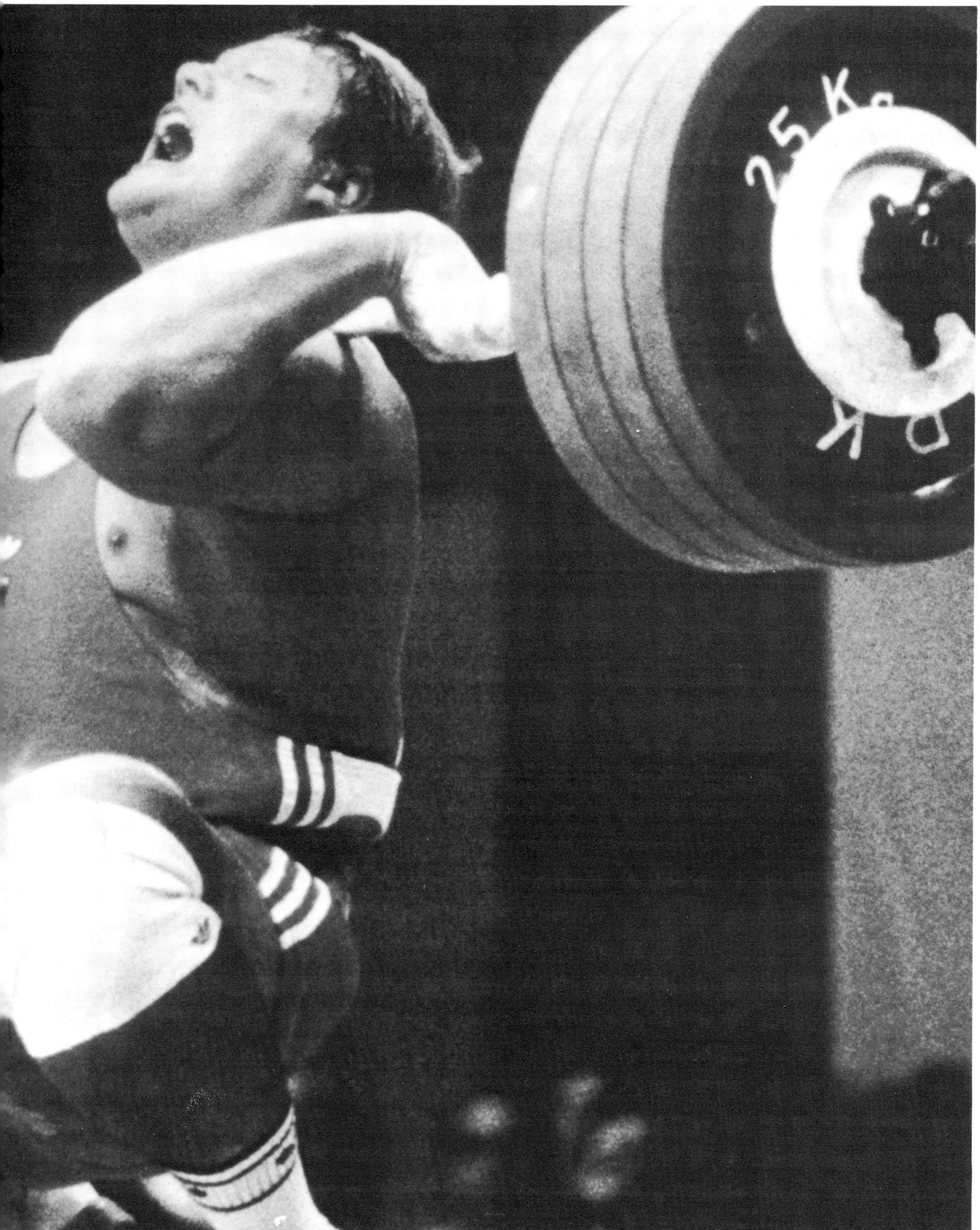
25 Kg

USING AVAILABLE LIGHT

Although a flashgun ensures that you can take pictures in almost every circumstance, it is sometimes either not desirable, or in some cases not permitted, to use it, and then it is necessary to make use of the available light. A common situation in which this technique is useful is when the lighting in a particular location or situation is a crucial element of its mood or appearance, when in a restaurant or disco for example. There are, however, a number of factors to consider when shooting in these conditions.

Firstly, it is likely that the level of illumination will be quite low and this will make it necessary to modify your usual camera technique. Even with the use of a faster film than normal, you will invariably need to use both slower shutter speeds and wider apertures. Both accurate focusing and a means of supporting the camera will consequently be needed to ensure sharp results. A tripod is the best type of support for fairly static subjects, but a monopod can also be helpful, and if nothing at all is available, then it is advisable to find some natural support, like a wall or door frame, against which you can brace your camera.

Supporting the camera and using a slow shutter speed is of course little help if the subject is moving and in these circumstances, it may be necessary to uprate and push-process the film to allow a faster shutter speed to be used. Most color laboratories offer a service whereby the speed of even very fast films can be further increased by one or two stops by modifying the development times. This will result in a loss of quality and an increase in the grain size of the image, but in many circumstances, this can add to the impact and mood of a shot.

Image contrast can also be a problem with this type of picture. Available light often creates areas of both deep shadow and bright highlights, and this can produce poor pictures if some care is not taken. The best solution is to choose a viewpoint and to frame your pictures in such a way that extremes of brightness are avoided. Ideally you should aim for the picture area to be either predominantly in shadow with only small areas of highlight, or to keep the shadow areas very small. As a general rule it is best to frame pictures quite tightly, in situations like stage lighting for example, where the brightness range can be very high.

For the same reasons, exposure calculations must also be made carefully. It is best to take close-up readings from the subject and to ensure that the meter is not influenced by either deep shadows or bright highlights. If it is not possible to take a close-up reading, as with, say, stage photography, then you can use the averaging method. This involves taking an average of the readings from each of the darkest and lightest areas in which you want to retain detail.

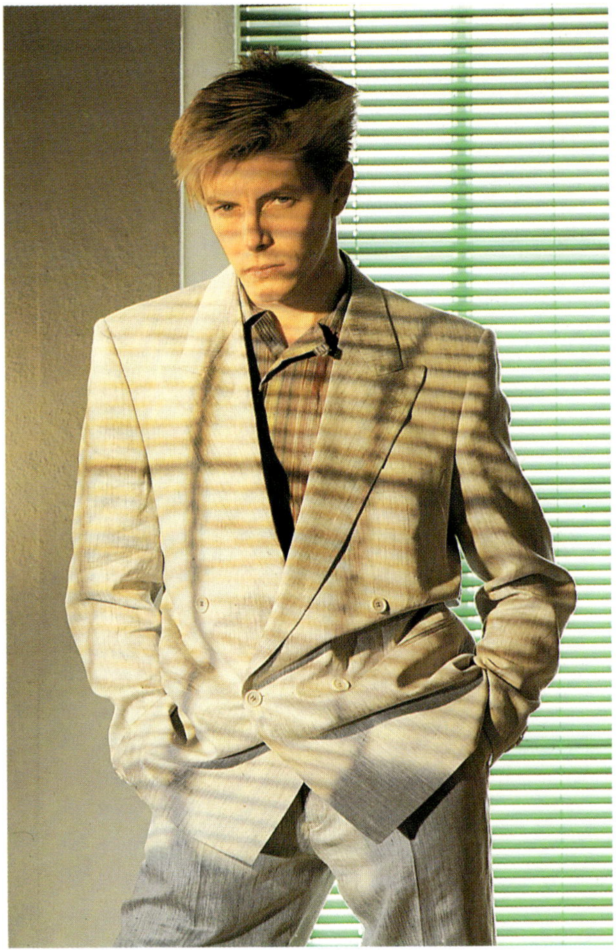

Contrast between light and shadow areas is often high with available light, and so exposure calculations must be made carefully, preferably taking a reading from, and exposing for, your model.

Available light in areas like this involves slow shutter speeds and wide apertures. For that reason, special care must be taken with the focusing and to avoid camera shake.

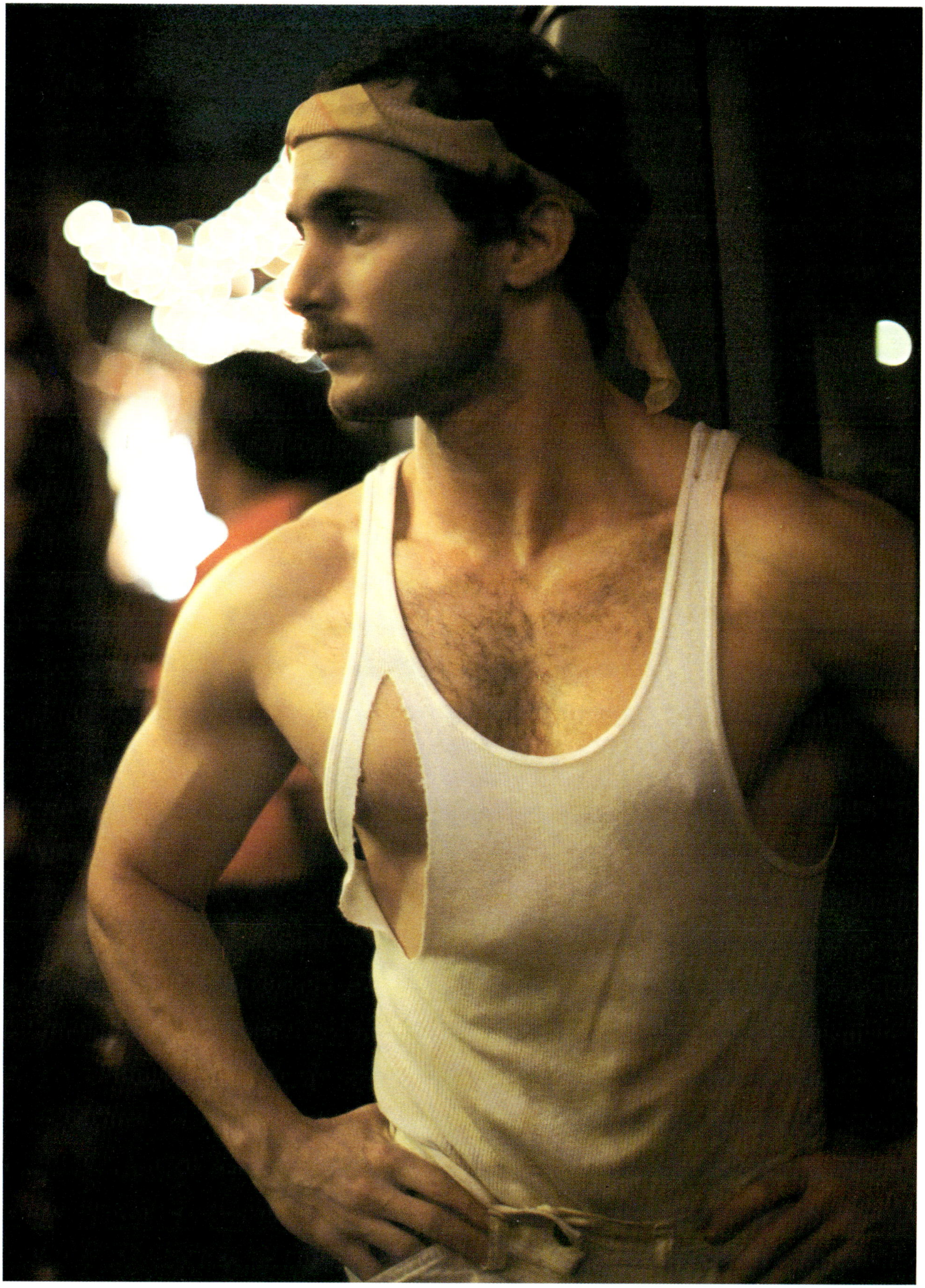

If you don't have access to a proper studio – or if you simply want to retain the spontaneity of pictures taken in a home environment – you may choose to use available light for posed pictures of the male such as those shown here. At home, though, there is greater control over the placement and orientation of lights than there is in a large public space.

Make the most of what light is available by moving the model and the light source closer together, by removing shades, and turning dimmer controls up to full power. Take care, though, that you don't create a level of contrast that is too high for the film to cope with; use reflectors wherever possible to fill in any large areas of shadow. If light levels are still too low for photography, try replacing the regular light bulbs with photoflood lamps. These resemble oversized light bulbs, and give out several times as much light. They also emit more heat than a regular lamp, so make sure that the bulbs are used only in the ceramic and metal lamp-holders which are resistant to heat. Though the bulbs will fit into ordinary plastic lamp-holders, this practise is not recommended, as the intense heat soon damages the plastic, creating a fire risk.

Light bulbs give out a very yellow glow compared to the colors of daylight, and for perfect color pictures with slide film, it is necessary to either fit a blue 80A filter over the lens, or to use special tungsten light balanced film. However, the warm orange tint that colors pictures taken on regular daylight balanced film is not always objectionable, and sometimes even adds atmosphere and presence to a picture.

Color negative film needs no corrective filtration – the colors can be put right at the printing stage. The final option, of course, is to use black and white film, as shown here, and thereby side-step the problems of color balance completely.

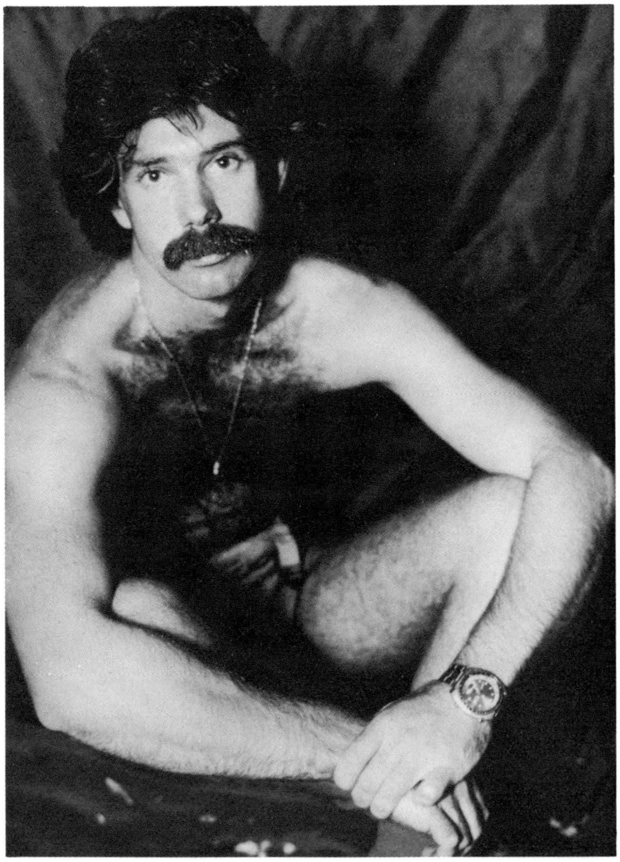

Dim light forces the use of wide apertures – and these in turn produce pictures that have shallow depth of field. Try to keep all the most important parts of your subject the same distance from the camera – and therefore all within the narrow zone of sharp focus. Here the subject's face and arms are acceptably sharp; other parts of his body are further away and therefore out of focus.

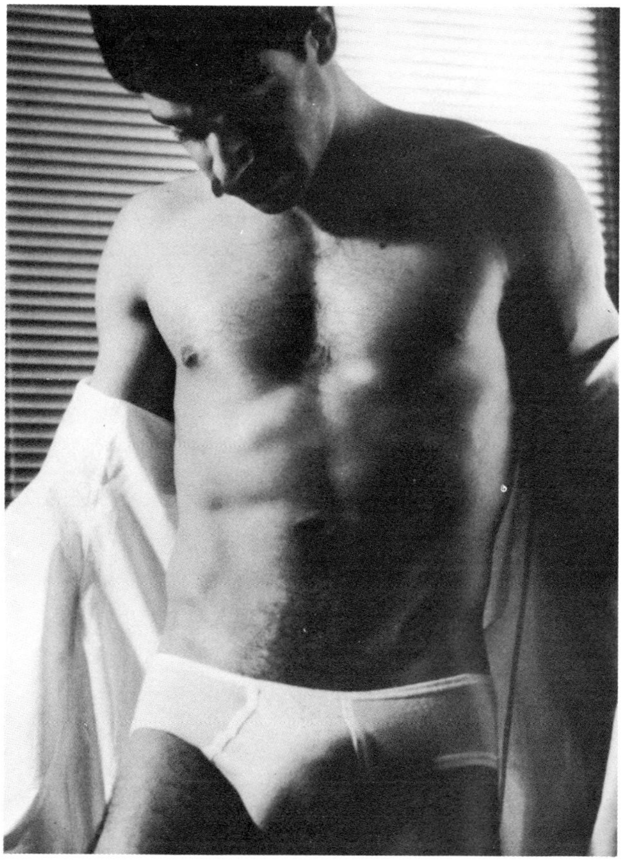

Available light often makes a pleasant change from the rather 'staged' look of studio lighting. Additionally, amateur models are easily intimidated by banks of bright lights, and may feel more comfortable if you use ordinary household lamps instead.

In available light, you may be forced to mount the camera on a tripod, and use exposures as long as a full second. So choose poses that your model can hold comfortably without moving while the shutter is open.

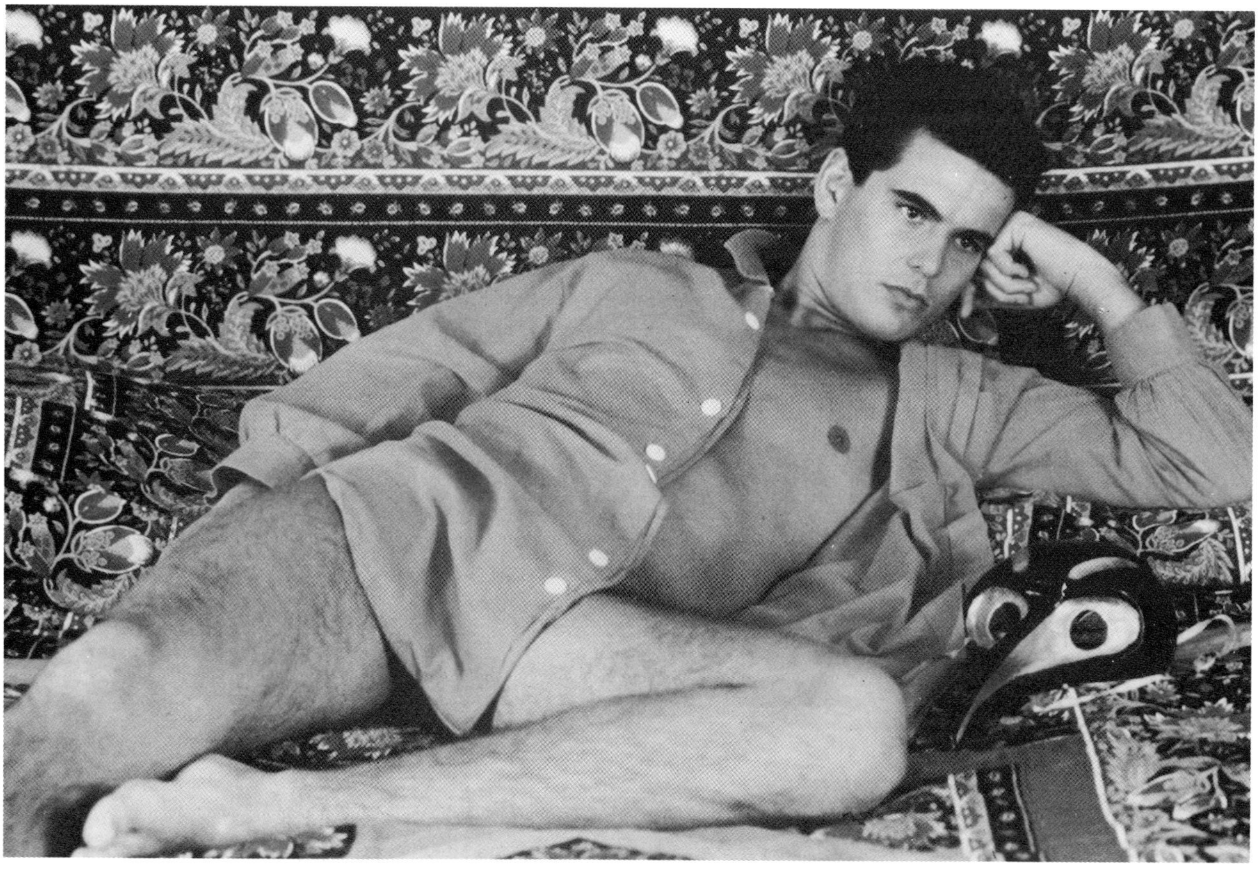

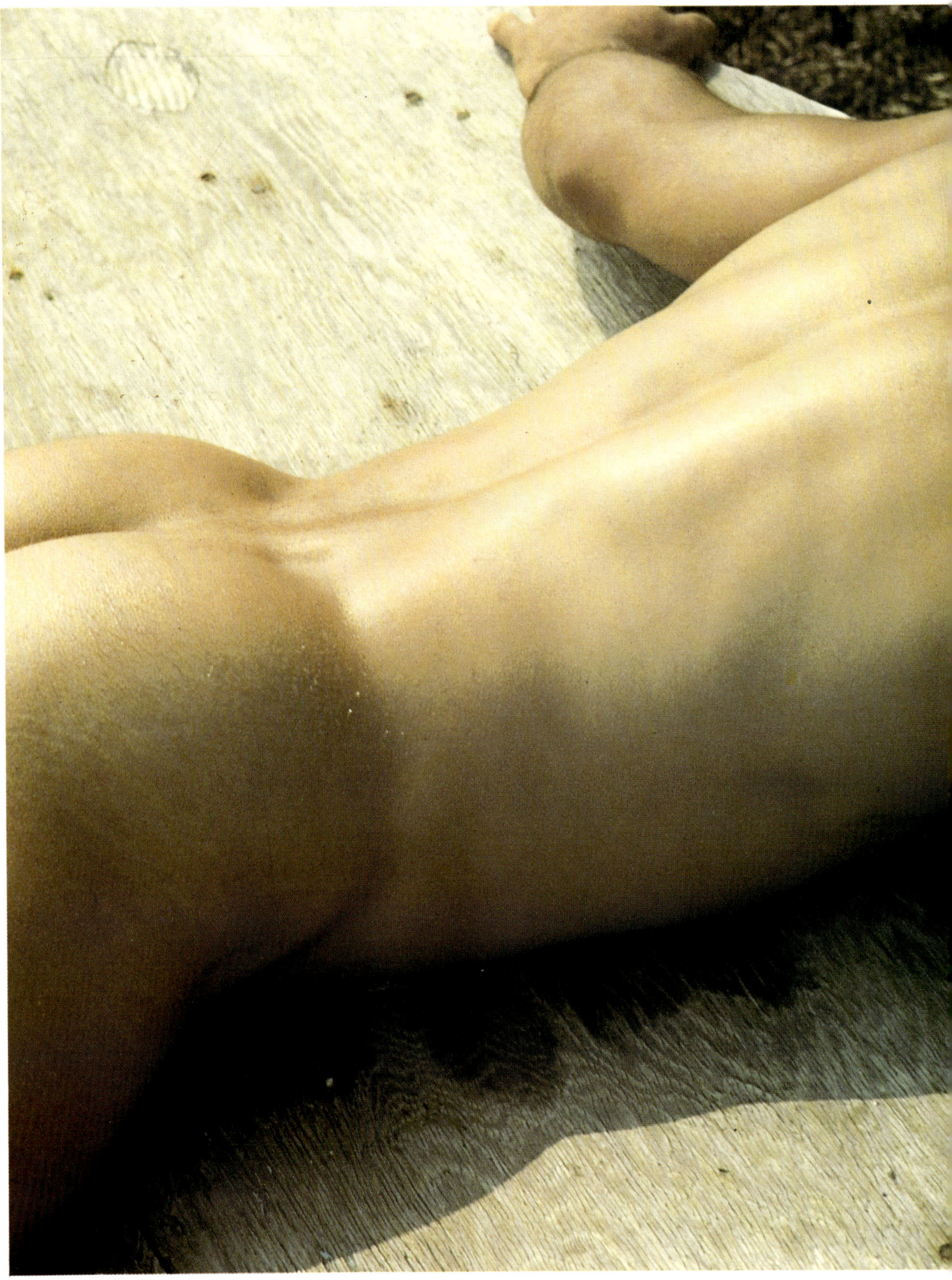

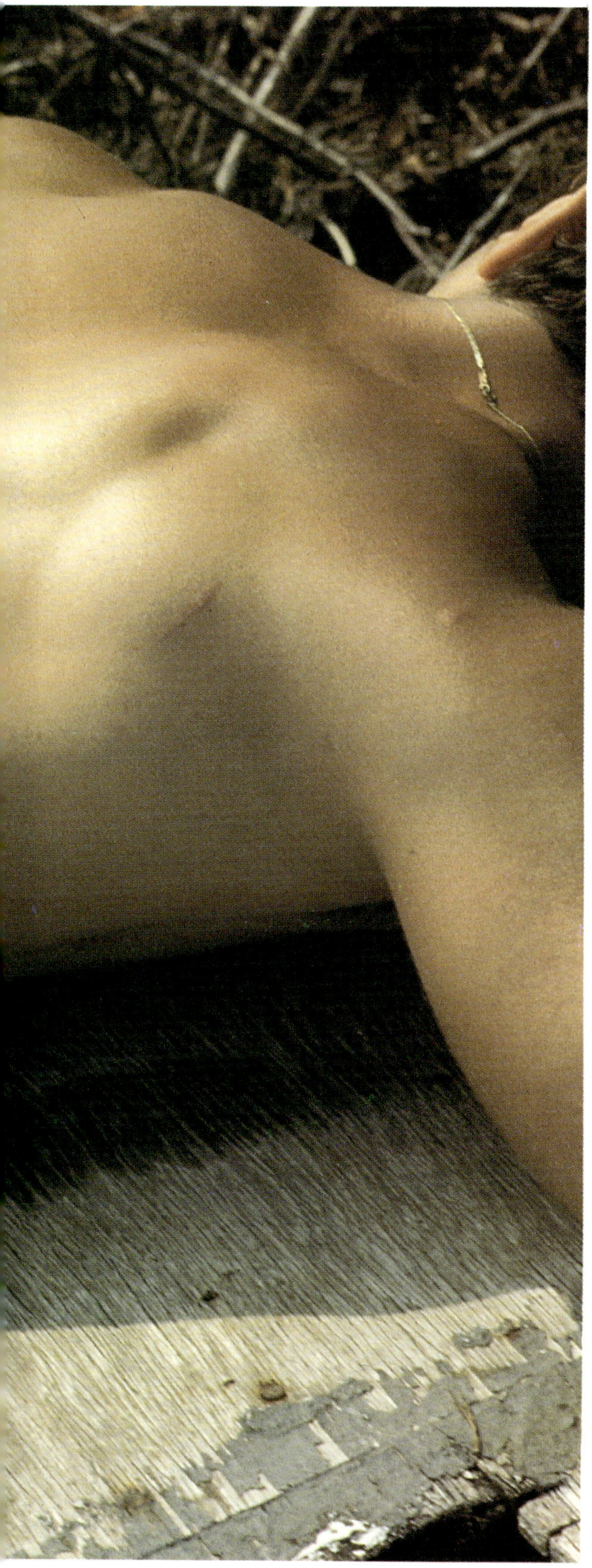

CAMERA TECHNIQUES

CHOOSING EQUIPMENT

The choice of equipment, for any type of photography, is an important consideration. Not only is it expensive to make mistakes, but the availability and range of equipment can be quite bewildering, particularly to the inexperienced. The right camera is of course the most crucial decision and for portrait, fashion and nude photography, the single lens reflex is the most widely used for a number of reasons.

Firstly, the viewfinder and focusing system of the SLR are ideal for this type of work since they allow the image created by the lens to be seen the right way up, and the right way round, on the viewing screen. In addition, the SLR can be focused with extreme accuracy as well as giving you the chance to see the actual effects of focusing. With cameras that have a preview button, the effects of depth of field at different apertures can also be seen. A further advantage of this system is that the effect of many filters or lens attachments which are fitted can also be viewed directly on the screen.

All modern SLR cameras also have through-the-lens metering systems which offer accurate control over exposure calculation and which allow for attachments or different lenses that might be used. In addition, it is also possible to have fully automatic exposure control for ease and speed of use. Last but by no means least, the SLR camera allows the use of a wide range of lenses of different focal lengths.

This is not intended to suggest that other types of camera are unsuitable for male photography. On the contrary, a camera is only a tool. In the right hands and aimed by a perceptive eye, any camera is capable of taking good pictures. However, the SLR does offer greater flexibility than cameras such as the viewfinder type and also has more potential as a system, enabling it to be added to as a photographer increases his expertise and interest.

Film format is another factor to consider when choosing a camera. As a general rule, the larger the image size, the greater the potential for image quality, but this in turn should be considered in terms of the ways in which the pictures will be used. Thirty-five millimeter cameras provide more-than-adequate quality for most amateur needs, allowing large prints to be made for exhibition and display as well as high-quality transparencies for projection and reproduction.

However, for professional use or where high image quality is needed, for very large prints or for high-quality reproduction, then larger formats should also be considered. SLR cameras are available in 120 rollfilm format and are designed to produce a variety of picture sizes, ranging from ten 6 × 7cm pictures on a standard roll to twelve 6 × 6cm or fifteen 6 × 4.5cm. Even the smaller formats such as the cartridge cameras using 126, 110 or Disc film can be used effectively, providing the limits of the format are appre-

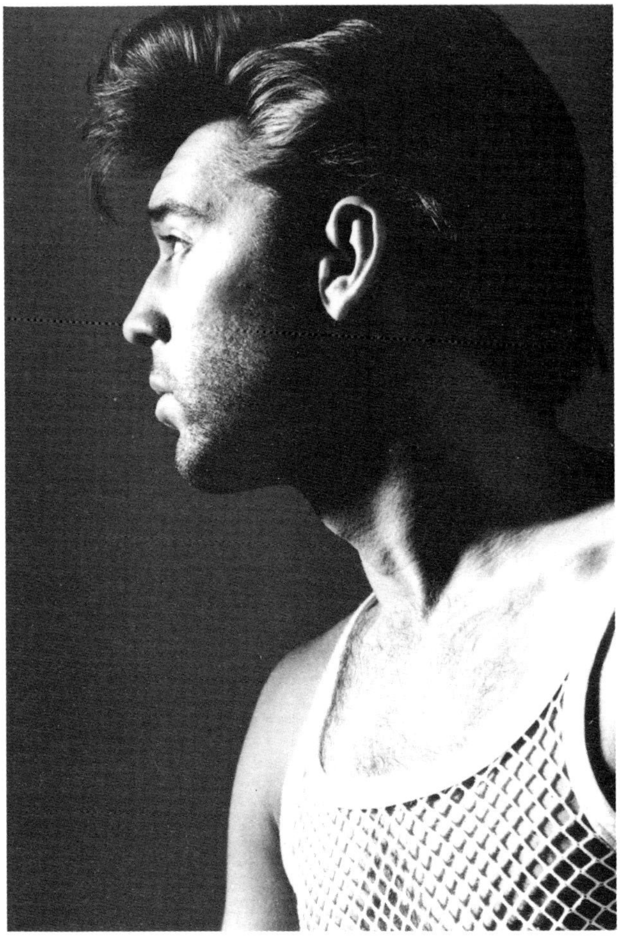

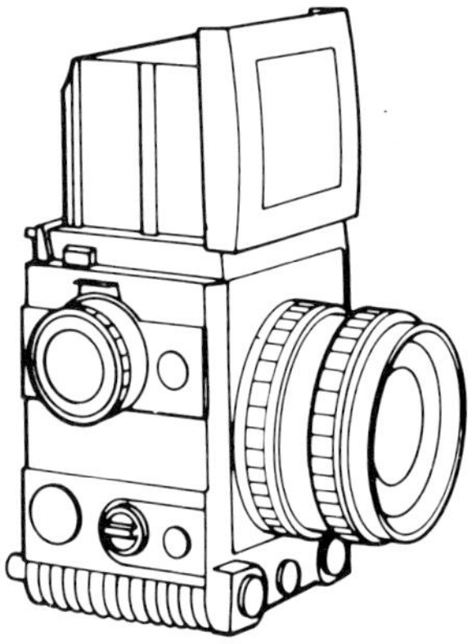

For pictures in the studio **(above)**, *quality is the primary consideration. Rollfilm cameras* **(right)** *produce negatives and transparencies several times the size of 35mm film, so are a good choice for studio photography.*

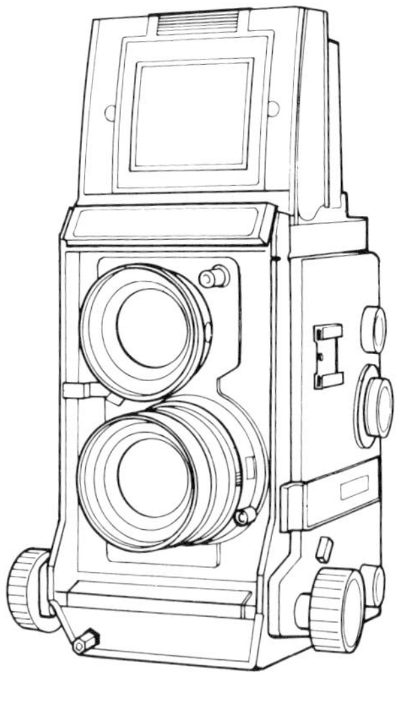

Twin lens reflex cameras are an economical way to quality. Widely available secondhand, these cameras use the same large-size film as rollfilm SLRs, but are a fraction of the price. However, they are not as convenient to use as SLRs.

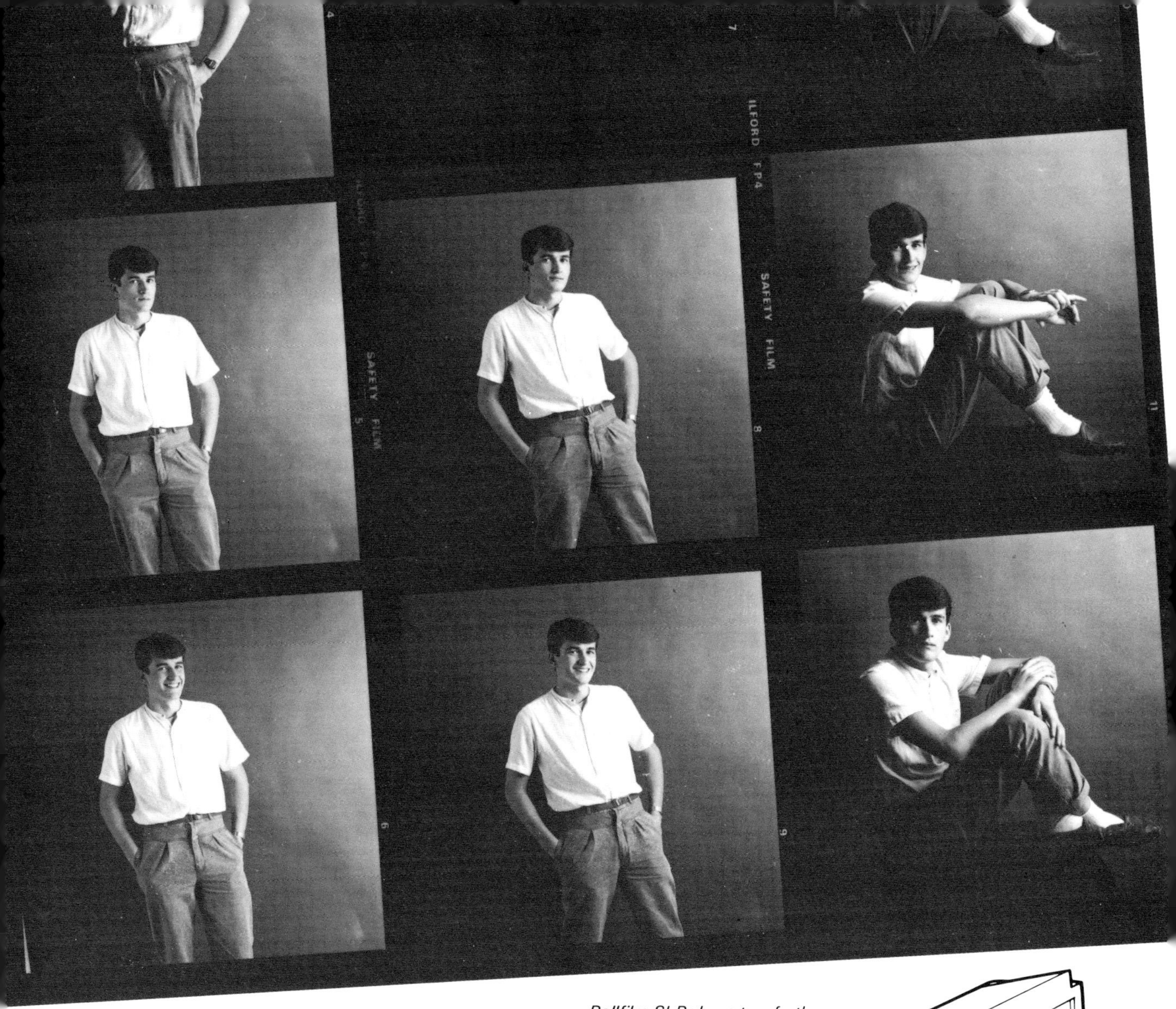

Rollfilm SLRs have two further advantages over their 35mm cousins: they produce images that are easy to look at, even without a magnifier **(above)***; and most accept interchangeable film magazines* **(right)***, which make it possible to change film in mid-rolls, and to use instant film for lighting tests.*

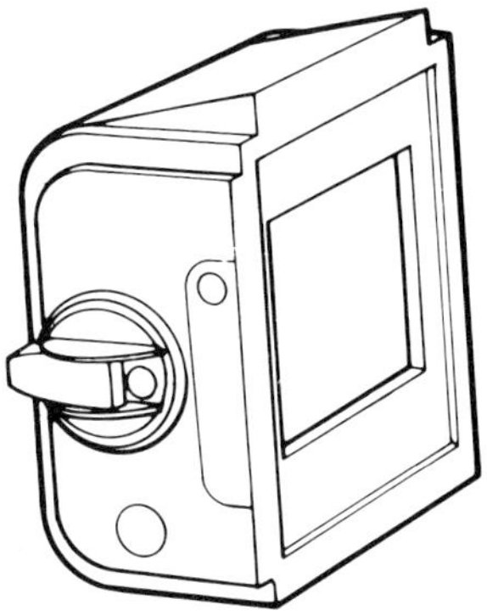

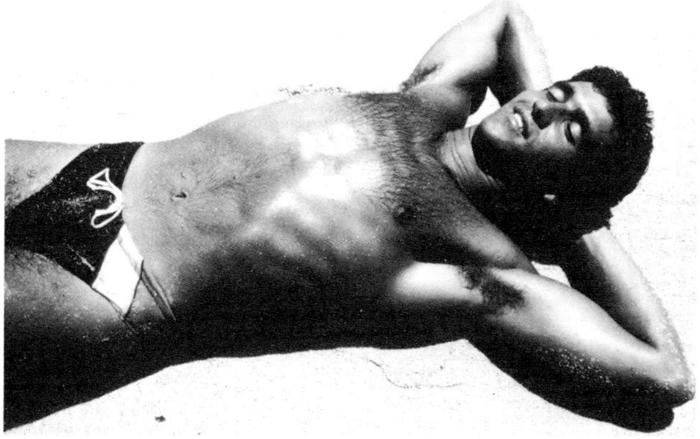

Quality is just as important on location as in the studio, but weight and size may also affect choice of equipment. When everything must be carried a mile or so from car to the beach in hot sun, a 35mm system is the most sensible choice.

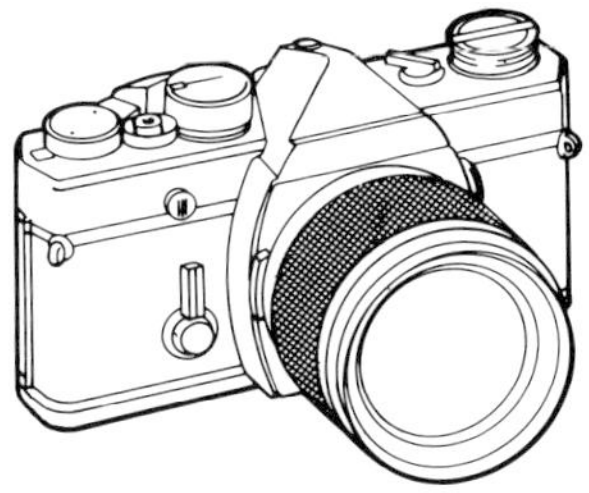

ciated and it is not intended to make large prints. It should be born in mind, however, that the choice of film type is more restricted in these formats than with 35mm or rollfilm.

The ultimate in image quality is achieved by the use of the large format view or field cameras taking 4 × 5 inch or 8 × 10 inch sheet film, but since these cameras must be used on a tripod and the image viewed upside down, reversed left to right on a screen, they are more suited to static subjects like still life, landscape and architecture than to portrait or fashion work.

The addition of different focal length lenses is a considerable asset that will increase the range and variety of your pictures. A telephoto lens is invaluable for portrait work since it allows a large image of the model to be obtained from a more distant viewpoint. This avoids the possibility of perspective distortion and allows a more comfortable and convenient working distance. A lens of between, say, 85mm and 150mm with a 35mm camera is ideal for this purpose and a zoom lens covering this range is particularly useful for this type of shot as you can alter the framing of the image without having to move the camera position. An even longer focal length would be desirable for subjects such as sport and action where it might not be possible to approach the subject more closely. For this, a 200mm, 300mm or even longer focal length lens would be the best choice.

A wide-angle lens can also be useful for male photography as a means of controlling perspective, for example. Because of its wider field of view, it allows both close and distant objects to be included in the frame, and it will accentuate the effect of perspective, increasing the impression of depth and distance in a picture. A very wide-angle lens such as a 20mm with a 35mm camera can be used to create dramatic effects of this type. In addition, this type of lens will be an asset when working in a confined space when it is not possible to include more of the subject by moving further back. It will also allow you to include a close-up image of the model in the foreground as well as a large area of background. The greater effective depth of field of a wide-angle lens can also be very useful for pictures of this type.

Other items of equipment which should be considered as part of a basic kit include a firm tripod for low-light shooting and more precise control over focusing and framing, as well as the elimination of camera shake. A small flashgun enables you to be independent of the available light when necessary as well as being able to supplement the existing light and to control contrast. A kit of filters should also be part of the essentials. The most useful are a selection of color correction filters for shooting in different lighting conditions and a polarizing filter and one or two graduated filters. In addition you might like to add some contrasting filters for controlling image quality when shooting in black and white, as well as a variety of effects filters and lens attachments for special effects.

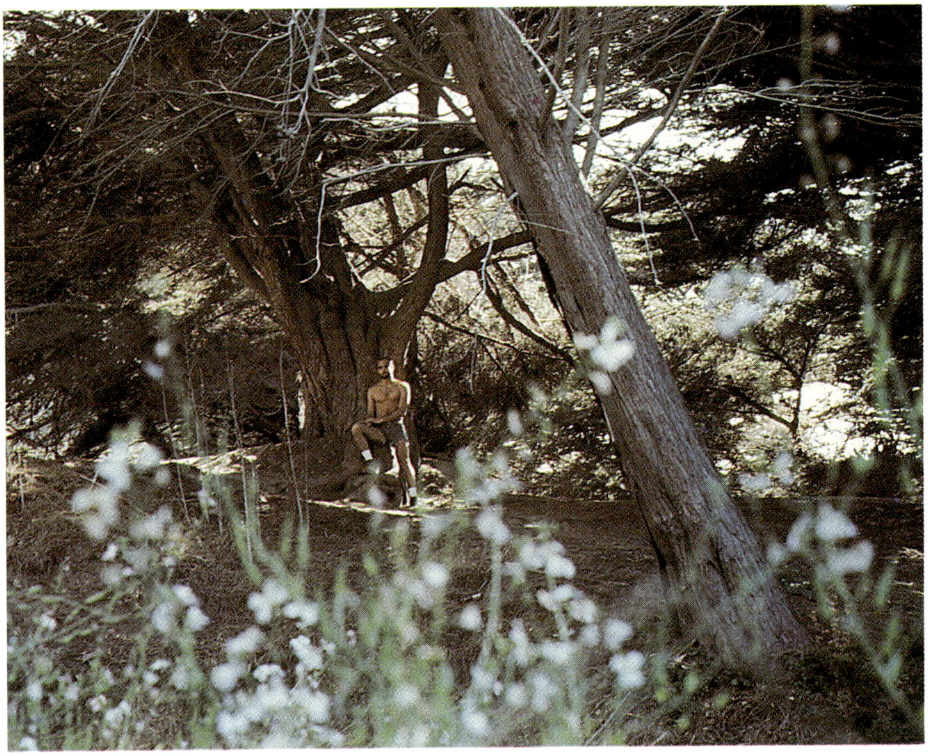

A selection of lenses allows you to quickly alter the composition without moving the camera. For this picture the photographer switched from a standard lens to a 28mm wide-angle to show the rural surroundings in which his model was posing.

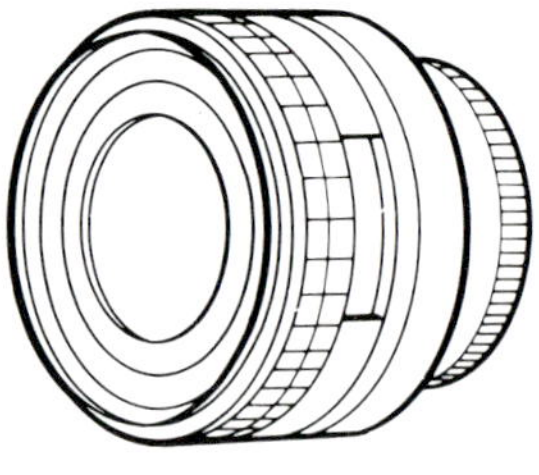

Telephoto lenses not only take in a narrower field of view than standard lenses – they also allow you to fill the frame with the figure from a greater distance. At these greater camera-to-subject distances, perspective seems flattened, so that figure and background appear pressed together. For this image, the photographer used a 200mm lens **(below)**.

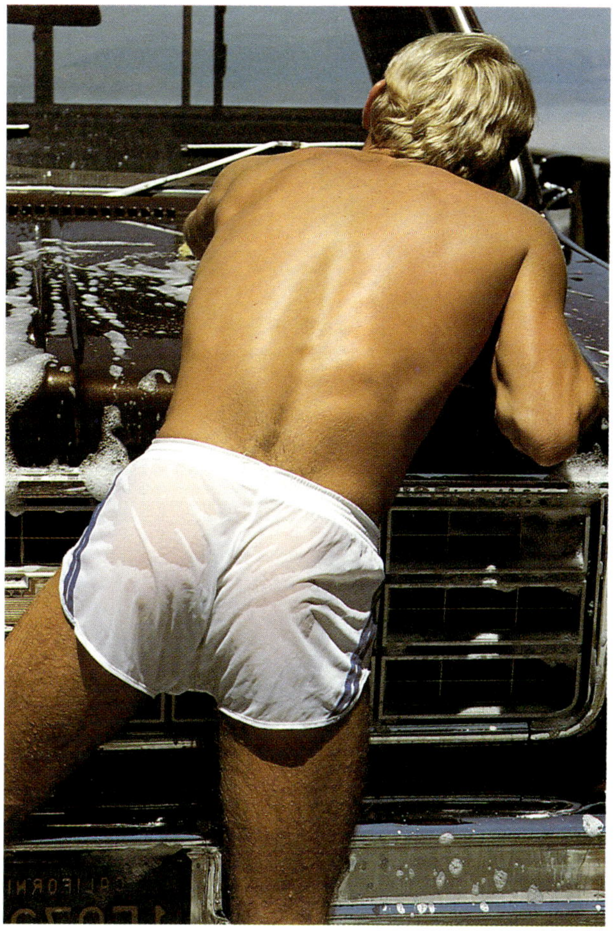

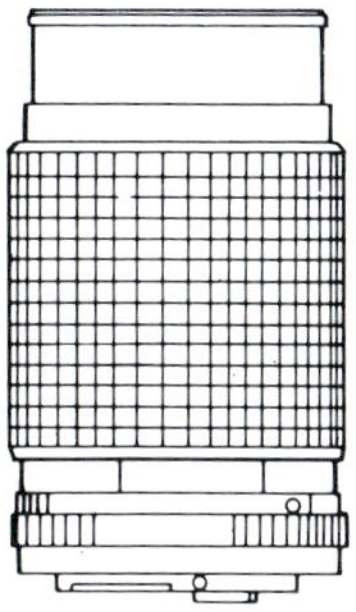

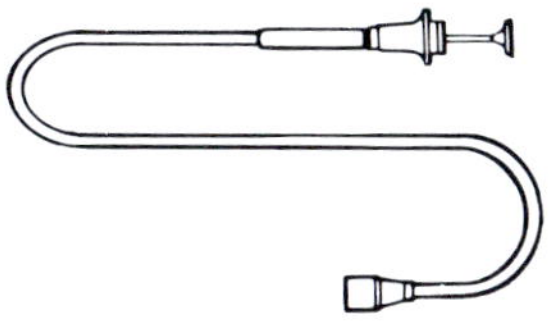

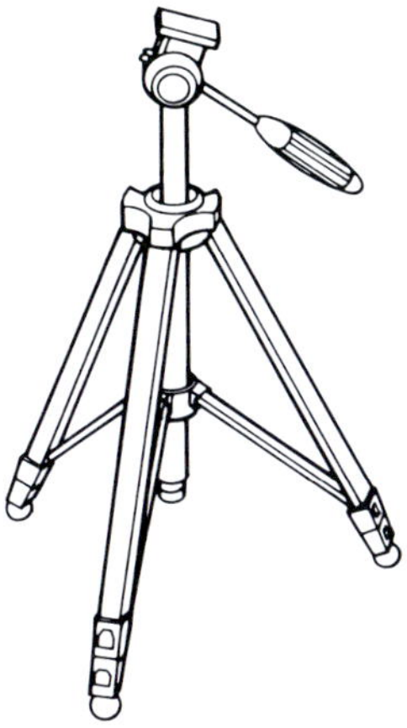

In dim light, the inevitable slow shutter speeds introduce the risk of camera shake. A portable tripod **(left below)** *eliminates the risk without adding too much weight to your equipment bag. A cable release* **(upper left)** *prevents vibration from the photographer's hands from jarring the camera during long exposures.*

A motor-drive **(right)** *may seem like an unnecessary luxury, but to the professional photographer it is a vital piece of equipment. For example, when the sun is setting there may be only three or four minutes to get the picture, and a motor drive makes the difference between a handful of saleable shots, and several rolls. The more sophisticated motor drives both wind and rewind film.*
Flashguns **(right)** *have an obvious role to play, not only after dark but in sunlight too, filling in harsh shadows.*

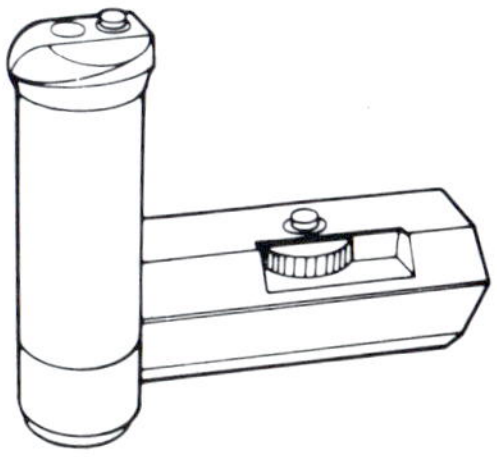

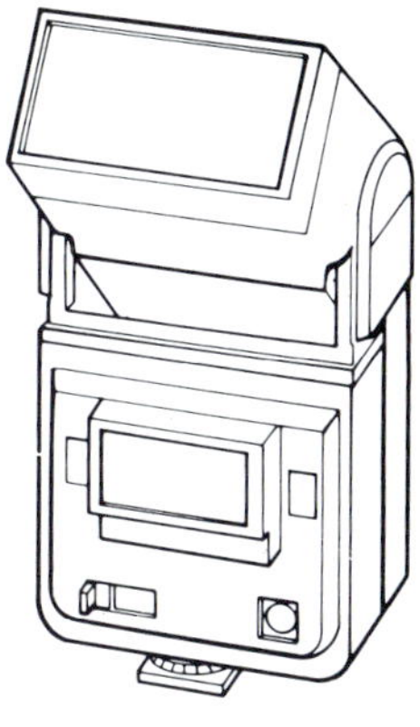

USING THE CAMERA

One of the essential requirements of a technically successful picture is that the image be recorded as sharply as possible where required. In most circumstances in male photography, it is vital that the subject himself is recorded sharply, although it may or may not be desirable for other parts of the image to be equally sharp.

It is essential that the camera is focused accurately upon the main point of interest, and with a camera that has a focusing device such as an SLR, a rangefinder or autofocus system, this should not present any problems. However, it must be appreciated that at distances of less than, say 12 feet, there is little latitude for error and with a simple camera where the distance has to be estimated, focusing this must be carried out with some care.

The aperture you select will also affect the sharpness of the image. When you focus on a subject at a certain distance from the camera, other details both closer to, and further from the camera will also be sharp. This range of sharp focus is called the depth of field. It varies according to the aperture selected and the distance at which the lens is focused. The depth of field increases as the aperture is made smaller and as the focusing distance is increased; it becomes less when the lens is focused at closer distances and when a wide aperture is used. Consequently, when you want to obtain maximum sharpness in both close and distant details you should use the smallest practicable aperture; when you wish to have the subject in sharp focus but other parts of the image, such as the background, out of focus, then you should use the widest possible aperture.

There is another factor which controls image sharpness, and this is connected with the choice of shutter speed. If the image moves on the film during the exposure, it will cause a degree of blur, governed by the choice of shutter speed. The movement can be caused either by the subject or by the camera moving during the exposure and the latter, known as camera shake, is responsible for a large proportion of unsuccessful pictures. The best way of preventing this is to use a tripod. For subjects like portraits it is preferable to do so anyway, as the effects of camera shake are accentuated with close-up subjects and when using a long-focus lens. If a tripod is not used, then it is best to select the fastest shutter speed practicable, particularly when using a telephoto lens. As a general rule, when the lighting permits, it is best to keep your camera set to at least 1/125 second when not using a tripod and 1/250 second or less with a long-focus lens. It will also help considerably to hold the camera firmly and to release the shutter with a smooth movement rather than a hasty jab of the finger.

When you are photographing a moving subject the same considerations apply. It is best to use the fastest

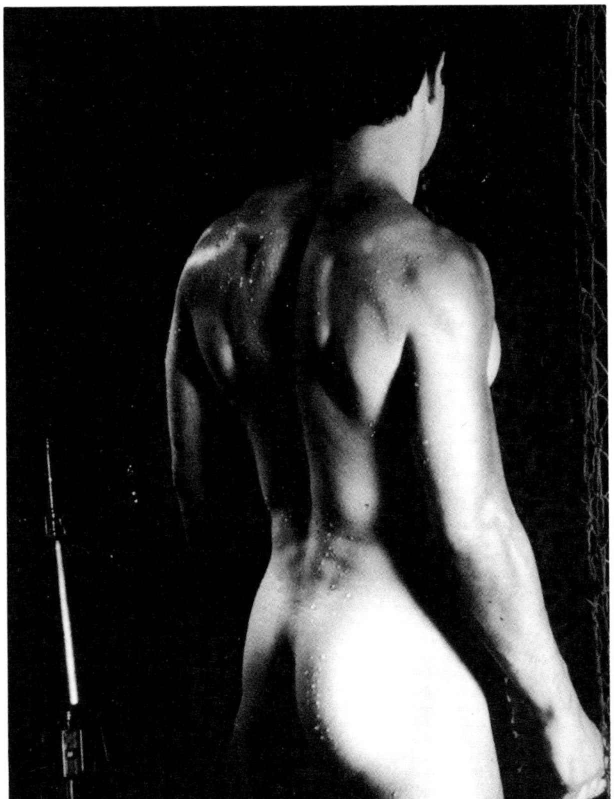

In some circumstances, a certain degree of soft-focus is acceptable or even desirable. This image, though, relies on the sharp renderings of every bead of perspiration on the model's back, so the picture must be sharp from corner to corner.

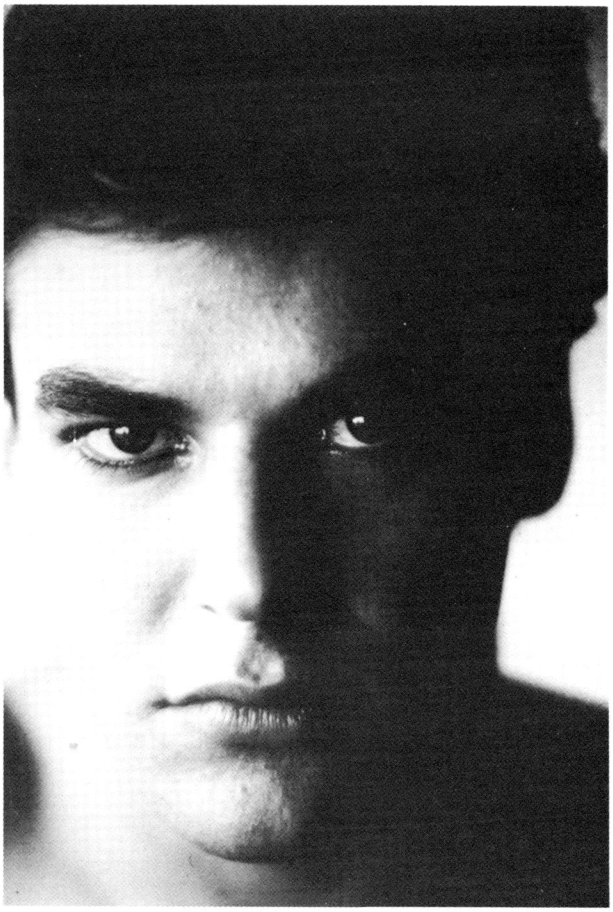

Sometimes low light forces the use of a wide aperture, and there is not sufficient depth of field to keep the whole image sharp. The best solution is to focus on the eyes – as long as these are clearly rendered, the viewer is usually prepared to accept unsharpness in other parts of the picture.

Programmed automatic cameras may not set shutter speeds fast enough to freeze rapid action. To catch every water droplet the photographer therefore switched to manual, and set a shutter speed of 1/1000.

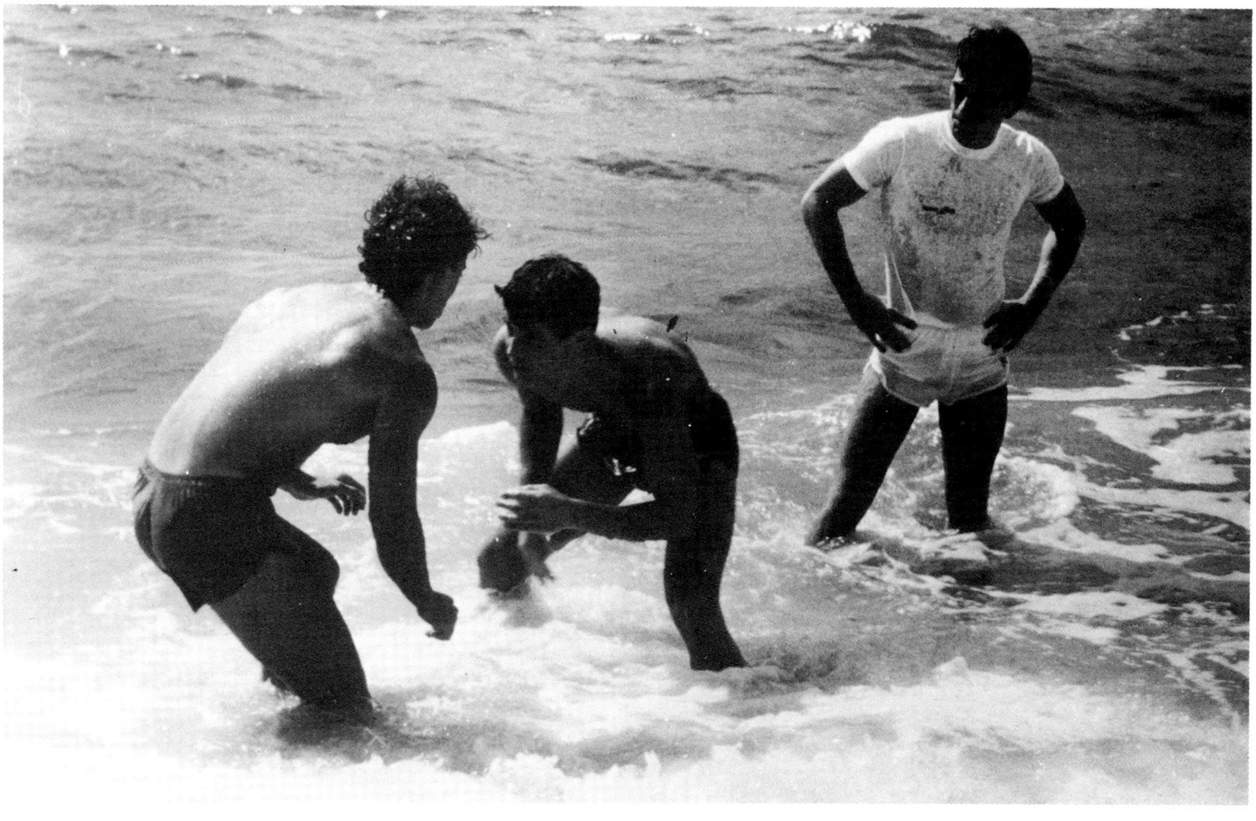

practicable shutter speed to freeze the movement. However, it is also possible to improve the chances of a sharp picture by selecting a peak moment of a movement to expose, when it is at its slowest, like an athlete reaching the apex of a jump, for example. Alternatively you can pan the camera when the subject is moving directly across the field of view. This involves swinging the camera in a smooth arc, keeping the subject steady in the viewfinder and exposing as you do so. This technique will also allow you to choose a fairly slow shutter speed and still obtain a sharp image of the subject but with the background blurred by the camera movement. In many cases this can convey the impression of speed and movement more effectively than a completely sharp image.

In addition to being sharp, a good photograph in the technical sense must also be correctly exposed and although most cameras now have built in, and often automatic metering, it is still vital for a photographer to understand the principles of exposure and how it can be used to control image quality.

An exposure meter is designed to measure the brightness level of the light which is reflected from the subject. This measurement is then converted into a reading which shows the correct aperture and shutter speed needed for a particular film speed. The exposure meter cannot think and it simply assumes that the subject at which it is aimed is of average tone and contrast. Exposure meters are, in fact, calibrated to read from a standard grey tone which is equal to a tone half-way between black and white. If the exposure meter is aimed at a man in a grey suit of this tone, the exposure it indicates will record the suit as grey in the photograph. The problem is that if it is aimed at a black or white suit it will not know this and simply assume that it is a grey suit with either more or less light reflected from it and will indicate an exposure in both cases that will still record it as grey.

The way the exposure meter is calibrated also assumes that when you aim it at a normal subject containing a range of tones from white through to black, these tones will average out to the standard mid-grey. In many situations this will be the case and the indicated exposure will be correct. But this is not always so and in other circumstances you must interpret or modify what the meter indicates before you set the exposure.

If the subject contains a large area of white the meter will indicate less exposure than is actually needed and you will underexpose the film; if a large area of black is included in the field of view, then more exposure than is needed will be indicated, resulting in an overexposed picture. Lighting too will affect this. If the subject contains very bright highlights, this will also fool the meter into believing the subject to be brighter than it is and will cause underexposure; if there are very deep shadows in the field of view, they cause overexposure.

The best way to avoid these problems is to take a close-up reading from the part of your subject which is equal to the mid-grey tone for which the meter is calibrated. Alternatively, you can take an average reading from both the lightest and darkest tones of the picture. It is important to appreciate, however, that in some instances, slightly more or less exposure than is strictly correct can often increase the impact of a picture and create interesting effects, particularly when you are shooting color transparencies. This is largely a matter of experience but it will often be beneficial to bracket exposures. This means making two or more exposures in addition to the one you have calculated as correct: one at, say, half or one stop more than that indicated and another at half or one stop less.

In dull weather, the range of tones on the subject is much lower than in sunlight, and the camera's built-in exposure meter is perfectly capable of setting exposure correctly without the photographer's intervention.

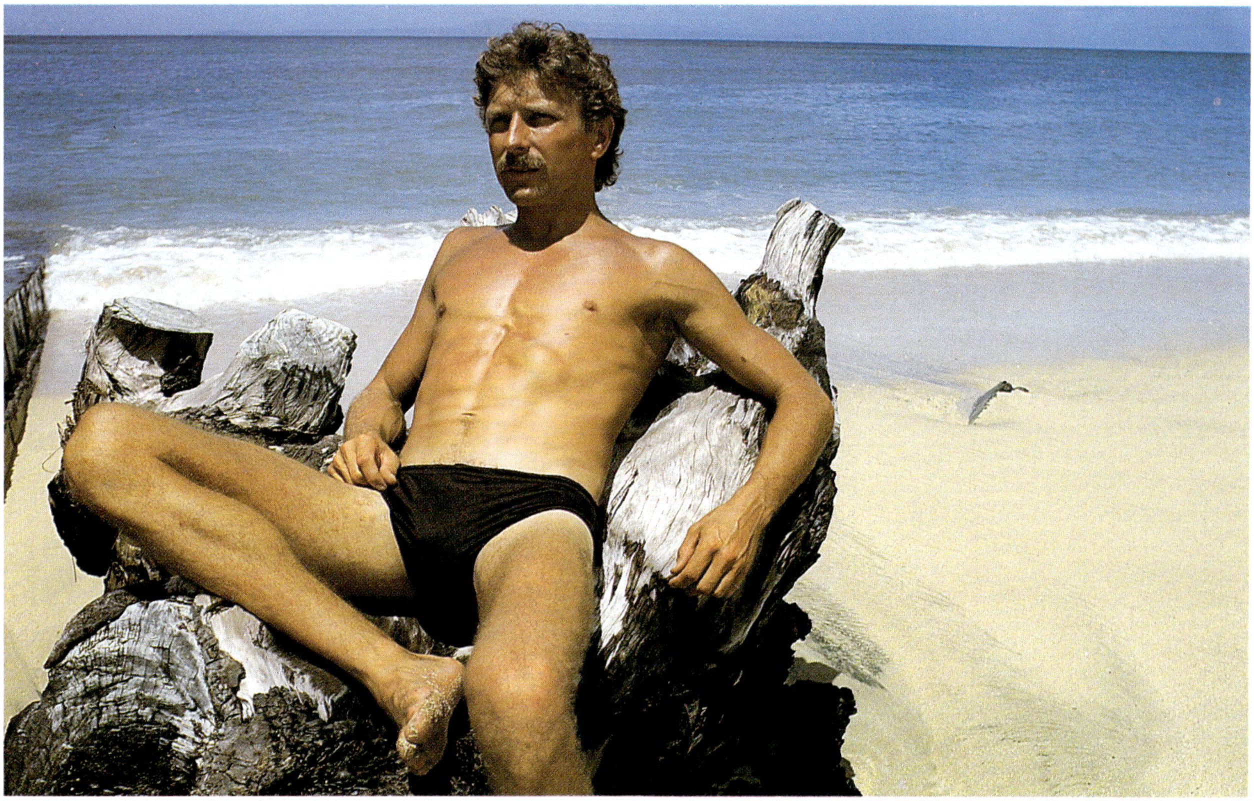

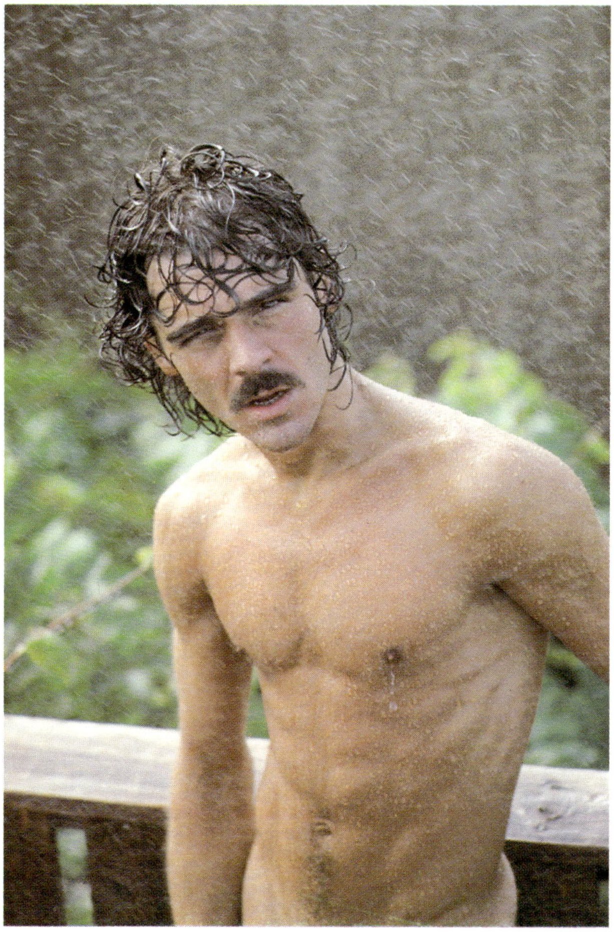

Brilliant sunlight creates very high contrast which stretches the exposure latitude of color transparency film to the limit. Even experienced photographers often shoot several pictures at different exposures, rather than miss a good opportunity.

When the contrast between highlight and shadow is very high, a spot-meter ***(below left)*** *provides a means of measuring the brightness of each individual area of light and shade. In experienced hands, this provides best method of evaluating and controlling exposure.*

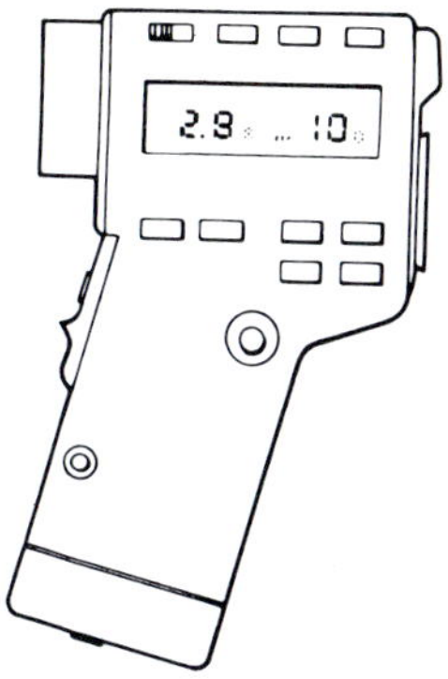

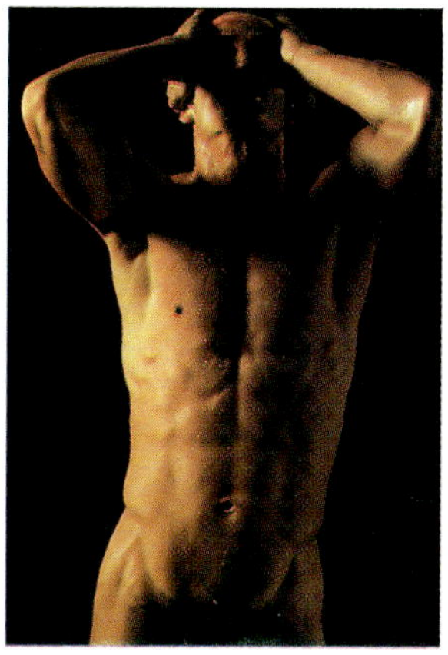

FRAMING THE IMAGE

The technical aspects of the camera are only part of the skill needed to produce good photographs. One of the most important elements of good technique is the use of the viewfinder. The success of a picture is very largely dependent upon what is left out, as well as what is included, in the picture. The camera viewfinder is to a photographer what a blank canvas is to a painter: it is entirely up to him what is put into it.

One of the most effective ways of framing the picture is to simply exclude all but the most crucial aspects of the subject. This can be very effective with a portrait when the subject's face is framed tightly and the emphasis is given to the model's features and expression. You can even crop into the face itself, maybe masking off the top of the head; or with a three-quarter-length shot, you could exclude all of the background and part of the body so that your model's image literally fills the frame.

Of course in many pictures this technique is undesirable. Often the background and surroundings play an important role in creating the mood of a picture or are needed to establish a situation or add to the meaning of the image. In this case, it is necessary to frame the picture in such a way that the subject of the photograph, your model, remains the focus of attention, although much more is included in the frame. Inexperienced photographers usually centre the subject in the viewfinder as if aiming a gun, but this is seldom successful because it tends to create a rather static and symmetrical image and makes it almost impossible to include other details or objects in a balanced and harmonious way. As a general rule it is better to frame the picture so that the model is placed about halfway between the centre and one of the corners of the image. Academically the strongest position for the centre of interest of a picture is considered to be at the intersection of lines which divide the frame into thirds, vertically and horizontally.

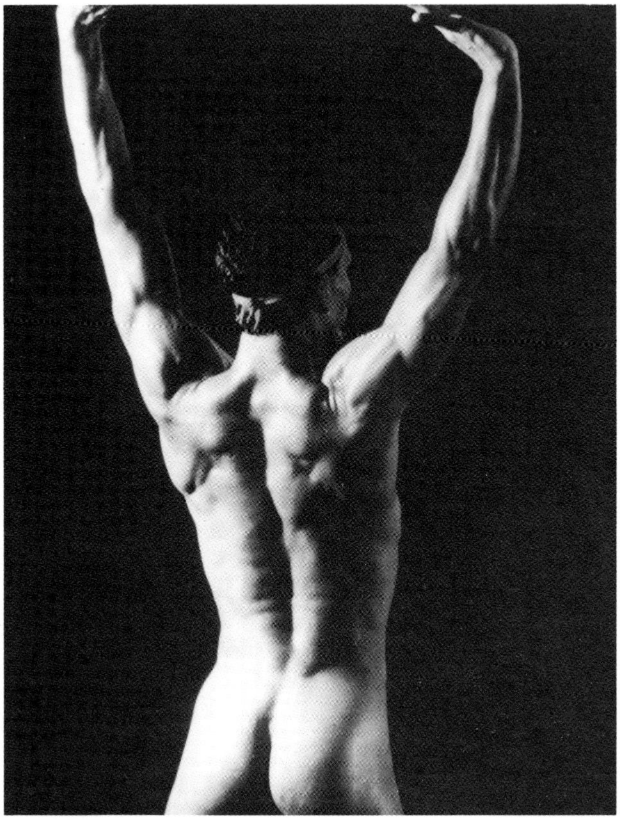

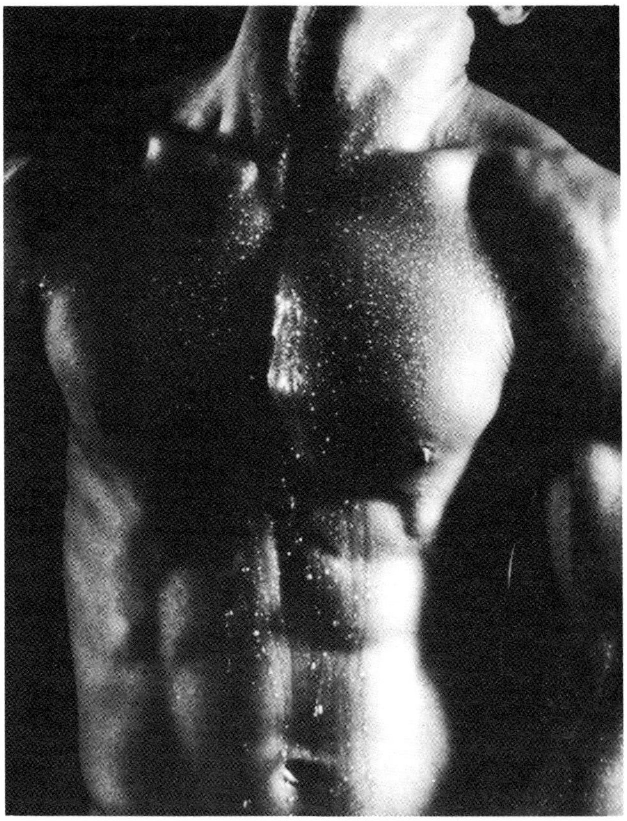

Don't feel obliged to include all of your subject in the picture. Often just a tightly-framed detail says more than a conventional view **(right and far right).**

Framing the image doesn't just mean centering the figure in the viewfinder. You should try also to look at the 'negative shapes' formed between the man's body and the edges of the frame **(opposite)**.

Asymmetrical compositions generally produce more dynamic pictures than carefully balanced images.

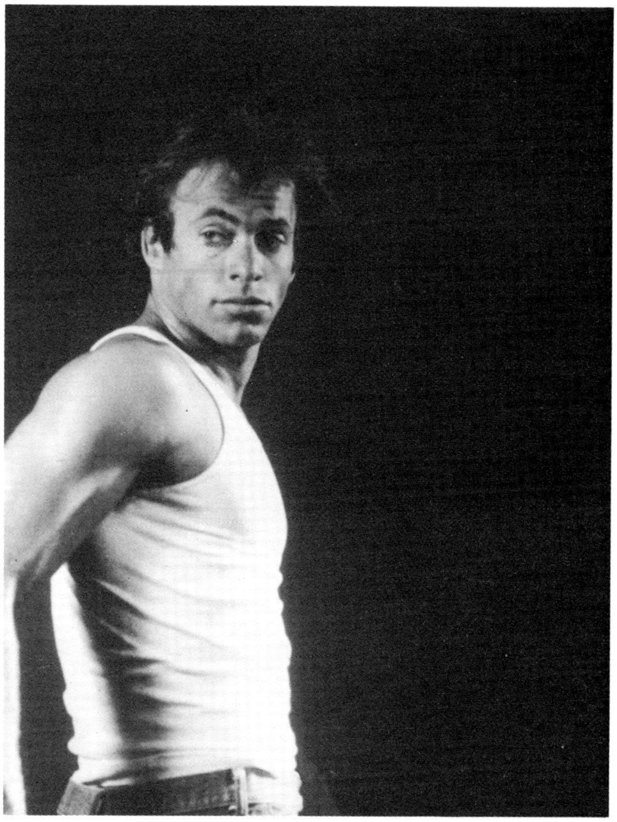

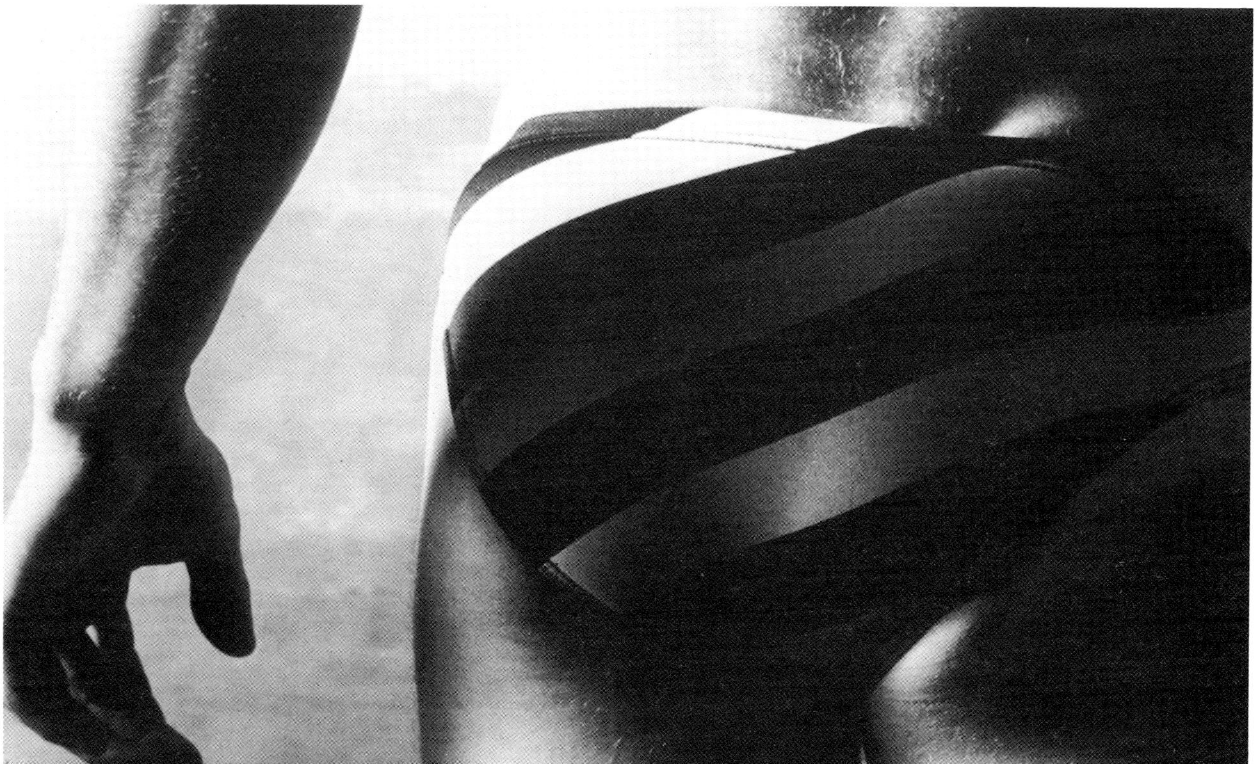

USING SHAPE, LINE AND PATTERN

One of the most effective ways of learning the art of composition is to become aware of your subject in terms of its visual qualities. It is, after all, how it will record as an image that is important. To adopt an analytical approach will help you be more selective and objective.

One of the most dominant elements of composition is that of shape, whether it is of the subject alone, a background object or detail, or simply the shape which the composition creates. A bold, well-defined shape can create considerable impact in an image and identifying and exploiting this element within a subject is an essential stage in composing a picture. The most elementary form in which a bold shape can be used is as a silhouette. In a sunset picture, for example, you could have the model silhouetted against a rich-toned sky. Alternatively an object in the background could be used in a similar way: in a beach location, a palm tree could be juxtaposed against the sea or sky with the model in the foreground.

Even when a pure silhouette is not used, a dramatic quality can be created by ensuring that there is a bold tonal or color contrast between the element of shape you wish to emphasize and the background. A red windsurf sail against a blue sky, for instance, or a dark brown, tanned torso against a white sand beach. The main way in which this quality can be emphasized is by the choice of viewpoint, as it is this which controls the juxtaposition of foreground features against more distant details. Both low and high viewpoints can also be used effectively: a low viewpoint enables you to use the sky as a background providing a plain, contrasting tone for the subject.

Line is a similarly dominant element in many pictures and can be created in a variety of ways. In the same way that shape is emphasized, line can be created where areas of bold tone, color or detail meet. In a landscape or seascape, for example, the horizon is invariably a powerful feature of the composition and can dictate the way in which the subject is positioned as well as the choice of viewpoint and the framing of the image. The existence and nature of the dominant lines in an image can also help to establish

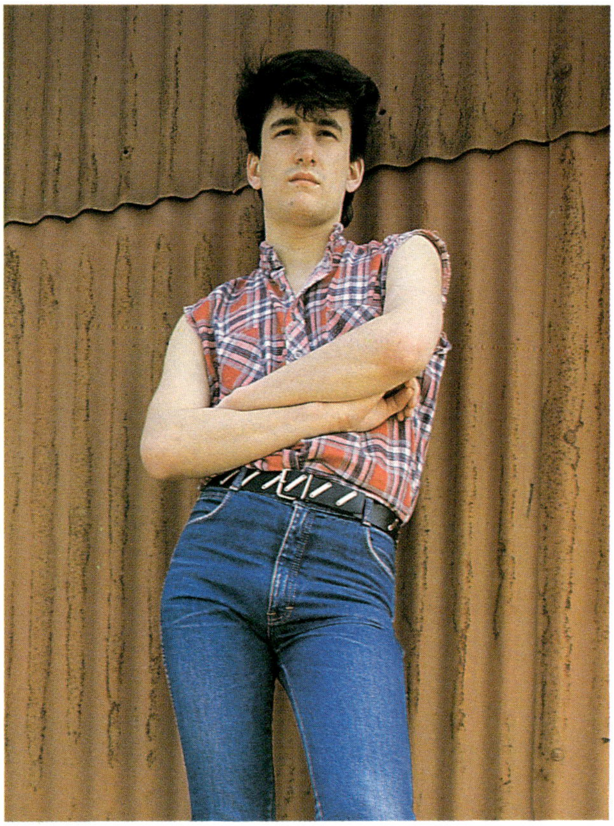

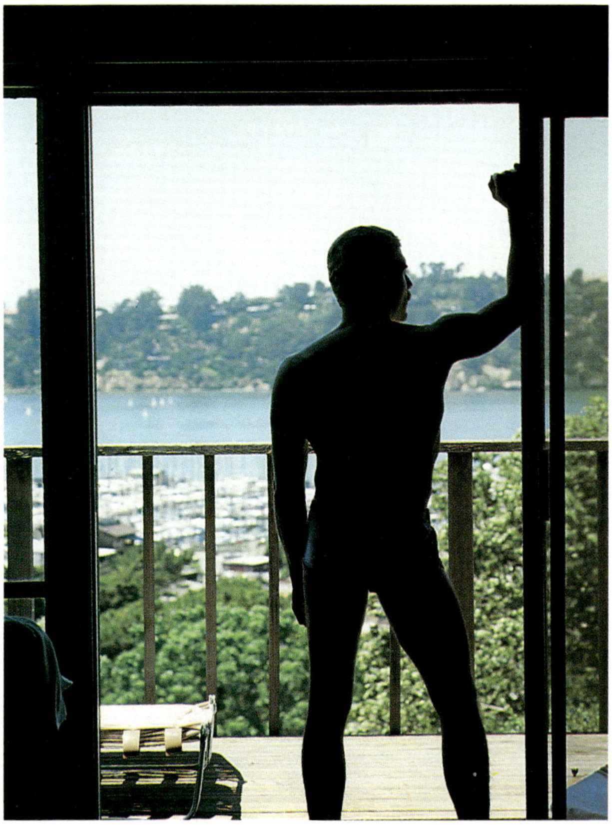

Look for repeated shapes that provide rhythmic backgrounds for your pictures **(top left)**. *Silhouettes work best when the model's pose makes a graphic shape against a brighter background* **(right)**. *Use line to lead the eye* **(top right)**: *here the model's gaze, the horizon and the shore all converge to a single point. Shadows* **(far right)** *help break up otherwise featureless areas of background with bold patterns.*

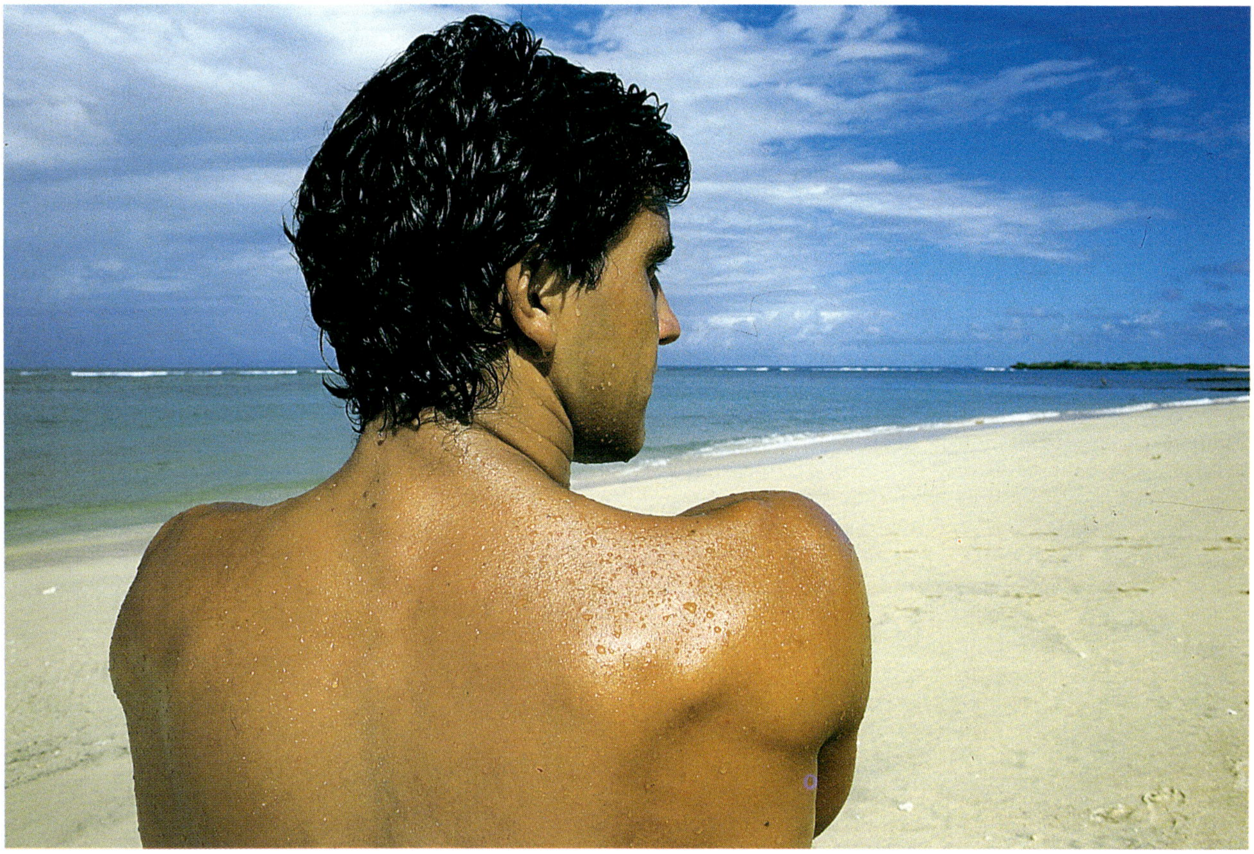

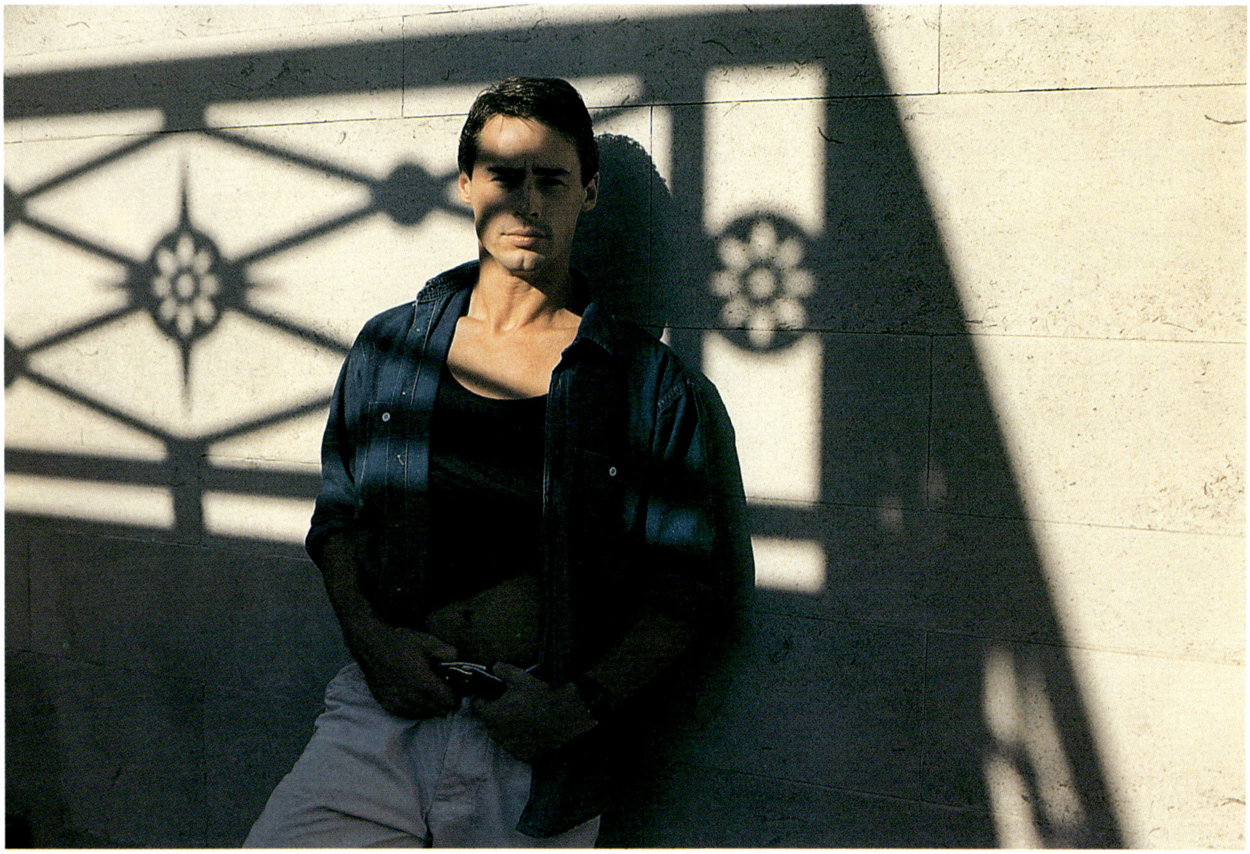

the mood and effect of a picture. In a setting such as a seascape, where the lines are primarily horizontal or essentially parallel, the mood will be quiet and harmonious, but when a strong line is introduced at an opposing angle, the effect will be to create a bold and more assertive quality.

Lines can also be created by the effects of perspective. When objects of a similar size recede from the camera, they appear to become progressively smaller. This, in turn, can create the impression of lines within the image and it can be used as a powerful force in the composition of the photograph. Choice of viewpoint is an important factor in emphasizing this quality. It is most effective when the camera is positioned and the image is framed to include objects or details in the foreground. The effect can be further accentuated by using a wide-angle lens.

In photographic terms, pattern is an effect which is created when similar shapes or lines are repeated within the image. Even if the similarity is only implied the effect can be strong. The effect does not necessarily have to even rely on the shape of an object or detail, it can often be produced simply by the presence of similarly-shaped highlights or shadows, like the ripples on the surface of water. The presence of a pattern in a picture can introduce a strong sense of harmony and balance, giving an image a cohesive, and sometimes almost mesmeric, quality. It can actually be too dominant unless used as an integral part of the overall composition.

One of the ways it can be used effectively in male photography is to provide an element of interest and contrast in the background. By using this repetitive and harmonious series of shapes, the model, positioned in front, will in effect break the pattern and in doing so become the focus of attention. Imagine, for example, a swimwear picture with the model lying on rippled, tide-swept sand, or a fashion shot with the model posed against a stack of crates or a row of railings. You must be careful that such pictures do not become too busy and distracting and if the background contains an element of pattern, it is essential that the model is wearing quite plain or boldly-contrasting clothes.

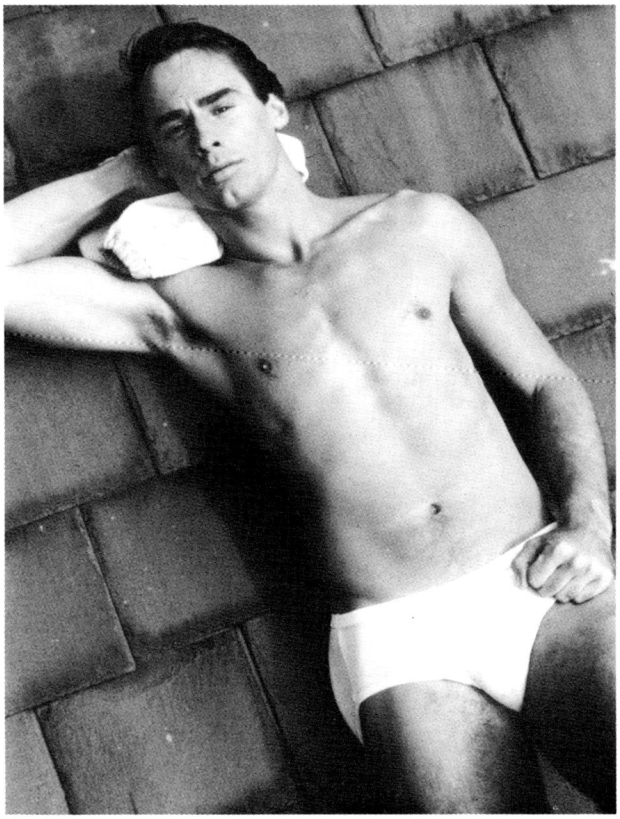

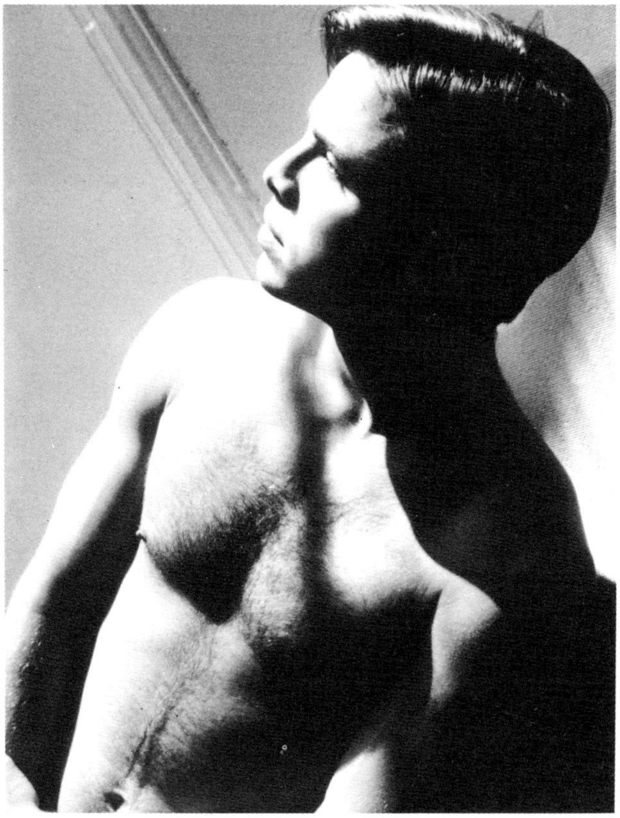

Rooftops **(top right and opposite)** *are good sources of heavily textured and strongly linear locations in which to set the male figure. Diagonal lines* **(near right)** *give images an air of dynamism and activity.*

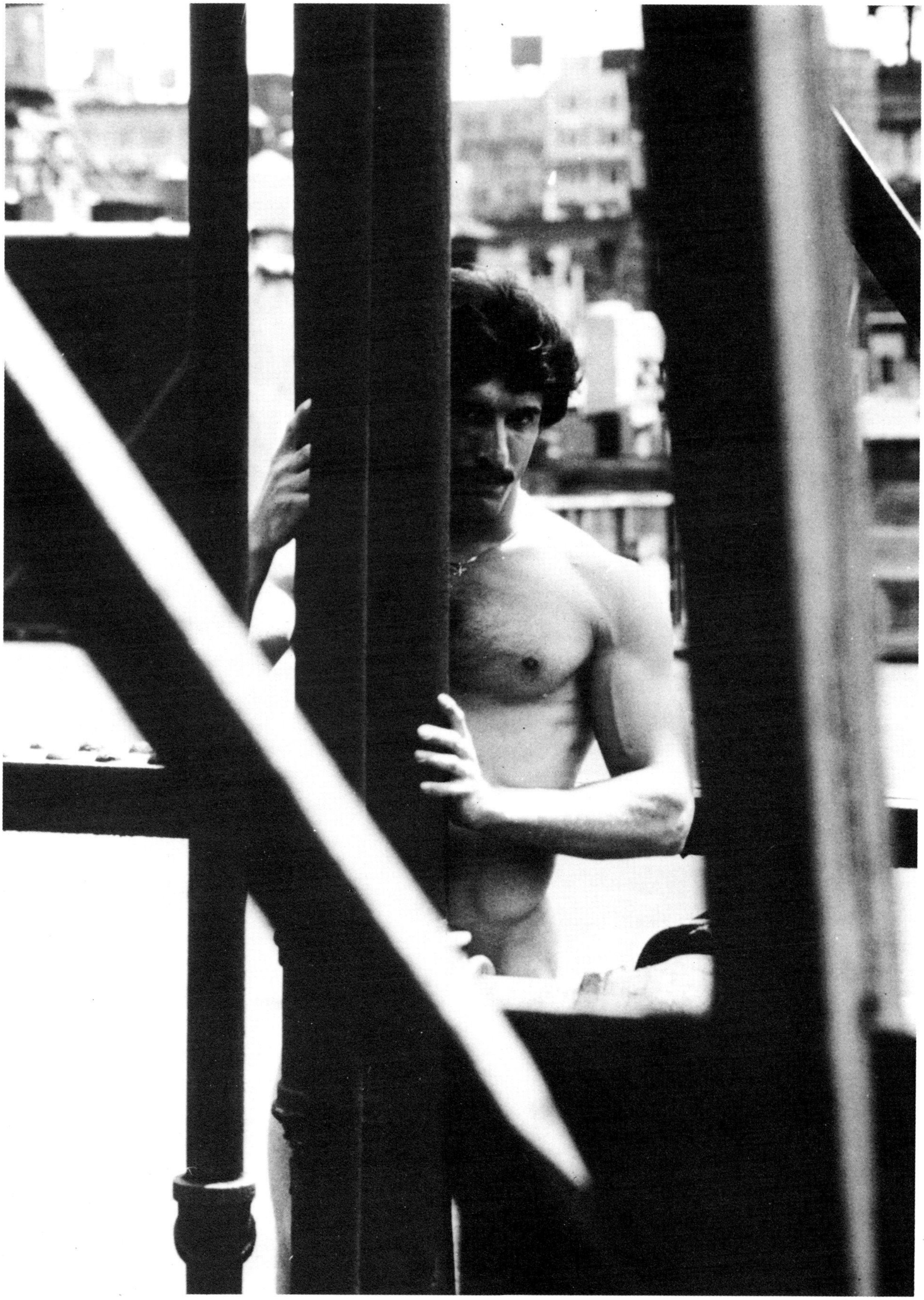

EMPHASIZING FORM, TEXTURE AND DEPTH

Whilst the visual elements of shape, line and pattern are responsible for creating the basic framework of the image, it is the qualities of form, texture and depth which gives it flesh. They are the elements which create the illusion of a solid, three-dimensional object on the flat surface of a print or transparency.

In portrait and nude photography, form is a crucial element as it is responsible for describing the features of a face or body. It is largely dependent on lighting since the impression of form is created by the subtle range of tones created within the outline of the subject. Using a portrait as an example, if you imagine a man's face lit by a single light close to the camera, it will create very little shadow or tone within its outline, resulting in a flat image. As the light is moved further to the side, the shadows will become progressively larger and more pronounced, and this will make the face appear more solid, giving it form as well as shape.

It is not only the angle and direction of the light which needs to be considered, the quality of the light source is also an important factor. A hard light, one in which the light from the sun or a bulb reaches the subject directly, will create a sudden transition from highlight to shadow, the shadows will be both dense and sharply defined and the range of tones quite small. A softer light, which is either diffused or reflected from a white surface, or which comes from the sun diffused by cloud, will create a more gradual transition from highlight to shadow and the range of tones will be greater.

It is this latter quality which creates the strongest impression of form in an image, and whether you are shooting pictures indoors with artificial lighting or outdoors by sunlight, you must be aware of how the lighting affects the tonal gradation of the image and how this can be controlled to emphasize the impression of form.

Texture is, in a sense, form on a smaller scale. It establishes the nature of a surface. Indeed it can be a powerful visual quality in a photograph as it allows us to sense how the subject might feel as well as how it appears visually. The same factors which establish the impression of form also control texture: it is in the nature of the transition of tone from highlight to shadow. However, since texture is usually a much more subtle type of form it requires a rather more directional light and sometimes a harder light than would be needed to emphasize form. Skin for example needs lighting which literally just skims along its surface to reveal its subtle qualities.

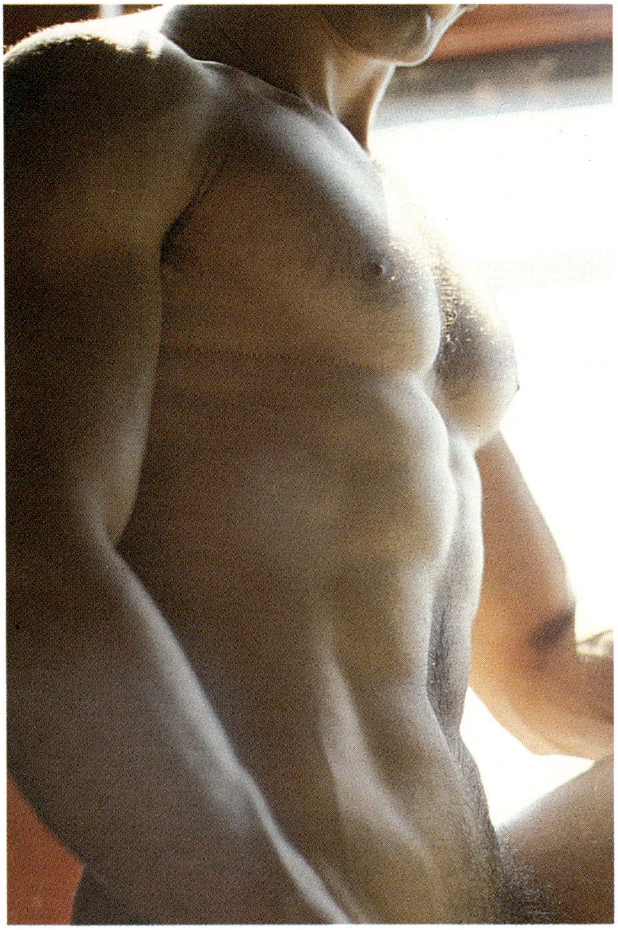

A model's pose profoundly influences the appearance of form and depth: pick postures that demand muscular tension **(above)**.

Sand **(opposite top)** *has a tactile quality that is compelling even in a photograph. Make sure, though, that the sand contrasts clearly with the model's skin, and stop the len well down so that every grain is sharp. Splashing water also looks good on film, particularly when softened to a smooth flow by a slow shutter speed. When emphasizing the forms of muscle and the texture of skin, pick a model without a trace of excess weight – the camera always make the body look heavier* **(far right)**.

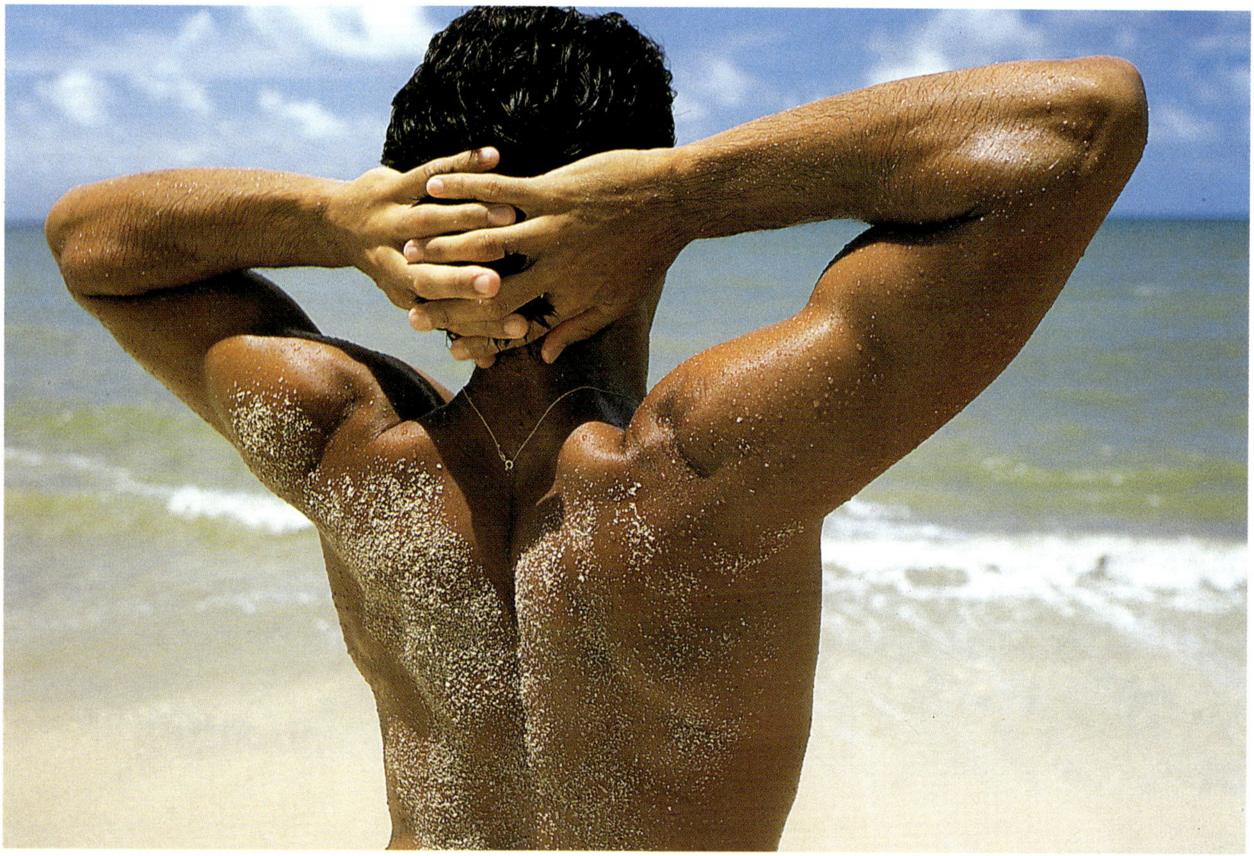

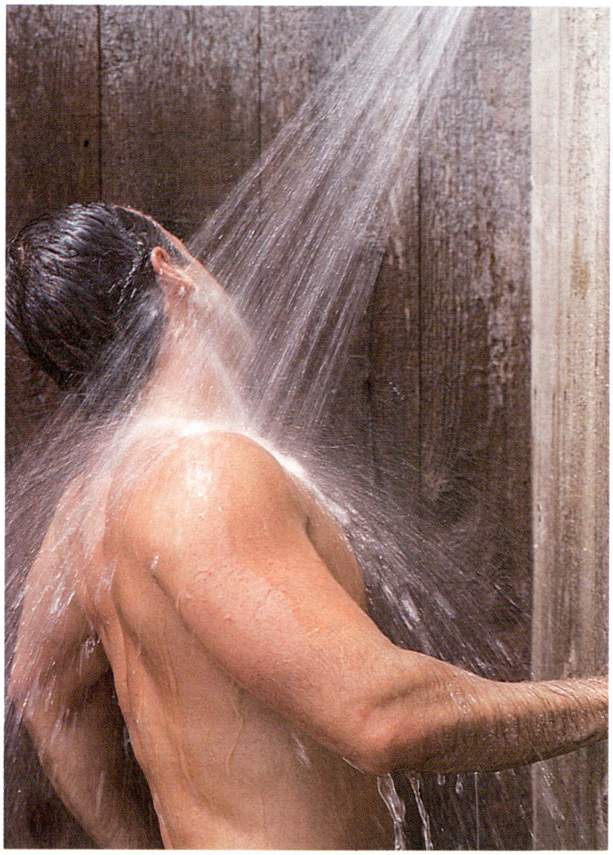

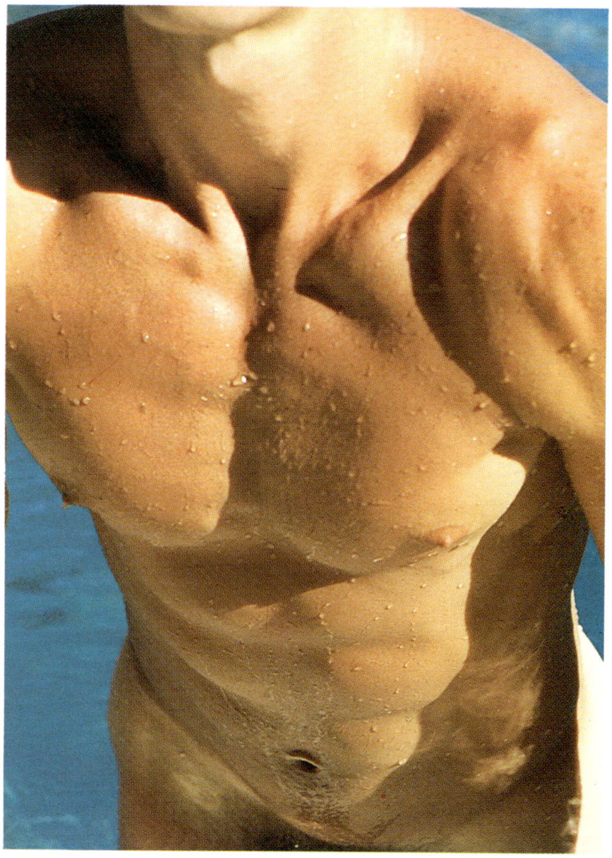

There is yet another factor which controls the impression of texture. Because the photographic process has an almost uncanny ability to recreate the tactile quality of different surfaces, it can often be heightened by juxtaposing one texture against another: sackcloth against silk for example. In male photography, skin texture can be a particularly crucial element in a photograph and the juxtaposition of skin against other contrasting textures is usually an effective way of creating bold, and visually strong, images. Imagine, for instance, the effect of water on skin, or skin against leather or sand. These images can be very powerful and the photographic quality can result in stunning prints and transparencies.

Image quality is also a vital factor in creating the impression of texture. The picture must be critically sharp – a slow fine grained film can be an advantage here – and exposure must be accurately assessed. As a general rule, a degree of underexposure will accentuate the quality of texture, whereas overexposure will reduce its effect.

Depth is a quality which can be emphasized in a variety of ways. Form, for example, also creates an impression of depth in a subject like a portrait or a nude. On a larger scale, in a subject like a landscape or similar, it is usually perspective which creates the impression of depth in an image. Perspective is created by the way objects appear to diminish in size the further they are from a particular viewpoint. A distant building can appear to be much smaller than a model standing close to the camera. This effect is heightened when both close, and distant, objects are included in the field of view, and for this reason, one of the most effective ways of emphasizing the impression of depth is to include foreground details in the picture.

The choice of lens will also affect the impression of perspective. A wide-angle lens will allow you to include both very close foreground details in the picture as well as distant objects, and this will exaggerate both the effect of perspective and the impression of depth compared to that of a standard lens. A telephoto lens will tend to exclude close foreground details and diminish the impression of depth and perspective.

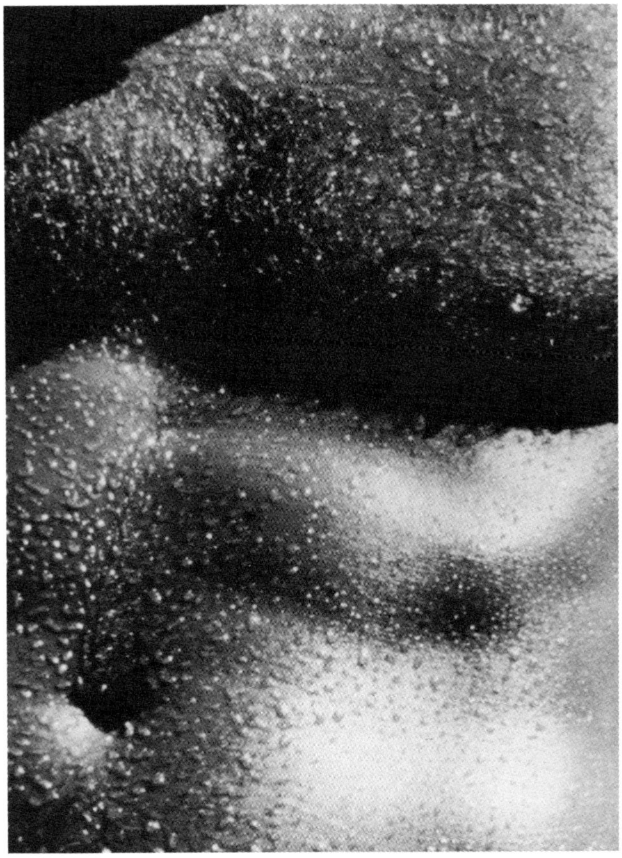

Water **(above)** *always helps bring out skin texture. The tiny droplets reflect sparkling highlights, and the water's cooling effect adds skin tone.*

Lighting direction is the principal control on the way that the form of the male body appears on film. In these three examples **(opposite page)** *raking sunlight glances across the model's body, creating the characteristic patterns of light and shade that suggest form, volume and depth.*

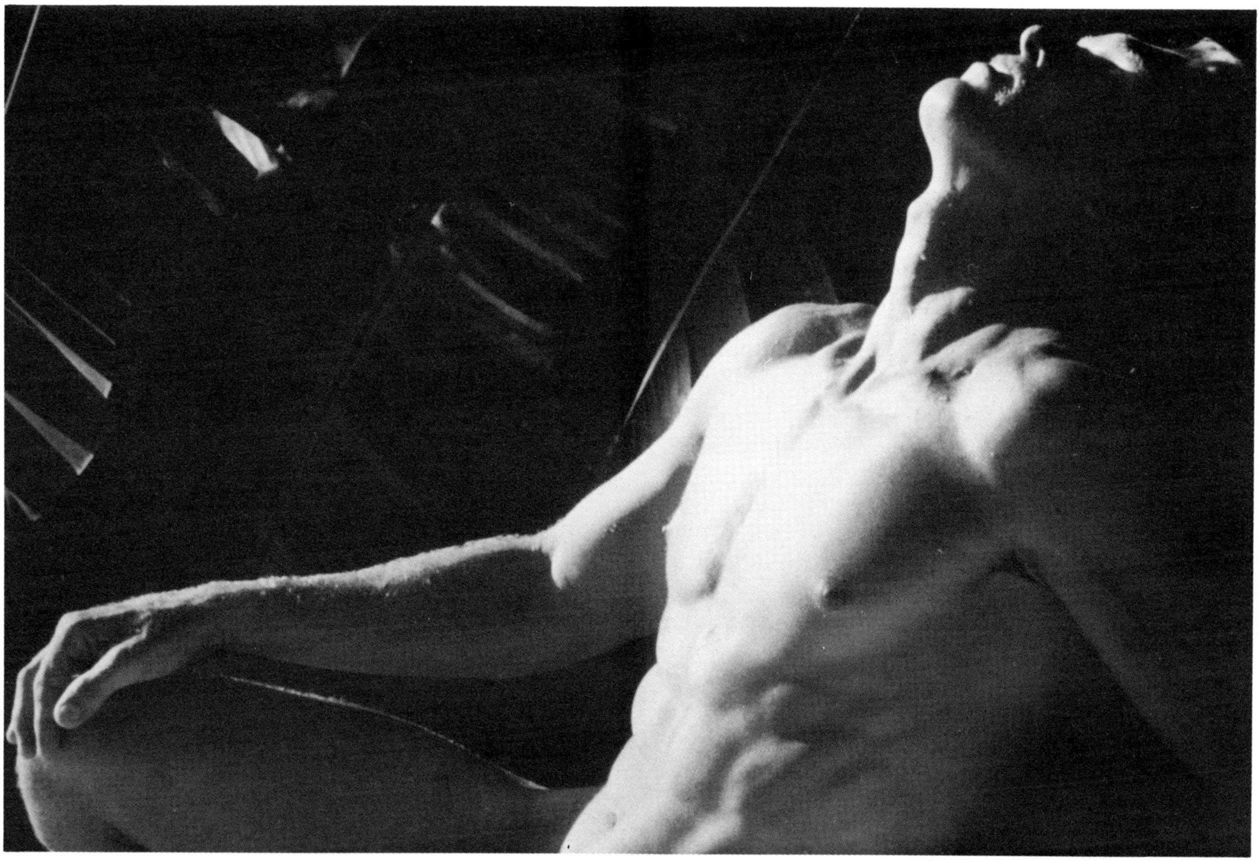

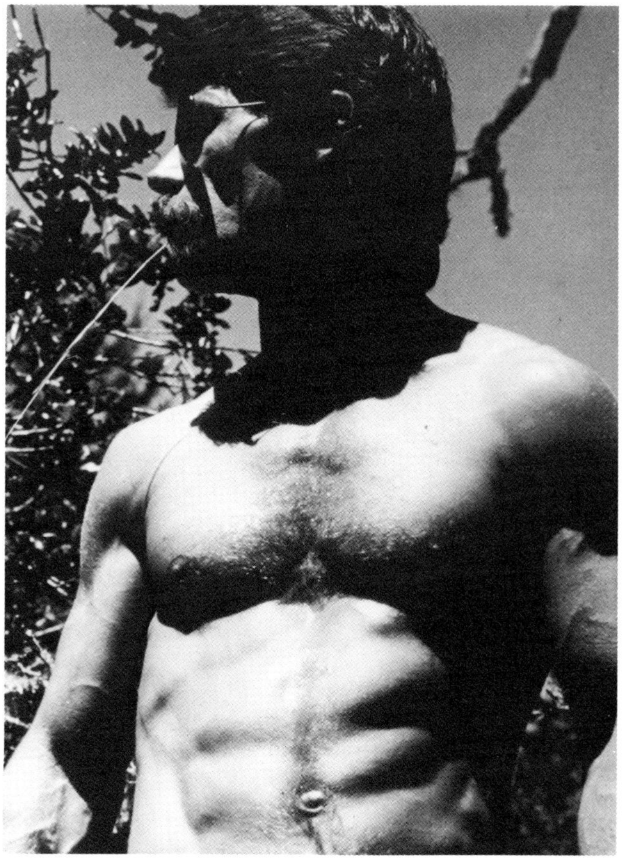

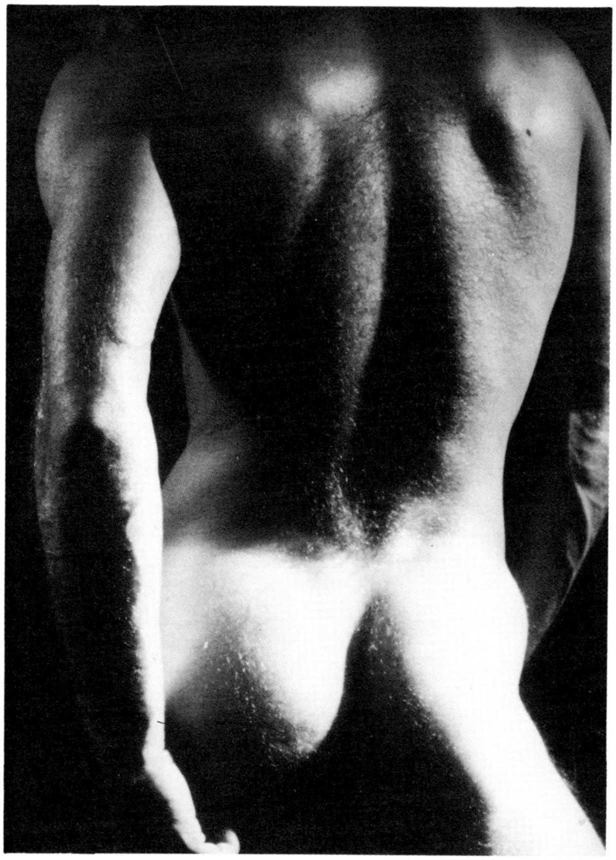

USING COLOR EFFECTIVELY

When shooting in color, color itself can be the most dominant visual element, and if this aspect of the subject is not given the same thought and care as the other elements of the image, the composition can be completely unbalanced. For this reason it is vital to be aware of each individual color within the field of view and also how each reacts with the others.

Color essentially have two different effects which can be used in an image: they either contrast with each other or they harmonize. Contrasting colors are created when they come from different sections of the spectrum. The further they are apart on the spectrum band, the stronger the contrast. Red and blue, for instance, create a bold contrast. Contrast will also be created when a bright color is opposed against a neutral tone such as black or white. In addition, fully-saturated colors will create a stronger contrast than weak or pastel colors.

The effect of bright, contrasting colors will be much greater and easier to control when they are limited to just two or possibly three hues. The most effective and dramatic use of color is seen when the subject contains a single, bold color which creates a contrast against an essentially monochromatic background or setting: a man in a red shirt against a blue sky. When there is a mixture of many different hues in a subject, the result can easily be confusing and distracting, no matter how well the picture has been composed in other respects.

Color harmony is created when the hues within the image come from a similar area of the spectrum such as green and blue. This is much easier to control and is less likely to overwhelm or disturb other aspects of the composition. Harmonious color is also more likely to be created when the hues are essentially weak or desaturated. In this case it is possible to combine a variety of different hues more successfully than when they are bold and fully saturated. Whereas contrasting colors evoke a lively and assertive quality in a picture, harmonious color quality tends to create a more peaceful and restful mood.

One of the most effective ways of using color is, in fact, to be sparing with it. Pictures that are almost virtually monochromatic, like a sunset scene or the soft blue cast that is created at dusk, can create effective and evocative images. In addition, it is also possible to use very small, bold areas of color within an otherwise contrasting or neutral setting to create maximum emphasis. Imagine the effect of a man in a blue shirt against a background of blue sea but wearing a bright red scarf.

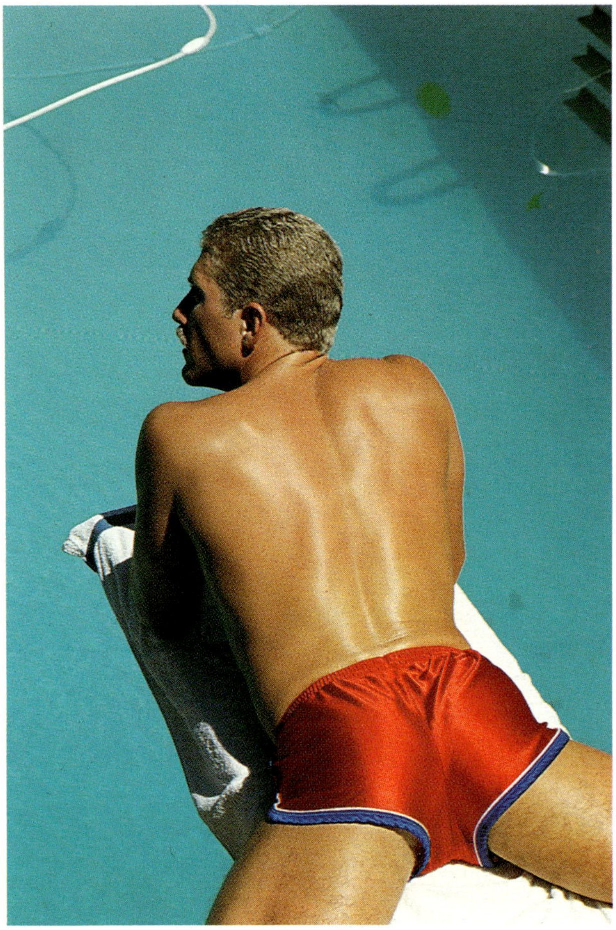

Red is most useful as a color accent, as in this picture. In large areas, red can be overpowering.

In the shade **(opposite, top)** *light from blue sky often creates a blue color cast. To record the subject in his true colors, use an 81A filter. For a richly saturated blue background, just tilt the camera up and frame the model against the sky* **(near right)**. *Look out for complementary color combinations, such as the yellow trunks and blue sky in the picture at far right.*

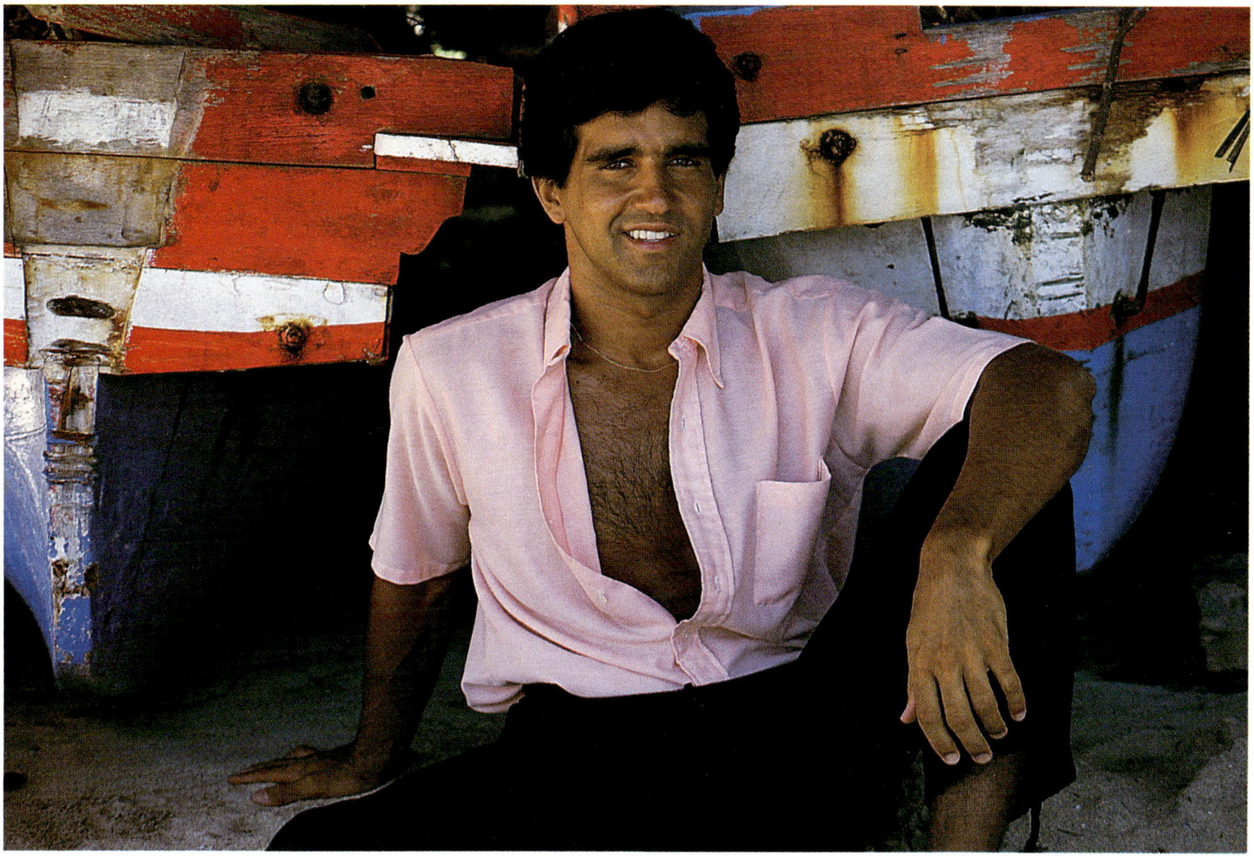

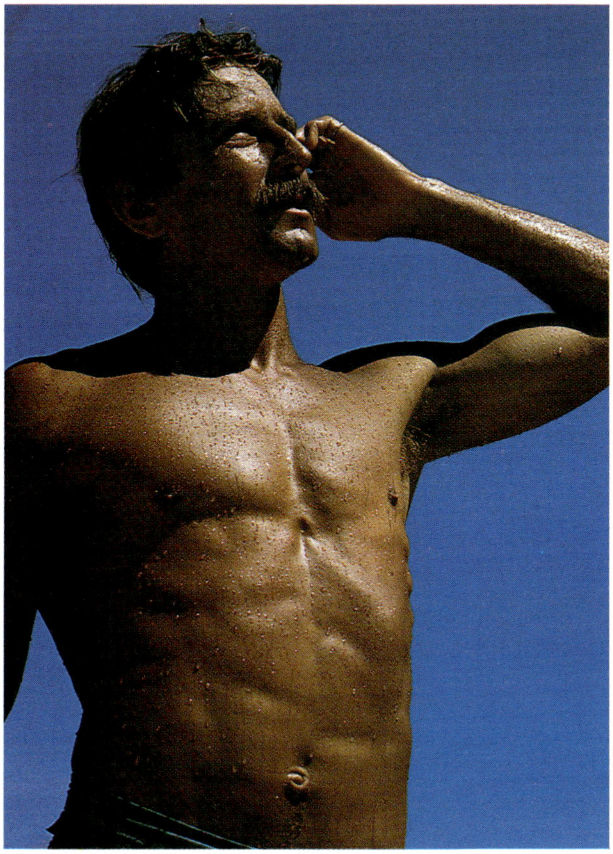

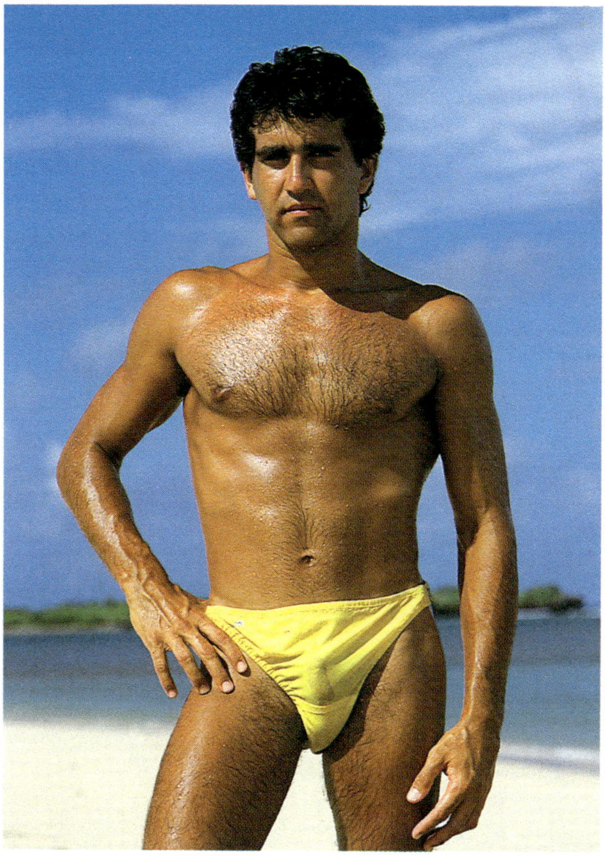

CREATING EMPHASIS THROUGH COMPOSITION

Composition is simply a term which is used to describe the way the visual elements of an image are arranged within the frame. In most cases this is done so that the viewer is unaware of any artifice, although there are circumstances in which it can be effective to draw deliberate attention to the subject in a more obvious, even 'clever' way. Sometimes this can be used to add impact to a picture where it is otherwise lacking.

Perhaps the most basic way of achieving this is to create a calculatedly bold contrast between subject and background. When shooting in color, you might select clothes and props to produce a violent clash or contrast to the background you are using. A similar effect can be created by juxtaposing opposing textures, patterns or shapes between subject and background, but remember that for this type of picture subtlety can be a negative factor. An unusual or ambiguous background or setting can be used in the same way.

Another method is to frame your composition so that the subject is placed in an unexpected part of the picture: almost at the top or bottom, for example, or right into one corner. Obviously this must be done in a way that retains a balance between the subject and the other elements of the picture, otherwise the result will simply be unattractive. Framing the image so that the subject or the background is cropped in an unfamiliar or surprising way can also be effective. Even tilting the camera so that vertical or horizontal lines are placed at an angle to the edges of the frame works well in some situations.

Exaggerated perspective is another method of creating impact: the deliberate use of a wide-angle lens to distort the appearance of the model or the setting can create bold and dramatic effects if handled in a controlled and considered way. The effect which is created when the camera is tilted upwards from a low viewpoint can produce quite stunning images when exaggerated with a wide-angle lens. In a similar way, a telephoto lens can be used to deliberately compress the effect of perspective and create images with a more graphic, two dimensional quality.

The choice of unusual viewpoints is also a useful means of drawing attention to the subject and of adding impact to the picture. Most photographs are taken from eye-level and the effect of using a low or significantly higher viewpoint, can have a surprising effect on the visual quality and mood of an image.

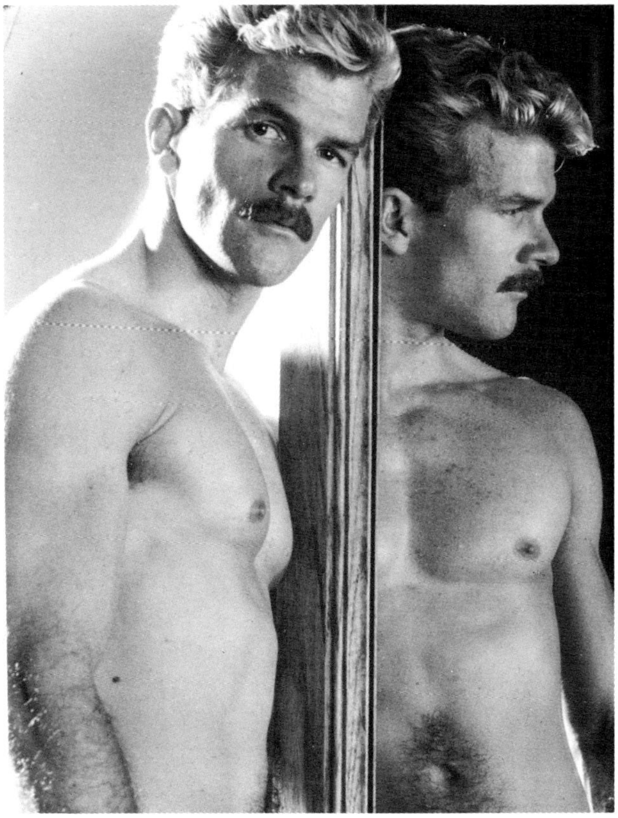

Reflections **(top)** *give the viewer two glances at the subject. Don't always try to fill the frame: contrasted with large plain areas, a small figure always catches the eye* **(right)**.

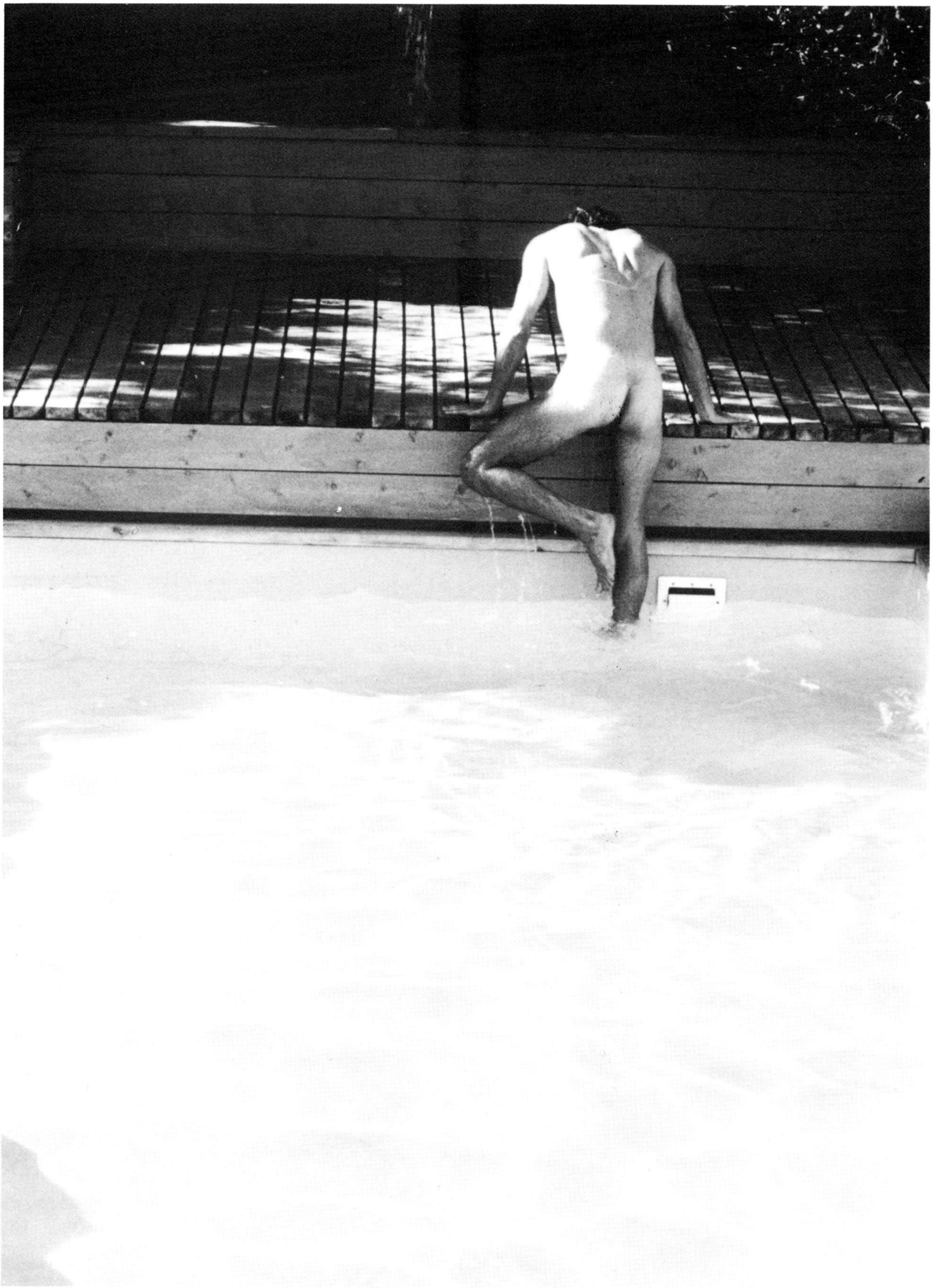

CREATING MOOD

Mood is a quality that can be difficult to define. Some pictures have it, others don't, and the factors that create it can be varied and sometimes elusive. It can be produced by things over which you have little control, such as a gesture or expression. In these circumstances, it is necessary to simply recognize it when it appears and to react quickly to record it. However, there are certain elements in an image which can be used and emphasized to evoke a particular mood or to create atmosphere in a photograph.

Because mood is largely a product of the imagination, it is less likely to be created in a picture that is boldly illuminated with every detail clearly defined. As a general rule, mood is something which is produced in the mind by the things that are implied rather than by those that are openly revealed. For this reason, lighting can be a vital factor since it can be used in a subtle way to allow glimpses of the subject with other details hidden in shadow or bathed in misty highlights. A low-key picture, comprised primarily of the darker tones, can be used to evoke a sombre or mysterious mood; in the opposite way, a high-key picture, with soft light tones, can be used to create a more peaceful or even romantic quality.

Focus too can be used to mask some of the detail in the picture and to leave more to the viewer's imagination. Using a telephoto lens or a wide aperture can enable you to focus sharply on the model but to throw more distant details of the setting or background out of focus. You can even use this effect by focusing on one feature of the model – his hands for instance – and to allow other details, like his face or body, to remain unsharp. Soft focus attachments can also be used to create mood and to mask detail. In addition to manufactured devices, it is also possible to create interesting effects with adhesive tape, petroleum jelly and gauze.

Color too can be an important element of mood. Individual hues have 'mood values' and if a picture is composed so that a particular color has a dominant effect, it will impart that mood to the image. Red, yellow and orange tend to create a bright, lively and often quite aggressive mood in a picture, while green and blue have a more restful peaceful quality. The darker hues of brown and purple tend to produce a more sombre or dramatic atmosphere.

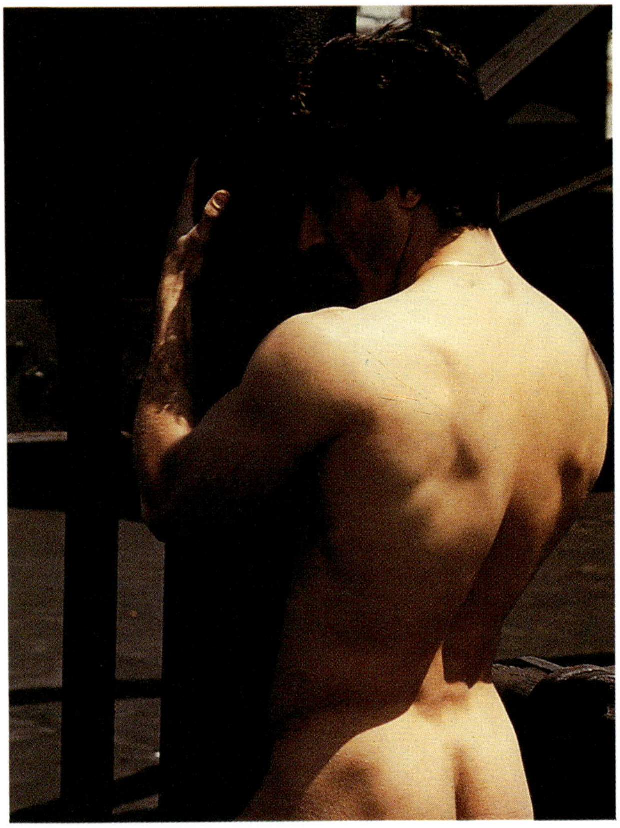

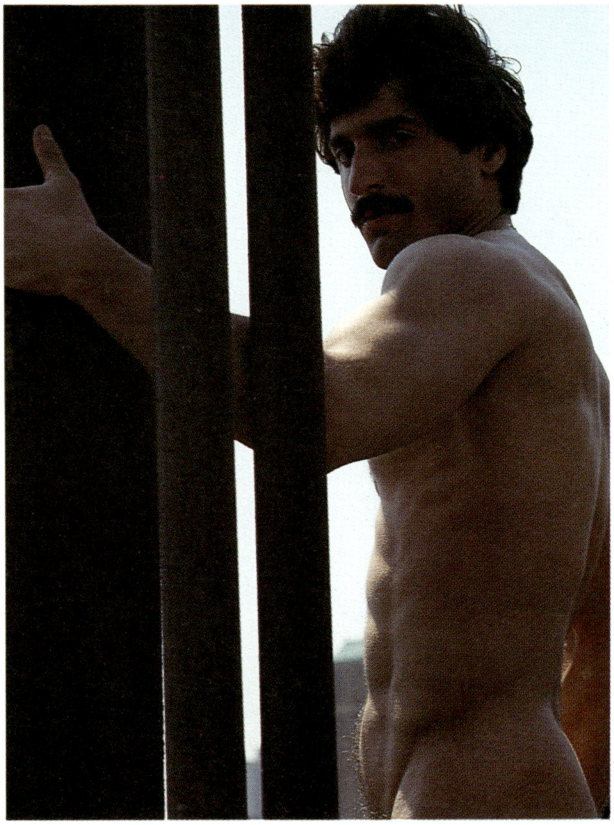

The most moody, evocative pictures are those that seem to seize a fleeting moment in time, such as the last rays of summer sunlight as the sun sinks over the horizon.

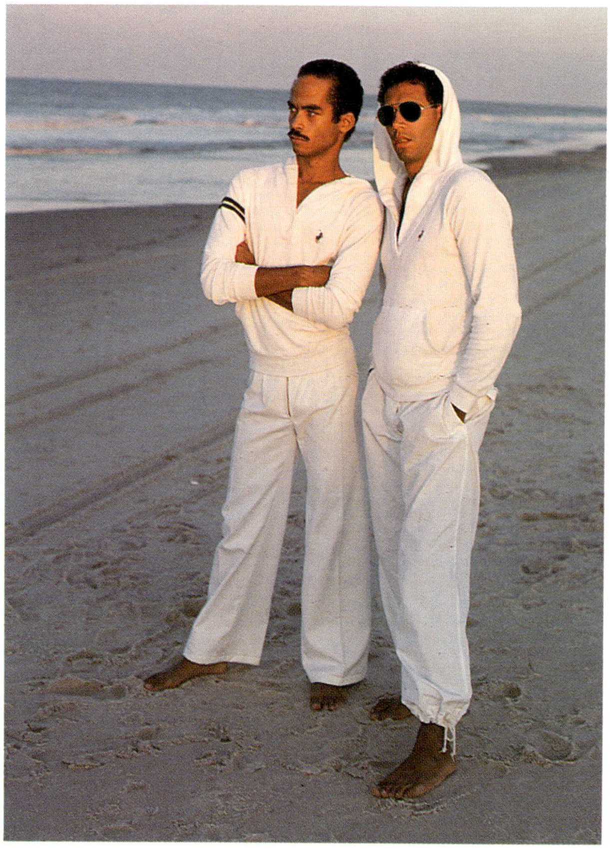

These two pictures, taken within minutes of each other, illustrate how small factors combine to make one image moody and brooding, while another similar one lacks atmosphere. In the upper picture **(opposite)**, *the model's face is turned away from the camera, shadows virtually hide his expression, and skin color is enhanced by the warm sunlight. The lower photograph is much cooler in color balance, and the model's face visible, so that mysterious mood of the upper image is dissipated.*

Shooting against the light **(below)** *emphasizes the translucent quality of clothes and props, giving the picture a light and airy mood.*

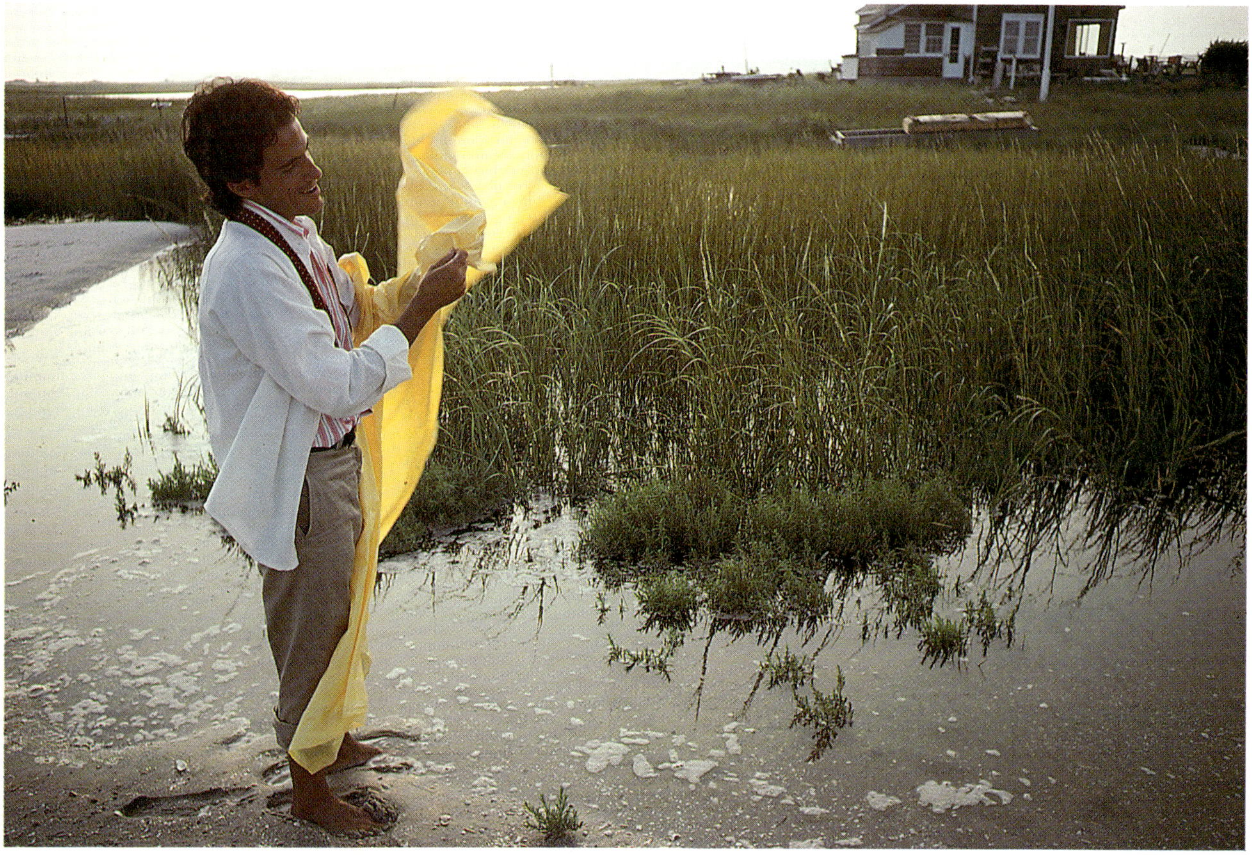

SHOOTING IN BLACK AND WHITE

Black and white photography requires a different approach than color work. Even experienced workers often find it difficult to shoot in both color and black and white during the same session. Just as it is vital to be aware of the color content of the subject when you are shooting in color, so black and white photography means that you must virtually ignore it and instead consider the image in terms of its tonal values alone.

A good example of how the color content of an image can be quite different in black and white terms can be given by imagining a situation where you have, for instance, a man wearing say a blue shirt with red trousers standing in front of a green tree. Viewed in color, this would create a bold and contrasty image. In black and white, the blue shirt, red trousers and green tree would all record as a similar tone of mid grey and the result would be flat and dull. If, however, he was wearing a pale blue shirt and a deep red pair of trousers, the picture would have more contrast and interest. In short, it is the variety of tone in the details and objects within the image that is important, not just the color.

The lighting too will affect this, since even with a subject of similar tones, light creates shadows and highlights which will introduce a much wider range of tones into the image. A man in a grey suit standing in front of a grey background would, if lit from the front with no shadows or highlights, appear flat and dull, but if the lighting was directed from one side, it would create both shadows and highlights, creating an image with a full range of tones from black and white.

Filters can be used to control the response of the film to individual colors and this, in turn, affects the tonal range and contrast of the image. A color filter passes light of its own color freely but holds back opposite or complementary colors. The complementary color of red is a mixture of green and blue called cyan, the complementary color to green is a mixture of red and blue called magenta; yellow, a mixture of red and green, is complementary to blue. In this way, a red filter can, for instance, be used to make greens and blues appear as a darker tone than they actually are and similarly a green filter will make reds and blues appear darker. A blue filter will create a darker tone where green and red is present.

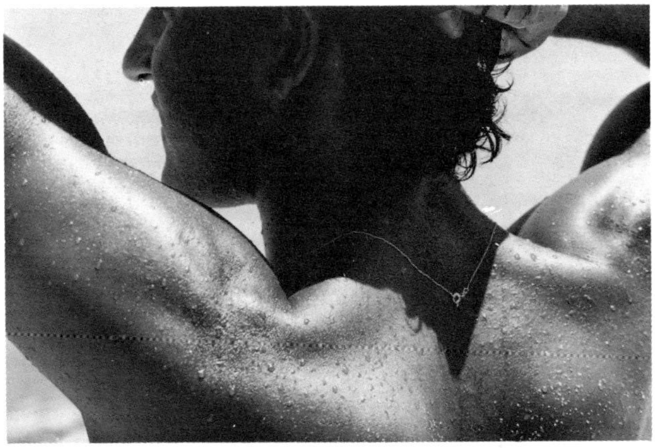

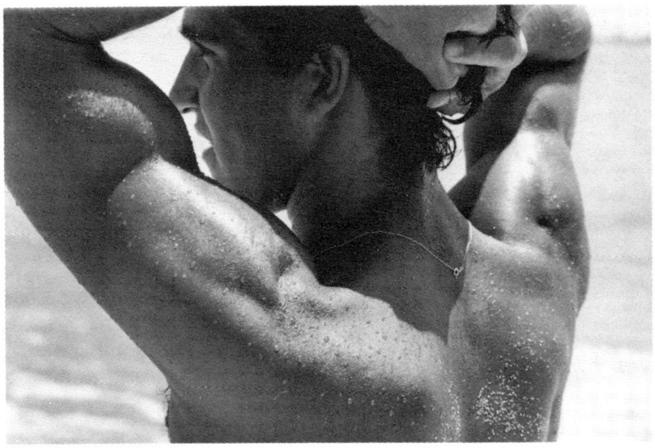

Black and white film offers the creative photographer of the male unrivalled control. The top image of these two was printed on hard, contrasty, paper, and as a result the model's face (and personality) are concealed. Printed on normal paper, much more detail is visible, and the picture becomes a portrait in the conventional sense.

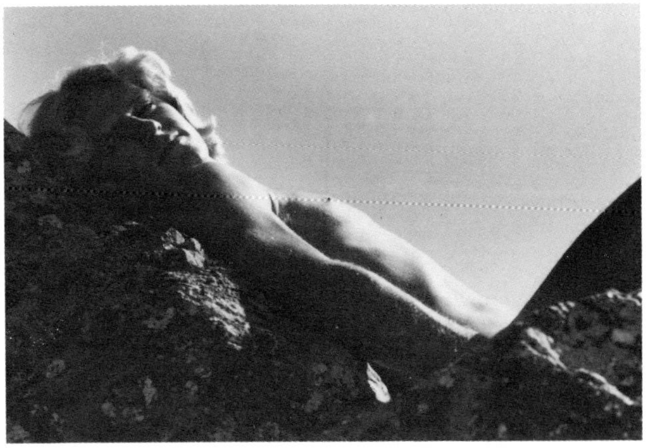

Taking pictures in black and white means thinking in terms of tone, and ignoring hue.

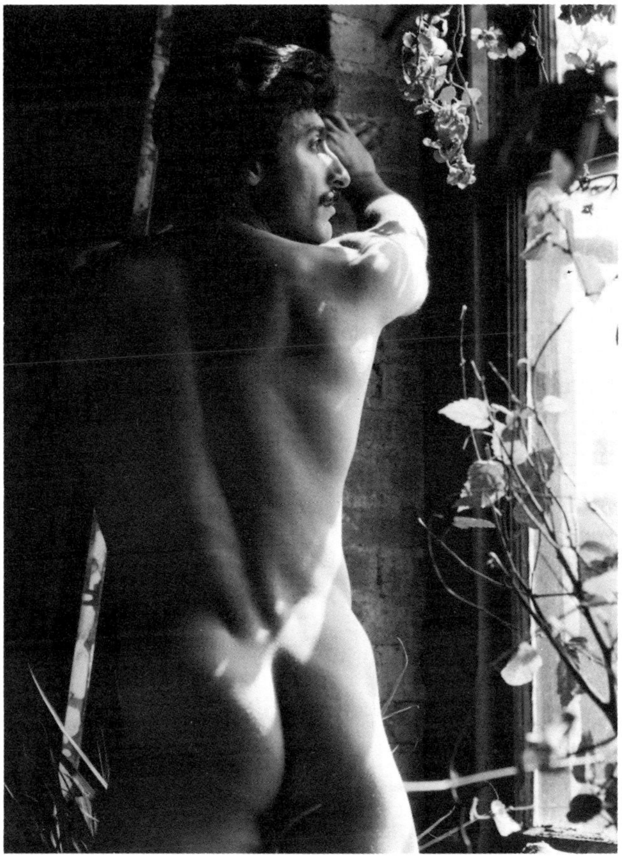

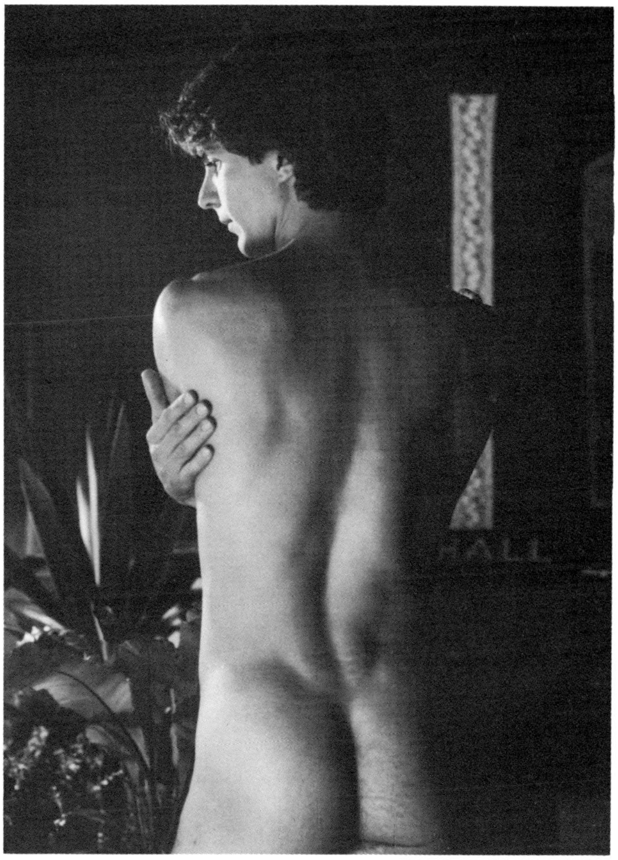

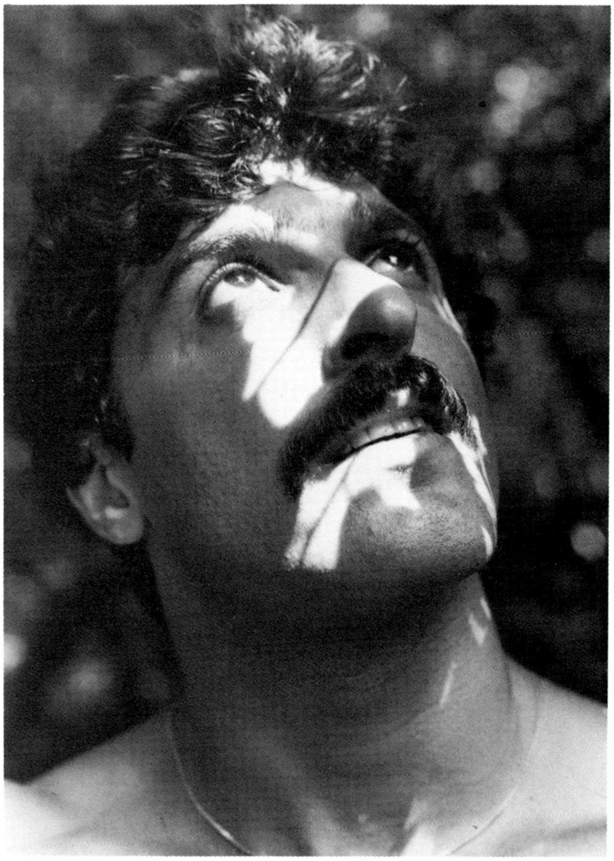

Black and white film has an enormous exposure latitude and will accommodate a far wider range of subject brightnesses than will color film **(above and right)**. *Indoors, black and white film can be used with impunity, without worry about color casts and filters* **(top right)**.

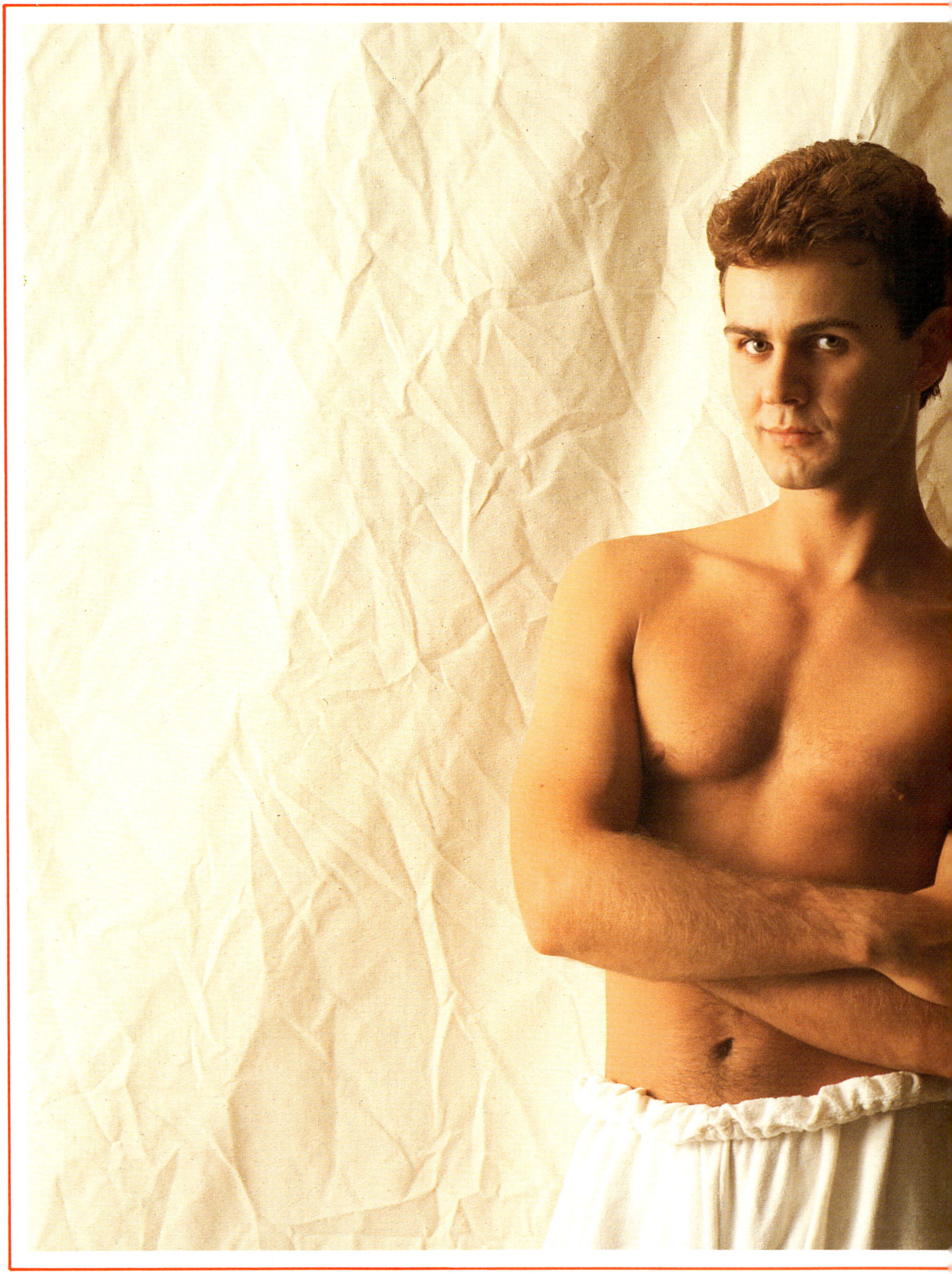

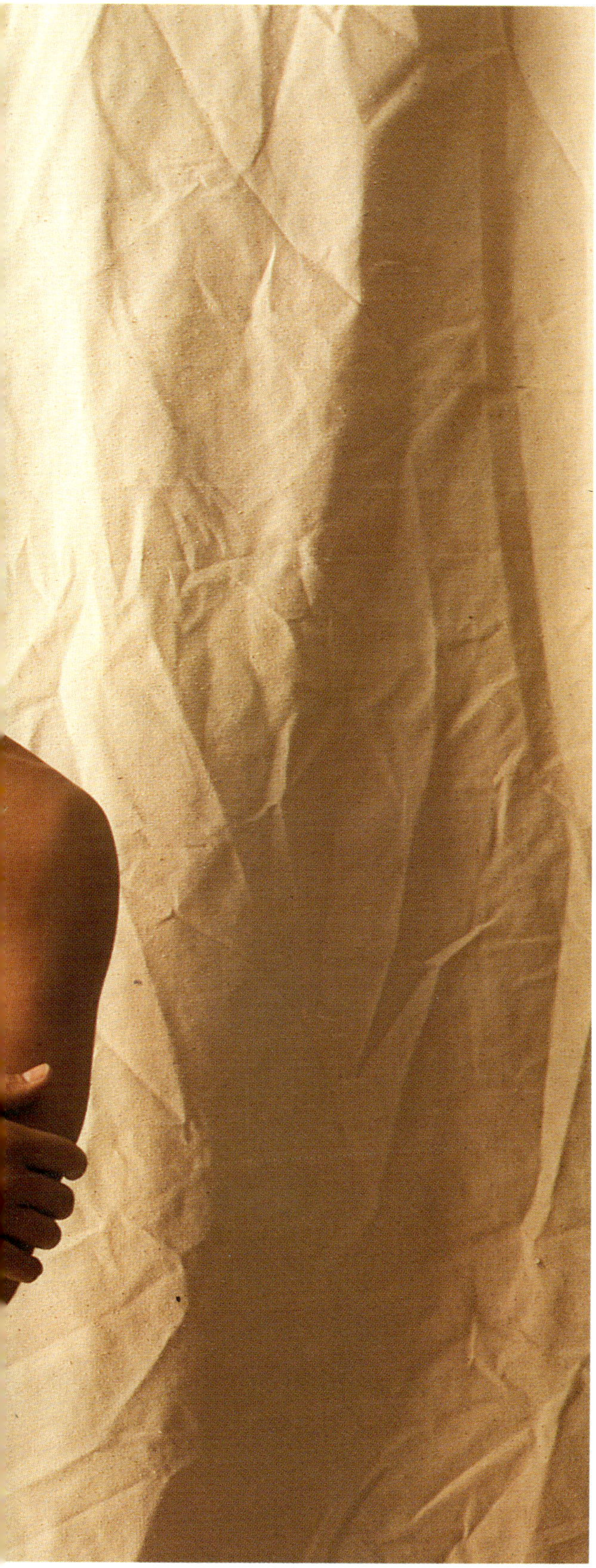

STUDIO TECHNIQUES

SETTING UP A MAKE-SHIFT STUDIO

Although outdoor locations and daylight indoor photography can be very satisfactory for portrait and fashion work, the opportunity to have complete control over lighting can be achieved only in a studio with artificial lighting. A studio does not have to be expensive or complex, particularly if it is to be used on a casual, part-time basis. Providing you have a room of reasonable size that can be partly cleared of furniture, it will only need a modest investment in some lighting equipment to expand both the range and the style of your pictures considerably.

The larger the room available, the better, but it is possible to cope with a wide range of pictures in a quite modest space. For portraits, you will need about 6ft between your camera and the model and around 3ft between him and the background. Naturally, for three-quarter and full-length pictures, you will need substantially more than this, but remember that you can always increase the distance between the camera and the model by shooting from outside the room and through a doorway. The width of the room will also be significant since you will need to have sufficient space each side of the model to position lights.

The most inexpensive form of photographic lighting is Photofloods. These are similar to ordinary, domestic bulbs but overrun to give a higher light output at the cost of a much shorter life. They can be used in standard bulb holders and reflectors and fitted to inexpensive, tripod-style, lighting stands. A more efficient and expensive form of lighting is found in tungsten halogen lamps. These are similar to the lights used for video work and have the advantage of being both compact and easily portable. They can be obtained in kit form with three or four lights, stands, reflectors and accessories fitting into an outfit case. When smoothing in color, it is necessary to use artificial light film with both of these types of lighting. It is also possible to use a normal exposure meter, or one built into the camera, with tungsten light.

Flash has the advantage of giving a very brief exposure so that you need not be concerned about subject movement as the speed of the flash will freeze it. However, small flashguns are not ideal, since you have no way of judging their effect. The more powerful flash units, run from the power cord, are more suitable for studio work because they have built-in modelling lamps. These are tungsten bulbs, incorporated with the flash tube within the unit to provide a visual indication of the direction, quality and effect of the light. The actual exposure, however, is made solely by the flash. Exposure measurement with flash has to be made with the aid of a special meter. Electronic flash enables you to use daylight type film when shooting in color.

If your room has plain, painted walls, these can be used as a background for your pictures. If you want to vary the color and tone, you can do so by using rolls of cartridge paper pinned to the wall. These can be obtained from professional photographic dealers. Alternatively you can use fabric, so long as it is stretched to be completely crease-free, otherwise it can look unattractive.

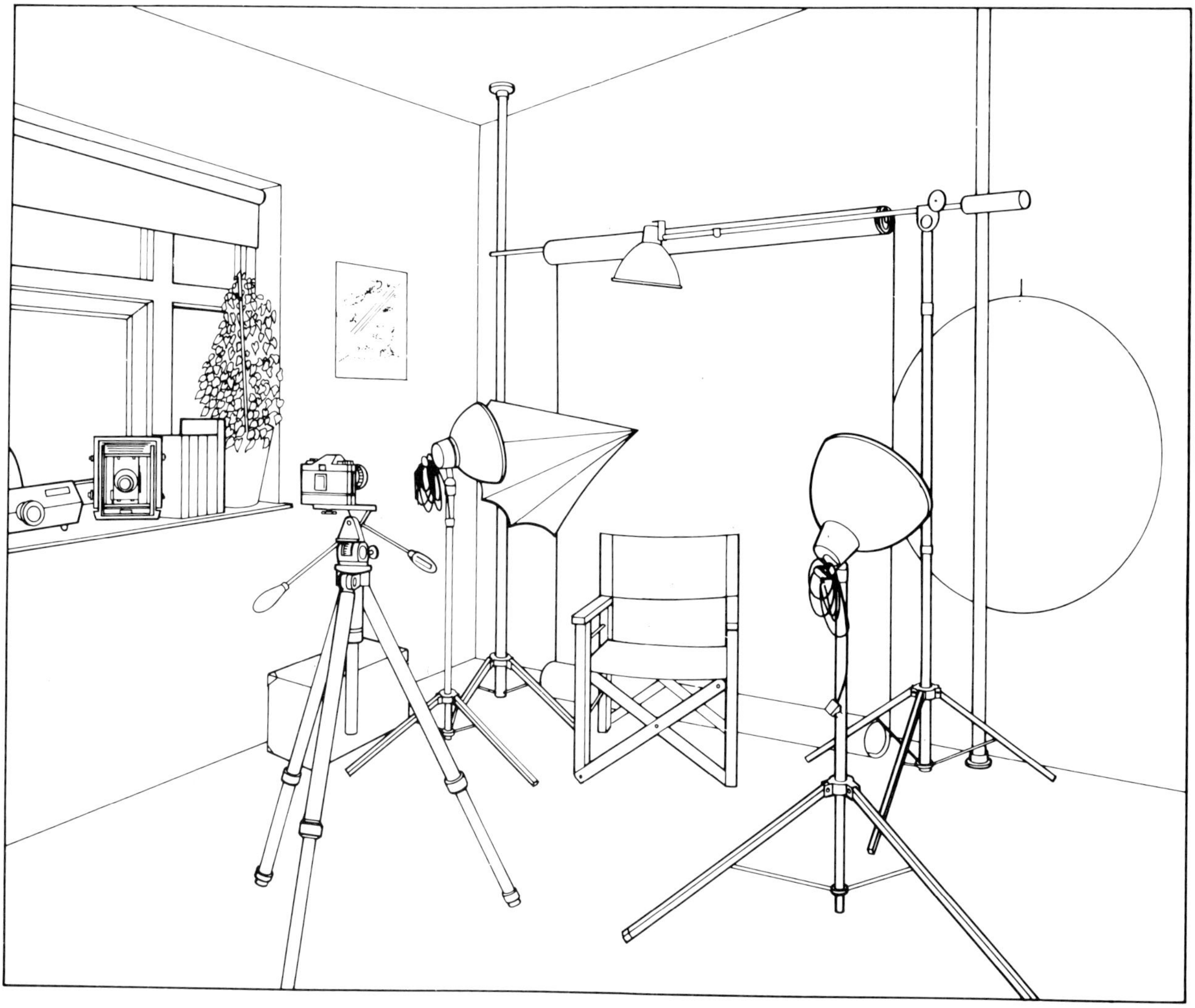

Equipping a home studio needn't cost a fortune. This one utilizes inexpensive tungsten lamps in simple reflectors. Telescopic alloy tubes support a roll of background paper; a circular reflector hangs on the wall behind.

A PERMANENT STUDIO

If you plan to carry out studio sessions frequently and have the space available, it is naturally more satisfactory to have a permanent facility. You will save a great deal of time in preparations and can arrange things so you have a comfortable and convenient working environment. The ideal space would be one in which you can shoot a full-length figure when using a standard lens. In some circumstances, it can even be an advantage to use a telephoto lens. Either way, it is worth setting up a trial shot in a proposed space before committing yourself to it.

If you are intending to use the professional cartridge paper background rolls, then you will also need at least 3ft each side of the 9ft paper width in order to position your lighting, making a minimum of 15ft studio width. Ceiling height can also be an important factor, especially for full-length pictures, since a 6ft model placed a couple of yards in front of the background, will need at least a 9ft high background to clear his head with comfort. If you use a low camera angle, an even higher ceiling will be needed. The cartridge paper rolls are ideal as backgrounds because they can be suspended and allowed to curve onto the floor, creating a smooth, seam-free sweep for full length shots.

The paper background rolls are best supported on specially-made stands or wall brackets. These can take up to three or more rolls at once, making background changing during a session a quick and simple affair. Lighting stands can also be chosen to make working more convenient. Wheel-based stands enable you to move lights easily and smoothly, although they are not portable. A boom stand is ideal for placing lights in awkward places such as directly above a model's head and a small floor-level stand is useful for placing a light behind the model for rim-lighting or to light the background.

A good, firm tripod or even a wheel-based camera stand should be considered an essential piece of studio equipment. A tripod with a centre column will enable you to adjust the camera height quickly and easily, while a camera stand will allow you to move it from floor level to around 9ft in seconds. For any type of model photography, some facility for changing and preparation is vital; even just a small curtained area with a good light and a full-length mirror is fine. A small bench for accessories and a garment rail with some hangers is also necessary.

The range of backgrounds can also be extended by the addition of two or three wall flats. These are simply hardwood frames covered in hardboard or plyboard. They can be clamped together in a variety of ways with G-clamps to create small room settings, covered with paper or fabric, or painted to create a variety of effects. A plinth is also useful. This can be constructed easily from a wall flat placed on a number of plastic bottle crates to raise it up to the required height, and the same crates can also be used to create different levels and supports, covered with fabric or cushions, as an aid to posing.

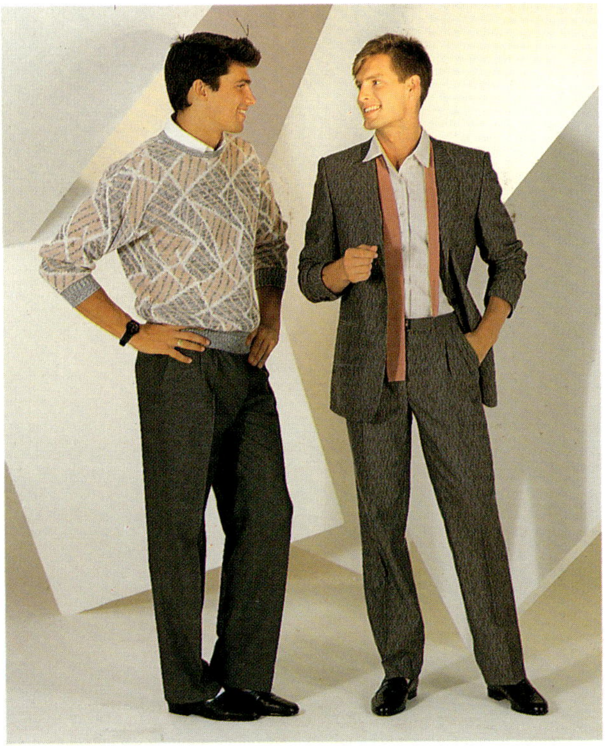

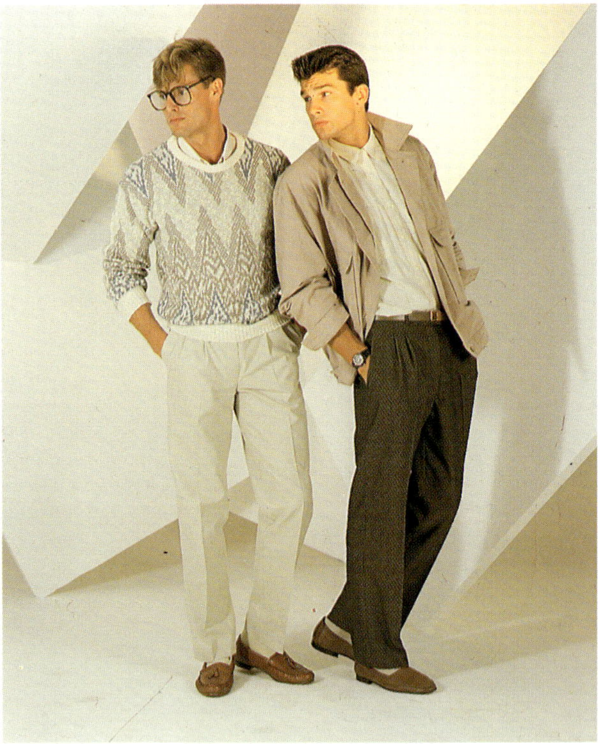

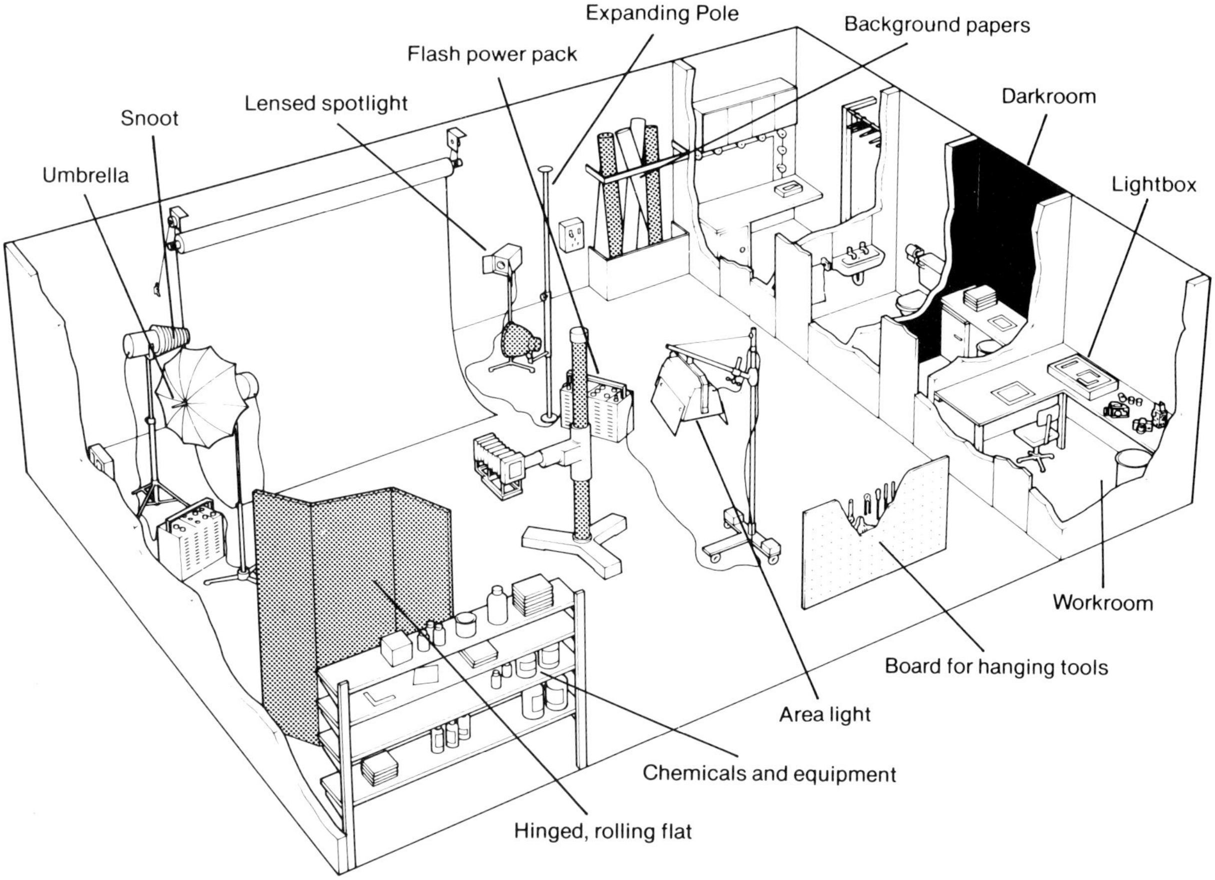

A permanent studio provides the ultimate in control over lighting and backgrounds. The ingenious photographer could, it's true, produce images such as these in almost any environment; a purpose-built studio, though, makes the task very much easier.

BASIC PORTRAIT LIGHTING

There are many different ways of lighting a portrait, depending upon a variety of factors: the model himself, the effect you wish to create and the purpose of the picture. However, the basic principles of portrait lighting are easily defined, and once learned and understood, it is a simple matter to adapt and modify the essential techniques to suit a particular circumstance.

The first principle is that of the key light. This is the name given to the predominant light source in a set-up and the one which is responsible for establishing the basic nature of the lighting and the modelling it creates. It is always best to start with this one light, experimenting with its position and angle relative to the model until it creates the most pleasing and effective quality. The way to judge the effect of this light on your subject is to look at the shadows it creates and to see how they affect his appearance. The nose shadow is a good indicator of the angle and quality of the light. When the key light is placed close to the camera, the nose shadow will be very small and the degree of modelling in your subject's face will be limited. When the light is moved further to one side or much higher, the nose shadow will become longer and more prominent and the modelling will also be greater.

As a general rule, a good starting place for the position of the key light is at an angle of approximately 30 or 40 degrees to the line between the model and the camera position and a foot or so above his eye level. With the model's face turned fairly square to the camera, this should create a strong degree of modelling without an excessively large nose shadow. However, the exact position of the key light will depend both on the angle of the model's head relative to the camera position, his physiognomy and of course upon the effect you want to create. You can learn a great deal about lighting by simply experimenting in this way with the position of the key light and judging the effect it has.

In addition to the angle and directions of the key light, you must also consider its quality. The direct light from, say, flood or an electronic flash with a

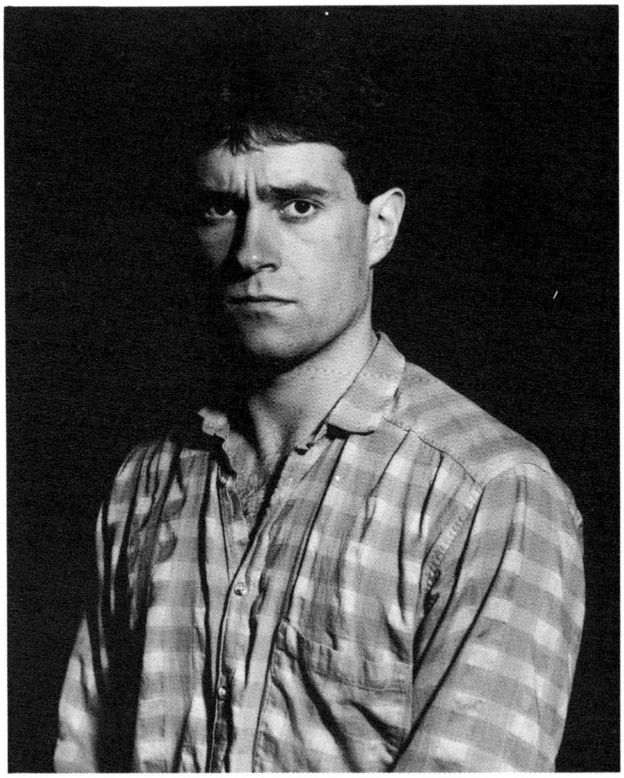

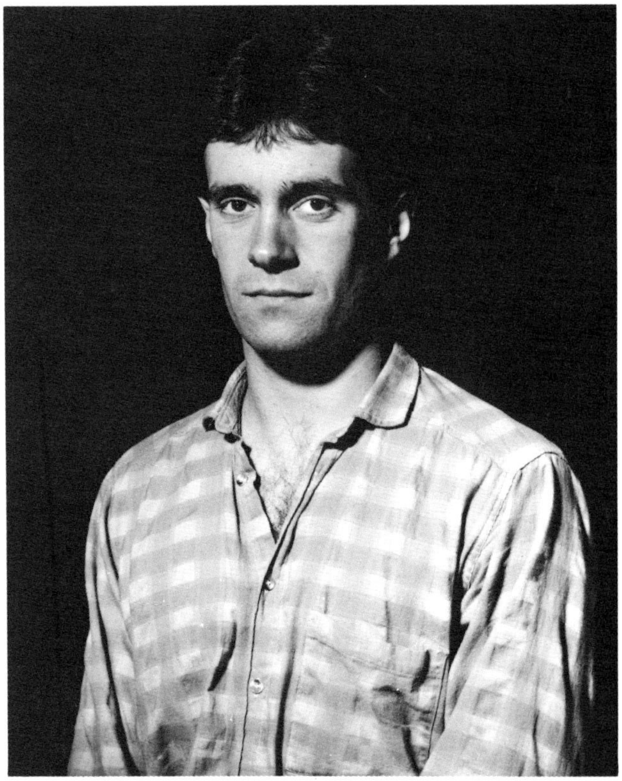

The position of the main light fundamentally changes the appearance of a portrait, and the change is most marked when the light source is small, or far away from the subject. These images show how the shadows change in depth and position when a small floodlight is moved around the model.

Light high

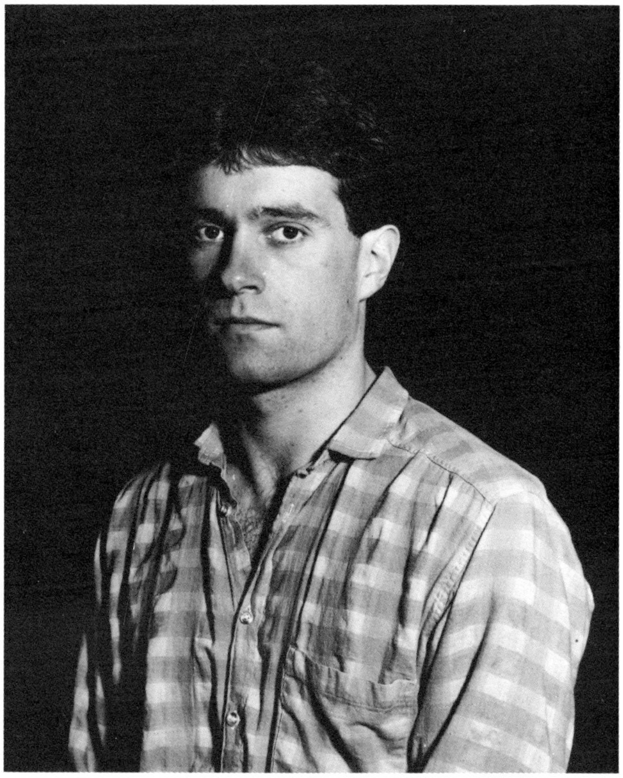

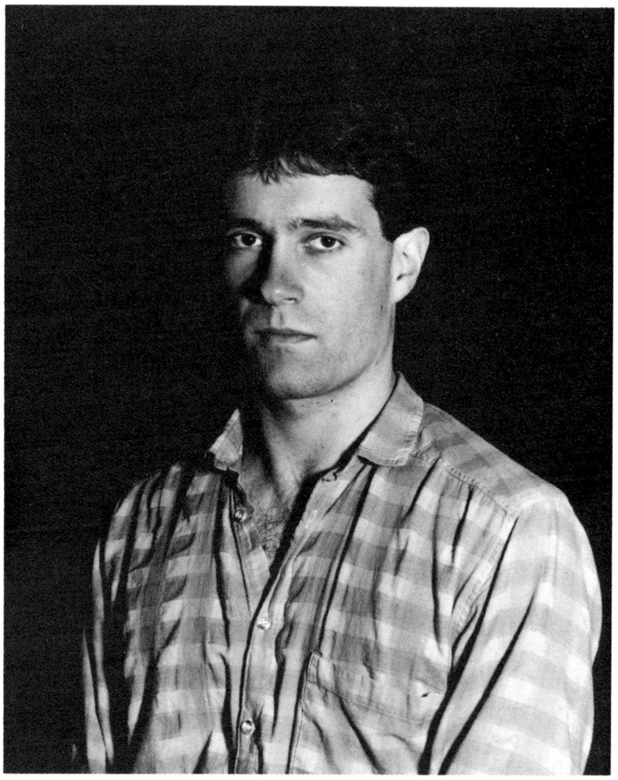

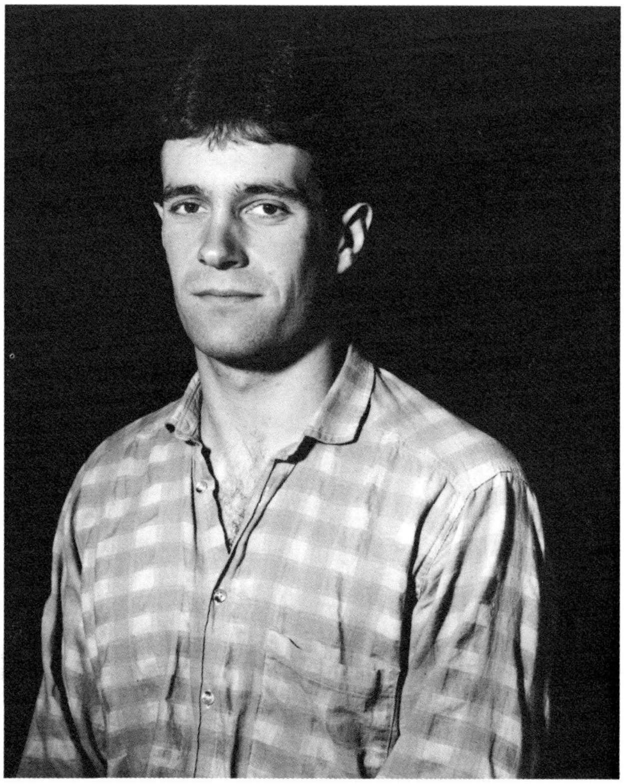

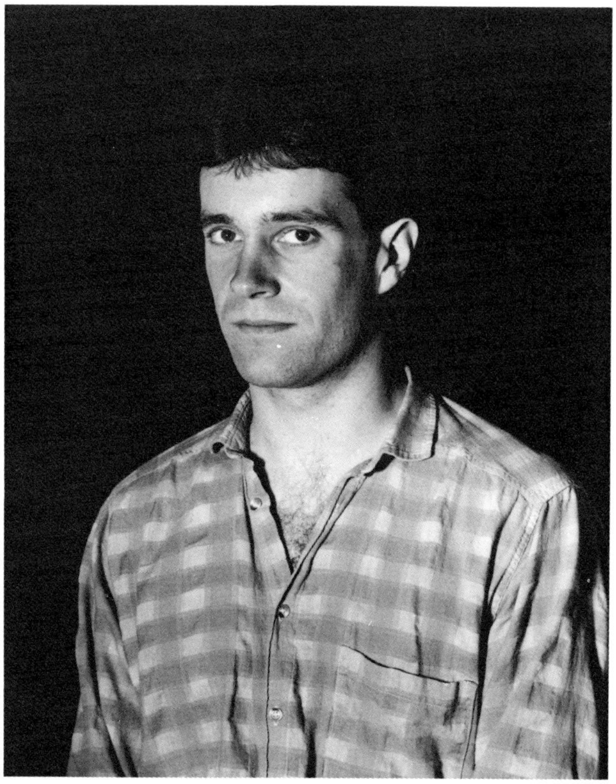

Light medium height

Light low

standard reflector, is hard. That is to say, it creates a dense shadow with sharply-defined edges. Although this type of light source can be effective in portrait photography, it does create considerable contrast as well as emphasizing skin texture. As a general rule if you want to produce an essentially flattering result, then it is preferable to use a softer and more diffused light. This can be obtained by using an umbrella reflector or a diffusion screen, or by reflecting the light source from a large white reflector.

You will also find that even with a more diffused light, the shadows created will, for many pictures, be darker than is desirable. This can be rectified either by using a second, less powerful and frontally-placed light to add to detail to the shadow areas, or to simply position a large white reflector close to the model on the shadow side. If you use a second light for this purpose, be sure that it does not create secondary shadows of its own, as this can look unattractive.

It is also important to consider how well the model is separated from the background. A portrait will inevitably have more impact if there is a bold tonal contrast between the two. This can be achieved by selecting a background which is either substantially lighter or darker than the skin tones, or one of a contrasting color. It can be even more effective to create this separation by the means of lighting. One method is to create a pool of light on the background by placing a light source behind the model and directed onto the background. If a spot light or a light fitted with a snoot or honeycomb is used, it is possible to create a distinct circle of light which can be aimed so that it forms a halo around the whole of the model's head or just the most important features.

Another method is to use an additional light source to create a highlight on the model's face or head. This can be achieved by rim lighting. For this, a light must be positioned behind and to one side of the model, aimed towards the feature you wish to highlight. With a full-face portrait, for instance, it could be made to skim along the side of his cheek, taking care that it does not spill onto the nose as this can look unattractive. A snoot or spotlight is also useful for this purpose as it limits the spill of the light and enables you to direct it precisely.

Lighting the model's hair can also be an effective way of creating separation between model and background, as well as adding interest and detail. This is most easily done with the aid of a boom stand since it is often best for the light to be positioned directly above the model's head. The brightness of this light must be geared to the colour of the model's hair. If the light is too strong with a fair-haired man, the detail can easily be burnt out and lost, but with dark hair, a very bright light will be needed to create highlights and reveal detail.

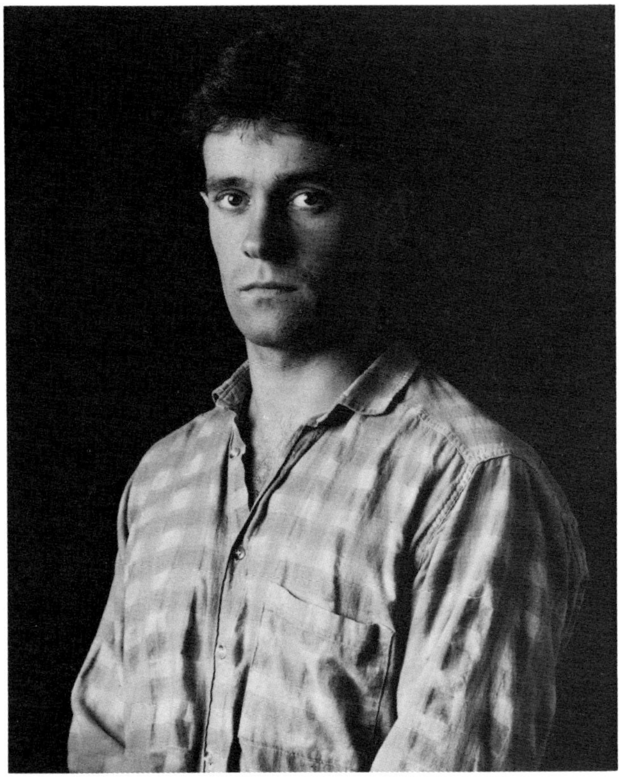

A large area light casts more flattering shadows on the model than does a small light source. However, only quite radical movements of a large light source will cause an appreciable change in the position of the shadows on the face. Here the light has been moved through a full 90° between the pictures on the **left** *and* **far right.**

Dark-haired models tend to merge into the background when lit normally **(near right).** *A hair light above and behind the model adds an extra highlight which separates hair from background* **(far right).**

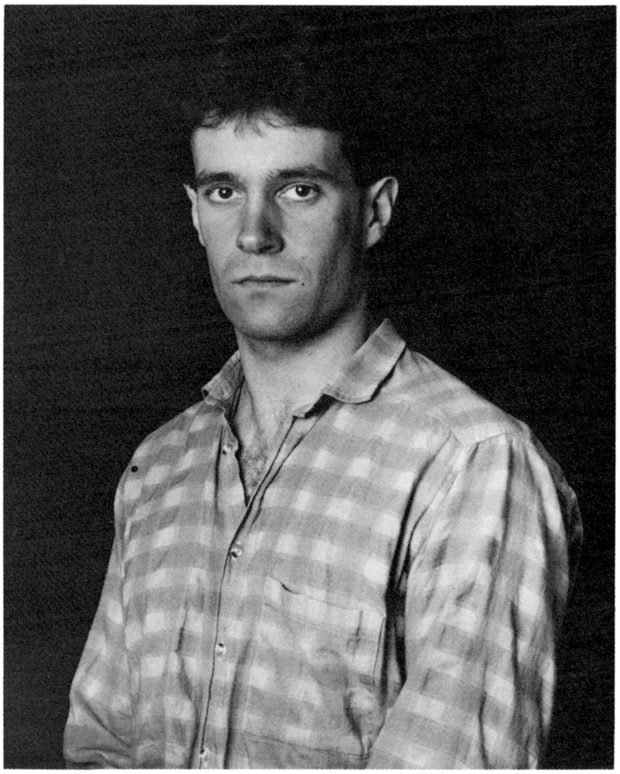
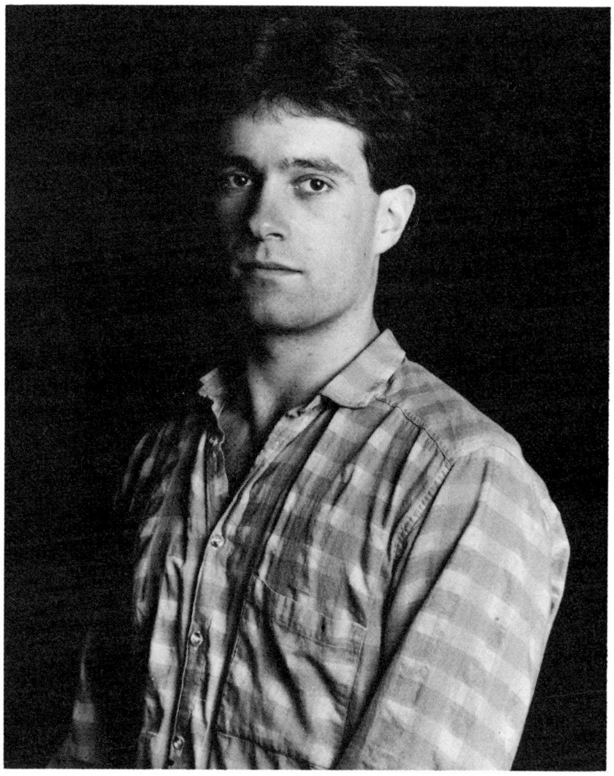
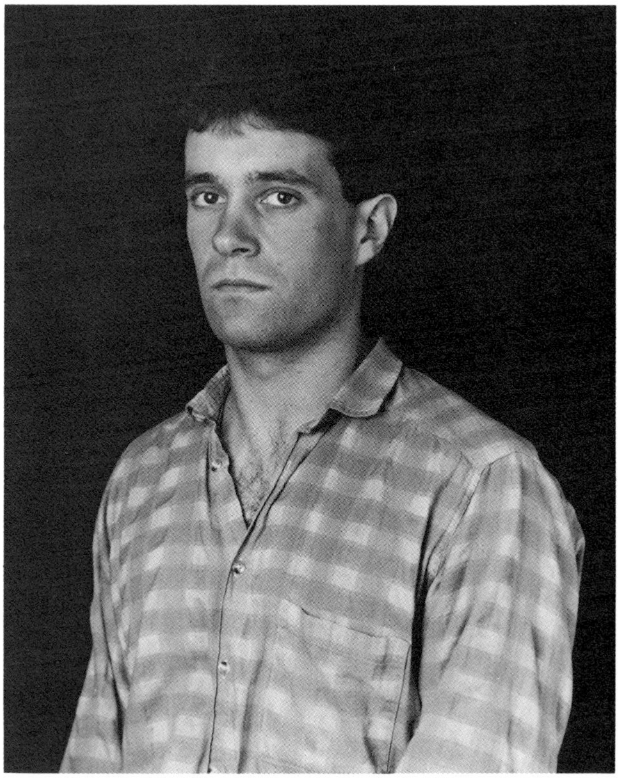
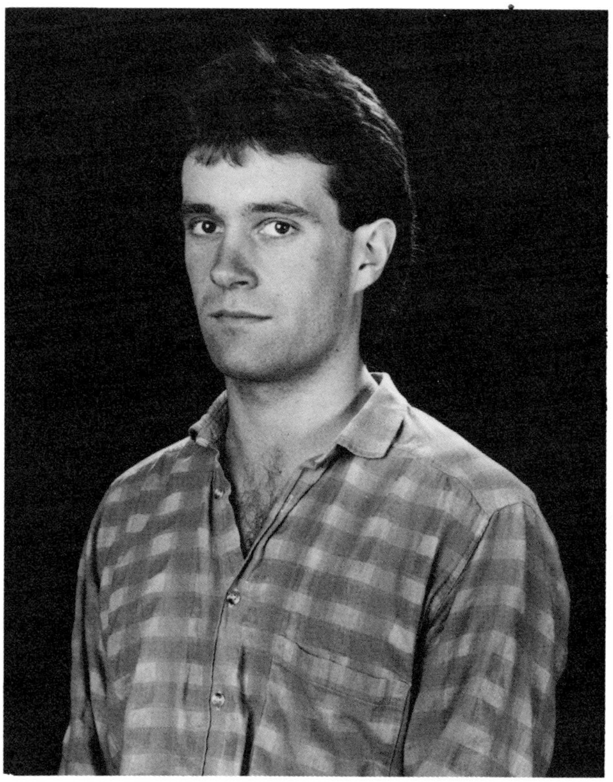

LIGHTING THE NUDE

Lighting for a nude is rather less straightforward than for a portrait, simply because there are many more permutations of possible angles for both the lighting and the body. In addition, there are many different effects that might be required from a nude photograph, ranging from abstract to beefcake and athletic images.

As in portrait photography, the best way to approach it is to start only with the key-light. It can be very instructive to spend a little time experimenting with the possible variations of model positions and lighting direction without actually taking any photographs. First you could ask your model to stand facing towards a point just to one side of the camera, next take a light with a standard reflector on a stand and with it raised to about the level of the model's shoulder, place it at right angles on the opposite side to the direction he is facing. From the camera position, make a careful note of the effect it has, and of the angle, direction and density of the shadows.

Next begin to move the light in stages towards a position close to the camera. At each stage, return to the camera position and study how the new lighting position has affected the appearance of the model, the mood and quality of the image. It will help considerably if you have an assistant who can move the light for you whilst you remain by the camera. You can continue this process until the light is at right angles on the opposite side of the camera. You can also move the light much higher, to maybe about 3ft or so above the model's head, or down to ground-level. You can extend this experiment further by setting the light up in a specific position and then asking your model to turn his body from one profile angle, round to the opposite side. These exercises will teach you a great deal more about the nature and effect of lighting than any other method of instruction.

In addition to direction, the quality of the light is also a crucial factor. To see how this affects your picture, select a lighting position which creates the most pleasing effect, and then see how it can be further adjusted by means of diffusion and reflection. Using a soft reflector, such as an umbrella instead of the standard direct light reflector, will make a significant difference. The shadows will not be as dense and they will have a softer, less defined edge.

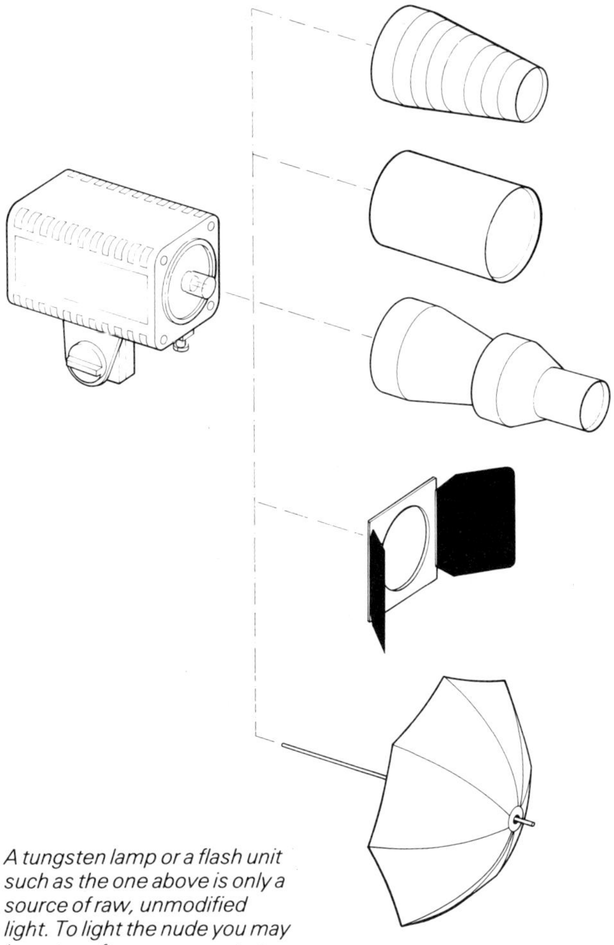

A tungsten lamp or a flash unit such as the one above is only a source of raw, unmodified light. To light the nude you may have to soften or concentrate the beam using the accessories shown alongside the unit. The top four – a cone, a snoot, a lensed spot, and barndoors – all narrow down the light from the flash. The umbrella at the bottom diffuses the light.

This lighting exercise demonstrates how the appearance of the male nude changes as the main light source is moved through 180° – from frontlighting to backlighting. Frontlit, the picture appears flat, and lacks modelling. Moving the light 45° to one side creates a more rounded appearance, and when the light is at one side, every muscle is picked out in high relief. Semi-backlighting and backlighting hide most of the body in shadow, and a reflector would normally be used to put back a little detail.

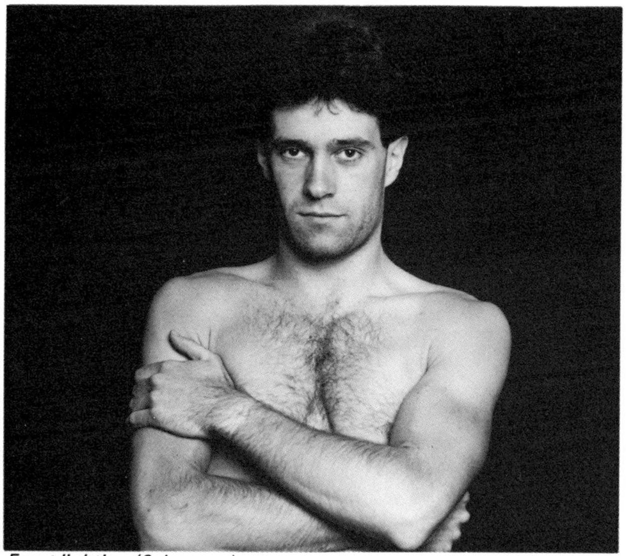
Front lighting (0 degrees)

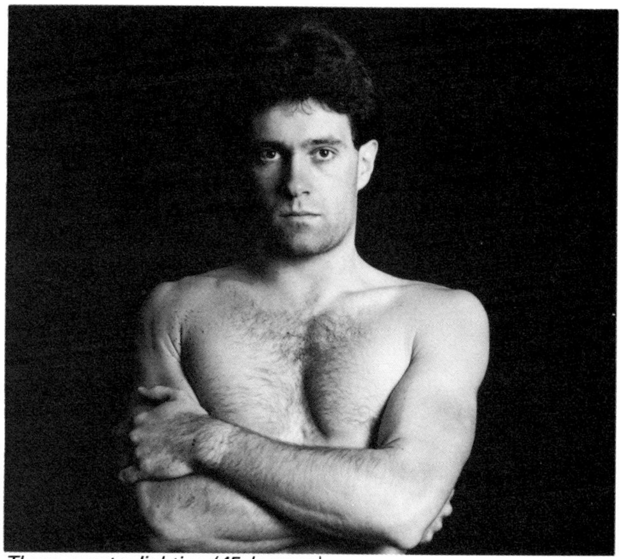
Three-quarter lighting (45 degrees)

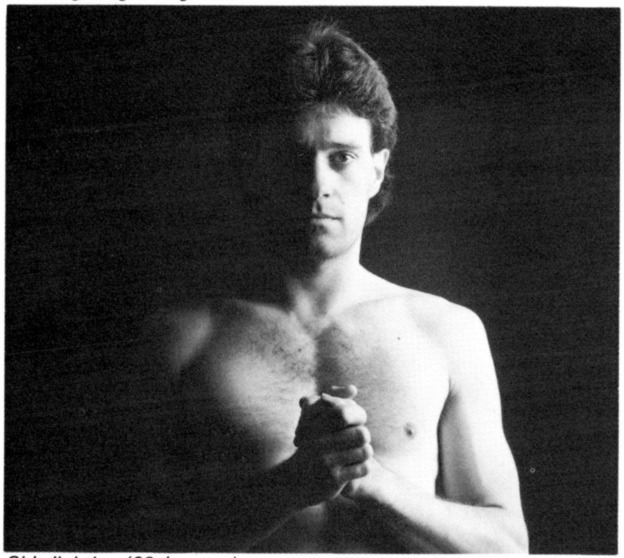
Side lighting (90 degrees)

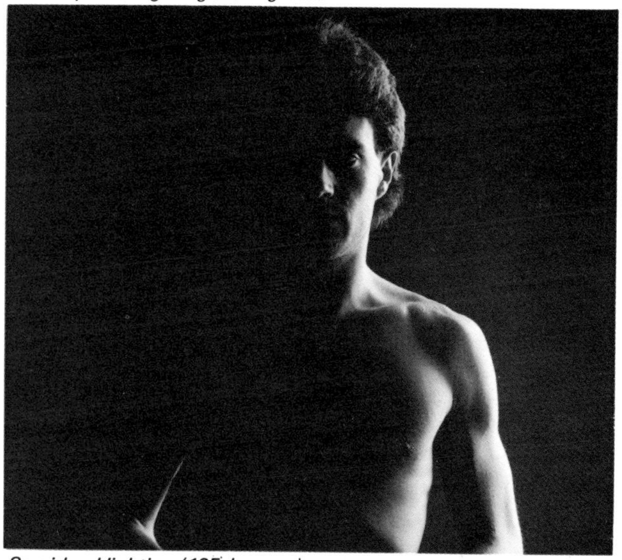
Semi-backlighting (135 degrees)

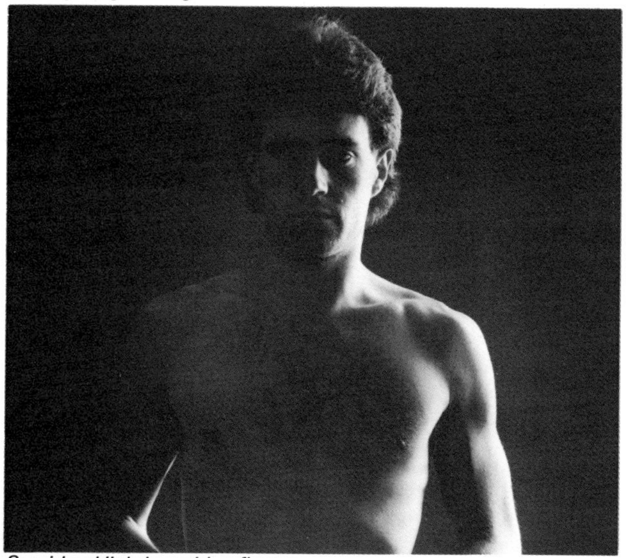
Semi-backlighting with reflector

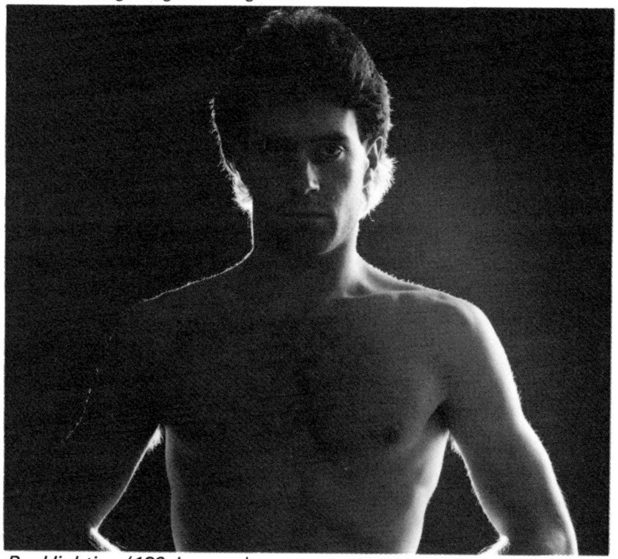
Backlighting (180 degrees)

Another effective way of achieving this quality for nude photography, particularly for full length pictures, is to place a large diffusing screen between the light and the model. This can be constructed easily by making a softwood frame, about 3×6ft and covering it with either tracing paper or white translucent plastic or fabric. The degree of diffusion can be controlled by altering the relative positions of the screen and light. A softer quality will be created with the light further from the screen and with the screen closer to the model. A soft light can also be created by bouncing the light from a large white reflector, placed at the selected angle to the model. A large reflector can be used to control the density of the shadows too, and reduce the contrast of the image, by placing it close to the model on the shadow side and angling it to reflect the light back into these areas.

The decision over type and position of lighting is entirely dependent on the effect and mood you want to create. As a general rule, a soft light placed at an angle to the model will tend to emphasize form and create a wide range of tones, while a hard, undiffused light with little or no fill-in, will emphasize texture and create a more dramatic quality when used directionally. Frontal lighting will minimize both texture and form, creating a more open, stark quality.

When you want to create a hard or dramatic quality, it is possible to use a black 'reflector' to reduce the amount of light being reflected into the shadows. One side of a normal reflector could be painted matt black, or you could simply drape a piece of black fabric over it. This can be a very useful technique if you are working in a small area which has light walls and ceilings; it will create a large amount of scattered light, diluting your lighting effects. More dramatic lighting can be achieved with the aid of a spotlight and this can also be used to create rim- and back-lighting in addition to the key-light.

These suggestions have been made essentially in relation to a model who is standing. When you are photographing a reclining body, even more variations are possible in the angle and direction of the lighting. There are, in fact, no hard and fast rules in lighting the nude. So much depends on subtle changes in position and angle of both the lighting and the model that it is impossible to create or even suggest a formula. It is purely a question of experiment, observation and experience.

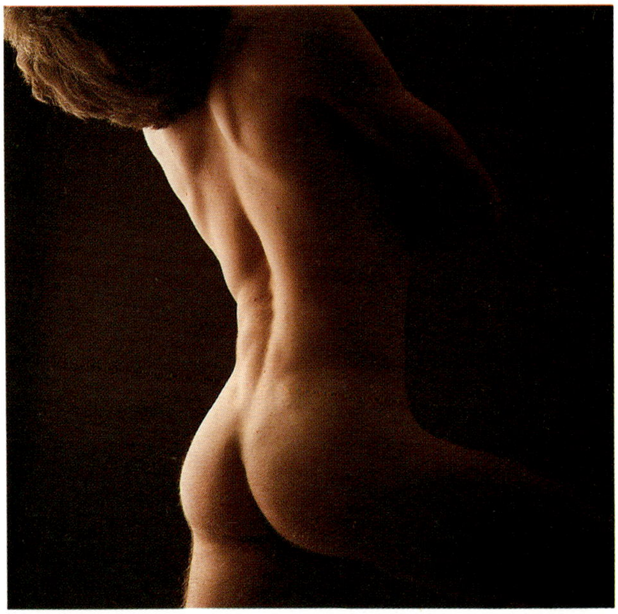

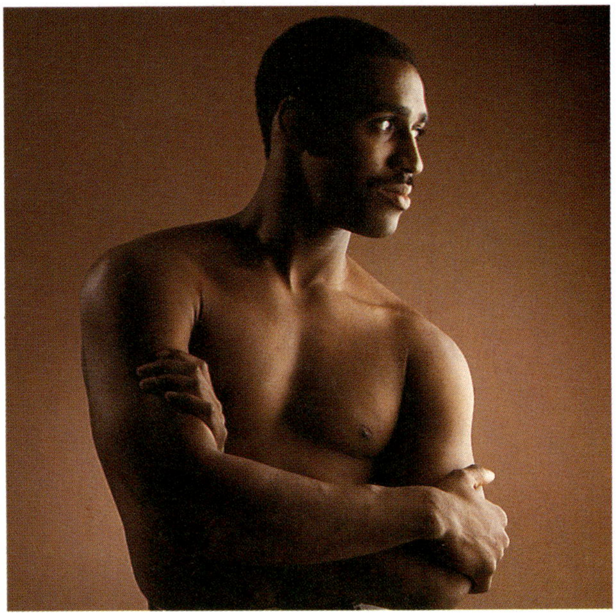

Soft but strongly directional lighting is perhaps the classic method of lighting the male nude. In the studio use: a large area light; a small light source diffused by a screen; or any light bounced from a white reflector. In the home, improvise by using light from a window.

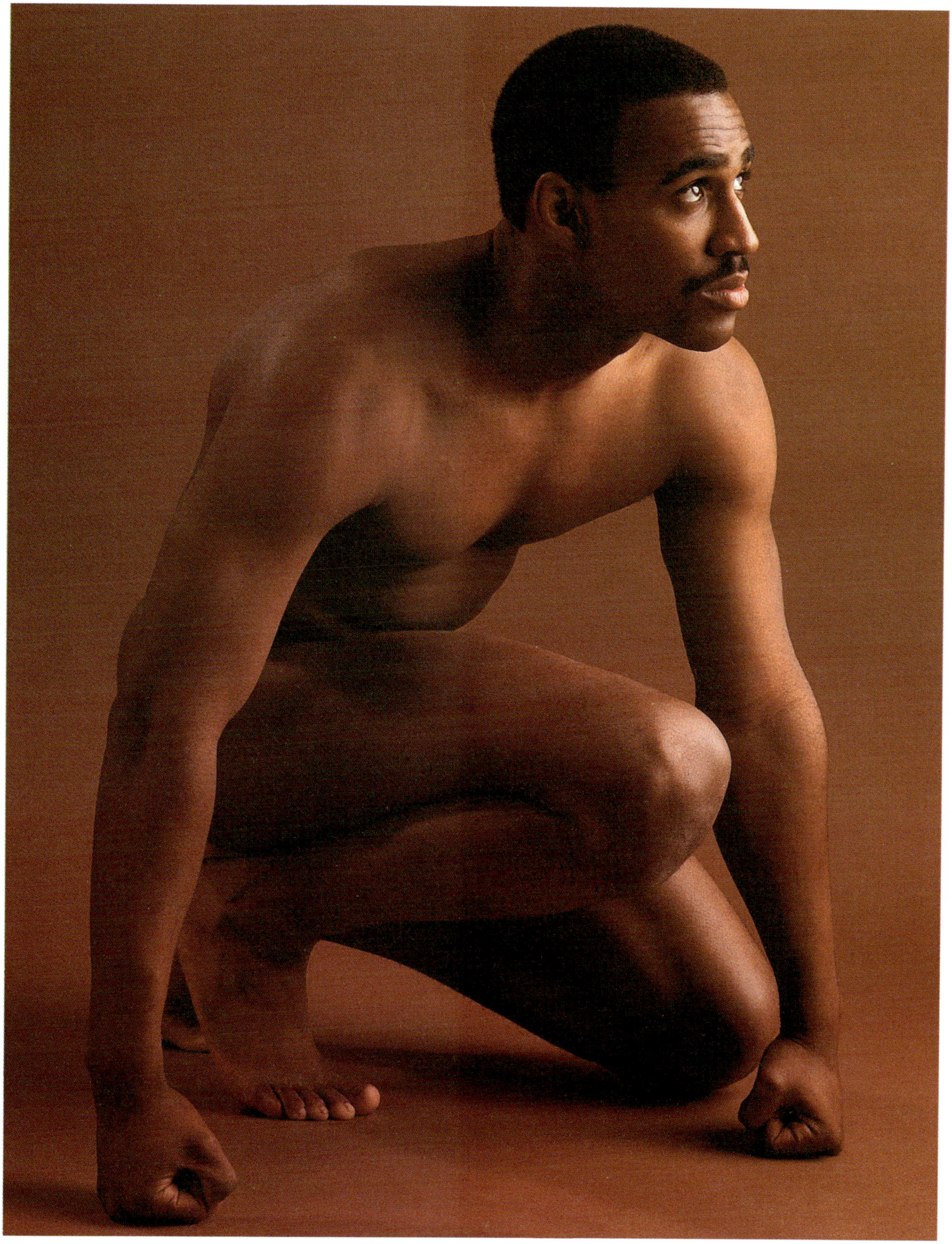

LIGHTING FOR FORM AND TEXTURE

The visual elements of form and texture are vital to both portrait and nude photography since they are largely responsible for creating an impression of depth and solidity within the borders of a two-dimensional image on film or paper. They are closely related, since texture can be considered to be the form created on a surface, but although there are similar considerations to be made when lighting the subject in order to emphasize either one or the other, there are also substantial differences.

Form is created in a photographic image mainly by the transition of tone as it changes from light to dark, in the same way that shading is responsible for the impression of solidity in a pencil sketch. With the human body, this is usually achieved effectively by a quite gentle and smooth transition since the contours of the face and body have similar attributes. As a general rule, the type of lighting which is most effective in creating this quality in a picture is one that is fairly soft but quite directional. In a studio, this is most readily provided by a diffused or reflected light placed at an angle of about 45 degrees to the line between the model and the camera. A large umbrella reflector is a convenient way of producing this type of light, or it can be achieved by bouncing direct light from a large white reflector placed to one side of the model.

Another effective way of creating a soft, directional light, is to position a light source with a normal reflector at the appropriate angle to the model and then to place a large, white translucent screen between them.

Even with a soft, diffused light source, however, it is still quite likely that the transition from light to dark tones will be too sudden; this can most easily be controlled by the use of a reflector. A large sheet of white cardboard, polystyrene or fabric can be placed close to the model on the opposite side to the light source to reflect light back into the shadows, and its effect can be controlled by moving it closer to, or further from, the subject.

The impression of form can be further enhanced by the use of a secondary light source to create additional highlights by rim-lighting or back-lighting. When lighting a nude, for example, the body can be lit from one side, creating highlights along that side, the tones gradually becoming darker towards the unlit side. If another light source is then placed on the opposite side of the model and slightly behind, it will create another area of highlight, relieving the darker tones and creating a rounded quality.

Because the form which creates texture is much more subtle and on a smaller scale altogether, the lighting needs to be more assertive in order to emphasize it. This is especially true of textures like skin and fabric which have a very slight relief. In these cases, the light can be considerably harder than you might use to create form and it can also be much more acutely angled. In many cases, it can be effective to use a very hard light such as a spotlight or an undiffused flood light, positioned so that it just skims the surface you are illuminating, and in some instances it can be very effective to use backlighting.

With a portrait, if a light source is positioned behind the model and to one side just outside the camera's field of view, it can be directed to skim the side of the model's face, creating bold textural relief. It should be appreciated, however, that this type of lighting can easily be unflattering and create an unattractive result if used inconsiderately, and it is often necessary to strike a balance between the maximum textural effect and a pleasing image.

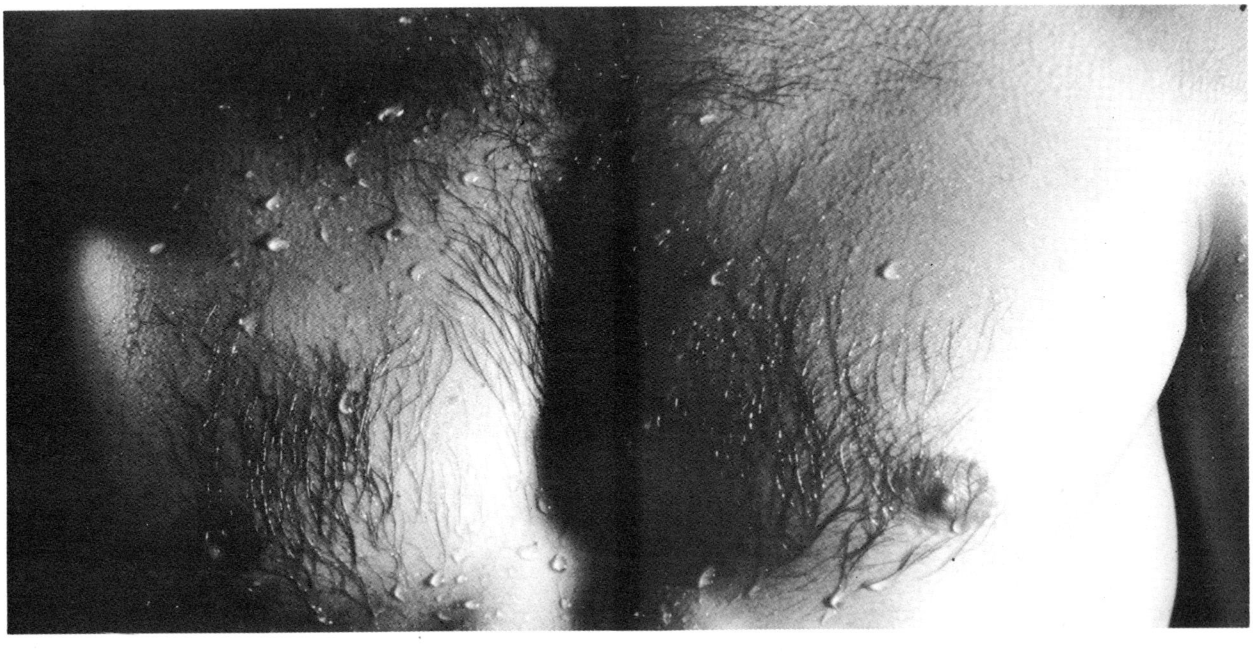

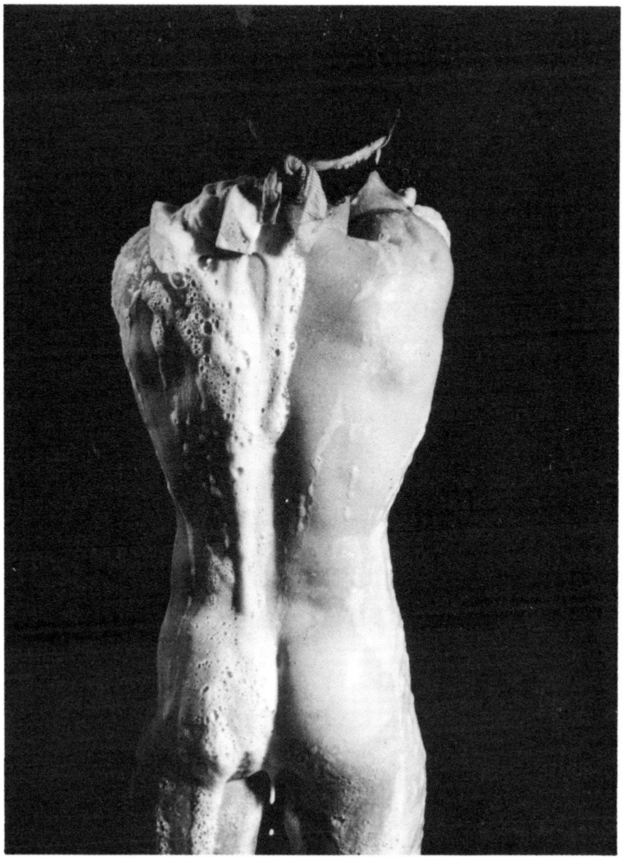

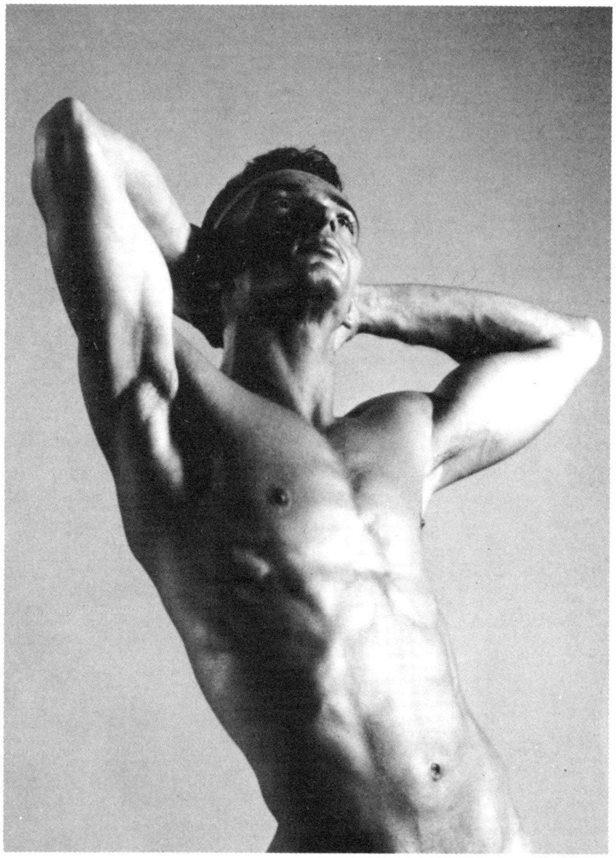

Any kind of moisture on the body enhances texture – suds and foam doubly so. Here the main light was to the right of the model; a weaker fill light was positioned on the left.

The smaller the light source, the more brilliant are the highlights it creates on the body. In these examples, the top picture was lit with a large soft light and the lower picture with a very much smaller light.

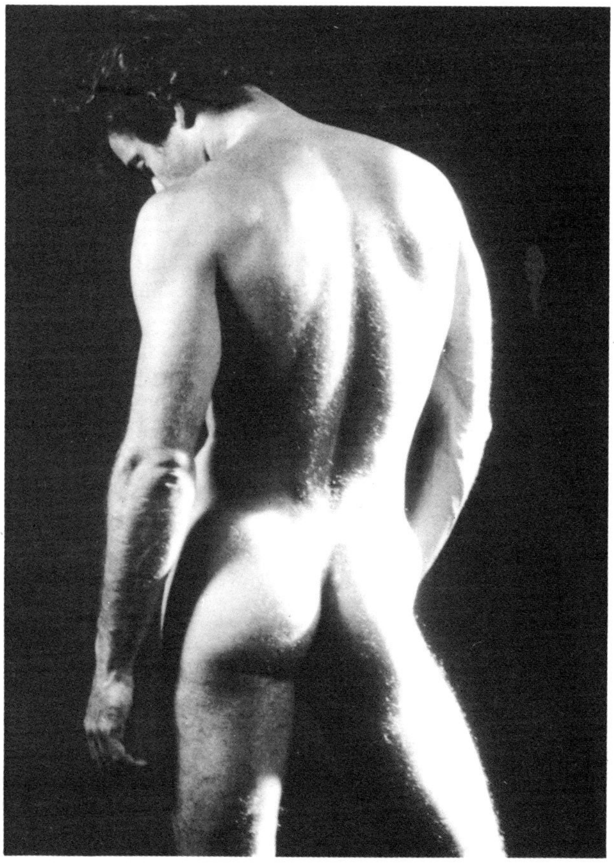

Filling shadows with a second light source – instead of a reflector – can be a useful way of adding attractive double highlights to the body. When using color film, try covering the fill light with a colored lighting filter to tint the second highlight.

LIGHTING FOR MOOD

Lighting is one of the most basic ways of creating mood in a photograph, and the opportunity to control this is greater in a studio than when shooting outdoors. As we have discussed in the sections on lighting for portraits and nudes, the direction and quality of light is responsible for creating the tones within the image and the tonal quality of a photograph is, to a large extent, responsible for creating mood and atmosphere.

An image with a full range of tones, from rich blacks to sparkling highlights will tend to create a lively and cheerful quality in a picture, whereas a picture with mainly dark tones suggests a more serious and dramatic mood. An image consisting primarily of light tones and highlights, evokes a more delicate and ethereal atmosphere.

A full-toned image requires straightforward lighting: a soft but directional key-light, with enough fill-in to give detail in the shadow areas, will establish the basic tonal range, while some back- or rim-lighting will create the highlights which add life and sparkle to the image.

A low-key image is one in which the tonal range is predominantly at the darker end of the scale and it can be used effectively to create a sombre or dramatic mood. Lighting to create this quality in a picture needs to be very directional in order to produce large areas of shadow. Back-lighting is an effective way of achieving this, using a light placed behind and to one side of the model and aimed towards him. The object is to reveal the essential features such as the outline of his head or body, but to leave large areas in quite deep shadow. It is important, however, not to create too much contrast, and for this reason it is preferable to use a soft, diffused light, as opposed to a direct light, and also to use a fill-in reflector so that the brightness range between the highlight and shadow tones is not too great. It is also important to ensure that the subject and background are of a fairly similar tone, because although it is possible to create a low-key image from a light-toned subject, one that contains a mixture of very light and dark tones will create too much contrast and too wide a tonal range.

Exposure too is important as overexposure will destroy the low-key effect and underexposure will lose all detail in the darker tones. When metering exposure, it is best to take a close-up reading from the lightest and darkest areas and then to take an average, giving around one or two stops less than that calculated. When shooting in black and white or with color negative film, it is possible to control the final quality and density of the image when making the print, but when shooting color transparencies it is vital to get the exposure exactly right.

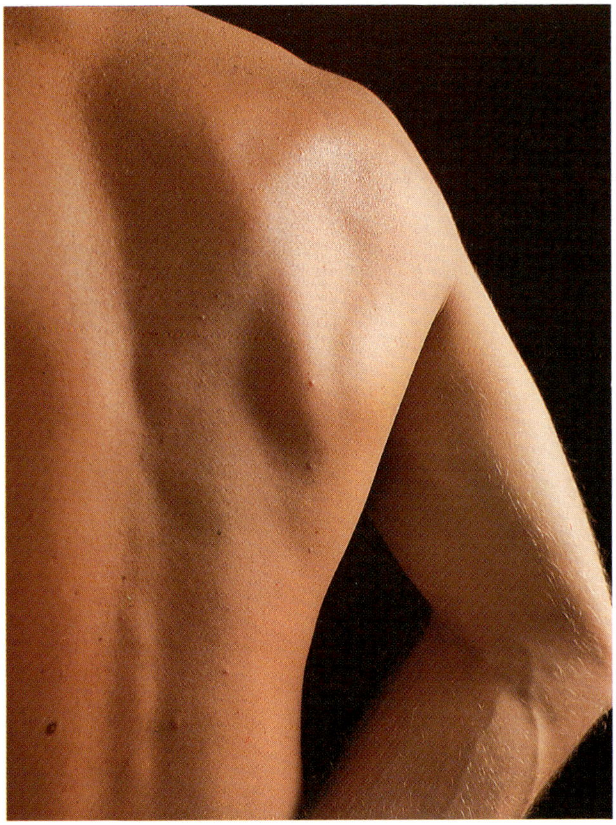

A change in lighting totally alters the appearance of the male body: here soft, moody lighting creates an image that is reminiscent of a gently undulating landscape.

A spotlight has a major advantage when lighting for mood: you can use its compact, highly directional beam to pick out small details of the model's face and body while leaving other parts in shadow.

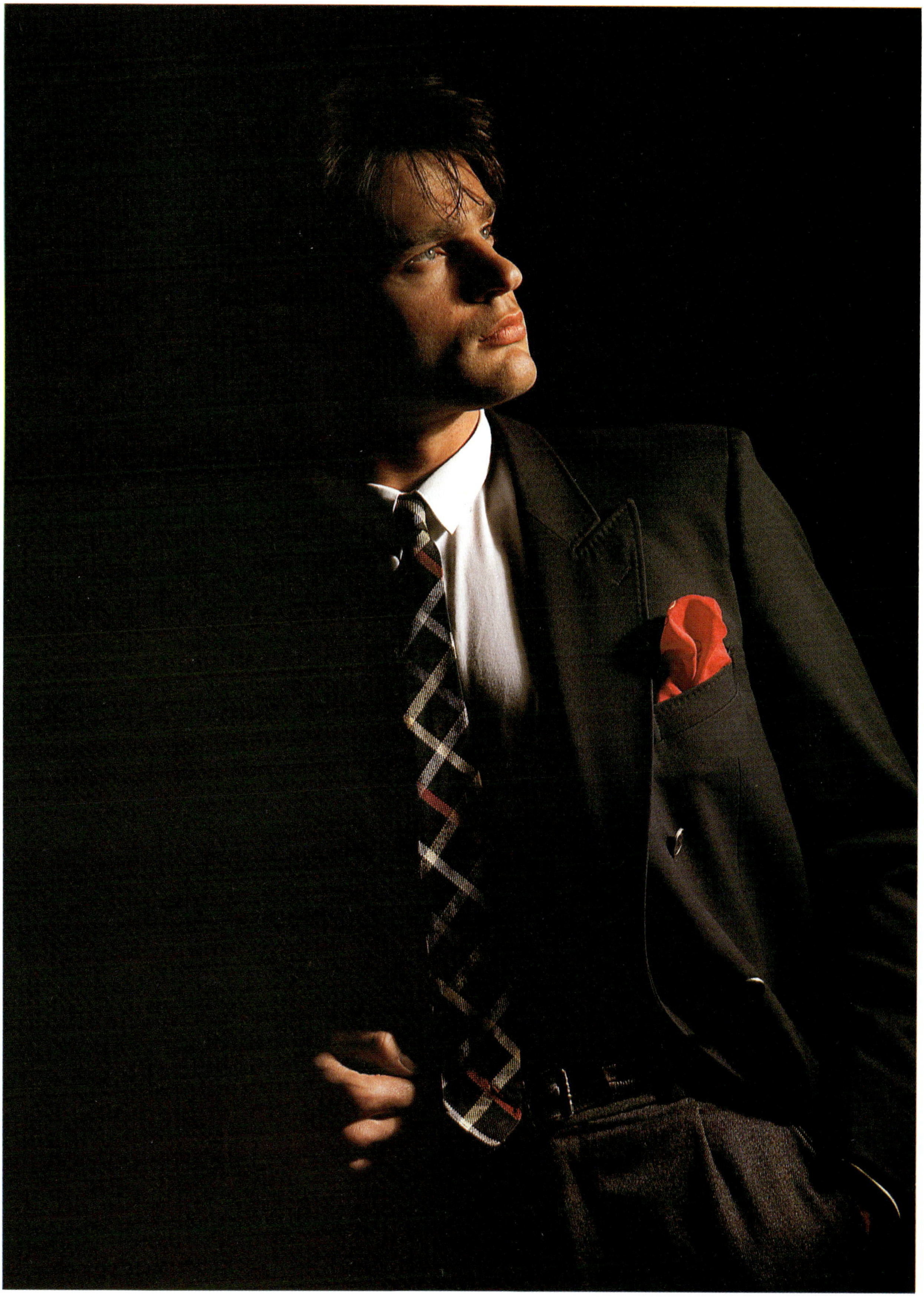

High-key lighting requires precisely the opposite conditions. The lighting must be arranged so that there are virtually no shadows and the subject must contain very few dark tones. Ideally everything within the frame should be as close to white as possible, with the exception of a few key features to give the image some definition. With a portrait, for example, a blond-haired man wearing a white shirt and placed against a white background would be a perfect subject for a high-key shot, just his eyes and mouth perhaps creating a darker tone to create a centre of interest.

Shadowless lighting is most easily achieved by using a very soft, diffused source as close to the camera lens as possible, with perhaps a separate light behind the model to illuminate the background, ensuring that is recorded as a pure white and is shadow-free. In addition it can help to use reflectors each side of the model and close to him; with a close-up portrait, you can use another small reflector placed just under his chin to eliminate any shadows that might be created under the eyes and jaw.

Exposure is also important with high-key pictures. Overexposure will result in subtle details being burnt out and lost, while underexposure will create a muddy, flat and grey image. The best way to take an exposure measurement for this type of subject is with an incident light reading. This requires a separate meter with a diffusion attachment, aimed towards the camera from the model's position. In this way, it reads the brightness level directly from the source rather than reflected from the subject. If you don't have such a meter, then you can take a reflected light reading in the normal way from a substitute, standard grey tone placed in front of the model. Kodak make a special Gray Card for this purpose. Remember, however, that a normal reading made directly from a light-toned subject will result in substantial underexposure.

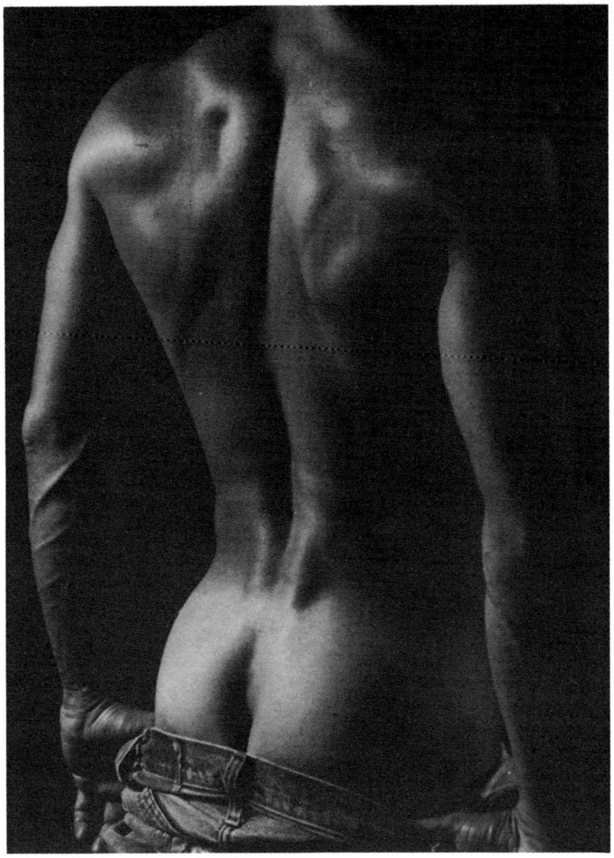

To swamp low-key images in shadow, use oblique or back lighting, and pose the model against a black or very dark background.

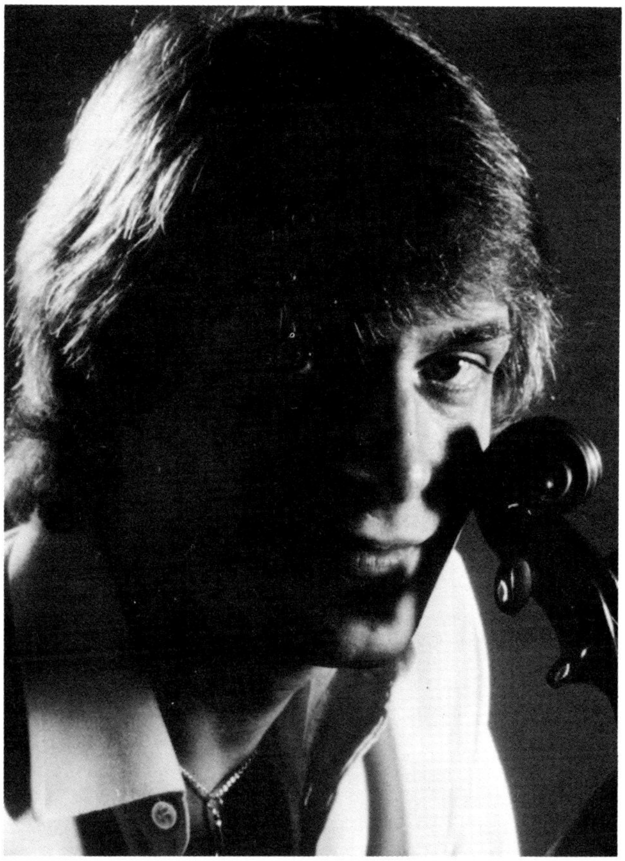

Two lights, each placed almost behind the model, throw shadows towards the camera, creating a brooding atmosphere. The rim lighting on the model's face, though, succeeds in conveying his personality.

Moody lighting needn't always be low key. These two figures are lit with very hard frontal light that is reminiscent of on-camera flash used by press photographers. The result is a picture that has remarkable directness, and a very contemporary atmosphere.

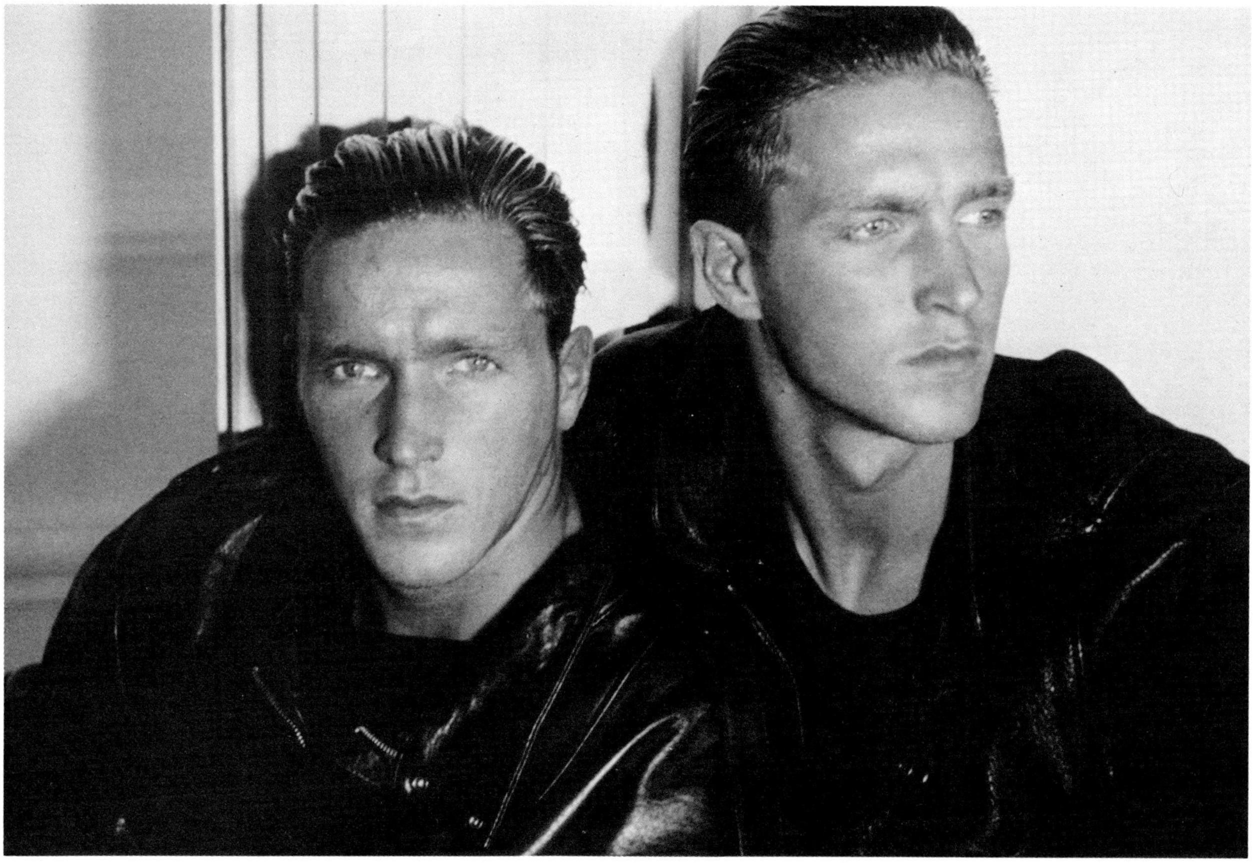

SPECIAL LIGHTING AND BACKGROUND EFFECTS

In normal circumstances, studio lighting is arranged to create a pleasing and effective quality, but in a way which does not draw attention to the lighting itself. In some situations, however, it is possible to use lighting so that it becomes an important and even dominant element of the picture. This can be carried out, either to add impact to a picture which would otherwise be a little dull or lifeless, or it can be used to create an unusual quality. High- and low-key lighting, described on the previous pages, are examples of this.

Extreme distortion and manipulation of the tonal range of the picture can be extremely effective for some subjects and very high contrast lighting is a simple way of achieving this end. When lighting a model for a picture of normal quality, it is necessary to ensure that the brightness range is within the tolerance of the film, but if the lighting is arranged so that it deliberately creates a high contrast image, the result can be both unusual and dramatic.

Direct, rather than diffused or reflected, light is the easiest way to achieve this and a spotlight can be particularly useful for this type of effect. When very high contrast is created in this way, you have the final control over the nature and effect of the picture by means of exposure. It is possible to calculate the exposure to give detail in the lighter tones, resulting in the darker areas of the image recording as solid black; of, if you give an exposure which will record detail in the shadow areas, the lighter tones will bleach out to pure white. These techniques can be useful with subjects in which you wish to emphasize bold shapes or lines; they can create a very harsh and dramatic image when the subject has a strong textural quality.

Lighting from an unconventional angle is another way of creating unusual and interesting effects. If a light is placed very high, for example, it can create unfamiliar shadows and even give the appearance of distorting features. A similar effect can be achieved with light from a very low position. With a portrait, it can suggest a sinister or mysterious mood.

When shooting in color, one way of creating unusual and dramatic effects with the lighting is to use color filters over the light sources. Professional photographic stores sell a range of such filters in large acetate sheets and these can be taped in position over the front of the reflector. Be careful, however, not to position the filter too close to the bulb as it will melt. A colored light source like this can be effective when

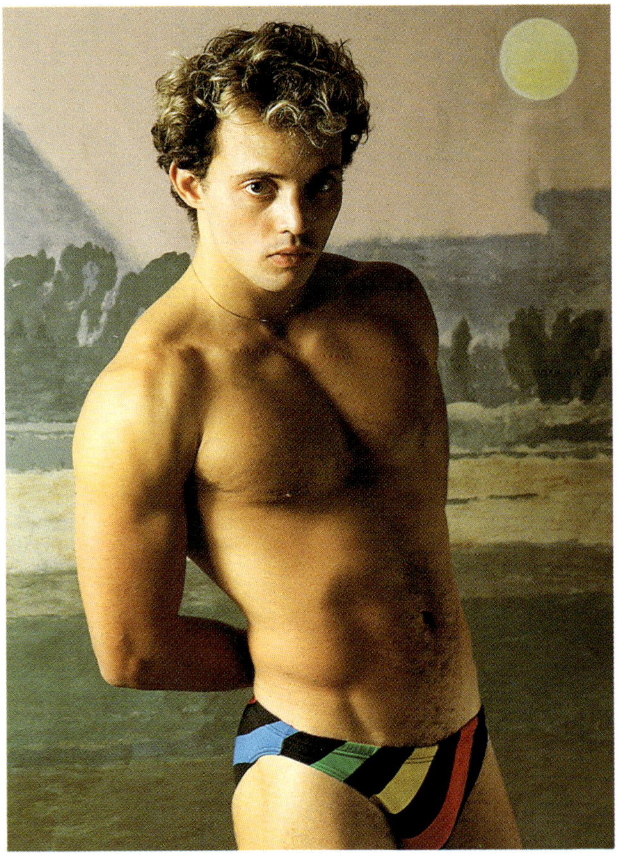

Painted backdrops rarely look truly realistic on close inspection, so either throw them out of focus, or just use them for decorative effect **(above)**. *A good source of suitable backdrops is a roller-blind shop. Movie supply houses hire out authentic and lifelike backgrounds, but the cost can be astronomical.*

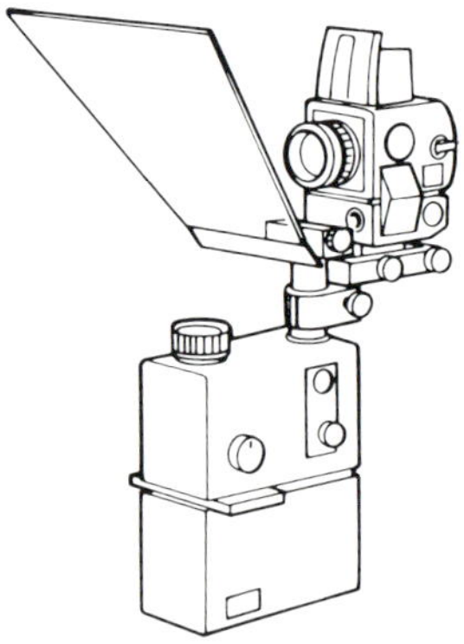

A front-projection unit works like a slide projector, throwing a slide of the photographer's choice onto a special screen behind the model. In seconds the background can thus be changed from a desert island to a city park. Though costly, these units are nevertheless far cheaper than a location shoot, and if the lighting on the model matches that in the projected background slide, the results are indistinguishable.

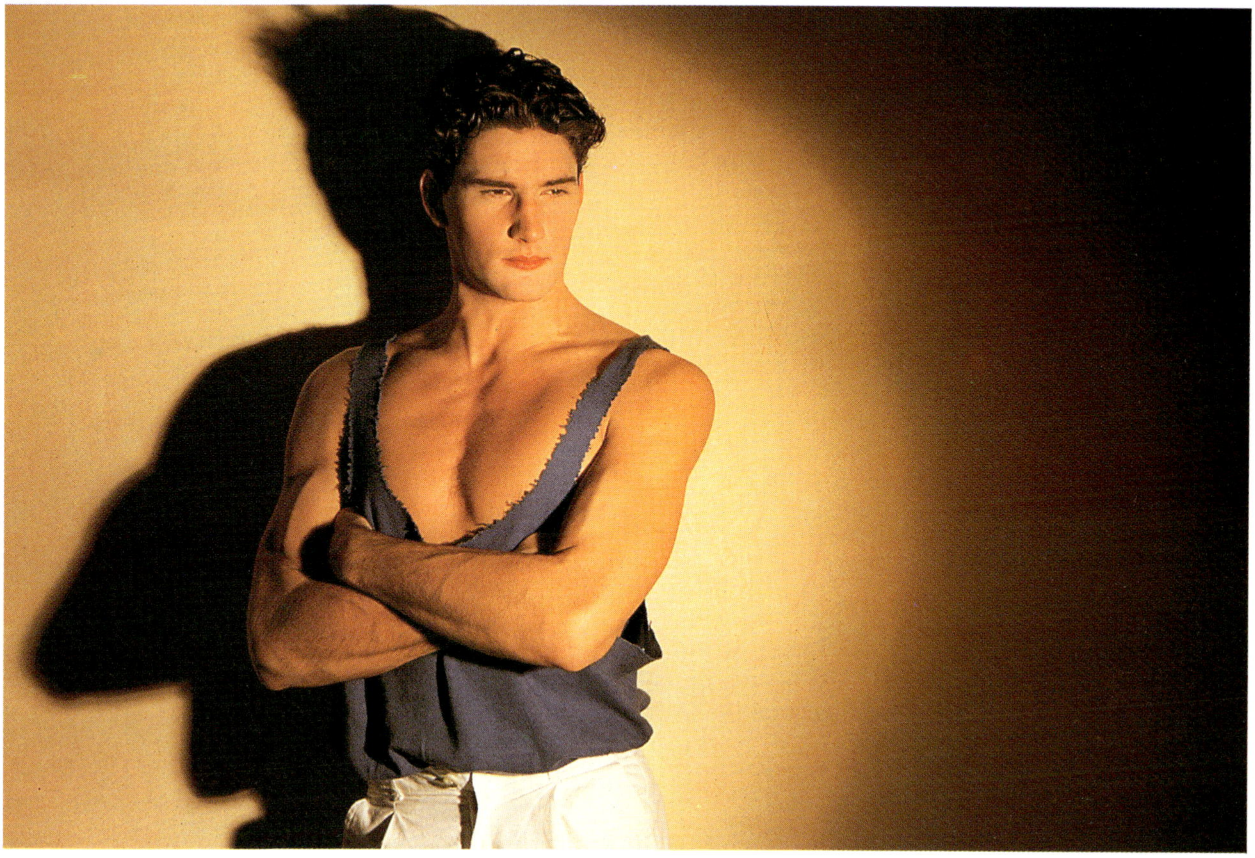

Original lighting creates exciting pictures. A cardinal rule of lighting is always to keep the lamp above the model's eye level. Here the photographer broke the rule and produced a striking picture as a result.

used as a rim-light or a back-light with the other lighting unfiltered. Another effect can be achieved by using two lights, each with a filter of a complementary color: red and its complementary cyan, for instance. If these two lights are placed in different positions, a normal color quality will be created where they overlap, but where each create a shadow, there will be a strong color cast.

Non photographic light sources can also be used to create effects: a candle or kerosene lamp, for instance, can be used both as a light source and as a prop, either in combination with other lighting or as a sole source. If used alone, you will need to use a fast film to avoid very slow shutter speeds, and of course you will have to use film balanced for tungsten light when shooting in color. Even so, the pictures will have a color cast, but this can contribute to the effect. Another interesting light source is the UV lighting that is used for window displays and stage or disco lighting. If used in a darkened room, UV light has the effect of causing objects and fabrics that have a fluorescent dye in them to glow with an eerie and vivid intensity. Again, a fast film will be needed, but best results are obtained with daylight type film, with the aid of a UV filter to absorb any scattered light, as this would degrade the image.

The background is another way of introducing additional interest and effects to an image. Even when using plain background papers it is possible to create an unusual quality with lighting. A spotlight or snoot can be used to create a pool of light on the background, and when shooting in color, a filter can be taped over the light for additional effect. In addition, a spotlight can be used to project patterns onto a plain background, by simply cutting stencils and shapes from stiff black card and suspending them between the spotlight and the background.

Instead of using plain paper backgrounds, there is also a wide variety of other materials that can be used for effect. A venetian blind can make a very effective background especially when combined with lighting, to create a pattern on the model. Other possibilities include lurex fabrics, metallic foils, plastic laminates and corrugated sheeting. Even ordinary textured surfaces like stippled paper, painted with a bright gloss paint and lit to create bold highlights, can give the desired result. A small store of such materials can add both interest and variety to your studio pictures.

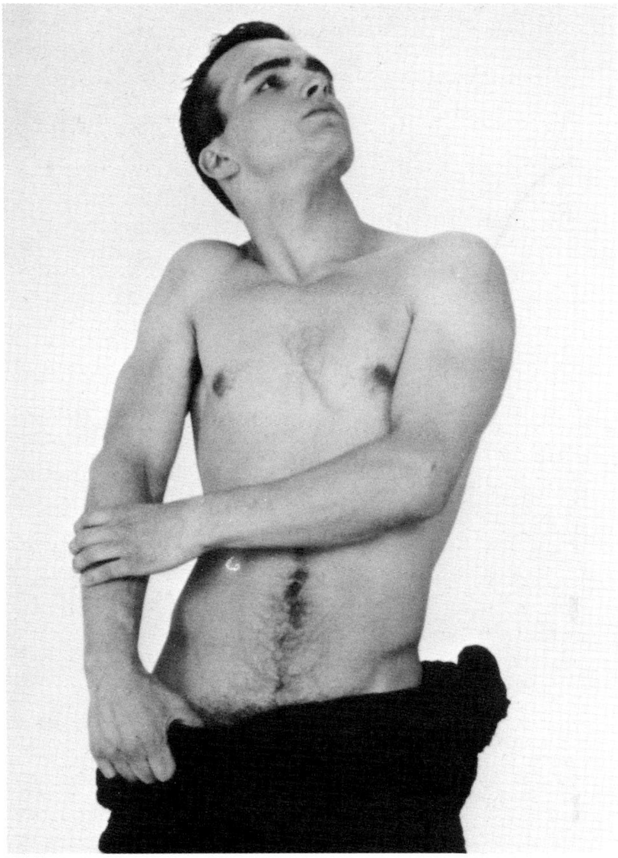

Plain white paper seems like the simplest of backgrounds, but the lighting required to ensure that the backdrop appears white, rather than grey, is not as straightforward. The best method is to light the background separately from the model – preferably with strip-lights on either side.

To cast dramatic shadows, move model and background close together. Here the photographer made the beam of the lamp narrower by using a snoot.

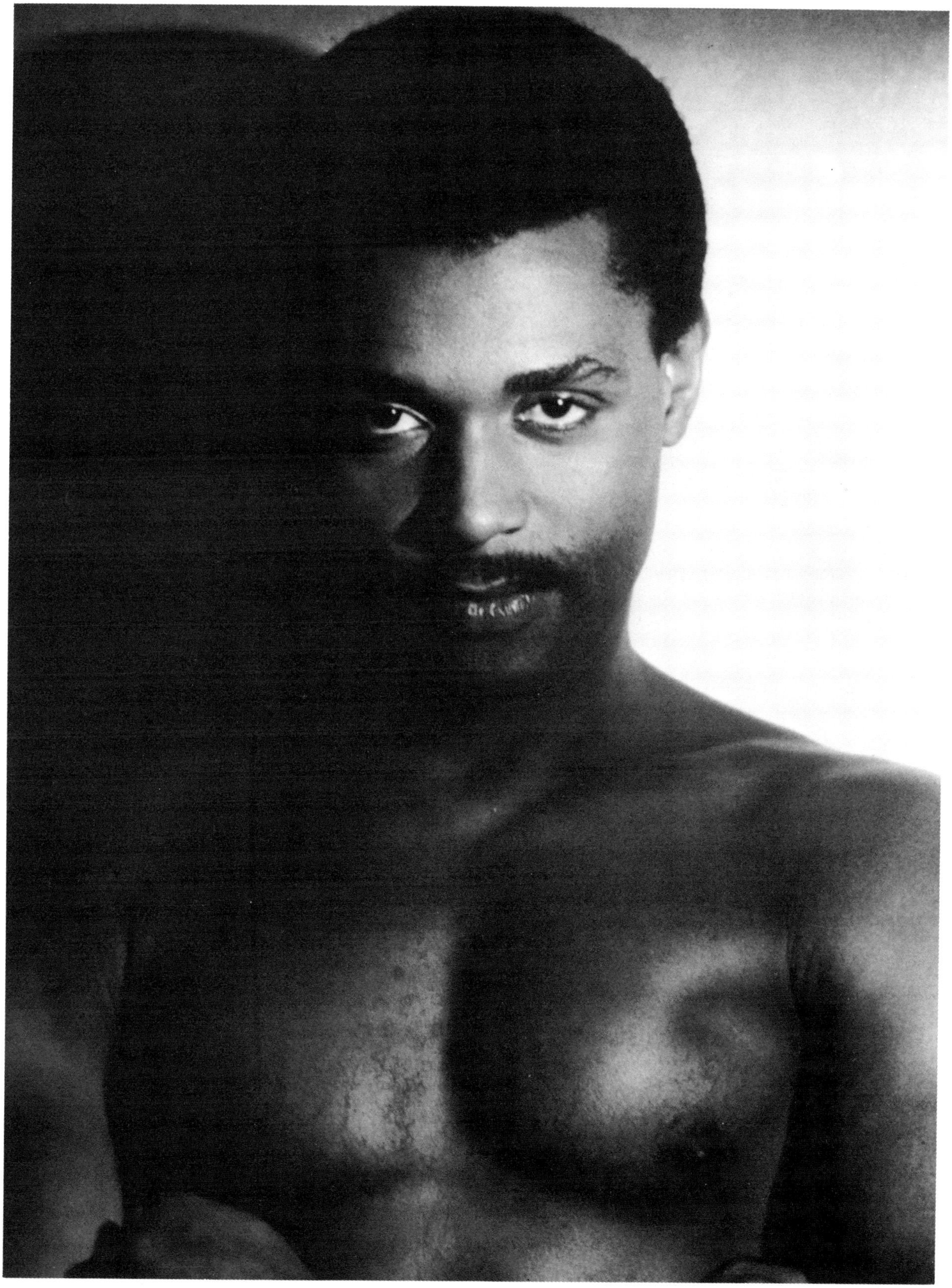

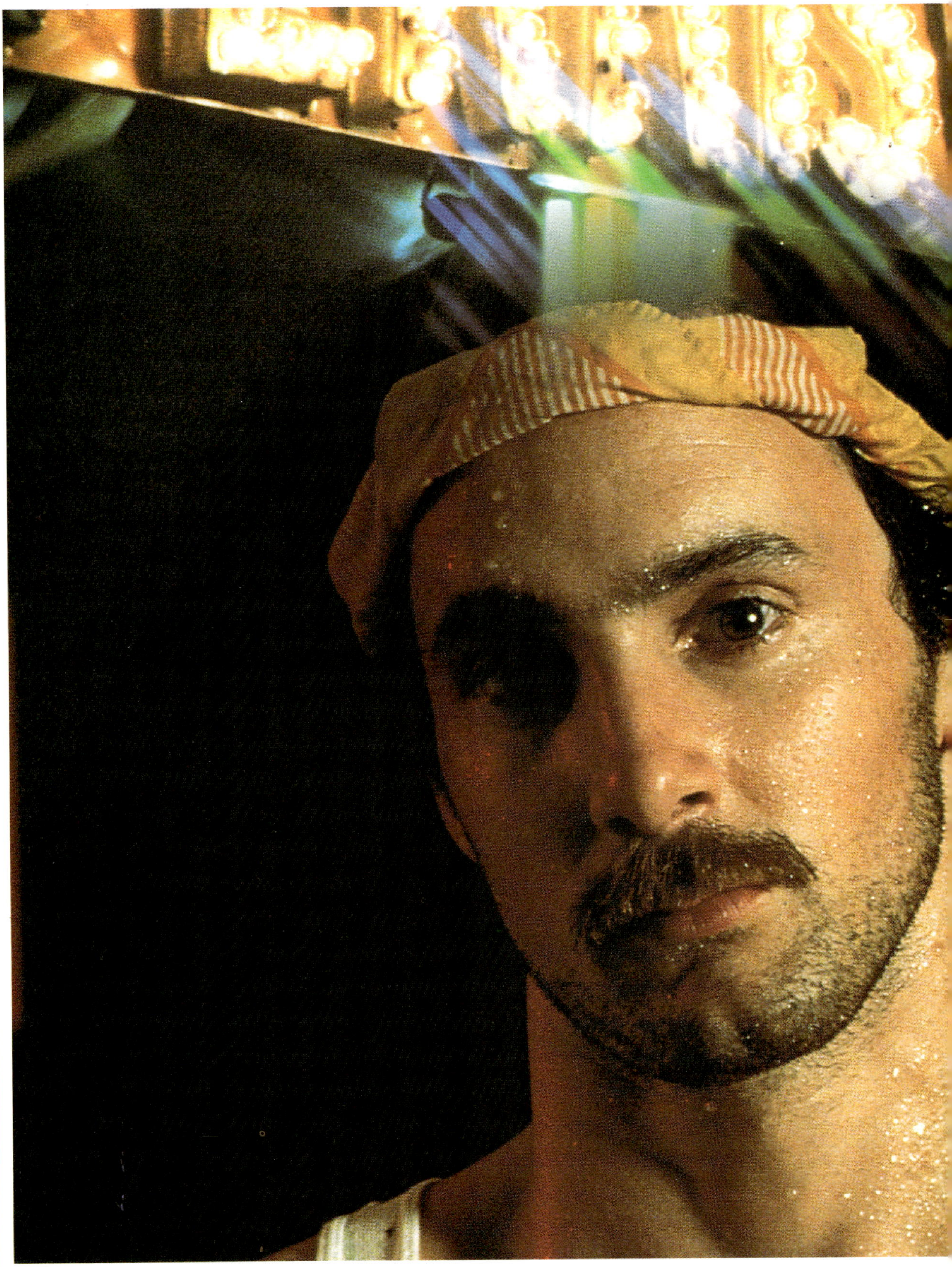

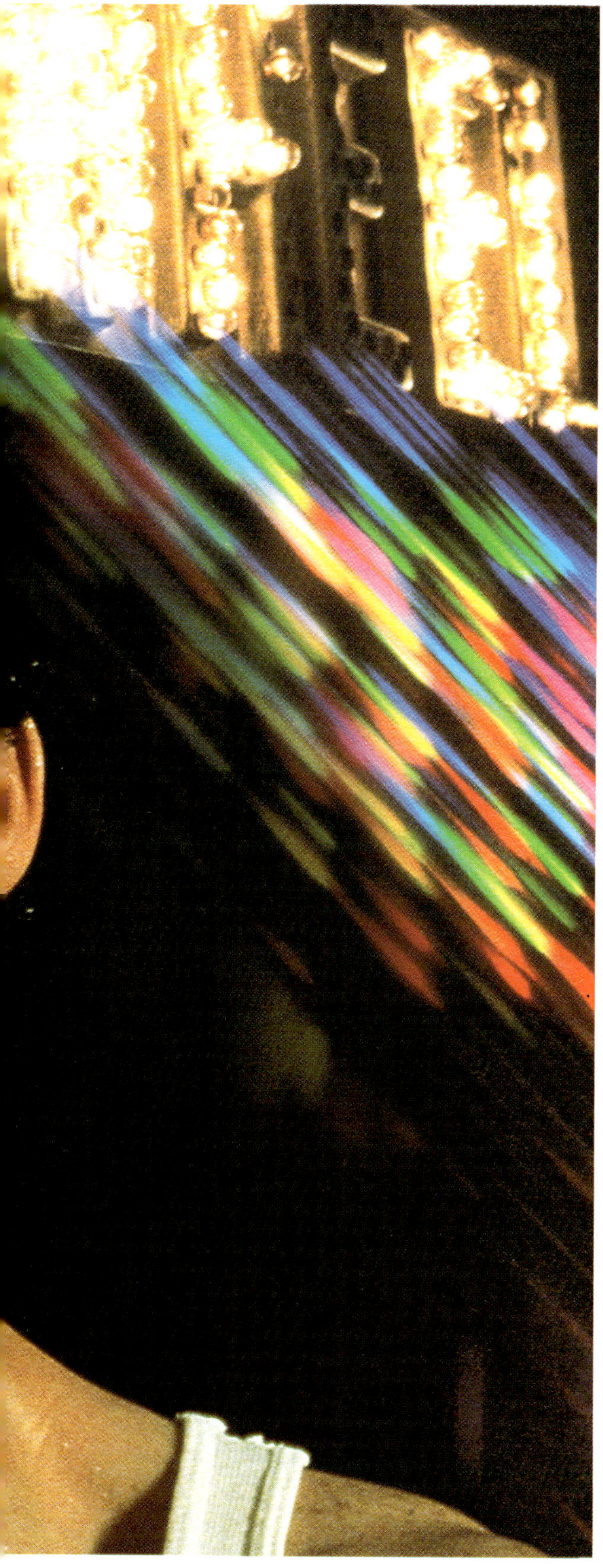

CREATING SPECIAL EFFECTS

DIFFUSING THE IMAGE

One of the prerequisites for a technically-perfect picture is that it should be sharp. Modern lenses are capable of resolving the finest detail with pin-sharp clarity, but this is not necessarily an advantage. It is sometimes more effective for an image to be slightly diffused, as a way of creating atmosphere and also for masking blemishes when taking portraits. Indeed, early portrait photography owed much of its charm and appeal to rather soft and diffused images, due in those times to the inadequacies of lenses rather than to the artifice of the photographer.

Soft focus effects are easily achieved by the use of lens attachments. There is a variety of types, but their basic principle is similar: a clear glass, or plastic disc or square, is engraved or moulded with a pattern that disrupts the image created by the lens and inhibits its ability to record sharp detail. They can be obtained in different grades, ranging from a very subtle image diffusion to almost hazy results. When used with the through-the-lens viewing system of a single lens reflex camera, the effect can be seen on the screen, and the choice of aperture will affect the degree of diffusion: small apertures reduce the effect. No exposure allowance is required and the attachments can also be used on simple cameras such as viewfinder types.

This technique is particularly effective with portrait and glamour pictures since it subdues skin texture and blemishes and has a very flattering effect, but in male photography, it is necessary to use it with some discretion as the results can be too soft and chocolate boxy. The result will be unmasculine if taken too far.

Soft focus creates a pleasing and atmospheric quality when shooting against the light, either outdoors into the sun or with back- or rim-lighting in the studio. The image diffusion creates a shimmering, halo-like effect where there are strong highlights, such as around the model's face or body. A further advantage is that the effect tends to reduce contrast and color saturation, and it can help to create a softer, more harmonious color quality.

In addition to the specially-manufactured attachments, it is also possible to use a variety of other materials to create image diffusion. Adhesive tape can be stretched across the front of a lens hood, leaving a clear hole in the centre, for the image to retain a basic core of sharpness. Nylon gauze also produces an interesting effect. Ladies' tights are ideal, but again it is necessary to leave a clear central area, the size depending both on the degree of diffusion and the aperture used. Clear petroleum jelly adds a further range of possibilities. If this is smeared onto a filter or piece of clear glass or plastic in front of the lens (with the clear, central hole) it can be teased and swirled around with a finger-tip or a cotton swab to produce an infinite degree of diffusion and also an enormous variety of streaks and blurs expanding from bright highlights within the subject.

A final suggestion for image diffusion is to simply use a very crude type of lens, such as a magnifying glass, in place of the camera lens. This can be mounted on the camera by means of a bellows extension or even with the aid of a cardboard tube. You will need to choose a lens with a convenient focal length, determined by holding it in front of a piece of paper, focusing the image of the sun onto it and measuring the distance between them. A camera with TTL, aperture-priority metering will give the correct exposure reading, but you will need to control exposure by means of the shutter speed alone as there will not be an adjustable aperture available.

Diffusion hides fine detail **(opposite top)**, *and spreads out the highlights. Compare the diffused image with the straight picture at near right.*

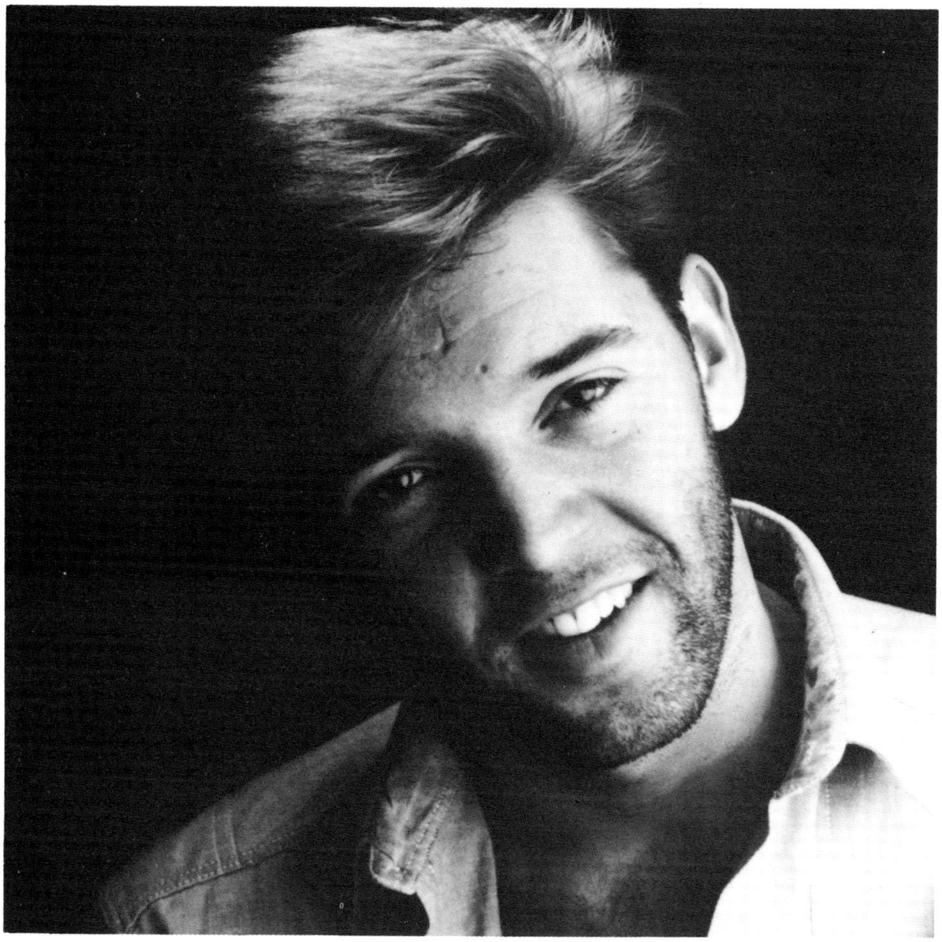

Soft focus effects are most appropriate when the aim is to produce an image which has nostalgic or romantic appeal **(below)**.

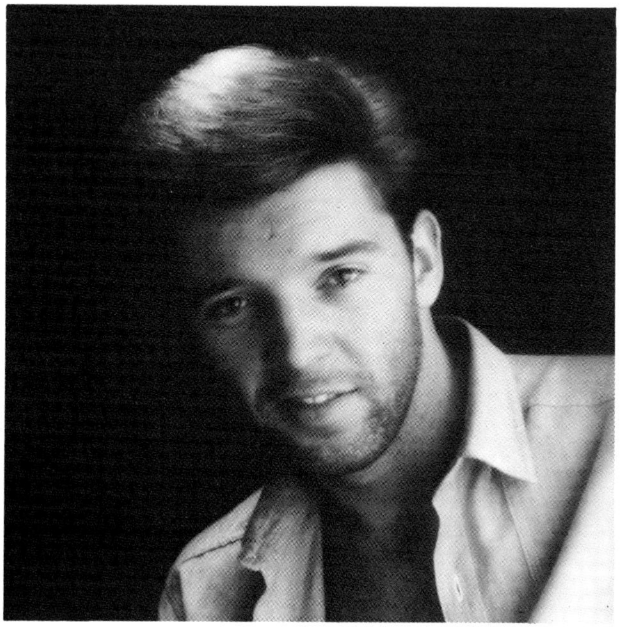

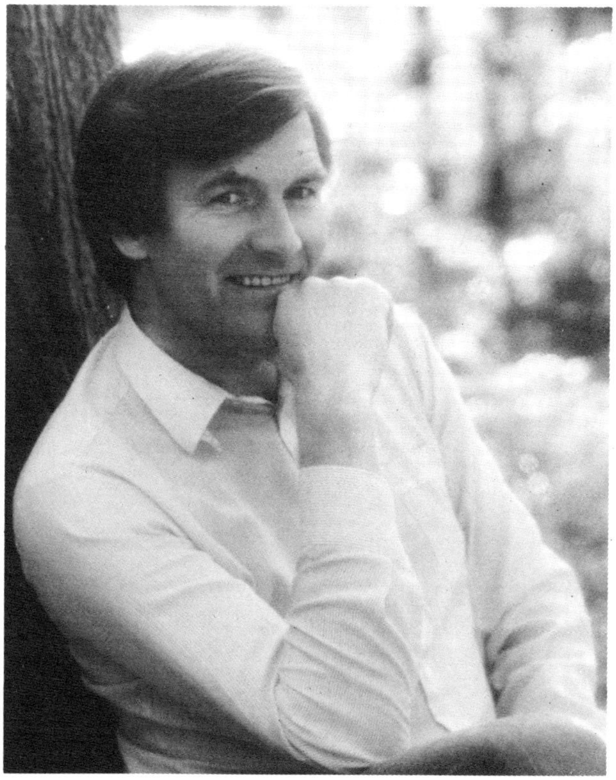

CREATING MULTIPLE IMAGES

One of the most effective ways of creating unusual and abstract images is by the use of multiple exposures. There are a number of ways in which this can be done. Double or triple exposing on to the same piece of film in the camera is quite easy, providing you have a camera which has a means of bypassing the double exposure prevention mechanism. If not, it is possible to rewind and run the film through the camera twice or more after having carefully marked its starting position.

The main point to consider when using this technique is that the film can be exposed twice or more only if it has been partially exposed the first time. This means that the second and subsequent exposures will only record effectively where the first exposure has left unexposed or dark areas. The second image will not register when juxtaposed against highlights or light tones in the original image. For this reason, it is necessary to plan your pictures quite carefully. A camera with a viewing screen upon which you can trace the outlines of the images is a positive advantage.

The simplest way of making a double exposure is to ensure that one of the images you use is essentially dark in tone, like a dark, moody landscape. You then need to ensure that your second image has quite bright highlights to define it, but is placed against a dark or even black background: this could be a rim-lit nude, for example. When combined, it will result in the lighter tones of the nude being recorded quite clearly against the darker areas of the landscape, but with the mid-tones merging nicely together. It is also important to appreciate that the exposures will have a cumulative effect, and for this reason it is necessary to give approximately half of each calculated exposure when making a double exposure. By giving proportionately more or less to one or the other, it is possible to make either images dominate the other.

An effective way of using multiple exposures in the studio is to simulate strobe effects with a moving figure. This can be done by positioning your model against a black background and making a series of exposures, asking your model to move slightly in a smooth action between each exposure. Rim-lighting is the most effective as it will record only the model's outline, defining the movement quite clearly. Be sure to mask stray light from both the background and the front of the model's body, as this will have a cumulative effect on subsequent exposures.

If you own a slide duplicator or an enlarger, it is possible to have more control over your double exposures since you can select individual images and juxtapose them to determine the best way of arranging them before you actually make the exposure. When using an enlarger, it is possible to use shading techniques to control the way the images blend.

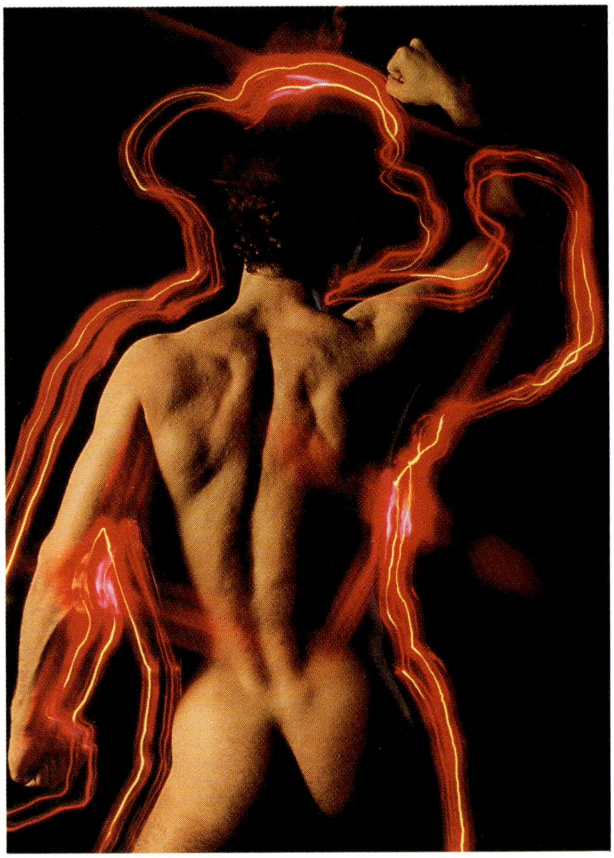

*When making fairly complex multiple exposures such as those shown here, **you will find** that it saves time to make a pencil sketch of the position of each element within the frame. If your camera has a removable prism, you can even sketch an outline drawing on the focusing screen, using a wax pencil, for absolute accuracy.*

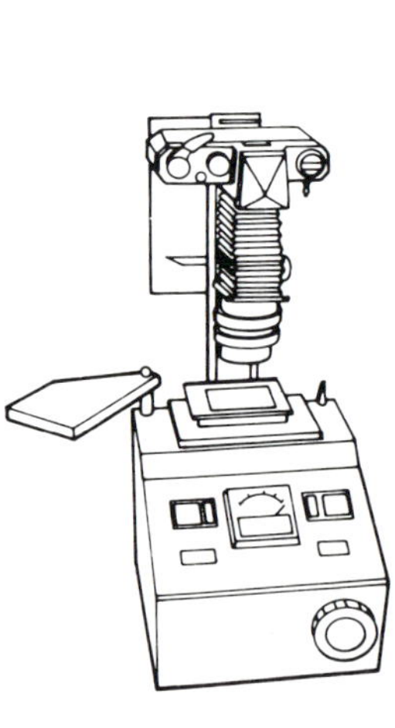

A bench-top copier **(left)** *allows you to shoot each element of the picture separately, then unite them on a single piece of film later on.*

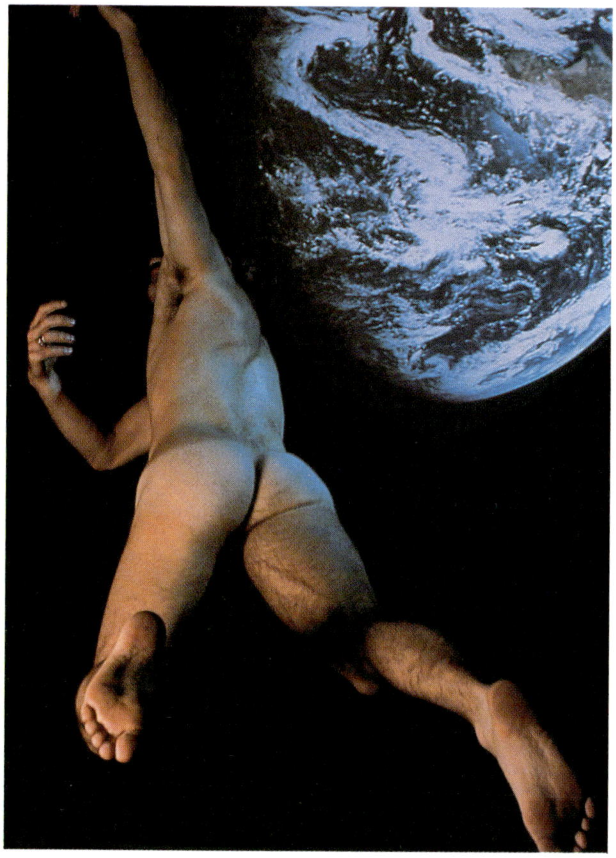

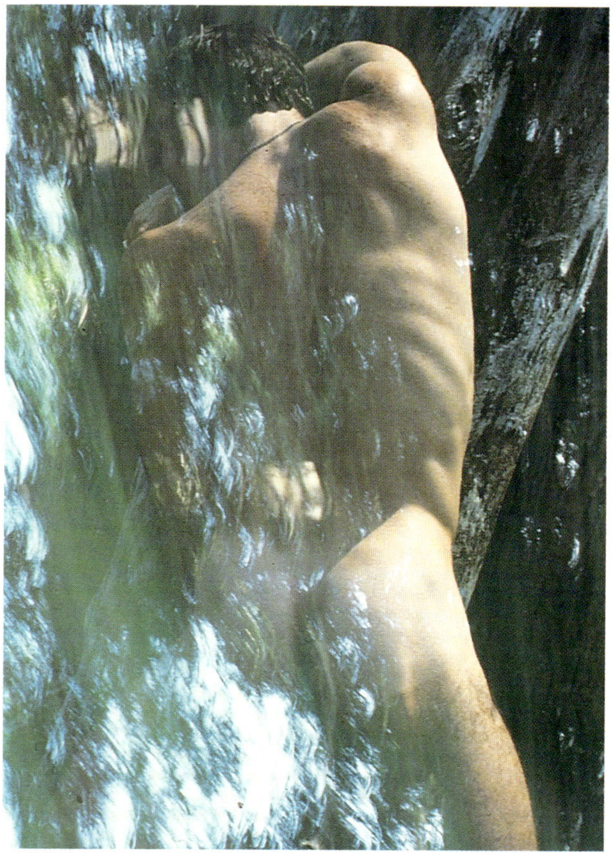

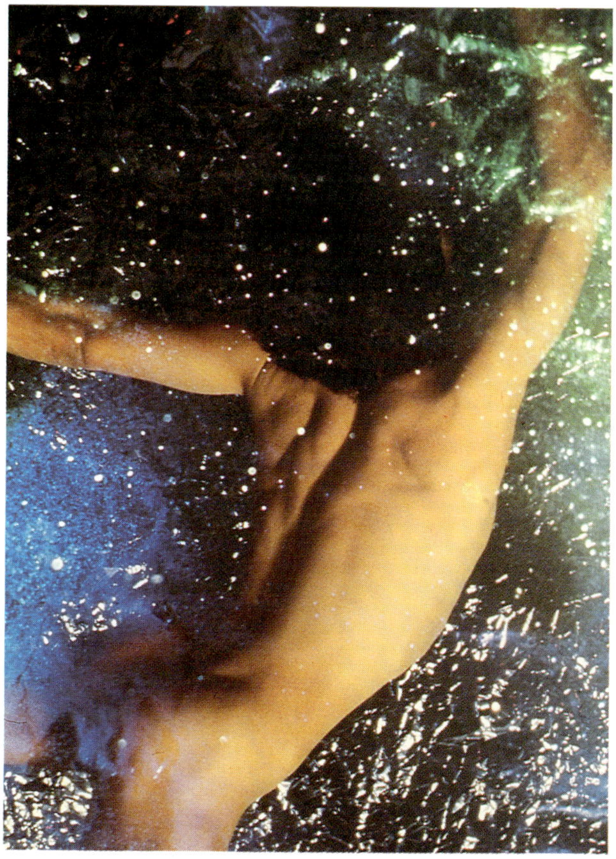

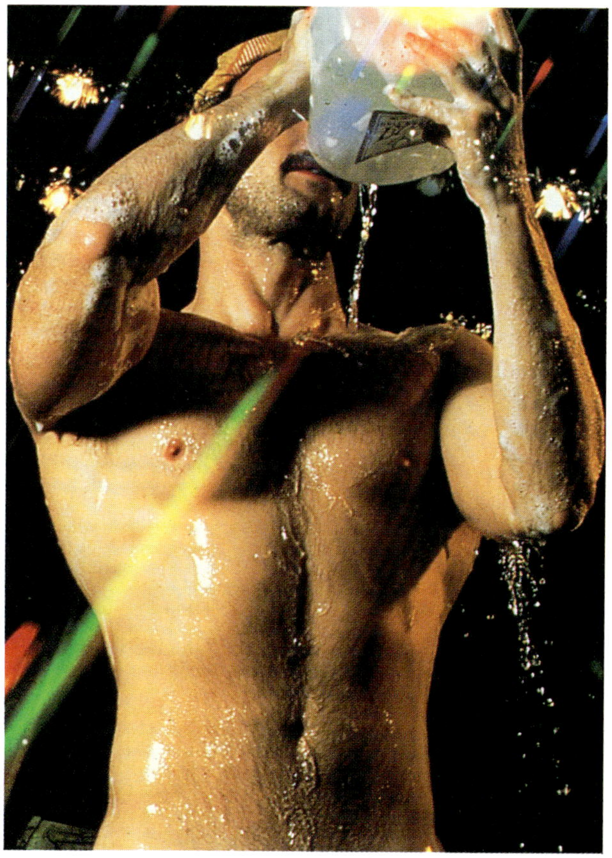

EFFECTS WITH FILM

In normal circumstances, a print is made in a way which reproduces the tones of the negative or transparency as faithfully as possible. However, there are a number of techniques which can be used to alter both the tonal range and the quality of the print, as well as its effect and mood. A simple method, and one which can produce strikingly bold images with little fuss, is that of tone elimination. This simply means reducing a normal image with a full range of tones to one in which there is just pure black and white. It can be particularly effective with pictures that have a strong shape or outline or an element of pattern or texture, and it can also be combined successfully with a very grainy image.

The effect is achieved by use of a special high-contrast emulsion made for lithography and reproduction processes. Kodak supplies a film called Kodalith, together with a specially-formulated developer. Tetenal also supplies a high-contrast paper, giving a pure black and white print direct from a normal negative, called Fotografik Document Paper. It must be used with its special developer. Lith film can be used to make a high-contrast negative direct from a color transparency, which can then be printed on conventional bromide paper. Exposure is the key to this technique as it determines the final effect. As the image will be divided only into black and white tones, the point at which their division takes place will be determined by the exposure. A short exposure will record all but the darkest areas of the image as black and all the rest as white, whereas a longer exposure will produce a black image from all but the very lightest tones in the original.

Another interesting effect can be created quite easily by the use of texture screens. These are simply weak images on film, usually on a texture or a small pattern, such as a printer's screen or perhaps a canvas or silk effect. The procedure is to place this film in contact with the negative or transparency and to make the print from the combination. It is possible to buy a selection of such texture screens from photographic stores, but it can also be interesting to make your own. The translucent paper used for negative storage envelopes, for example, can create an attractive crystalline effect.

The Sabattier effect or solarization is the result of re-exposing a negative during development to produce a partial reversal of the image and to create a line around the affected areas. Its effect is rather unpredictable and for this reason it is best to experiment with a copy negative rather than an original. A similar effect can also be created directly on a print or negative by purely chemical means, and this can be controlled rather more easily. This chemical is available from Colorvir as part of their special effects kit and also from Tetenal under the trade name Fotografix.

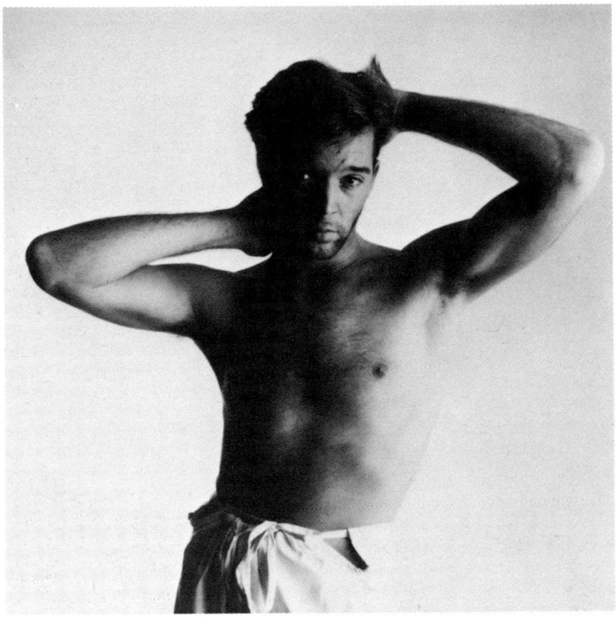

Grainy films produce moody, heavily textured images **(right)** *compared to photographs shot on regular black and white film* **(above)**. *A similar effect can be produced in color, using the new generation of ultra-speed films such as Kodak VR 1000 (for negatives) or Ektachrome 800 – 1600 (for slides). Slide film can additionally be underexposed and then pushed – overdeveloped – to further increase grain.*

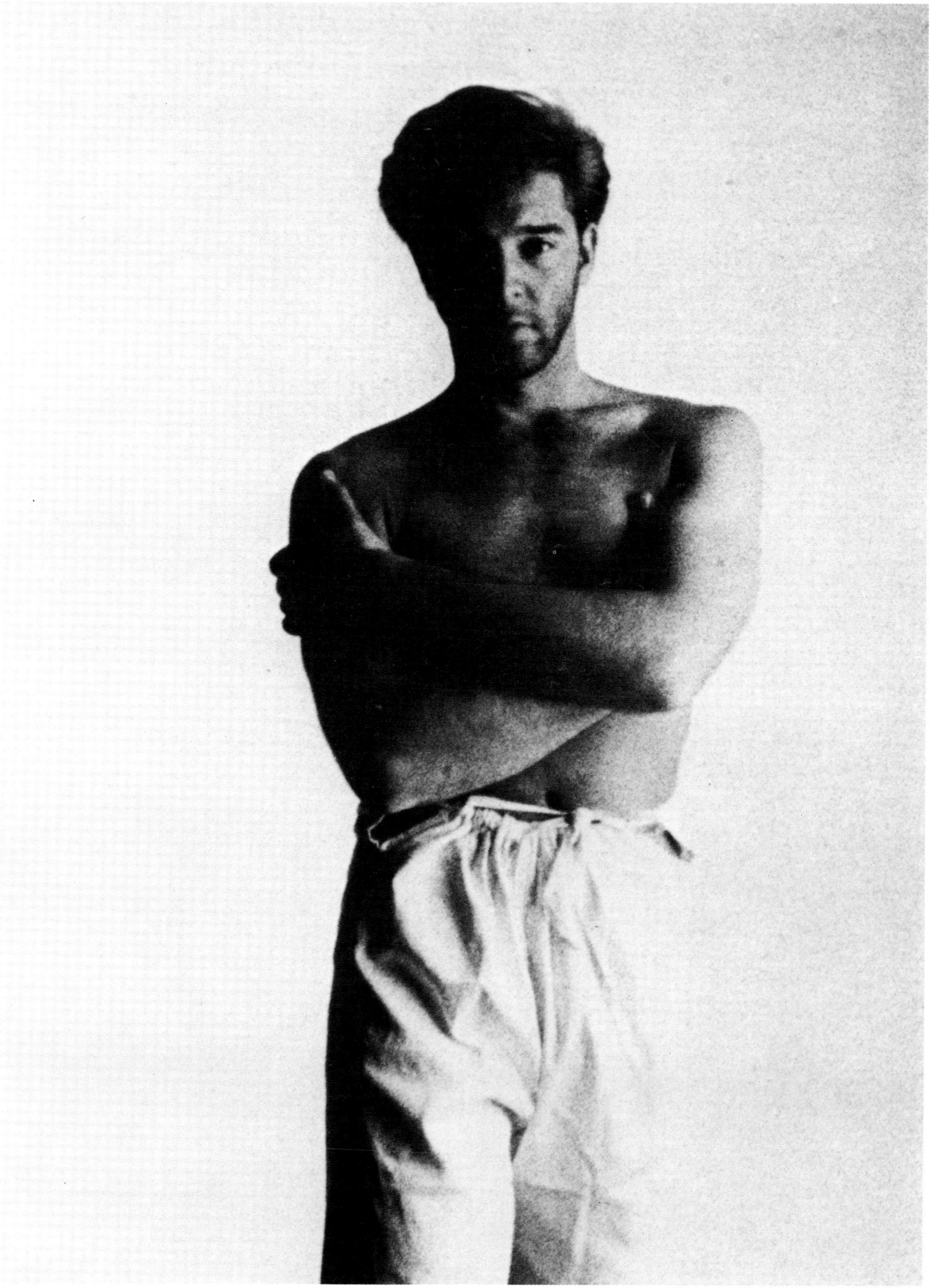

PROJECTED IMAGES

If you own – or can borrow – a slide projector, there is a variety of ways in which it can be used to create interesting and even abstract pictures. You will also need a darkened room, ideally some photographic lighting and a large screen or piece of white cardboard.

One way in which a projected image can be used creatively is to superimpose a transparency onto your model. You simply place the selected slide into the projector and use your model as a screen. With a light-skinned model, you can use his bare body or face as a background but you can of course also use a light-toned item of clothing or prop. It can be very effective if you choose a fairly abstract image for the projector such as a pattern or texture shot, in close-up. It also needs to be quite bright and contrasty as it will lose something when projected; there will also be a degradation of the projected image if the room is not effectively darkened. If you place your model against a black background, the projected image will simply take on the shape of his outline when the projector is positioned close to the camera. If you move the projector to one side of the camera, it will create a degree of modelling and also some shadows in addition to the image.

It is also possible to combine lighting effects with the projected image. In this way, part of the body can appear normal but the shadow areas will allow the projected image to be revealed. For this reason, rim-lighting can be most effective since it will clearly define the model's outline, but create large areas of shadow where the projected image dominates.

You can also use a white background for this technique. If you place your model close to a large piece of white cardboard or paper, the projected image will spill over onto the background and the result will tend to be more like a montage, with the projected image and the model blending together. If the projector is placed to one side of the camera, it will also throw a shadow on the model onto the background, adding another element to the composition.

In addition to projecting a slide onto the model, you can also reverse the procedure and project a slide of the model onto a surface or object. This can also be done either with or without additional lighting to vary the extent to which either image dominates. You could rim-light a still life of a light-toned vase so that the projected image would appear as part of the decoration, or you could simply project the image of the model onto a textured surface to create a canvas or wood-grained effect, for example.

When shooting in color, you will need to use artificial light type film and if the projected image is quite large, you will probably need to use a fast film to avoid using a slow shutter speed. To ensure a sharp image, the projector must be firmly supported and the camera mounted on a tripod. Providing the projected image is of normal tone, an exposure reading taken in the usual way should produce a good result.

Slides that look nondescript projected on a screen may look great when shining on a torso. The best images are those that have a strong linear structure, or a repeated motif.

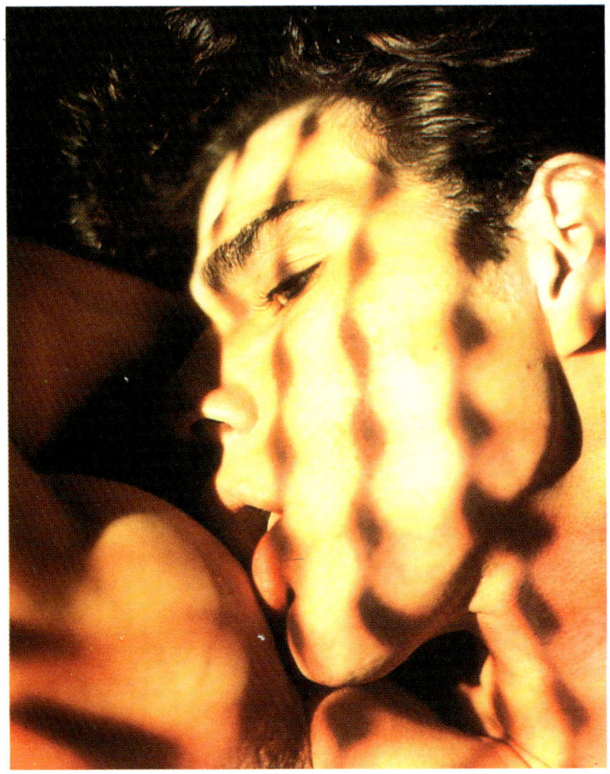

Projected images conform to the shape of your model's body, picking out his curves in a manner similar to the contour lines on a topographical map.

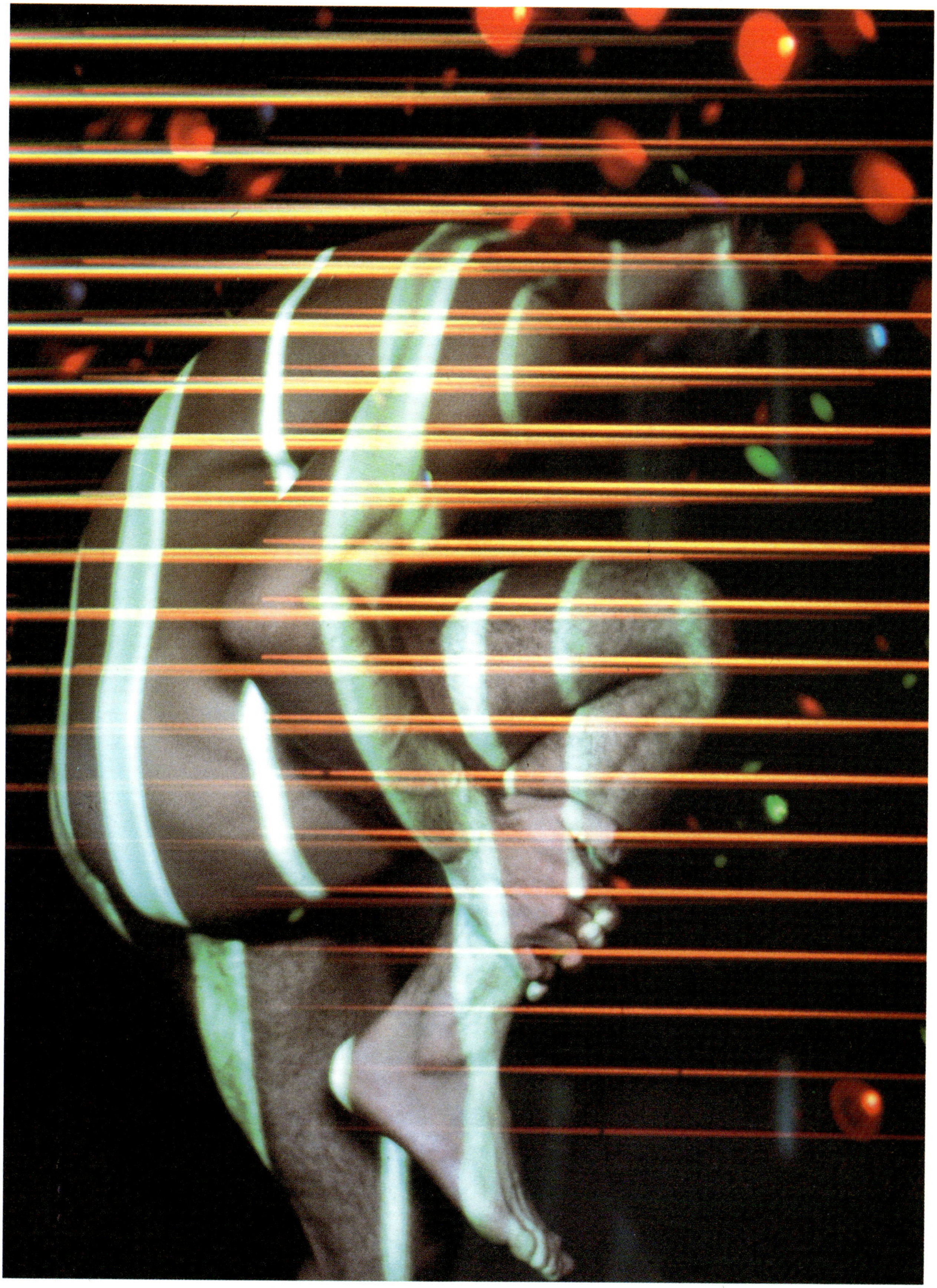

MAKING A SLIDE SANDWICH

A slide sandwich is a simple, yet effective, way of combining two images. Unlike a multiple exposure, it allows you to control both and judge the effect more easily. Essentially, you simply place one slide on top of another, but the effect will depend on your selection of slides and upon their quality. As the combined effect will also have a combined density, it is best to choose slides that are a little thin, or slightly over-exposed. It will help if you have a light box upon which you can spread and sort your images and to make the juxtapositions.

The most basic, and in some ways the most effective way, of producing a slide sandwich is to combine a slide that has a quite even and regular tone or quality with one that has a predominantly bold shape or line. It is best to think of the individual images in terms of subject and background. You might, for instance, choose a pattern or textural image, like a field of corn as the background image with, say, a picture of your model almost silhouetted against a white or very light-toned background as the more dominant image. It works best when the two images produce a degree of contrast with each other: a dark image against an essentially light one, or a bluish picture juxtaposed with, say, a red image.

It will help if you choose slides that are not too tightly framed, as this will allow you to alter their relative positions more freely and to vary the juxtaposition. In fact, it can be a benefit to combine slides of a larger format, say 6 × 6cm, with 35mm.

Once you have found the best juxtaposition for your slides, you can simply tape them together along two edges and then place them in the same mount. It can now be projected in the normal way if desired or you can make a color print or a duplicate transparency from the result.

Although you will probably make your first attempts with slides you have already on file (they might even be rejects), it is much more satisfying to plan your final image and to shoot them specially for the purpose. This will allow you to frame your picture in the best way and to adjust exposure, color quality and other elements of the two images to create the best effect. You could try shooting the 'background picture' a little out of focus, or with blurred movement, to create a stronger relief with the more dominant image, or you could shoot one with a color filter to create a color contrast. It can help to sketch out your ideas beforehand and to work out where you need light and dark areas, or other types of contrast, in each of the two pictures to obtain maximum impact.

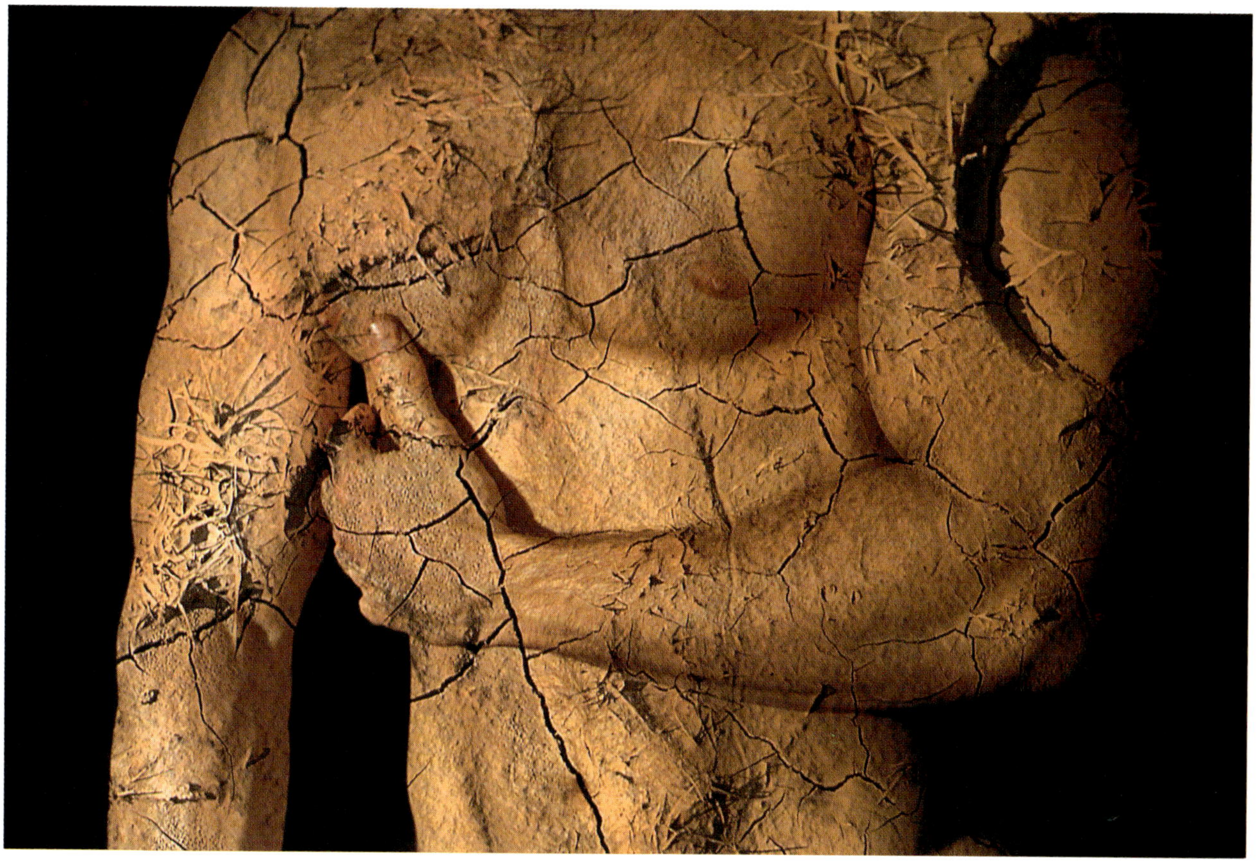

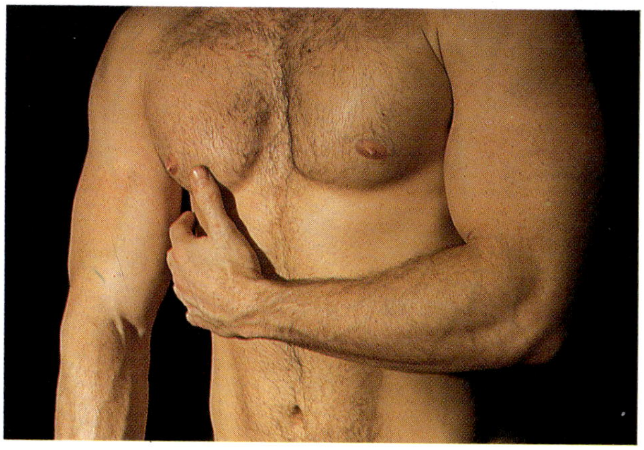

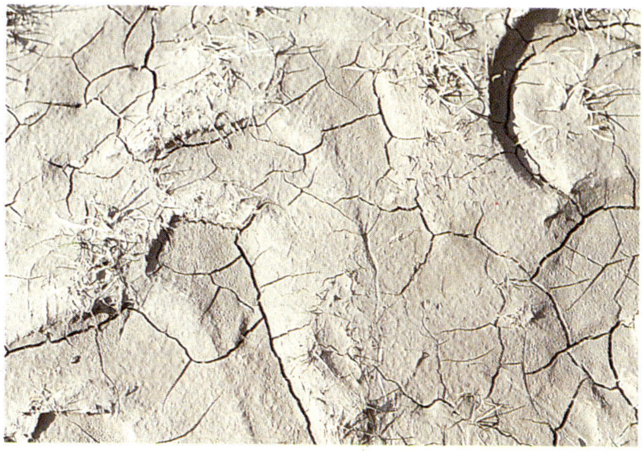

Choose images for sandwiching carefully. Neither should be too dark – overexposed pictures work best. The main picture should be quite bold in composition, with a good range of tones from highlight to shadow **(bottom left)**. *The background image should be very much paler* **(bottom right)**. *Sandwiched together, the two pictures should complement each other, not clash.*

MAKING A MONTAGE

A montage involves a technique in which two or more separate images are combined to produce a single photograph. It can be worked so that the result appears to be uncontrived, or it can be calculatedly unnatural or ambiguous. Unlike a slide sandwich or a multiple exposure, a montage uses negatives and prints to achieve the final effect and requires the use of a darkroom.

It is first necessary to select the images you wish to combine and, at the same time, to plan the final effect. To avoid a complicated and confusing result and to create a bolder effect, it is best to plan your picture so that the darker tones of one image are juxtaposed against lighter tones in the other.

Once you have made your selection, place the first of your two (or more) negatives in the enlarger carrier and size it up according to the paper you are using. When it is focused and framed correctly, place a piece of plain paper the size of the final print into the masking frame and trace the most important outlines of the image onto it with a black marking pen. You can now make a test strip and process it in the normal way. Next, you must replace the first negative with the other and, with the tracing placed back into the masking frame in exactly the same position, size up, frame and focus this image in relation to the first, according to the effect you want. You can now make a test strip from this negative.

Once you have determined the correct exposure for each of the negatives you are using, you can make the first attempt at a montage. After checking its position on the tracing and the focus, expose the negative you last used in the normal way, after having marked the paper to ensure that you know which way it was placed in the masking frame. Place this exposed print in a light-tight box and replace the other negative in the enlarger, using the tracing to size and position it. You can now re-expose the piece of paper with the second image, after ensuring the paper is in the masking frame the same way as for the first exposure. This can now be processed in the normal way.

It is unlikely that your first print will be completely satisfactory, since the effect of a montage depends to a large extent upon the way the two images blend. It is important to appreciate that the exposure you assessed is correct when it is made on a piece of unexposed paper but, if it is combined with an existing image, it will be darker. Consequently, in most cases, you will need to adjust the exposures and also use shading techniques to make the images blend according to the way they are juxtaposed and to the effect you want. When a darker detail is juxtaposed against a light one, it will be more dominant so you can control the effect by shading back areas of one image in order to emphasize the other.

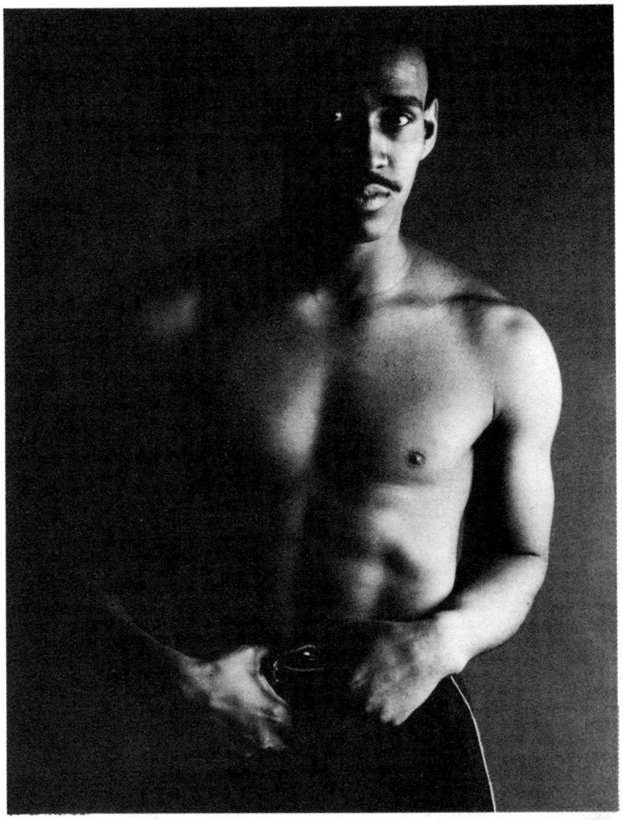

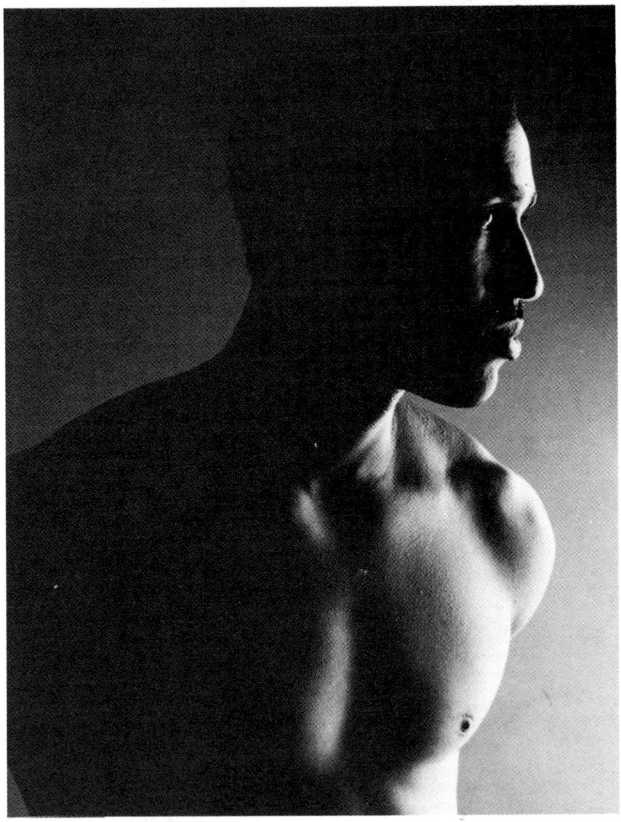

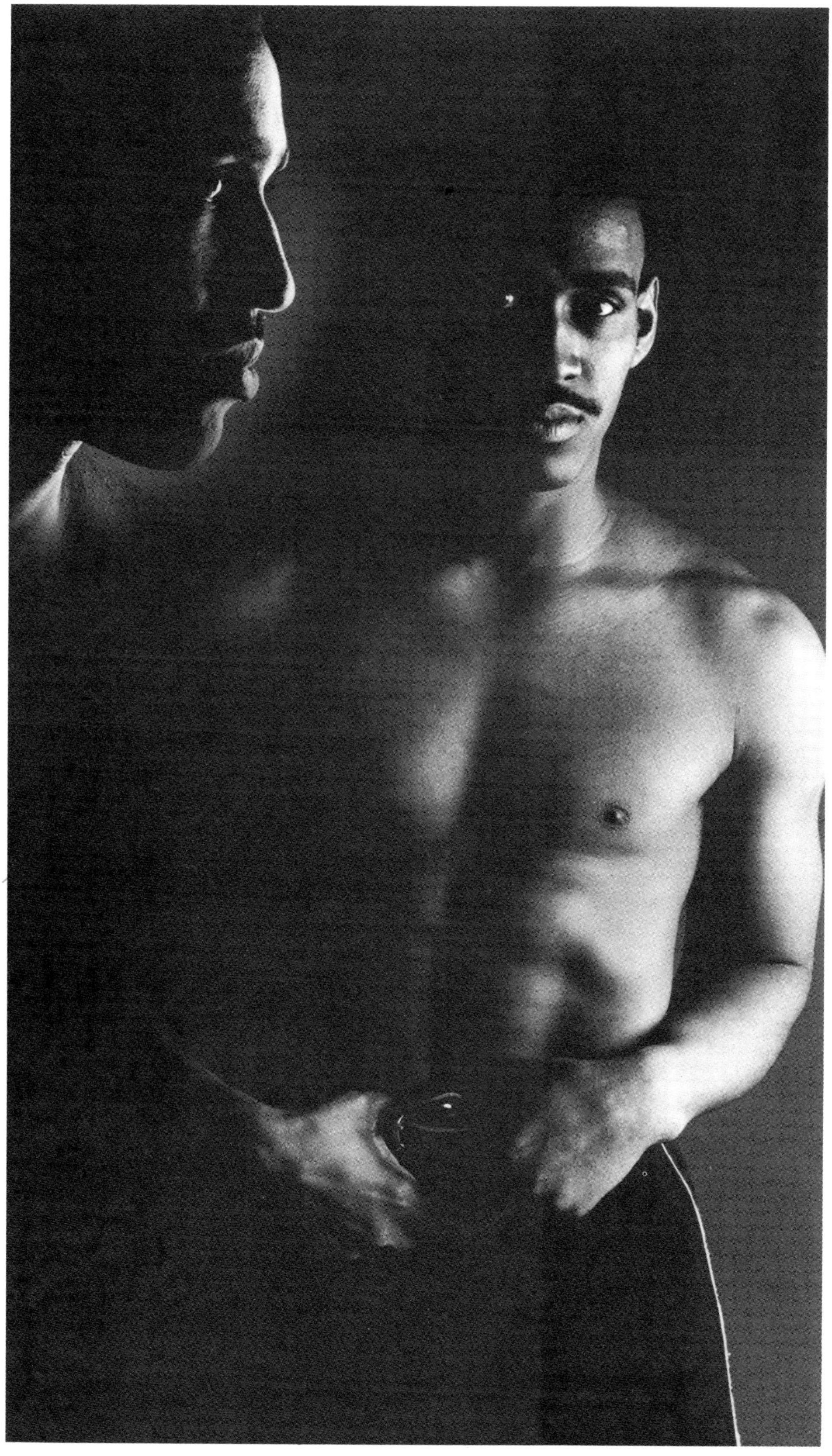

Using the montage technique described opposite, you can show several images of your subject in a single print, or perhaps combine several completely incongruous images.

TONE MANIPULATIONS

In normal circumstances, film is chosen to simply record the image as sharply and accurately as possible, but both interesting and unusual effects can be produced by either modifying the film's response, or by the use of special film. The use of the film's grain structure is a particularly striking and simple way of creating dramatic, evocative images. All films have a grain structure, although with slow or medium-speed films it is very fine and will not be noticeable at normal degrees of enlargement. High-speed films, however, have a marked and coarse grain structure which becomes visible at even modest degrees of enlargement. This technique is most effective when the grain is particularly pronounced and there are a number of ways of achieving this end.

Firstly, select the fastest practical film. When shooting in black and white, you can use a special film made by Kodak and available in 35mm cassettes. It is called 2475 Recording Film and has an attractive, gritty quality. Failing that any fast film will give you a result. In addition, the film can be uprated by push-processing. This will significantly increase the grain size, and when shooting in color, it is best to use transparency film since this can be push-processed more effectively. Since the effect of the grain will be more pronounced the greater the enlargement, it is also best to compose your pictures so that only a small central area of the negative or transparency is needed. A useful trick here is to compose your picture using a standard or telephoto lens, then switch to a much shorter focal length for the exposure. The full effect of the grain will only be realized if the prints are pin-sharp and it is vital to ensure that the enlarger is focused accurately, using a small aperture for the enlarging lens to produce maximum definition right into the corners of the image.

In addition to grain, the tonal quality of the film can also be used to create unusual effects. Infra-red film is particularly interesting and can be obtained in both black and white and color emulsions in 35mm cassettes. A Wratten 12 filter, deep yellow, is recommended for use with the Kodak infra-red color film, but it is interesting to experiment with other filters: a sepia-colored filter is worth trying, for instance. When used on a sunny day outdoors, green foliage will record as a bright red tone with the recommended filter and skin tones will appear almost normal. A wide range of other effects can be created, according to the filter used, the lighting conditions and also the exposure.

The black and white infra-red film can be used with a special infra-red filter, but it is also very effective with a deep red one, creating almost black tones from a blue sky with skin tones as a chalky white and green foliage also as a near white tone.

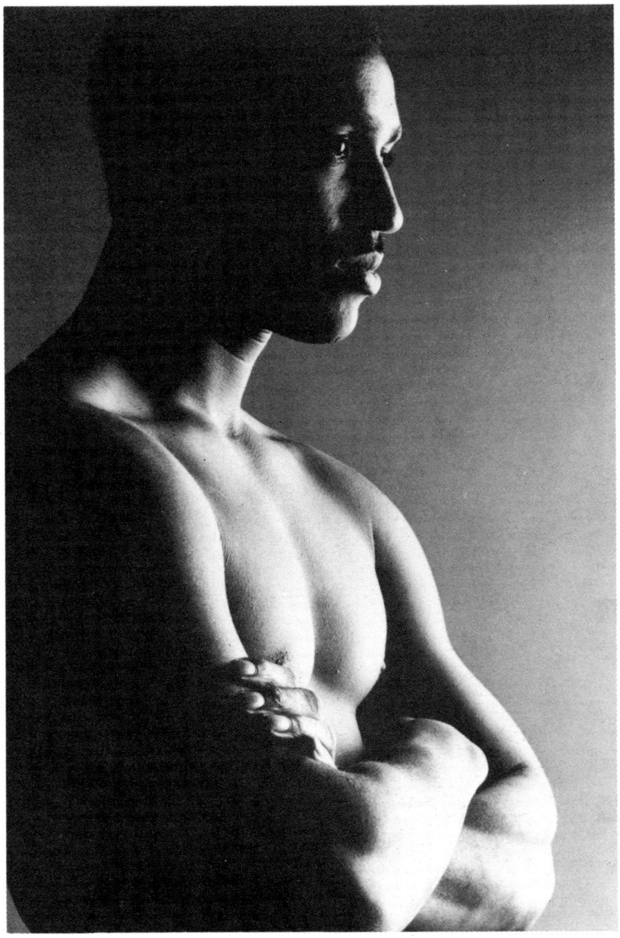

Tone elimination works best when the original negative itself has quite high contrast, as this one does. Though the conventional route to solid black-and-white images with no mid tones involves the use of special film and chemicals, you may be able to produce similar effects using a regular office photocopier.

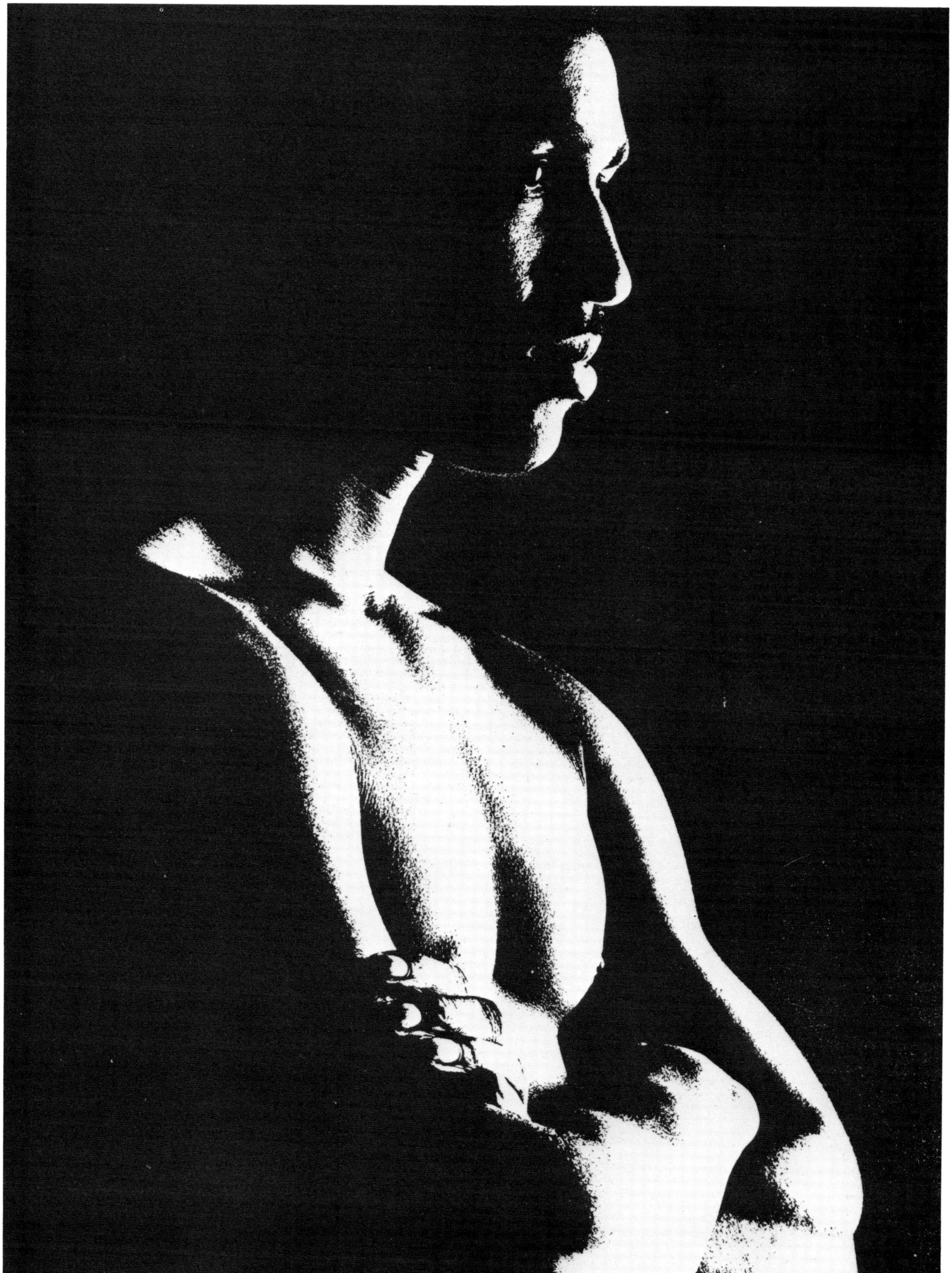

COLOR FROM BLACK AND WHITE

There are a number of ways to produce a colored image from a black and white original and, although there is little point in attempting to emulate the effect achieved by shooting on color film, there is considerable potential for creating unusual and intriguing images with these techniques. There are a number of paper manufacturers who produce bromide papers with colored bases, allowing a single-colored image to be produced directly from a conventional black and white negative. Kentmere Kentint and Argenta Autone are two such papers, available in a wide range of colors including metallic.

A much wider range of effects can be created by the use of toners and dyes. These are applied to a black and white print after normal processing and drying and the process can be carried out in daylight. Toning enables the metallic silver image to be converted to a chemical dye, producing a picture in which the whites are unaffected by the grey and black tones are given a color. Dying results in the whites and lighter tones taking up the color of the dye, leaving the blacks and darker greys neutral. Sepia is the best-known type of toner and can create a very pleasing effect, but there is also a wide range of other colors from red and orange to blue and green which can be produced by this method. Some processes require that the black and white print is first bleached and then redeveloped, others simply use a single bath to tone the print. It is also possible to combine toning and dying within the same print to create a multicolored effect. There are kits, such as that made by Colorvir, which provide a variety of chemicals and dyes to be combined in a number of ways to create different effects.

Hand-coloring is a technique which was widely used before color film was invented and it can still be used today to produce controlled and selective color effects. A variety of coloring mediums can be used from oils to felt tip pens. A very simple method is to use transparent photo dyes applied with a brush or cotton-wool swab to a damp-dry print. These have the advantage of being absorbed into the emulsion and leave no visible trace on the surface of the print.

Whichever method is used, it is best to start with the larger areas of tone and detail and with the softer, weaker hues leaving the bolder colors and smaller details until last. It is not always most effective to attempt to color every detail in the image, because often a much more striking effect can be created by leaving the print mainly monochromatic and simply picking out small details with the application of color. It is often helpful to use a sepia-toned print as the basis for hand coloring as it will tend to degrade the colors less than a full-toned black and white print.

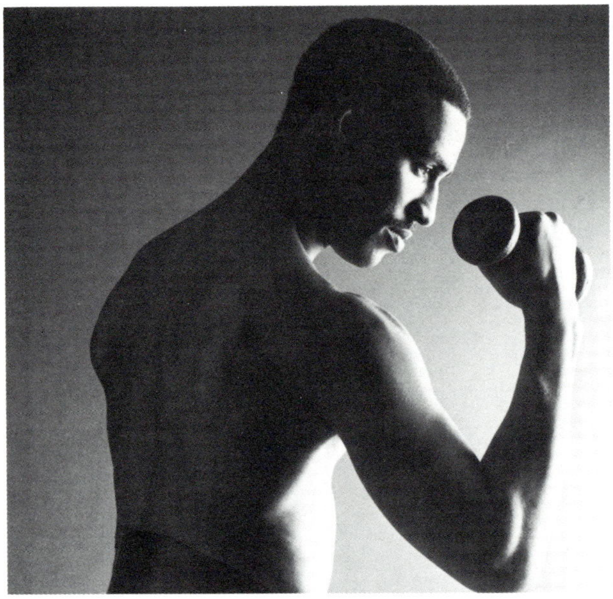

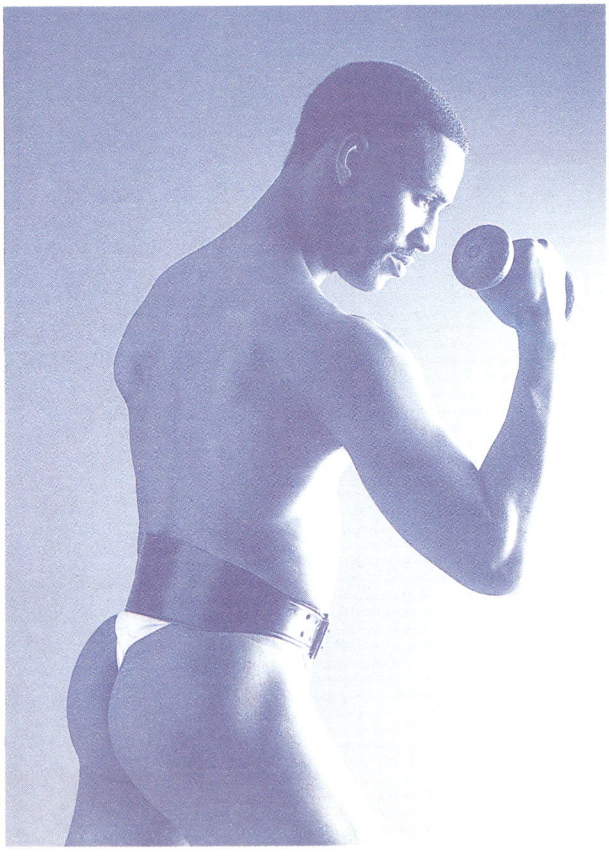

Iron toner **(near right)** *tints black and white prints bright blue, and intensifies the image, so start with a pale, flat print. Most types of sepia toner, on the other hand, reduce contrast, so it is best to print your pictures on harder paper if you plan to sepia tone them* **(far right)**.

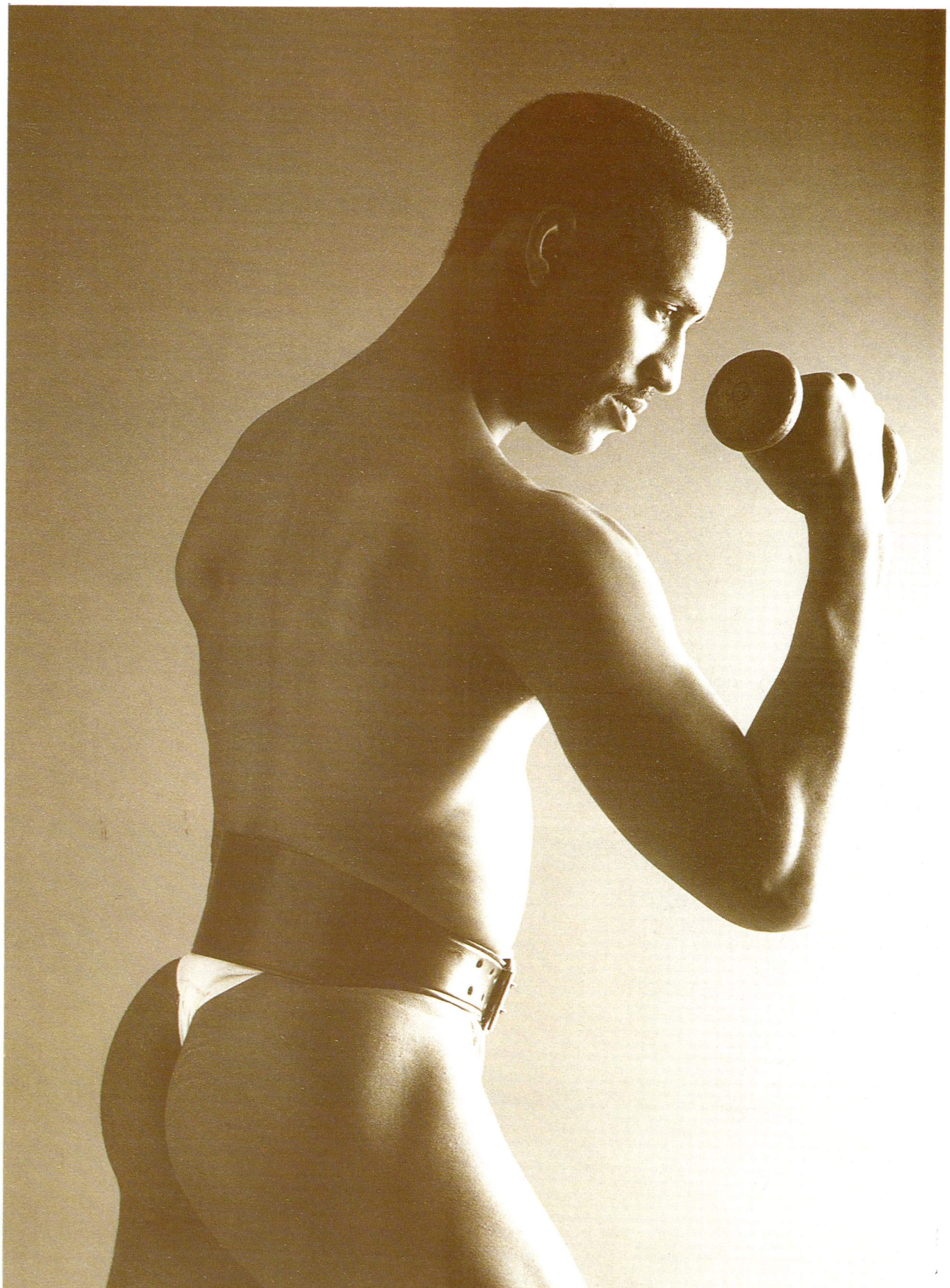

PRESENTATION AND DISPLAY

A great deal of the pleasure of photography is in being able to show your work to others, and in this context the method and style of presentation is a vital consideration. It is important to appreciate that even the best picture will lose some of its impact if poorly or indifferently finished and presented. A portfolio is an ideal means of displaying your prints and a convenient way of carrying and protecting them. There are a number of different types. A simple box or folder in which individually-mounted prints can be kept is an ideal way of displaying them occasionally, but constant handling can damage the unprotected surfaces. For a more practical and protective presentation, a folder with detachable plastic sleeves can be a better choice. Individual, mounted prints can be placed inside the sleeves and the prints can be easily changed around to suit a particular occasion.

A mounted print tends to look far more pleasing and professional than an unmounted one, and this alone can improve the initial impression of your work. Prints on resin-coated paper can be quite satisfactorily mounted with the aid of an aerosol spray adhesive, but fibre-based prints will have a flatter and smoother finish when dry-mounted. In addition to mounting, it is also vital to ensure that all dust spots and blemishes have been removed from the print. This can be done by the careful application of water colour paint or dye. A very fine brush is used to fill in white marks, using a color and tone which matches the surrounding area. Black marks can be removed either by a bleach or use of the scalpel to carefully shave away the emulsion where the mark is until it approximately matches the surrounding area.

The best method of presenting color transparencies is undoubtedly by projection and a well-chosen selection of slides, shown on a large screen in a darkened room can have considerable impact. In other situations, it is impressive to mount color slides in black card mounts. These are designed to hold a number of transparencies, usually twelve 6 × 6cm or twenty 35mm. The complete sheet is then placed into a protective plastic sleeve, usually with a frosted back which allows the slides to be viewed against any convenient light source, such as a window.

The effect of photographs for display, either in the home or office or on an exhibition wall, can also be greatly enhanced by sympathetic framing. There is a number of frame kits available which are particularly suitable for photographs, the aluminium type, for example, or even the simple clip frame in which the print is sandwiched between a piece of glass and the mount and held together by small metal clips. In addition to mounting, a framed print can also benefit by adding a cut-out overlay or matt. This is a piece of card cut to fit the frame with an aperture cut to the size of the print. The result looks particularly effective if a thick overlay card is cut with a bevelled edge and its tone or print is chosen to complement the print.

Sorting, selecting and mounting prints and slides is a great deal easier if you have the right tools for the task. A pair of black cardboard 'L' shapes will help you decide which framing looks best **(top left)**, *and a wax pencil is a handy way of marking a crop on the print – you can wipe off the lines with spirit. For slides, the most valuable accessory is a light box. This is a back-illuminated sheet of white glass or acrylic, and it enables you to look comfortably at twenty or more slides. Storing the slides in clear plastic file sheets makes this easier still. A powerful magnifier enables you to weed out pictures that are unsharp or have other faults.*

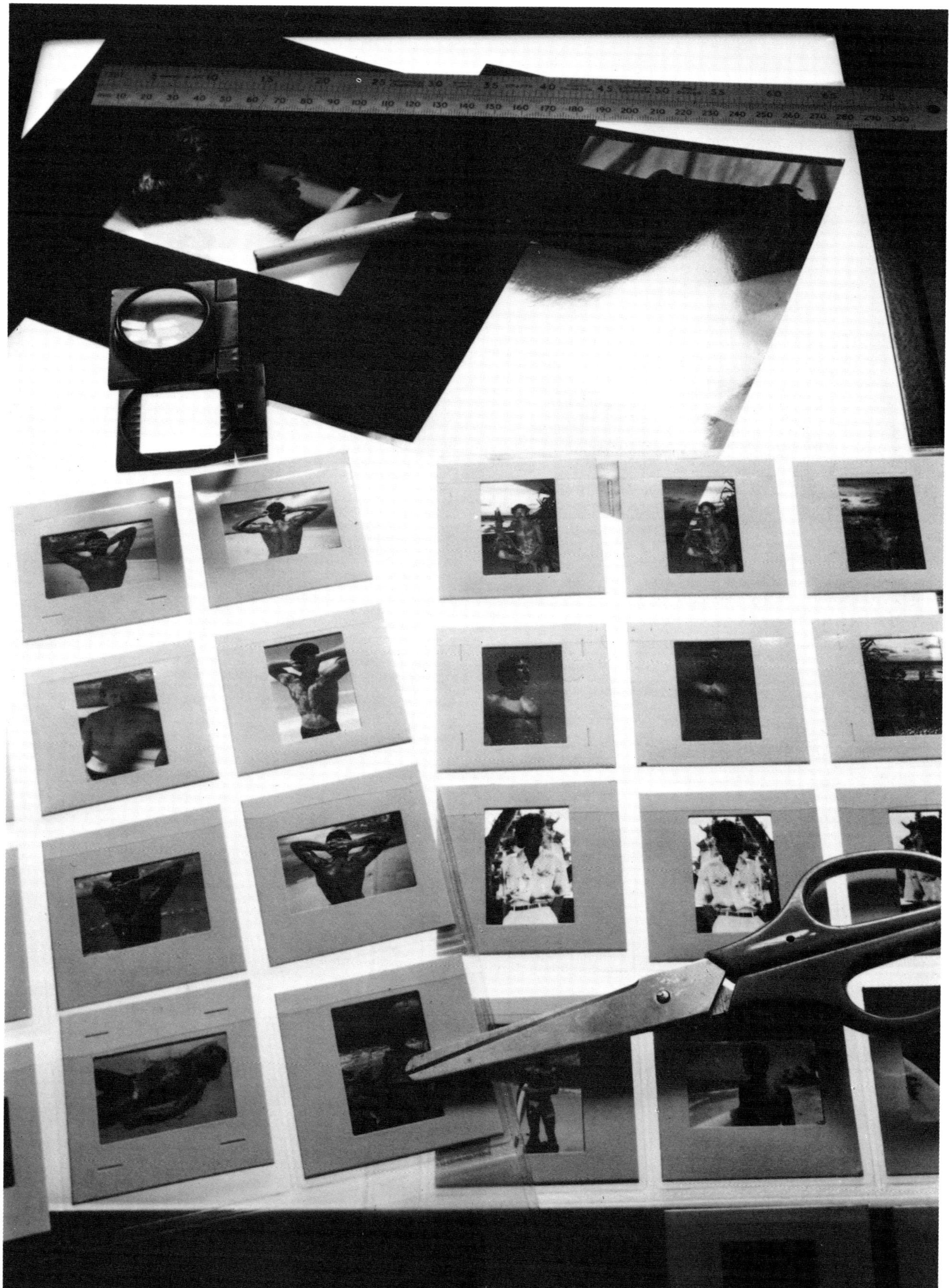

GLOSSARY

ASA
Measure of film speed now superseded by ISO scale, to which it is numerically equal.

APERTURE
Adjustable hole made by several small metal leaves between the elements of a camera's lens. Used to control the intensity of light reaching the film and thus also the exposure
See also STOP.

BLEACH
Chemical used to remove silver from photographic image, thereby reducing density. On prints, applied locally to lighten small areas.

BRACKETING
Process of making several pictures of the same subject, but giving each picture a different exposure to ensure that one is perfect. For example, a photographer might make one exposure at the setting indicated by the meter, then give one picture half a stop extra exposure, and a third half a stop less. This acts as an insurance policy, and is a particularly useful technique in high-contrast situations where exposure is critical.

CABLE RELEASE
Flexible cable inside a pliant tube. One end screws into the camera's shutter release; pressing a plunger at the other initiates the exposure without vibration being transmitted to the camera.

CENTER-WEIGHTING
Term used to describe TTL exposure metering systems that are more sensitive to light reflected from the central area of the subject than to the outer areas of the frame. Most TTL meters are center-weighted, but some much more heavily than others.

CLOSE-UP LENS
Add-on-lens resembling a filter. Reduces camera's minimum focusing distance, thereby permitting close-up pictures.

COLOR CAST
Usually undesirable wash of color uniformly covering the whole of a photograph.

COLOR SATURATION
Term loosely used to connote richness and depth of color.

COLOR TEMPERATURE
Scale used by photographers to describe color of light. Bluish light, such as that from an overcast sky, has a high color temperature. Yellowish light like candle-light, a low color temperature. Usually measured in kelvins.

CONTRAST
Difference between lightest and darkest areas. On a print or slide, contrast refers to the difference in the amount of silver or dye in the darkest and lightest areas of the image. In a scene before the camera, contrast is the difference in brightness between different parts of the scene as perceived from the camera position.

DAYLIGHT FILM
Film manufactured to give lifelike colors when daylight or electronic flash illuminates the subject.

DEPTH OF FIELD
Amount of a scene or picture in focus, measured outwards from the camera.

EXPOSURE
(1) Term used loosely to mean amount of light received by film or printing paper. Exposure is affected by three factors: brightness of light reflected by subject; how long the shutter is open; and size of aperture.
(2) Often used to mean picture or frame, as in 'make three exposures'.

EXPOSURE LATITUDE
Ability of film or paper to tolerate over- or underexposure.

F-NUMBER
Measure of aperture size, marked on camera lens in a standard scale. Alternate f-numbers double, so the scale runs 2, 2.8, 4, 5.6 etc. Changing from one f-number to the next double or halves the amount of light passing through the lens. Large f-numbers connote small apertures, and vice versa.

F-STOP
Term used interchangeably with aperture.

FIELD OF VIEW
The amount of the scene in front of the camera that a particular lens takes in. Wide-angle lenses have a broad field of view, telephoto lenses a narrow one. See also FOCAL LENGTH.

FILL-IN FLASH
Flash used in sunlight to illuminate shadows and thereby reduce lighting contrast.

FILM SPEED
Measure of the sensitivity of film to light. Measured in ISO values.

FLARE
Non-image-forming light which forms either regular disc-shaped marks on film, or veils the whole picture, reducing contrast.

FOCAL LENGTH
In practical terms, a dimension in millimetres indicating the field of view of a lens. Long focal length lenses (telephoto lenses) take in a narrow field of view; short focal length lenses (wide-angle lenses), a wide one. On a theoretical level, focal length is an actual distance corresponding to a physical measurement between the film and the notional centre of the lens, when focused on infinity.

FOCUSING
Act of adjusting distance between lens and film in order to render the subject sharply.

GRAIN
Grit-like texture of film's structure that appears when picture is greatly enlarged. More evident with fast films than with slow.

HIGHLIGHT
Brightest areas of subject or image.

ISO
Numerical measure of film speed. Fast films have high ISO ratings and vice versa.

INCIDENT LIGHT
Light falling on a subject, as opposed to that reflected from it.

INCIDENT LIGHT METER
Hand-held meter that measures the above. Has the advantage that it is not misled by subject tones, and therefore gives reliable indications even when setting exposure for dark or light subjects. See also LIGHT METER.

IRIS DIAPHRAGM
Arrangement of metal blades that together forms the aperture within a lens.

LIGHT METER
Instrument that measures the light intensity, and, when programmed with film speeds, indicates which combinations of shutter speed and aperture will yield correctly exposed pictures.

MODELLING
The appearance of form and depth created by the light falling on a subject. Side-lighting creates a lot of modelling – the appearance of high relief.

MODELLING LIGHT
Tungsten lamp fitted into studio flash units to simulate the quality of illumination created by the flash tubes themselves.

OVEREXPOSURE
Usually undesirable effect of allowing too much light to reach the film or print. Yields images that are too light, or lack highlight detail.

PERSPECTIVE
The appearance of depth in a scene.

PULLING
Reduction of film developing time to compensate for overexposure.

PUSHING
Extension of film developing time to compensate for underexposure.

RANGEFINDER CAMERA
Type of camera that has one lens for use as a viewfinder and a separate one to form the image on film. Rangefinder cameras are focused indirectly: the photographer turns the focusing ring until twin images of the subject in the viewfinder merge to form a single image.

REFLECTANCE
Amount of light reflected by a subject, relative to the amount that falls on it. Thus light-toned subjects have a high reflectance.

REFLECTED LIGHT METER
Instrument that measures the light reflected by the subject. See also LIGHT METER.

SLR
Abbreviation for Single Lens Reflex camera: highly versatile and convenient design of camera that uses just one lens: both for viewfinding and focusing the image; and for making the exposure. Principal advantages are that the subject appears in the viewfinder exactly as it will on film, so close-ups are simple to take, and when lenses are changed the photographer can see immediately the changed field of view.

SHADOW
Darkest areas of a subject or print – not necessarily those in the shade.

SHUTTER
Device fitted into cameras to regulate the duration of exposure. Closed, the shutter stops all light from reaching the film; open, a shutter allows light to reach the film unhindered.

SHUTTER SPEED
Measure of the time for which the shutter remains open. Usually calibrated in doubling steps, so that each setting admits light for twice or half the time as the adjacent settings.

SPOTMETER
Reflected light meter that measures light from a very small area of the subject

STOP
Term used very loosely, but generally one unit of exposure, always used in relative terms. For example . . . 'give one stop extra exposure' means doubling the exposure, by opening up the aperture to the next, wider setting or choosing the next slower shutter speed.

STOPPING DOWN
The process of using a small aperture, to reduce exposure or to increase depth of field.

STUDIO FLASH
Powerful flash unit operated from mains electricity.

SYNCHRONIZATION
The firing of a flash unit at the precise moment when the camera's shutter is open.

TTL METERING
Abbreviation for Through The Lens metering. Method of

metering that reads light reflected from the subject, using light-sensitive cells within the camera body itself.

TELECONVERTER
Optical device that multiplies the focal length of the lens to which it is fitted.

TUNGSTEN FILM
Film manufactured to give correct colors when subject is illuminated by photographic tungsten lights.

TUNGSTEN LIGHT
(1) Any lamp that produces its light by the heating of a metal filament inside an evacuated glass envelope.
(2) The light given out by (1).

UNDEREXPOSURE
Usually undesirable effect of allowing too little light to reach the film or print. Yields images that are too dark, or lacking shadow detail.

INDEX

Numbers in italics refer to captions

PICTURE CREDITS

T = top, B = bottom, L = left, R = right, C = center

Allsport: 12, 13, 72, 100.
Godfrey Argent: 24T.
Michael Busselle: 11, 16, 17, 50, 56, 57TR + CR, 58, 59TL + BL + BR, 61, 65, 69, 70-1, 73T + BR, 74, 81, 83, 87B, 88-91, 94, 97T, 98, 116-7, 123T, 125B, 126, 127T, 131T, 135, 140T + C, 142, 154-5, 158, 169, 172-3, 178-9, 180-1, 182-3.
Colorific: 47.
John Freeman: 15B, 25.
Mike Freeman: 20, 46.
Phil Flasche: 8, 23T, 27T, 59TR, 60, 66, 67T, 72BL, 82T, 87T, 92, 93TR + TL, 96, 97, 97B, 99R, 100-7, 111, 112, 113T, 114, 118-121, 123B, 124, 125T, 129, 130, 131BL + BR, 132-4, 136-8, 140B, 141, 156, 157TL + BR, 160-2, 166, 170-1, 174-5, 177.
Joachim Frederick: 6, 9, 14, 53B, 57TL + B, 62-4, 68, 76-7, 82B, 93B, 99L, 113B, 127B, 128, 139, 157TR, 159, 163-5.
Laurie Lewis: 15TL + TR, 19, 26, 27BR + BL, 67B.
John Miller: 148-153.
Richard Platt: 184.
Royal Photographic Society Collection: 28-33, 36-41, 44-5.
Nick Scott: 18. Nick Scott/ courtesy of Vanity-Edizioni Condé Nast: 21, 48, 49, 53T.
Victoria and Albert Museum collection: 34-5.
Brian Ward Photographic: 110, 146-7.
Zefa: title page, 22, 23B, 78.